"The translation of novels, stories and plays from Indian languages is now a flourishing field. The translation of scholarly and critical works, however, is much less developed. This landmark volume presents a wide-ranging and richly informative history of Odia literature through its translation of major essays in literary criticism. The contributions cover different genres – folk tales, village songs, epics, novels, poems and plays. They discuss literature with regard to its aesthetic aspects as well as in its social and historical context. The book is further enriched by a brilliant introduction by the editors, which provides a magisterial overview of literary production in Odia from oral traditions and palm-leaf manuscripts to print culture."

Ramachandra Guha, *historian and biographer, Bengaluru, India*

"All literary traditions are constantly evolving and, in this volume, we find this happening before our eyes in the case of Odia. The twenty-five extracts selected here from the critical debates that took place in the modern period convey a vivid sense of the contestations over tradition and modernity, the shaping of the literary public sphere, and the formation of the canon. The editorial headnotes are a model of their kind in their erudition and perspicacity. *Critical Discourse in Odia* will serve to enrich and refine our understanding of Odia literature substantially."

Harish Trivedi, *critic, scholar and former Professor of English, University of Delhi, India*

"The twenty-five carefully chosen essays in this excellent volume, competently translated from Odia into English, enlighten us on the origin and the development of literary criticism in Odia, the evolution of the idea of literature, and the gradual emergence of a responsive readership of critical discourse in this language. The introduction to the volume embodies outstanding scholarship. Specialists and general readers will certainly find reading this book an enjoyable and enriching experience."

Bibudhendra Narayan Patnaik, *linguist, scholar, and former Professor of English and Linguistics, IIT Kanpur, India*

Critical Discourse in Odia

This volume forms part of the Critical Discourses in South Asia series, which deals with schools, movements and discursive practices in major South Asian languages. It offers crucial insights into the making of Odia literature and its critical tradition across a century. The book brings together English translations of major writings of influential figures dealing with literary criticism and theory, aesthetic and performative traditions, and re-interpretations of primary concepts and categories in Odia. It presents twenty-five key texts in literary and cultural studies from the late nineteenth century to the early twenty-first century, translated by experts for the first time into English. These seminal essays explore complex interconnections between socio-historical events in the colonial and post-Independence period in Odisha and the language movement. They discuss themes such as the evolving idea of literature and criteria of critical evaluation; revision and expansion of the literary canon; the transition from orality to print; emergence of new reading practices resulting in shifts in aesthetic sensibility; dialectics of tradition and modernity; and the formation, consolidation and political consequences of a language-based identity.

Comprehensive and authoritative, this volume offers an overview of the history of critical thought in Odia literature in South Asia. It will be essential for scholars and researchers of Odia language and literature, literary criticism, literary theory, comparative literature, Indian literature, cultural studies, art and aesthetics, performance studies, history, sociology, regional studies and South Asian studies. It will also interest the Odia-speaking diaspora and those working on the intellectual history of Odisha and Eastern India, and conservation of language and culture.

Jatindra Kumar Nayak is a former Professor of English, Utkal University, Bhubaneswar, Odisha, India. He is recipient of the Hutch-Crossword Book Award, 2004, and the Katha Translation Award, 1997. He is a member of the English Advisory Board, Sahitya Akademi. His English translations of classic Odia novels include Chandrasekhar Rath's *Yantrarudha* (*Astride the Wheel*, 2003), Fakir Mohan Senapati's *Mamu* (*The Maternal Uncle*, 2007) and J.P. Das's *Desh Kal Patra* (*A Time Elsewhere*, 2009). He has co-edited *Reminiscences: Excerpts from Oriya and Bangla Autobiographies* (2004) and *Memory, Images, Imagination: An Anthology of Bangla and Odia Writings on Colonial Burma* (2010).

Animesh Mohapatra teaches English literature at Delhi College of Arts & Commerce, University of Delhi, India. His research interests include literary history, modernity studies, translation and print culture. He has co-edited a selection of critical essays by eminent Odia critic Natabara Samantaray in English translation, which was published in 2017. He has recently contributed a chapter on Odia devotional songs to a volume titled *Bonding with the Lord: Jagannath, Popular Culture and Community Formation* (2020).

Critical Discourses in South Asia

Series Editors: Avadhesh Kumar Singh and Kiran Singh, AURO University, India

South Asia, and especially India, has a long and rich tradition of critical discourses in its languages. These discourses are unique in their own ways without being exclusive and they form an integral part of the regional intellectual traditions. Each critical discourse has its specificity, while it is also related with other critical traditions in an interlingual and interliterary way. However, there is a considerable amount of insulation among such critical traditions primarily because of lack of translation of seminal texts in major South Asian languages.

This series broadly deals with critical discourses in major South Asian languages representing various schools, movements and discursive practices. Each individual volume in the series brings together English translation of major writings dealing with theoretical formulations, literary criticism and theory, re-interpretations of critical concepts and categories, and critical movements in the concerned language that go into the making of its critical tradition.

The volumes in the series not only offer a comprehensive picture of critical discourses in major South Asian languages but also facilitate a comparative understanding of critical traditions across the world.

Editorial Advisory Board:

G. N. Devy, Chairman, People's Linguistic Survey of India; Founder Director, Adivasi Academy, Tejgadh, Gujarat; and former Professor of English, M.S. University of Baroda, India.

Subha Chakraborty Dasgupta, former Professor of Comparative Literature, Jadavpur University, Kolkata, India; and former Visiting Professor, University of Delhi, India and Tokyo University of Foreign Studies, Japan.

Critical Discourse in Bangla
Edited by Subha Chakraborty Dasgupta and Subrata Sinha

Critical Discourse in Telugu
Edited by K. Suneetha Rani

For more information about this series, please visit: https://www.routledge.com/Critical-Discourses-in-South-Asia/book-series/CDSA.

Critical Discourse in Odia

Edited by
Jatindra Kumar Nayak and
Animesh Mohapatra

Routledge
Taylor & Francis Group

LONDON AND NEW YORK

First published 2022
by Routledge
2 Park Square, Milton Park, Abingdon, Oxon OX14 4RN

and by Routledge
605 Third Avenue, New York, NY 10158

Routledge is an imprint of the Taylor & Francis Group, an informa business

© 2022 selection and editorial matter, Jatindra Kumar Nayak and Animesh Mohapatra; individual chapters, the contributors; individual translations, the translators

British Library Cataloguing-in-Publication Data
A catalogue record for this book is available from the British Library

Library of Congress Cataloging-in-Publication Data
A catalog record has been requested for this book

ISBN: 978-1-138-50480-6 (hbk)
ISBN: 978-1-032-12485-8 (pbk)
ISBN: 978-1-003-22477-8 (ebk)

DOI: 10.4324/9781003224778

Typeset in Sabon
by Deanta Global Publishing Services, Chennai, India

Contents

Figures

Acknowledgements

We acknowledge our deep indebtedness to the late Avadhesh Kumar Singh for his spontaneous generosity and unfailing support. We benefited immensely from his erudite advice and his warm encouragement. This volume is a humble tribute to his cherished memory.

In preparing this volume we have incurred numerous debts of gratitude. We are sincerely grateful to J.P. Das, our indulgent mentor, who not only went through the introduction and some chapters, but also deftly translated proverbs and songs we had considered untranslatable. Without the ungrudging guidance of eminent scholars like Debi Prasanna Pattanayak, Gaganendra Nath Dash, Sudarsana Acharya, Debendra Dash and Basant Kumar Panda, we would not have been able to complete this project. The comments and suggestions we received from Sumanyu Satpathy, Nivedita Mohanty, Kalidas Misra and Jyotirmaya Tripathy were illuminating and helpful. We gratefully remember the support we received from Gourahari Das and Bijayananda Singh. It is a pleasant duty to acknowledge a debt of thanks to our friends Subha Chakraborty Dasgupta, John Creyke, Rohit Manchanda, Pinky Hota, Malavika Menon, Lalit Kumar, Gautam Choubey, Jyotiprakash Nayak, Aruni Mahapatra, Umasankar Patra, Hara Mohan Nayak and Shaswat Panda for their constructive criticism. We stand deeply obliged to Falguni Ray, Aurobindo Behera, Kishor K. Basa, Biraj Mohan Das, Anil Pradhan, Manoj Mohapatra, Sudhansu Pradhan, Asis Nanda and Bigyan Ranjan Das for their timely and valuable help.

Copyright holders were very generous with their permissions and we thank each one of them for their kind cooperation. The website odia-bibhaba.in hosted by Srujanika and *Sahityakosha*, a companion to Odia literature published by Sambad-Aama Odisha proved to be invaluable resources. We feel deeply obliged to Nikhil Mohan Pattnaik, Srujanika and Soumya Ranjan Patnaik, *Sambad* for placing these at the disposal of the general public.

Our sincere thanks are also due to Kiran Singh for her patience and kindness. We express our heartfelt gratitude to Rimina Mohapatra for guiding us at every step of the way, and to all members of the Routledge team who were responsible for giving a final shape to the volume. We gratefully acknowledge the unstinted cooperation we have received from all the translators. Without their hard work and commitment this volume would not have seen the light of day.

Translators

Urmishree Bedamatta teaches at the Department of English, Ravenshaw University, Cuttack, India. Currently, she is leading research projects on linguistic aspects of Sarala Das's *Mahabharata* and the Bhakti texts of Odisha. She has written introductions to the English translations of *Tika Gobindachandra* (2015) and *Mathuramangal* (2016), two precolonial Odia texts which enjoy abiding popularity.

Amrita Chowdhury is a prospective PhD student in Asian Languages and Cultures at the University of Wisconsin-Madison, USA. Her research focuses primarily on colonial Indology, especially the episodic *Ramayanas* composed in Bengal Presidency during the nineteenth and early twentieth centuries, and their reception. She has translated with Ujaan Ghosh Upendra Bhanja's Odia *kavya*, *Baidehisha Bilasa* into English. Their co-authored article on the same has appeared in the *Journal of American Academy of Religion* (2020).

Snehaprava Das is a well-known translator and taught English at several colleges in Odisha, India. She co-translated *Padmamali* (2005), the first Odia novel, into English. Her other translations include Gopabandhu Das's *Prison Poems* (2017), Manoj Kumar Panda's *One Thousand Days in a Refrigerator* (2016) and Paramita Satpathy's *Colours of Loneliness and Other Stories* (2019).

Ujaan Ghosh is a doctoral student at the Department of Art History, University of Wisconsin-Madison, USA. His PhD research focuses on the colonial history of Odisha, especially the urban history of Puri. His paper "Chariots of the Gods: The Many Histories of Jagannath, 'Juggernaut,' and the Rathayatra in the Nineteenth Century" was published in the journal *History of Religions* in 2018. He translates precolonial Odia poetry into English.

Sangram Jena is a well-known Odia poet, translator and cultural historian. He was Senior Fellow at the Department of Culture, Government of India in 2011–13. He has received several awards including the Sahitya Akademi Award for Translation (2011) and Bhanuji Rao Memorial

Award for Poetry (2016). He has been editing *margASIA*, an international journal, since 2013.

Aruni Mahapatra is Assistant Professor, Department of English, at the University of Alabama at Birmingham, USA. He obtained his PhD in English from Emory University, Georgia, USA in 2020. His doctoral thesis "Irreverent Reading" examines scenes of reading in vernacular Indian and Anglophone postcolonial novels. His writings have appeared in several books and journals, most recently in the *Cambridge Journal of Postcolonial Literary Inquiry*.

Kalidas Misra is a retired Professor of English, Sambalpur University, Odisha, India. He was a Post-doctoral Fulbright Fellow at Colorado State University, USA in 1992, and a Shastri Indo-Canadian Faculty Research Fellow at the University of Manitoba, Canada in 1996. He was associated with a University of Heidelberg (Germany) project on Bhima Bhoi's poetry, which resulted in the publication of *Bhima Bhoi: Verses from the Void* (2010). His doctoral dissertation on "The War Novel in America: A Study of Changing Response" received the Best Dissertation Award from the ASRC, Hyderabad in 1989.

Aditya Nayak works at *Sambad*, a daily newspaper published from Bhubaneswar, Odisha, India. His English translation of Jalandhar Dev's travel narrative *Diaryra Kiyadansha* [Fragments of a Diary: A Trip to Sri Lanka] was published in 2020. He has also translated into English Gopinath Mohanty's *Utkalmani* [The Gem of Odisha].

Haramohan Nayak teaches English Literature at Kabi Samrat Upendra Bhanja College, Bhanjanagar, Odisha, India. He is also pursuing doctoral research at the Center for Comparative Literature and Translation Studies, Central University of Gujarat, Gandhinagar, India. His areas of interest include colonial urban culture, cyberculture and translation.

Shaswat Panda teaches English literature at Maharaja Sriram Chandra Bhanja Deo University, Keonjhar Campus, Odisha, India. He is pursuing his PhD at the Department of English, University of Delhi, India. His research interests include life-writing, popular visual culture and book history. He has contributed a chapter on Jagannath iconography to *Bonding with the Lord: Jagannath, Popular Culture and Community Formation* (2020). He has translated the critically acclaimed novel *Ghachar Ghochar* into Odia (2020).

Asim Ranjan Parhi is Professor and Head of the Department of English at Utkal University, Odisha, India. He has authored a book titled *Indian English through Newspapers* (2008). Specializing in linguistics and English language teaching (ELT), he takes an active interest in translation studies and children's literature. His forthcoming publications include an edited collection of essays on Gopinath Mohanty and a monograph on Rajkishore Pattanaik.

Umasankar Patra is Assistant Professor of English in the Department of Humanities and Social Sciences, National Institute of Technology, Tiruchirappalli, Tamil Nadu, India. He earned his PhD degree from the University of Delhi, India, writing a thesis on the discourse of the autobiographical in the works of Christopher Isherwood. He recently contributed a chapter on the food economy of Jagannath culture to *Bonding with the Lord: Jagannath, Popular Culture and Community Formation* (2020). He received the Christopher Isherwood Foundation Fellowship, Huntington Library (USA) in 2015. His research interests include Anglo-American modernism, autobiography studies, queer studies and modernity in India, with a special focus on Odisha.

Sumanyu Satpathy is Professor of Eminence at K R Mangalam University, India. A former Professor and Head of the Department of English, University of Delhi, he was a Fellow at the Indian Institute of Advanced Study, Shimla; and Distinguished Fellow at Michel J Osborne Centre, La Trobe University, Melbourne, Australia. As visiting professor, he has taught at University of Granada, Spain; Frankfurt University, Germany; Exeter University, UK among several others. His areas of specialization include modernism, queer theory and Odisha studies. His major publications include *Will to Argue: Studies in Late Colonial and Postcolonial Controversies* (2017); *Southern Postcolonialisms: The Global South and the 'New' Literary Representations* (2009); *Reading Literary Culture: Perspectives on Odisha* (2007). He has co-edited *Natabara Samantaray: A Reader* (2017); *The Tenth Rasa: An Anthology of Indian Nonsense* (2007), and *Signifying the Self: Women and Literature* (2nd ed. 2019).

Niroj Kumar Sethi is Assistant Professor of English at Kuntala Kumari Sabat Women's College, Balasore, Odisha, India. He wrote a doctoral dissertation on narrative technique in Manoj Das's fictional works. His research interests include narrative theory, short fiction and translation.

Jyotirmaya Tripathy is a member of the faculty of Humanities and Social Sciences, Indian Institute of Technology Madras, India. His broad areas of interest are cultural development thought and contemporary India with specific focus on the way institutional development questions converse with everyday practices. He has published on these topics in various journals. He has co-edited *The Democratic Predicament: Cultural Diversity in Europe and India* (2013), *Becoming Minority: How Discourses and Policies Produce Minorities in Europe and India* (2014) and *Bonding with the Lord: Jagannath, Popular Culture and Community Formation* (2020).

Introduction

Jatindra Kumar Nayak and Animesh Mohapatra

This volume comprises twenty-five critical essays exploring various aspects of Odia literature, and forms a part of the larger project titled "Critical Discourses in South Asia". These essays were published between the closing decade of the nineteenth century and the second decade of the twentieth. We expect them to help readers trace the journey of Odia literature from its beginnings rooted in orality to the modern era characterized by print literacy. They also shed light on the changing idea of literature and reveal evolving criteria of critical evaluation. We hope the essays will enhance one's understanding of the context in which literary change unfolded and the factors that vitally contributed to it. Some of the essays show how debates and arguments over questions of decorum, relative merits of tradition and modernity, sources of influence, and experiments with poetic techniques led to the expansion and revision of the literary canon, established new reading practices, and brought about crucial shifts in aesthetic sensibility. Several of the essays transcend disciplinary boundaries and explore key issues affecting human creativity. The critics featured in the volume, thus, include a historian, teachers of philosophy, political activists, inspired amateurs and creative writers, who provide refreshingly insightful perspectives on the relationship between life and literature. Taken together, the essays contribute to widening the scope of discussion of Odia literature by linking it to diverse domains of human experience.

Over the past few decades, literature in Indian languages has reached a wider readership through translation. Literary criticism written in various Indian languages, however, has not received similar attention from translators. As a result, readers outside these linguistic communities have not been able to access and appreciate the vibrant richness of critical thought expressed in Indian languages. This series, "Critical Discourses in South Asia", therefore aims to introduce readers to literary critical traditions in these languages. We sincerely hope that in presenting twenty-five Odia critical essays in English translation we are contributing to this initiative in a modest way. In what follows, we chart the course of modern Odia criticism from about the middle of the nineteenth century to the latter half of the twentieth. Since a substantial part of this introduction focuses on the literary and cultural changes taking place in Odisha in the nineteenth century, a brief note on the political status of Odisha in this period seems warranted here.

Located on the eastern seaboard of India, Odisha went by different names such as Kalinga, Utkal and Odradesha in the past. In the nineteenth century, during British rule, different parts of present-day Odisha were placed under three different centres of administrative control – the Bengal Presidency, the Madras Presidency and the Central Provinces. Odisha became a separate province in 1936 on the basis of language. Later, a number of feudatory states were merged with it and Odisha as a state of the Republic of India was formed. Well into the early decades of the twentieth century, "Utkal" was widely used to refer to both the land and its language.

As regards the names of authors included in this volume, we have chosen to use their first and middle names instead of surnames, deviating from the standard practice. We have done so in order to avoid confusion that might result from the fact that several authors share the same surname.

From *pothi* to print

Although it is well known that modern critical discourse took shape in Odisha in the late nineteenth century, one should not suppose that literary criticism in the form of evaluation and commentary was absent earlier. Poets self-consciously reflected upon the art of composition and the employment of appropriate devices of literary embellishment. Odia poets were deeply influenced by and sought to emulate Sanskrit and Prakrit poetic conventions, and so early modes of criticism were largely confined to demonstrating defects or merits of poetic works with reference to prescribed rules. Deviations from prescriptions enshrined in *alamkara shastras* were regarded as defects. Criticism was, thus, focused more on form than on content. Systems of patronage which sustained the practice of literature in pre-print Odisha also promoted this preoccupation with form. Moreover, there were annotators whose task it was to bring to the reader's attention beauties latent in a *kavya*. Texts were also written to educate aspiring poets and these were known as *kavishikshatmaka granthas* [treatises on educating poets]. Notable among such texts were Jadumani Routray's (late seventeenth century) *Kavikalpadruma* and Upendra Bhanja's (c. 1675–1730) *Rasapanchaka*. In *kavyas* written by celebrated authors like Upendra, Dinakrushna Das and Abhimanyu Samantsinghar, one also comes across instances where the poet laid down rules to be followed for evoking aesthetic delight in the reader.[1] However, these critical maxims were dispensed through verse and no separate space existed for literary critics to engage in arguments about the nature of literature and ways of understanding and evaluating it. The milieux in which literature was created, interpreted and appreciated laid emphasis on aesthetic effect and rules of decorum, and left little room for discussion of literature in relation to its social and historical context.

Like elsewhere in India, modern literary criticism in Odisha emerged in the late nineteenth century in the wake of the introduction of print culture. A printing press was established in Odisha for the first time in 1837 by missionaries, Charles Lacey (1798–1852) and Amos Sutton (1798–1854). Earlier, a few books in Odia had been printed at Serampore Press in neighbouring Bengal. Graham Shaw provides the following account of the activities carried out by the Cuttack Mission Press:

> By 1858 … the press had printed, in twenty years since its establishment, a total of 952,700 tracts of between twelve and thirty-six pages, 77,000 Gospels, 31,050 miscellaneous portions of Scripture, 25,575 "bona fide religious volumes", and 34,750 volumes or parts of educational series. These figures do not include the editions of the Old and New Testaments and Sutton's dictionary and do not take into account the relatively small amount of work done in English and the considerable amount in Oriya undertaken for the government.[2]

It is clearly evident from the above account that the initiatives of the Mission Press were directed primarily at the dissemination of religious texts, and to a very limited extent at school textbooks and administrative documents. Matters relating to Odia literature were conspicuous by their absence in its publications. The periodicals, *Gyanaruna* (1849), *Prabodh Chandrika* (1856) and *Arunodaya* (1861) were also brought out by the Press. While all issues of the first and the last are irretrievably lost, a few issues of *Prabodh Chandrika* survive.[3] The articles published in them have little to do with Odia literature though they carried essays and news of a secular nature, and translations from Sanskrit texts. However, it must be acknowledged that the use of prose became more extensive through missionary interventions, and it emerged as the preferred medium of critical discourse in Odisha. The role of periodicals, which reflect and produce a cultural ethos, in creating conditions congenial for the emergence of literary criticism cannot be underestimated. However, for the rise of such periodicals, Odisha had to wait for a few more years.

Cuttack Printing Company, the first printing press owned and managed by Odias who had received modern education, was set up in 1865. The following year, in the middle of a terrible famine that devastated Odisha, the most influential Odia periodical of the nineteenth century, *Utkal Dipika* [The Lamp of Odisha], a weekly newspaper, came to be launched by the same company. Although the chief aim of the weekly was to publish factual reports on the social and economic condition of Odisha, it also sought to awaken its readers to the urgent need for cultural regeneration. *Utkal Dipika*, therefore, made room for poetic and fictional compositions despite its primary preoccupation with publishing news stories. The Company also actively engaged in bringing out annotated editions of palm-leaf manuscripts of Odia *kavyas* and epics. One of the first *pothis* to be printed in book form was Upendra Bhanja's *kavya Premasudhanidhi* [The Nectar of Love]. In the 8 December 1866 issue of *Utkal Dipika*, readers were informed of its forthcoming publication:

> Much labour has gone into preparing a reliable version of *Premasudhandhi* written by the famous poet Upendra Bhanja, in which all the difficult words have been explained. The printed book will be available for sale by the 15th of this month. The price of a soft-bound copy is 10 *annas* [62.5 paise] and that of a hard-bound one is 12 *annas* [75 paise]. Those who will purchase 50 copies of the book will get a 5% discount and those buying 100 copies or more will receive a 10% discount.
>
> Since only a small number of copies of the book have been printed, those desirous of procuring copies of the same will not get them if they do not place their orders at the earliest.[4]

This is the first instance of a *pothi* finding its way into print and getting transformed into a saleable commodity targeting anonymous readers in an impersonal marketplace. It is not surprising, therefore, that around this time, Rangalal Bandyopadhyay (1827–1887), eminent Bengali poet, scholar, and administrator, at the inaugural meeting of Utkal Bhashoddipani, Sabha held on 19 May 1867, advised its members to ensure that Odia palm-leaf *pothis* be collected and printed at the earliest. A letter written by Bichhanda Patnaik (1838–1887) and published in the 7 March 1868 issue of *Utkal Dipika* provides yet another telling instance of this transition from *pothi* to print.[5] It informed readers that the palm-leaf *pothi* of Krushna Singh's (1739–1788) Odia version of the *Mahabharata* (which also included *Harivamsha*) was going to be presented to them in the form of a printed book. It mentioned that the *pothi* version of these two texts cost about fifty rupees and stated that readers would have to pay less than half the amount, i.e. twenty rupees, for a copy of the printed book comprising almost 1500 leaves. Potential buyers were urged to make advance payment or commit themselves in writing to buying the book when it came out. Thus, new marketing strategies, such as raising subscriptions, were adopted and the printed book was vigorously promoted at the expense of the palm-leaf *pothi*. Soon afterwards, people arrived at the Cuttack Printing Company carrying *pothis* hoping that the printing press would miraculously and instantly convert the palm leaves into printed pages.[6] It becomes clearly apparent that a new technology and an emerging market combined to create a public sphere where the evaluation and interpretation of literature took on new dimensions.

Book reviews and literary periodicals

With the arrival of the printed book as a cultural commodity, book reviews increasingly became an essential feature of periodicals. This can be explained in terms of the growing need of a nascent publishing industry in Odisha to recommend publications to anonymous buyers. In the absence of modern literary texts, *Utkal Dipika* initially carried reviews of non-literary books and textbooks. On 8 December 1866, *Dipika* published a review of an English book on the famine in Odisha written by Gopal Chandra Haldar.[7] One can find a template for future reviews in this early attempt. This rather unfavourable review contained a brief summary of the book, drew the reader's attention to its shortcomings, pointed out factual errors, and placed the argument of the book in a larger context. A similar pattern is also discernible in the reviews of school textbooks which assumed a special significance in the context of the growing awareness of the importance of modern education. In the first year of its publication, *Utkal Dipika* repeatedly voiced concern over the way school textbooks were taught in the classroom and the role of school inspectors in improving the quality of teaching Odia in schools.[8] It is but natural that textbooks came to be reviewed on the pages of *Utkal Dipika* and, their strengths and limitations were diligently analyzed. Gourisankar Ray (1838–1917) subjected Fakir Mohan Senapati's (1843–1918) *Bharatabarsara Itihas* [A History of India] to penetrating scrutiny in the 10 April 1869 issue of the periodical. In the review, Gourisankar, while full of praise for Senapati for having filled a vacuum in the field of textbook writing, took him to task for the preponderance of Bangla inflections and syntax in the book. The comment reflects the reviewer's anxiety about the incursion of Bangla into Odisha's cultural space. That such critical reviews were taken seriously is evident from the fact that Fakir Mohan followed Gourisankar's suggestions while writing the second volume of the book.

One comes across, arguably, the earliest review of a literary text in the 13 February 1869 issue of *Utkal Dipika*. The book under review bore the title *Bhramabhanjan*, Jaganmohan Lal's (1838–1913) Odia adaptation of Thomas Parnell's *The Hermit* (1714). Jaganmohan received due praise from the reviewer for eschewing the method of literal translation, and successfully employing traditional melodic modes and Odia poetic conventions in presenting the English text to the Odia reader. The reviewer used this occasion to dwell on the disadvantages of translating Bangla texts which resulted in the employment of an impure, Bangla-infested Odia. He articulated his preference for traditional Odia literature over its potential rival, modern Odia poetry. However, he approved of Jaganmohan's attempt to receive western influence while remaining rooted firmly in indigenous poetic traditions. For this reason, the reviewer recommended *Bhramabhanjan* to be prescribed as a textbook for schoolchildren in the hope that it would enable them to access and appreciate works of great Odia poets like Upendra Bhanja. Curiously, the review anticipates the traditional-modern controversy that erupted towards the end of the nineteenth century. On 10 April 1869, *Utkal Dipika* carried an impassioned and thoroughgoing rebuttal of a review of *Bhramabhanjan* published in *Bodhadayini o Balasore Sambad Bahika* (founded in 1868), a periodical brought out from Balasore, early issues of which are irrevocably lost. In the rebuttal presented in the form of a letter to the editor, its anonymous writer set out to define the function of criticism:

> Reviewing a book is a highly responsible task. The reviewer has to express an opinion on the book only after carefully assessing its merits and defects. Criticism should not be confined merely to dwelling on the defects of a book.[9]

Such vibrant exchanges and arguments about the function of criticism in the public sphere contributed to the formation of a modern critical sensibility. In this context the caption "Nutan Pustakara Samalochana" [review/criticism of new books] given to the book review section in *Utkal Dipika* draws attention to itself. It may be noted here that modern critical discourse in Odia in its early stage took the form of book reviews. Interestingly, in *Purnachandra Bhashakosha*, Gopal Chandra Praharaj (1874–1945) defined the word *samalochana* as "criticism or review of any matter, thing or person".[10]

Although periodicals like *Utkal Dipika* and *Balasore Sambad Bahika* were primarily devoted to the diffusion of news, they nevertheless strove to create conditions conducive to the promotion, appreciation and evaluation of Odia literature. However, the need for a periodical exclusively dedicated to the pursuit of literature began to be felt with great urgency. *Bodhadayini*, edited by Fakir Mohan, was brought out to focus upon publishing creative literature rather than topical news. Since copies of the periodical are not available, *Utkal Darpan* [The Mirror of Odisha], which appeared in 1873, is considered to be the first literary periodical in Odisha. It was followed by a few short-lived literary magazines before the publication of the long-running and influential *Utkal Sahitya* in 1897. An anonymous and playfully ironic letter to the editor published in the April 1873 issue of *Utkal Darpan* underscored the importance of book reviews as a powerful critical tool.[11] The letter advised an aspiring writer on how he could acquire fame ordinarily achieved in a decade within the space of a single year. It urged the young man to contribute articles to newspapers for the latter were gymnasia for would-be writers. The correspondent offered hilariously sly instructions on how to do a book review:

> You must review books in newspapers. The authors whose books you review should be labelled as modern and subjected to ridicule. When you categorize others as modern, you would automatically assume the hallowed mantle of a traditional or an experienced author. Single out authors from Balasore for censure. Do not uniformly denigrate the work under review; if you do so, others would look upon you as a malicious person. If you begin by praising the work, everyone would be convinced that it is not your real intention to malign the author. Reserve your

dismissive depreciation for the remainder of the review and pretend as if it is not your intention to disparage the author. Adopt a neutral tone which will make others believe that only you, and no one else, could remedy the deficiencies in the literary sphere in Odisha. Others who entertain the ambition of becoming writers merely display their audacity. They should leave you to worship Goddess Saraswati [the goddess of learning] and retire from the scene.[12]

The above quotation affords a glimpse of the techniques contemporary book reviewers adopted to make or mar the reputation of an author. It also indicates the growing rivalry among periodicals in Odisha. It is very likely that *Utkal Dipika* and its style of reviewing books were the target of this anonymous correspondent. Most importantly, it reveals battle lines, however faint, drawn between continuity and change. As we shall see later, this tension flares up into a full-scale literary controversy and determines, to a large extent, the future course of criticism in Odisha.

Classrooms as cradle of criticism

Over the course of the next two decades a new body of writing began reshaping the literary landscape in Odisha. This comprises the poetic works of Radhanath Ray (1848–1908) and his close associate, Madhusudan Rao (1853–1912), among others. Their works brought about a momentous shift in aesthetic sensibility and challenged established conventions relating to taste and decorum. As early as 1876, *Balasore Sambad Bahika* published a brief review of *Kabitabali*, a collection of poems jointly authored by Radhanath and Madhusudan, which stated, "We are convinced that these poems provide the first examples of *adhunik* [modern] poetry in Odisha".[13] Radhanath went on to compose several long narrative poems after publishing the above collection, and Madhusudan wrote a number of poems informed by his Brahmo outlook on life. Their "modernity" consisted in moving closer to western literary models, and absorbing new forms and techniques. Radhanath based many of his celebrated poems on European narratives such as *Metamorphosis, Agamemnon* and "Siege of Corinth". He also introduced into his narratives tragic endings which were, generally speaking, absent in traditional Odia *kavyas*.[14] Moreover, Radhanath and Madhusudan boldly experimented with poetic techniques. For instance, in *Kabitabali*, one comes across a poem written in the Spenserian stanza. And later, Radhanath employed *amitrakshar chhanda* in his magnum opus *Mahayatra* (1892).

Not content with composing pathbreaking works, Radhanath and his followers actively sought to create a climate of critical opinion receptive to their innovations. Recipients of modern education and ensconced in powerful official positions, they made a concerted effort to train a generation of school students in appreciating and interpreting modern Odia literature.

Since a new literature called for the interventions of exponents of new critical thinking, they ensured that the questions set in school examinations would prepare students to interpret and evaluate modern literature. Here one may refer to *Sahitya Bisayaka Adarsh Prashnabali* [Model Questions on Literature] (1879) compiled by Bhubaneswar Dutta and endorsed by Radhanatha Ray, which played a decisive role in the formation of a new literary taste.[15] Close scrutiny of the questions reveals the aims they sought to fulfil. Natabara Samantaray (1918–2000) perceptively defines some of these aims. One clearly discerns a conscious attempt to reduce the importance of grammar in the teaching of literature in order to place greater emphasis on the literariness of a literary text. Attention was increasingly directed at the content of a literary work. To illustrate this, the following question (no. 52) may be cited: "What event is the poem 'Nirabasitara Bilap' [The Lament of an Exile] based on?"[16] It may be noted here that this well-known poem is Madhusudan's adaptation of William Cowper's "The Solitude of Alexander Selkirk". Many of the questions set in school examinations were very similar to the questions given in *Adarsh Prashnabali* and attempted to make students aware of the distinction between traditional and modern Odia literature. A question set in 1885 makes this point amply clear: "Does Upendra Bhanja's poetic diction depart from modern Odia in Certain ways? If yes, give illustrative examples".[17] Moreover, with Madhusudan's active involvement and under his patronage, a monthly periodical *Siskshabandhu* [A Friend of Education] came to be published in 1885. It aimed to acquaint teachers with new methods of teaching various subjects, especially Odia literature, publishing model questions, book reviews, and articles on aspects of pedagogy. In the February–March 1886 issue of the magazine one comes across a question set in the middle school scholarship examination which asked students to compare the *Ramayana* with the *Iliad*.[18] *Siskshabandhu*, thus, can be seen to be advancing Radhanath and Madhusudan's agenda of orienting students towards western literature.

Furthermore, textbooks also played a significant part in disposing students to be more warmly responsive to modern trends in literature. Before 1868, the chief aim of textbooks was to dispense general knowledge, and literature formed no part of the syllabi. After 1868, textbooks of literature acquired a vibrant new dimension as emphasis shifted to writing essays, learning grammar, and dividing literature into poetry and prose. Natabara Samantaray argues that the study of prose, especially essays, provided students access to a western worldview. Defending the introduction of Madhusudan's collection of essays *Prabandhamala* in the syllabus, Radhanath, in the 7 October 1880 issue of *Balasore Sambad Bahika*, offered a more inclusive view of literature:

Textbooks need to cater to the taste and disposition of students. Hence textbooks cannot afford to be unidimensional as they aim at the all-round growth of fertile young minds. For this reason, in many civilized countries, literature that is prescribed in school syllabi is multidimensional and is necessarily an anthology. ... This book [*Prabandhamala*] consists of essays on history, politics, psychology, physical sciences, geography, biography, *nabanyas* [novels], *alamkara* etc. Many educated people in this country treat literature as a subject distinct from the ones mentioned above. The anemic condition of our literature is a result of such a narrow outlook. With the advancement of Odia language, these parochial ideas will be dispelled and Odia literature will gradually move beyond the world of imagination towards the realm of knowledge and truth.[19]

Radhanath's inclusive view anticipates the definition of literature advanced by Biswanath Kar (1864–1934) in the inaugural issue of *Utkal Sahitya* in 1897.[20] It may be mentioned here that in the 1870s writing school textbooks became a highly profitable business. This exacerbated the already existing rivalry among various publishing houses. As Natabara Samantaray observes,

> Thus, individuals like Sitanath Ray and zamindars like Baikunthanath Dey transformed book publishing into a business venture. The above transformation sometimes led to controversies and Joint Inspector of Schools, Radhanath Ray became the first target of such controversies.[21]

The growing dominance of Radhanath and his followers over educational institutions and policies, and the textbook market inevitably led to a backlash. Their privileging of modern literature created antagonists, who now pitted traditional literature against it.

Magazines at war

Attacks on Upendra Bhanja who embodied Odia pride during the language agitation in Odisha in the late 1860s were launched from time to time by well-known intellectuals. Their views were imbued with the puritanical outlook associated with Brahmoism. What they found particularly objectionable in Upendra's poetry was the element of explicit eroticism and its intricate ornateness. However, as a major modern Odia author had not appeared on the literary scene yet to be pitted against Upendra, their response remained shallowly negative. With the ascendancy of Radhanath Ray as the foremost literary figure in the 1880s, the picture dramatically changed. Moreover, Radhanath's controversial role in the selection of textbooks had earned him vocal opponents who also championed the poetry of Upendra. A fierce literary controversy was triggered by Lala Ramnarayan Ray's (d. 1896) essay on Upendra Bhanja serialized in *Utkal Prabha* between December 1891 and April 1893. Ramnarayan undertook a meticulous analysis of Upendra's poetic techniques and then went on to mount a scathing attack on the "pervasive" element of obscenity in his poetry. Although his focus was purportedly on Upendra, he subtly sought to present Radhanath Ray in a favourable light. His chief objective was evidently to replace Upendra with Radhanath as the greatest Odia poet.[22] Commenting on the preponderance of *adirasa* [the erotic sentiment] in *Baidehisha Bilasa*, he made the following observation:

> Dear Readers! How does Lord Rama differ from a lowly beast driven by sexual desire? Even in the hour of extreme distress, he can disrobe Sita in his mind and caress her body with his nails. How can one consider Ramachandra an ideal human being? If *Baidehisha Bilasa* is regarded as a great and exemplary *kavya*, and if the protagonist of this *kavya* is adored and worshipped by the young men of this land, one wonders if Odisha will ever make any progress![23]

Such a provocative stance on Upendra and the ill-concealed attempt at promoting Radhanath at the former's expense led to a deluge of opinions opposing and supporting Ramnarayan. Two major newspapers of the time provided space for opinions for and against the two poets: *Utkal Dipika* published articles defending and celebrating Upendra, and *Sambalpur Hitesisini* featured articles attacking Upendra and championing Radhanath. Soon, however, the newspapers found it difficult to accommodate the barrage of opinions, and two partisan literary periodicals, *Indradhanu* [Rainbow] (1893–97) and *Bijuli* [Lightning] (1893–94), were launched to fight this literary battle. While a few copies of *Indradhanu* have been collected and published in the form of a book, all the copies of *Bijuli* are lost without a trace. The battle between the two magazines could be fought with fervent vigour because by the 1890s an informed community of readers had come into being largely as a result of the new methods of teaching of Odia literature adopted in schools in the 1870s.

Even after *Bijuli* ceased publication, one of its contributors, Damodar Mishra (b. 1871) published a booklet *Dosa Darshan* [Detection of Defects] (1895) devoted entirely to pointing out imperfections in Upendra's poetry. Five years later, after *Indradhanu* stopped getting published, in another booklet titled *Gunadarsha* [Poetic Virtues] (1900), Buddhinath Kavyatirtha Sharma provocatively presented those very same imperfections as poetic virtues.[24] At first sight it may appear that the controversy in which the rival camps took part, represented by the two magazines, contributed little to the advancement of Odia critical discourse as they obsessively dwelt on the relative defects and merits of Upendra and Radhanath. The arguments for and against their icons often degenerated into mudslinging, malicious vituperation, colourful abuse and even violent threats. However, closer scrutiny would reveal that the controversy did introduce new ways of thinking about Odia literature. To begin with, the controversy motivated many educated young Odias to engage in a close reading of literary texts and offer arguments about them in writing. Traditional Odia literature was no longer meant to be sung or recited but subjected to new reading protocols which treated it as a body of written texts to be studied, interpreted and evaluated. In the process, it began losing its intimate contact with the world of orality. The controversy also made some participants aware of the limitations constraining critical practice in Odisha. Gopal Ballabh Das (1860–1914), a prominent contributor to *Indradhanu,* for instance, drew attention to the vital importance of biographical information on an author in assessing their work. He also emphasized the need for making the entire oeuvre of an author available in print to facilitate a holistic evaluation of their poetic achievement. Sudarsana Acharya's (b. 1939) introduction to *Indradhnau: Unabimsha Satabdira Eka Bismruta Patrika* [Indradhnau: A Forgotten Magazine of the Nineteenth Century] (1991), an excerpt from which titled "War of Words: Aspects of a literary Controversy" has been included in this volume, shows how this apparently narrow-minded literary controversy actually widened the literary horizon in Odisha:

> Through its initiatives the realisation dawned that, no matter how rich an ancient literature might be, it can never fulfil the aesthetic needs of a new, changing world. Even when the contributors to *Indradhanu* venerated Upendra Bhanja, their writings reflected a departure from the conventions of ancient Odia poetry. Although they harshly criticized Radhanath Ray, they acknowledged, in spite of themselves, that his poetry embodied the modern sensibility more effectively. They also helped Radhanath shift his focus away from his preoccupation with conveying aesthetic pleasure to more sensitively exploring his own world and its social values.[25]

Moreover, some of the prominent participants in this controversy, especially Lala Ramnarayan and Gopal Ballabh, displayed a remarkable ability to combine in their essays traditional methods of analyzing literary texts with habits of western thought. It is very likely that attempts at retrieving precolonial Odia texts and subjecting them to critical and scholarly scrutiny made by a few colonial officials might have exercised a decisive influence on them. Therefore, a discussion of their contribution, albeit written in English, to laying the foundation of modern critical practices may be in order.

Mapping local culture

As several scholars have persuasively argued, after 1857, the character of imperial governance in India underwent a dramatic transformation. Greater emphasis began to be laid on acquiring an intimate understanding of Indian culture at a micro level. Information assumed immense significance and was recognized as an essential tool for governance.[26] In Odisha, we get to see the pivotal outcome of such a shift of emphasis in the 1870s. In 1872, W.W.

Hunter (1840–1900) appended a list titled "The Literature of Orissa: Being an Analytical Catalogue of 107 Uriya Writers, Alphabetically Arranged; With a Brief Description of 47 Mss. of Undetermined Authorship" to his *Orissa* (vol. 2).[27] The inclusion of such a catalogue in a historical account indicates the growing recognition on the part of colonial authorities of literature as valuable data. And interestingly, this data is presented within an information grid which reflects the prioritization of linearity. Two major features are discernible in Hunter's catalogue: (1) the idea of attributing particular works to individual authors; and (2) an attempt at ascertaining the period in which the authors lived and composed their works.[28] This constitutes a marked departure from the pre-colonial practice of attribution of authorship to texts and the notion of literary past.

The same year, John Beames (1837–1902), a colonial official then posted in Balasore and a philologist, published another list of eighty-two Odia literary texts as part of an essay titled "The Indigenous Literature of Orissa" in *Indian Antiquary*.[29] A distinctive feature of Beames's catalogue is his attempt to classify these texts on the basis of their content; his taxonomy comprised categories such as religious poems, hymns to Jagannath, poems on Hindu ceremonies, erotic poems, youth of Krishna, history of Rama, ceremonial observances and Hindu laws. Describing Dinakrushna Das's *Rasakallola* [Waves of Delight] as "the most celebrated" Odia poem, he went on to examine the same in detail in an article published a few months later.[30] Remarkable features of his "Notes on Rasakallola" include his reconstruction of the poet's biography from legends, situating the writer in a specific historical period and in the larger context of Vaishnavite poetry in India, and a scrupulous examination of the techniques employed in the poem. As will be observed later, this approach would be adopted by Odias who had received modern education in their study of literature. It may be mentioned here that Rangalal Bandyopadhyay's essays on Dinakrushna Das and Upendra Bhanja published in Bangla in 1864 anticipate Beames's approach to the poet in significant ways.[31] Interestingly, Beames's own Victorian reservations about the erotic were echoed by the denigrators of Upendra Bhanja in the *Indradhanu-Bijuli* controversy. For all his sophistication as a scholar, Beames was not able to conceal his view of Indian literature as a source of useful information required to govern the colonized. As he observed in "Folklore of Orissa",

> Human nonsense, like human sense, is very much the same everywhere, and it is only because in ruling men one must take their nonsense into consideration quite as earnestly as their sense, that these scraps of folklore are worth recording at all.[32]

This bears evidence of not only the comprehensiveness of his interest in Odishan culture, it also shows how he believed that understanding literature could be employed as an instrument of control. Moreover, Beames's interest in folklore adumbrates the growing preoccupation with folk narratives in the early twentieth century in Odisha.[33]

Monmohan Chakravarti's (1863–1916) influential essay "Notes on the Language and Literature in Orissa"[34] was published at a time when Odia criticism entered a phase of unprecedented stability. Criticism no longer derived its impetus from controversies and moved towards a sober interpretation and assessment of literary texts and issues. In the hands of Monmohan, the fragmentary efforts made by Hunter and Beames in their catalogues and notes on single authors were transformed into an initiative to construct an integrated and coherent narrative of the development of Odia literature. Unlike Hunter and Beames, Monmohan offered a set of reasons for the chronological arrangement of authors he adopted in the "Notes". He used both textual and extra-textual evidence to arrive at a probable date of composition of a literary work. He closely studied the phenomenon of literary change and presented an insightful account of it. Here one may consider his explanation for the rise of literature in Odia:

> To summarise, the difficulties of composition in the dead Sanskrit, the example of the early developed Telugu, the influence of Vaishnavism and the supersession of the Hindu rule by Mahomedans – all tended to swell the tide in favour of the vernaculars.[35]

An explanation of this kind indicates a new and broader approach to the study of literature in Odisha. Another noteworthy feature of Monmohan's study is the classification of the texts into two broad generic types – "songs" and "religious poems". He employed the encompassing term "songs" to include various genres such as *chautishas*, *chhandas* and *chapois*, and different tunes (*banis* and *bruttas*) such as *chakrakeli*, *abakasha* and *bhagabata*. "Religious poems", in his classificatory scheme, included translations into Odia of four major Sanskrit works: *Bhagabata*, *Ramayana*, *Mahabharata* and *Harivamsha*. Bringing "religious texts" within the purview of literary criticism was a bold and striking intervention. Generally speaking, references to these were conspicuous by their absence in the *Indradhanu-Bijuli* controversy. Importantly, in the early decades of the twentieth century, a number of seminal essays on Sarala Das came to be published in the leading literary periodicals, establishing him as the *adikavi* [first poet] of Odisha. It is quite likely that Monmohan Chakravarti's essay played a crucial role in expanding the Odia literary canon.

Widening the critical horizon

As has been observed earlier, in the closing years of the nineteenth century, literary controversies ceased to supply criticism its energy and direction. A new climate of critical thinking came to prevail and the literary critic emerged as a figure in their own right. Founding of the literary monthly

Utkal Sahitya in January 1897 provided a lively forum for a new generation of critics. An ambitious undertaking, it continued to be regularly published for thirty-eight years unlike its short-lived predecessors. Following the example of *Utkal Prabha* (1891), the magazine announced on its cover *samalochan* [criticism] as one of its central functions.[36] The beginnings of *Utkal Sahitya* were rooted in the Alochana Sabha [discussion forum], which was established in Cuttack Training School a few years earlier to promote the cause of Odia literature. This forum merged with several others and grew into the leading literary institution in Odisha called Utkal Sahitya Samaj in 1903. The same year, a political forum named Utkal Sammilani [Utkal Union Conference] was also established to unify Odia-speaking tracts. This organization laid great stress on the preeminent role literature plays in building the identity of a community. *Utkal Sahitya*, for its part, shared the central objectives of these organizations and remained closely associated with the activities they engaged in. It not only regularly published the proceedings of meetings organized by these institutions, it also featured the papers presented and lectures delivered there. Mohini Mohan Senapati's seminal essay "Odia Folktales" serialized in *Utkal Sahitya* was originally presented at the Alochana Sabha. Essays winning the prestigious medal instituted by the king of Talcher were also brought out in the magazine. *Utkal Sahitya* published Mrutyunjay Ratha's medal-winning essay on Dinakrushna Das's *Rasakallola*, among many others. The alliances *Utkal Sahitya* formed with emerging pan-Odishan institutions mentioned above lent it stability and made it part of a larger movement which strove to shape the destiny of a linguistic community.

In the inaugural issue of *Utkal Sahitya*, the editor Biswanath Kar announced a truce in the battle between the champions of tradition and advocates of modernity. The following observation reveals Biswanath's judiciously balanced perspective:

> It will be utterly foolish to resist the forces of progress out of blind loyalty to the past. At the same time, however, it would be equally terrible to dismiss ancient traditions out of immoderate admiration for the modern. Only those who can successfully negotiate between these two worlds are wise. The great and the good in all enlightened ages and developed lands have upheld this ideal. So long as we remain alive we would sincerely follow this golden precept.[37]

The catholicity of spirit inherent in this editorial principle allowed the literary critic to access and reflect on a larger cultural and intellectual world, and participate in a richer and more cosmopolitan conversation on literature. Echoing Radhanath Ray's definition of literature cited earlier, Biswanath Kar widened its scope by including *kavyas*, plays, science, philosophy, education, industry, agriculture, commerce, religion, and ethics within its ambit. In other words, *Utkal Sahitya* purposively set out to treat literature as a knowledge system. The magazine and the literary critics who contributed to it actively sought to train the aesthetic sensibility of the Odia reading community. For instance, Abhiram Bhanja's (1880–1918) lecture published in *Utkal Sahitya* rued the fact that Odia readers were wasting their time on authors like Mrs. Henry Wood and Marie Corelli.[38]

In the closing decade of the nineteenth century, the need for a history of Odia literature was articulated with a mounting sense of urgency. Attempts were made to move beyond Upendra Bhanja and expand the Odia literary canon by situating Odia authors in a longer historical time frame. Possibilities for accomplishing this task were created in no small measure when Monmohan Chakravarti brought "religious poems" within the realm of literary history and criticism. In the early decades of the twentieth century, a number of contributors to *Utkal Sahitya* devoted their energies to tracing the origin of Odia language and literature. Notable among them were Mohini Mohan Senapati (1881–1945), who wrote a perceptive essay on Odia folktales (1902), and Tarini Charan Ratha (1883–1922), who tried to offer an answer to the question "Utkalara Pratham Kavi Kie" [Who is the First Odia Poet] (1912). A noteworthy outcome of this intense concern with literary history led to the rediscovery and rigorous assessment of Sarala Das. The process was initiated by Shyam Sundar Rajguru (1866–1909) in the landmark essay on Sarala Das's Odia *Mahabharata* where Shyam Sundar located him in the fifteenth century and recognized him as the earliest among major Odia poets. This investigation was conducted on a more ambitious scale in a series of essays written by Gopinath Nanda Sarma published in *Utkal Sahitya* in thirty instalments between 1911 and 1915. In this pathbreaking study, Gopinath perspicaciously compared Sarala Das's *Mahabharata* with Vyasa's epic, closely examined its language and literary quality, and reconstructed the life of the author from information available in the text and local legends. Around the same time, Mrutyunjay Ratha's (1882–1924) "Adikavi Sarala Das", an account of the poet's life, came to be serialized in *Mukur* [Mirror] (1905–1930), the other major literary monthly of the time.[39] In this way, Sarala was canonized as the *adikavi* [first poet] of Odisha. However, it should not be presumed that these critics confined themselves only to a celebration of Sarala; they wrote scholarly essays on several lesser-known Odia poets such as Matsyendranath, Gorakhnath, Dhananjay Bhanja, Haladhar Das, Nisankaray Rani, Dasarathi Das, Gopal Kavi, Kavi Hari Krushna and Kanhu Das. It is interesting to note here that critical attention visibly shifted away from Upendra Bhanja and the ground was prepared for writing a history of Odia literature. In 1916, Tarini Charan Ratha, a noted contributor to *Utkal Sahitya*, published the first history of Odia literature in book form. This powerful urge to reconstruct the rich literary heritage of Odisha stemmed from the need to assert and consolidate Odia linguistic identity. While for colonial administrators, literature was valuable as useful information, for the Odia intelligentsia, it was a means of asserting their distinctive cultural worth. The preoccupation of *Utkal*

Sahitya with developing a historical understanding of Odia literature continues to dominate the literary critical landscape in Odisha even today.

To publish and critically respond to modern literature was another important task *Utkal Sahitya* had set itself. This task, as we have already seen, was earlier performed to some extent by book reviews. Although book reviews constituted a salient feature of *Utkal Sahitya*, criticism was now expected to perform a more serious and comprehensive task, and rise above the ephemeral immediacy of a book review. It is not surprising, therefore, that several essays focusing on the function of criticism and responsibilities of the critic frequently appeared in *Utkal Sahitya*. In the earliest of these, appropriately titled "Samalochana" (1897), Krushna Prasad Choudhary (1865–1927) made a few pertinent observations.[40] He assigned the critic a "sacred and highly elevated place" in the world of letters and expected them to display an unswerving commitment to objectivity. Lamenting the dearth of thoughtful critical engagement in Odisha, he urged the educated young to energetically undertake critical evaluation of their own literature, for only through probing criticism could literature attain excellence. In another essay titled "Siksha o Samalochana" [Education and Criticism], Kamapal Mishra (1875–1927) distinguished different types of criticism and brought in English literature and criticism as key reference points.[41] The continuing concern of *Utkal Sahitya* with laying out the role and responsibilities of a literary critic manifested itself in an essay published almost two decades later. Girija Sankar Ray (1886–1967) in "Samalochanara Dhara o Lakshya" [Literary Criticism: Trends and Objectives] classified criticism into two broad categories, synthetic and analytic, and set a lofty goal before the critic.[42] He insisted that the critic should strive to evaluate national literature in the light of the standards of world literature, and in the process raise the former to a higher level of accomplishment. Thus, a number of essays exploring the nature and function of criticism were published in *Utkal Sahitya* between 1897 and 1935, emphasizing the role of criticism in enriching literature.

The two leading literary periodicals of the early twentieth century in Odisha, *Utkal Sahitya* and *Mukur*, have been rightly described as "training ground" for new writers.[43] It may be added that in these, several new literary forms such as the novel, short story, sonnet, lyric and essay were zealously nurtured. A substantial body of new literature now awaited sustained critical attention. The function of the critic, thus, consisted in revising old criteria of evaluation, forge new ones and explain innovation. A notable earlier initiative in this regard was represented by Madhusudan Rao's foreword to Radhanath Ray's unfinished epic *Mahayatra* [The Great Journey] (1896).[44] In the foreword, Madhusudan defended Radhanath's employment of *amitrakshar chhanda* as a pioneering experiment with poetic technique. When Fakir Mohan Senapati's "Rebati", the first Odia short story, was published in the October 1898 issue of *Utkal Sahitya*, it was followed, three months later, by an anonymous review titled "Samalochana" in which two imaginary characters discussed various aspects of the story.[45] In their play-ful dialogue, they seem to be groping towards an adequate critical response to an unfamiliar literary form. They grapple with issues such as the short-ness of the story, unmerited suffering undergone by innocents, the death of all the characters featured in the story resulting in unrelieved gloom, and the depressingly stark realism of the narrative. The author is justified during the course of the conversation through compelling parallels drawn between the fictional universe and the real world. Similar unease character-ized Gopal Chandra Praharaj's critical response to Fakir Mohan Senapati's novel *Chha Mana Atha Guntha* [Six Acres and a Third] (1902).[46] Gopal Chandra also expressed his discomfort with the way poetic justice operates in the novel in which quite a few innocent characters suffer and perish. In his analysis of Fakir Mohan Senapati's novel *Mamu* [The Maternal Uncle] (1913), Ashraf Ali Khan (1875–1959) employed *rasa* theory, traditionally applied to *kavyas* and *natakas*, to a realistic novel.[47] In the same essay, he also invited the reader to see the novel as a history of contemporary society. Madhusudan Rao's *Basant Gatha* [Song of Spring] (1903) prompted a dis-cussion of this alien literary form and later generated a lively debate. In an essay titled "Chaturdashapadi Kavita", published in the January 1904 issue of *Utkal Sahitya*, Chandra Sekhar Nanda briefly explored the history of the sonnet in Europe and astutely commented on its Odia adaptations.[48] In 1920, when Mohini Mohan Senapati examined the spiritual content of Madhusudan Rao's *Basant Gatha* [Song of Spring] from the point of view of a materialist and an atheist, he was sharply taken to task by the editor of *Utkal Sahitya* and Lakshmi Narayan Sahu (1890–1963).[49] A few years later, Annada Sankar Ray (1904–2002) presented Madhusudan as an innovator who introduced into Odia literature a European literary form like the son-net and the personal lyric.[50] *Utkal Sahitya* and *Mukur* can be said to have contributed to the development of Odia critical discourse in yet another significant way. The demise of major modern writers such as Radhanath Ray (1908), Madhusudan Rao (1912), Fakir Mohan Senapati (1918) and Gangadhar Meher (1924) led these two literary periodicals to pay fulsome tributes to them which comprised biographical sketches and assessment of their contribution to Odia literature. These tributes combined to create con-ditions favourable to a fuller understanding of the achievements of modern authors.[51]

If criticism can be considered an argumentation about literature, then *Utkal Sahitya* can be credited with laying down the ground rules for mature and enriching literary debates. The magazine encouraged the articulation of alternative, and at times conflicting, views which illuminated unexplored dimensions of texts and issues. The attempts to reconstruct the literary past of Odisha led several contributors to *Utkal Sahitya* and *Mukur* to initiate the process of writing a detailed history of Odia literature. This process culmi-nated in the publication of richly comprehensive narrative histories of Odia literature in the 1960s which include Mayadhar Manasinha's *History of*

Oriya Literature (1962) in English and *Odia Sahityara Itihas* (1967) in Odia; Surya Narayan Das's *Odia Sahityara Itihas*, vol. 1 (1963), vol. 2 (1965), vol. 3 (1966) and vol. 4 (1971); and Surendra Mohanty's *Odia Sahityara Adi Parva* (1963) and *Odia Sahityara Madhya Parva* (1968). The magazines also introduced new literary forms, ushered in new modes of interpretation and helped forge a new critical idiom. Publishing translations and adaptations of western literary texts, they expanded cultural understanding and encouraged writers to experiment with new modes of creative expression. Moreover, through their pan-Odishan presence, they contributed seminally to building a new Odisha based on its linguistic identity. In hindsight, what appears remarkably striking is the fact that *Utkal Sahitya, Mukur, Satyabadi* (1915) and a few other literary periodicals shaped and sustained a tradition of critical inquiry into Odia literature for years before its study came to be included in the curricula of institutions of higher learning.

Criticism academized

Although Ravenshaw College, the first college in Odisha, was founded in 1868, the study of Odia literature did not find a place in its curriculum. In an article titled "Vishwavidyalayare Odia Bhasha" [The Place of the Odia Language in the University] (1901), Krushna Prasad Choudhary informed the reader of the inclusion of Odia as a subject in the University of Calcutta to which Ravenshaw College was then affiliated: "It has been notified that from next year onwards questions will be set for students in composition in Odia in FA [First Arts] and BA examinations".[52] He greeted this welcome development with great enthusiasm mixed with considerable anxiety. Krushna Prasad was apprehensive that the academic resources required to prepare for the examinations were not available and, therefore, he outlined a desirable course of action:

> Traditional Odia literature is available mostly in palm-leaf manuscripts; only a few of these have been printed in the past fifty years. How would students access texts that have not been published in book form? How would they form an idea about the development of Odia language? How would they compare one writer with another? What would help them learn in what distinctive ways different authors have used language? How would they answer questions regarding Odisha's past? In order to help Odia students overcome the above difficulties, the collected works of, at least, the major writers need to be published; a history of Odia literature ought to be written and a comprehensive history of Odisha has to be put together. Two other essential requirements are a good dictionary and a reliable grammar of Odia language.[53]

This statement prophetically laid out the map of academic study of Odia literature in future and almost anticipated the publication of Bijoy Chandra

Mazumadar's (1861–1942) *Typical Selections from Oriya Literature* (vol. 1, 1921; vol.2, 1923; vol. 3, 1925).

Bijoy Chandra's three-volume anthology was prepared as a textbook for postgraduate students in Odia at the Arts Department, University of Calcutta. In the "Outlines of a Scheme for the Advanced Study of the Indian Vernaculars" included in its first volume, Ashutosh Mukherjee (1864–1924), a visionary educationist, explained the purpose the scheme was meant to serve:

> The duty has, indeed, been officially imposed on one of the Indian Universities to encourage research in Indian literatures and languages and to foster their growth, by the publication of critical editions of early texts, by historical investigations of their origins, early development and ramification into a variety of dialects. I have long maintained the view that a subject so extensive in scope, so well calculated to rouse intellectual curiosity, may fittingly be included in the scheme for our highest degree Examinations. ... My proposal in substance is that the services of competent scholars, wherever available, should be secured to prepare a series of volumes of Typical Selections, dealing with the chief Indian vernaculars and illustrating the origin and development of both the language and the literature. The selections will be made from sources published and unpublished, and manuscript materials will be utilized to the fullest extent desirable. ... Each volume will be furnished with an introduction, glossary, notes and appendices.[54]

One notices here a visible turn towards academization of vernacular literatures in India. Emphasis was, thus, placed on the need for a well-defined scholarly and critical apparatus. Teaching of Odia language and literature at the postgraduate level began at the University of Calcutta in 1919 and Nilakantha Das (1884–1967) joined the University as a lecturer. When he left the University to take part in the Non-Cooperation Movement, Binayak Mishra (1894–1971) succeeded him in 1921. Bijoy Chandra, Nilakantha and Binayak were the earliest teachers of Odia in a postgraduate department. During its three decades of existence, about thirteen students earned their MA degree in Odia from Calcutta University. Of them, Raj Kishor Ray (1913–1998), Kunja Bihari Das (1914–1994), Kanhu Charan Mishra (1922–2001) and Chintamani Behera (1927–2005) later distinguished themselves as academic critics of Odia literature. Notable outcomes of the academic engagement with Odia literature at Calcutta University were Binayak Mishra's *Odia Bhashara Itihas* (1927) and *Odia Sahityara Itihas* (1928),[55] and Priyaranjan Sen's *Modern Oriya Literature* (1947).

It may be observed here that the situation obtaining in Odisha with reference to the teaching of Odia literature in an institution of higher learning presents a strikingly different picture. At Ravenshaw College, there was no department devoted exclusively to the teaching of Odia language and literature.[56] In 1907, Kasinath Das was appointed as lecturer in Sanskrit and Odia composition.[57] In 1936, the year Odisha became a separate province, Odia was introduced as a subject of study, and the honours programme at the undergraduate level started in 1942. When the postgraduate department was opened in 1946, Karunakar Kar was appointed the first professor of Sanskrit and Odia.[58] At this time Odia was taught by teachers of Sanskrit and philosophy like Kasinath Das, Artaballabh Mohanty (1886–1963), Lakshmikant Choudhary (1898–1942), Karunakar Kar (1895–1968), Ratnakar Pati (1889–1969) and Narayan Mohan De (1889–1963). Artaballabh and his associates, who included Lakshmikant and Karunakar, founded the *Prachi Samiti* in 1926, which undertook the publication of critical editions of Odia texts available in palm-leaf manuscripts. These laid a firm foundation for an academic study of Odia literature, and opened up possibilities for writing comprehensive literary histories. In 1951, a postgraduate department of Odia was created at Visva-Bharati, Santiniketan. Meanwhile, opportunities for conducting doctoral research became available to scholars. Three postgraduate departments of Odia were established in Berhampur, Sambalpur and Utkal universities in Odisha between 1968 and 1969. Thus, an institutional framework for academizing Odia criticism came to be put securely in place.

Over the years, as a result of the developments mentioned above, a community of college and university teachers of Odia was created.[59] The locus of literary critical activity gradually shifted from public fora such as Utkal Sahitya Samaj and Kalinga Bharati to colleges and universities. An early indication of this shift can be found in Nilakantha Das's insightful and groundbreaking lecture entitled "Odia Sahityara Krama-parinama" [Odia Literature: A Historical Enquiry] delivered at the newly-established Balasore College on 29 September 1947. On public demand, this lecture was later expanded into a book of monumental import. Not long afterwards, Odia came to be recognized as one of the thirteen scheduled languages of India by its constitution. Institutions such as Sahitya Akademi and Odisha Sahitya Academy also fostered literary critical activity through publishing journals and books, and organizing events. What compels one's attention here is the fact that contributors to these journals and literary magazines mostly included teachers of Odia literature.

A defining characteristic of the criticism generated by this community of scholar-teachers is the increasing focus on the centrality of research to critical practice. One cannot do better than quote Natabara Samantaray, an iconic practitioner of modern criticism in Odisha, to illustrate this point:

The importance of the foundation for future criticism which has been laid by critical practice over the last decade [1947–56] can never be underestimated. This foundation has been built only through research. ... Criticism should always be guided by a scientific and rational outlook. Lack of consistency in thought, inability to coherently develop an argument and neglecting to locate a text in its temporal context are the enemies of good criticism. ... Essays based on research written during this period have sought to combat these enemies. Their number may now be very small; it is hoped that in future more such essays will be written and works of criticism in the true sense of the term will be published.[60]

This observation in a way establishes the criteria that would be used to evaluate Odia criticism in future, and the works of some of the best practitioners of Odia criticism produced during the latter half of the twentieth century exemplify these.[61] It might be pointed out in this context that the rise of literary criticism in the form of academic research in Odisha indicates a discernible weakening of the earlier impassioned preoccupation with building Odia identity through literature and criticism. The idea of literature as a marker and agent of the progress of a community which animated the Odia intelligentsia in the early twentieth century gradually lost its grip over the consciousness of literary critics and the reading public alike. In the process, the space for enlightened laypersons responding to and evaluating literature in an informed manner has considerably shrunk. Of course, one comes across brilliant exceptions such as Surya Narayan Das (1908–1982), Gopinath Mohanty (1914–1991), Surendra Mohanty (1922–1990), Chitta Ranjan Das (1923–2010), Sachchidananda Mishra (1930–2015) and Fanindra Bhusan Nanda (b. 1959) but it cannot be denied that an arid academicism often threatens to dominate the literary critical world. The experience of deriving pleasure from the text has, generally speaking, given way to an oppressively solemn engagement with it.

A note on editing the volume

The process of selecting essays for this volume posed formidable difficulties since we had an overwhelmingly large number of excellent essays to choose from. We decided to make our selection reflect the fascinating diversity of critical opinions and methods, and, to the best of our ability, chose essays which represent significant inflection points in the development of modern critical discourse in Odisha. The revival of interest in Sarala Das's *Mahabharata* towards the end of the nineteenth century was an event of momentous significance that led to the revision and expansion of the Odia literary canon. This is the reason why as many as four essays on Sarala Das have been included in this volume. Given the crucial role played by the literary monthly *Utkal Sahitya* (1897–1935) in shaping modern Odia critical discourse and literature, it is not surprising that eight out of the twenty-five essays featured in this volume were published in this magazine. We also seek to offer the reader a synoptic account of the beginnings of Odia literature in oral traditions, its preservation and dissemination through scribal production of palm-leaf manuscripts, and transformations it undergoes with the arrival of print culture. Therefore, the order in which the essays are arranged here follows the pattern of this transition, and is not based on the years in which these essays were first published. As far as possible, we have included essays by critics who have written primarily in Odia. Given our emphasis on the above-mentioned pattern of evolution of critical discourse in Odisha, we inevitably left out many trends and movements which eminently deserve attention. To our regret, we could not include some excellent essays written by celebrated critics on account of the constraint of space. We decided not to incorporate in this introduction comments on the essays featured in the volume because to each essay is added a biographical sketch of the author and the specific contribution the essay makes to the development of literary criticism in Odisha. We earnestly hope that our effort, for all its inadequacies, will expand the not-so-substantial corpus of works on critical traditions in South Asia.

Notes

1 For more discussion on pre-colonial Odia literary criticism, see Umacharan Pujari, *Odia Samalochana Sahityara Kramabikash* [The Development of Odia Criticism], Digapahandi: Gitarani Devi, 1963. pp. 2–5.
    Sudarsana Acharya, *Odia Kavya Kaushal (1500–1850)* [Odia Poetry: A Study of its Techniques], Cuttack: Friends' Publishers, 2002 [1983], pp. 122–163.
    Harihar Kanungo, "Prak-unavimsha Satabdira Odia Samalochana Sahitya" [Pre-nineteenth Century Odia Literary Criticism], *Odia Samalochana Sahitya* [Odia Literary Criticism], Bhubaneswar: Odisha Sahitya Akademi, 2015 [1989], pp. 105–133.
    Pradipta Kumar Panda, "Prachin o Madhya-kalin Sahitya Samalochana" [Literary Criticism in Ancient and Medieval Odisha], *Sahityapatra*, Cuttack: Department of Odia, Ravenshaw University, 2016–17, pp. 178–191.
2 Graham W. Shaw, "Cuttack Mission Press and Early Oriya Printing", *The British Library Journal 3* (1977), p. 41.
3 Bansidhar Mohanty, Ed., *Prabodh Chandrika (1856)*, Vani Vihar: Utkal University, 1984.
4 Bansidhar Mohanty, Ed., *Atharasha Chhasathi (Utkal Dipika)* [Eighteen Sixty-six (*Utkal Dipika*)], our translation, Cuttack: Friends' Publishers, 1978, p. 189.
5 Bansidhar Mohanty, *Odia Bhasha Andolana* [Movement for the Odia Language], Cuttack: Sahitya Sangraha Prakashan, 2nd ed., 2001, pp. 233–235.
6 Mrutyunjay Ratha, *Karmayogi Gourisankar*, Cuttack: Granthamandir, 2005 [1925], p. 16.
7 Bansidhar Mohanty, Ed., *Atharasha Chhasathi (Utkal Dipika)* [Eighteen Sixty-six (*Utkal Dipika*)], Cuttack: Friends Publishers, 1978, p. 187–189.
8 Ibid., pp. 21, 46, 158–159.
9 *Utkal Dipika*, 10 March 1869, appendix.
10 Gopal Chandra Praharaj, compiler, *Purnachandra Odia Bhashakosha*, vol. vii, Cuttack: Utkal Sahitya Press, 1940, p. 8193.
11 Arabinda Giri, Ed., *Odishara Prathama Sahitya Patra: Utkal Darpan* [The First Literary Periodical of Odisha: Utkal Darpan], Rourkela: Pragati Utkal Sangha, 2007, pp. 116–122.
12 Ibid., our translation, p. 119.
13 *Balasore Sambad Bahika*, 16 November 1876, our translation, p. 51.

14 Debi Prasanna Pattanayak, "Introduction", *Kabilipi* [Letters of Poets], Santiniketan: Odia Gabesana Bibhag, 1957, p. 12.
15 Recent scholarship has attributed the authorship of *Adarsh Prashnabali* to Radhanath Ray himself. See, Prasanna Kumar Mishra and Debendra Dash, Eds., *Radhanath Granthabali*, Cuttack: Grantha Mandir, 2010 [1998], pp. 402–417.
16 Ibid., p. 414.
17 Natabara Samntaray, *Odia Sahityara Itihas: 1803–1920*, Bhubaneswar: Prafulla Kumar Dhala and Hrudananda Bhola, 1964, p. 139.
18 *Sikshabandhu*, vol. 2 & 3, February–March 1886, p. 17.
19 Natabara Samantaray, "Genesis of the Modern Odia textbook", trans., Umasankar Patra, in *Natabara Samantaray: A Reader*, New Delhi: Sahitya Akademi, 2017, p. 46.
20 See the chapter "The Need for a Literary Periodical" in this volume.
21 Natabara Samantaray, "Genesis of the Modern Odia textbook", trans., Umasankar Patra, in *Natabara Samantaray: A Reader*, New Delhi: Sahitya Akademi, 2017, p. 44.
22 Sudarsana Acharya, *Odishara Asmita Sandhan o Upendra Bhanja Kabyalochana* [Upendra Bhanja and the Search for Odia Identity], Cuttack: Agraduta, 2013, p. 73.
23 Lala Ramnarayan Ray, "Kavi Upendra Bhanja", cited in Sudarsana Acharya, *Odishara Asmita Sandhan o Upendra Bhanja Kabyalochana* [Upendra Bhanja and the Search for Odia Identity], our translation, Cuttack: Agraduta, 2013, p. 270.
24 For a discussion of the two booklets, please see Debendra Dash's introduction to the reproduction of Damodar Mishra's *Dosa Darshan* in *Esana*, Vol. 41, Cuttack: Odia Gabesana Parisad, December 2000, pp. 2–6.
25 Sudarsana Acharya, "Indradhanu", *Indradhanu: Unabimsha Satabdira Eka Bismruta Patrika* [Indradhnau: A Forgotten Magazine of the Nineteenth Century], Berhampur: Centre for Regional Studies, Berhampur University, 1991, p. xlix.
26 See Pritam Mukherjee, "William Wilson Hunter and Colonial Bengal: Historiography, Literature, Modernity", unpublished dissertation, Jadavpur University, 2015, p. 27.
27 William Wilson Hunter, *Orissa: Or the Vicissitudes of an Indian Province under Native and British Rule*, vol. 2, London: Smith, Elder & Co., 1872, Appendix-IX, pp. 199–210.
28 Animesh Mohapatra, "The Local and the National in Oriya Public Sphere: 1866–1948", unpublished dissertation, University of Delhi, 2016, p. 107.
29 John Beames, "The Indigenous Literature of Orissa", *Indian Antiquary*, vol. 1, 1 March 1872, pp. 79–80.
30 John Beames, "Notes on the Rasakallola, An Ancient Oriya Poem", *Indian Antiquary*, vol. 1, 5 July 1872, pp. 215–217; 4 October 1872, pp. 292–295.
31 Debendra Dash, "Odia Sahityara Itihasa-rachana o Monmohan Chakravarti" [Monmohan Chakravarti and Literary Historiography in Odisha], *Esana*, vol. 20, Cuttack, June 1990, p. 179.
   Gaganendra Nath Dash, *Punascha Janasruti Kanchi-Kaberi* [Revising the Legend of Kanchi-Kaberi], Bhubaneswar: Rama Devi, 2014, p. 154.
32 John Beames, "Folklore of Orissa", *Indian Antiquary*, Vol. 1, 7 June 1872, p. 168.
33 In 1901, two compilations of Odia folktales – Gopal Chandra Praharaj's *Utkal Kahani* and Suchitra Devi's *Katha Lahari* – were published. Mohini Mohan Senapati's seminal essay on Odia folktales, serialized in *Utkal Sahitya* in 1902–03, has been included in this volume.
34 Monmohan Chakravarti, "Notes on the Language and Literature of Orissa", parts III and IV, *Journal of the Asiatic Society of Bengal*, vol. LXVI, no. IV, Calcutta: Asiatic Society, 1898, pp. 332–386.

35 Ibid., p. 333.
36 Priyaranjan Sen, *Modern Oriya Literature*, Calcutta: self-published, 1947, p. 49.
37 Biswanath Kar, "Suchana", *Utkal Sahitya*, vol. 1, no. 1, Cuttack, 1897, p. 2. See Aditya Nayak's translation of this essay included in this volume.
38 Abhiram Bhanja, "Utkal Sahityara Bartaman o Bhabisyat" [Odia Literature: Its Present and Future], *Utkal Sahitya*, vol. 7, no. 11, Cuttack, 1904, p. 342.
39 Mrutyunjay Ratha, "Adikavi Sarala Das", *Mukur*, vol. 5, nos. 1, 2 & 3, and 4 & 5, Cuttack, 1915, pp. 2–12, 60–72, 74–87.
40 Krushna Prasad Choudhary, "Samalochana", *Utkal Sahitya*, vol. 1, no. 6, reprinted, Cuttack: Sahityika, 1972 [1897], pp. 141–144.
41 Kamapal Mishra, "Siksha o Samalochana" [Education and Criticism], *Utkal Sahitya*, vol. 2, nos. 2 & 4, Cuttack, 1898, pp. 27–35 & 99–107.
42 Girija Sankar Ray, "Samalochanara Dhara o Lakshya" [Literary Criticism: Trends and Objectives], *Utkal Sahitya*, vol. 22, no. 10, Cuttack, 1919, pp. 453–458.
43 Umacharan Pujari, *Odia Samalochana Sahityara Kramabikash* [The Development of Odia Criticism], Digapahandi: Gitarani Devi, 1963, p. 38.
44 Madhusudan Rao, "Mukhabandha" [Foreword] to *Mahayatra*, *Radhanath Granthabali*, Shashi Bhusan Ray: Cuttack, 1916 [3rd ed.], pp.165–169.
45 Shri, "Samalochana", *Utkal Sahitya*, vol. 3, no.1, Cuttack, 1899, pp. 12–14.
46 Gopal Chandra Praharaj, "Duikhandi Odia Pustak" [Two Odia Books: A Review], *Utkal Sahitya*, vol. 6, no. 6, pp. 130–135.
47 Ashraf Ali Khan, "*Mamu* – Samalochana" [Fakir Mohan Senapati's *Mamu*: A Review], vol. 18, nos. 2 & 3, Cuttack, 1914, pp. 111–115 & 149–152.
48 Chandra Sekhar Nanda, "Chaturdashapadi Kavita" [Sonnet], *Utkal Sahitya*, vol. 7, no. 10, Cuttack, 1904, pp. 296–297.
49 See the following issues of *Utkal Sahitya* for this lively debate on *Basant Gatha*: vol. 23, nos. 10 & 12 (1920); vol. 24, no. 3 (1920).
50 Annada Sankar Ray, "*Basant Gatha*" [Madhusudan Rao's *Basant Gatha*: A Perspective], *Utkal Sahitya*, vol. 28, nos. 9, 10 & 11, Cuttack, 1924–25, pp. 316–321, 362–371 & 405–414.
51 Sumanyu Satpathy & Animesh Mohapatra, "Introduction", *Natabara Samantaray: A Reader*, New Delhi: Sahitya Akademi, 2017, pp. xiii–xiv.
52 Krushna Prasad Choudhary, "Vishwavidyalayare Odia Bhasha" [The Place of Odia Language in the University], *Utkal Sahitya*, vol. 5, no. 1, our translation, Cuttack, 1901, p. 16.
53 Ibid. pp. 16–17.
54 Ashutosh Mukherjee, "Outlines of a Scheme for the Advanced Study of the Indian Vernaculars", in *Typical Selections from Oriya Literature*, vol. 1, Ed. Bijoy Chandra Mazumdar, Calcutta: University of Calcutta, 1921, pp. i–ii.
55 Binayak Mishra's *Odia Sahityara Itihas* (1928) provoked a prompt response from Karunakar Kar – then principal of Sankrit college, Puri – in the form of a book titled *Sri Binayak Mishranka Odia Sahityara Itihasra Samalochana* (1929).
56 Kunja Bihari Das, *Mo Kahani* [Autobiogrpahy], Cuttack: Orissa Book Store, 1976, p. 207.
57 Nivedita Mohanty, *Ravenshaw College: Orissa's Temple of Learning, 1868–2006*, Jagatsinghpur: Prafulla, 2017, p. 95.
58 Krushna Charan Behera, *Akhira Dekha Pranara Katha* [What I have Seen and What I have Felt], Cuttack: Akshar, 2018 [2009], p. 63.
59 Umacharan Pujari, *Odia Samalochana Sahityara Kramabikash* [The Development of Odia Criticism], Digapahandi: Gitarani Devi, 1963. pp. 79–80. See also, Natabara Samantaray, "Swadhinata-para Odia Samalochana Sahitya: Samalochanara Parinam, Pattabhumi o Gati-prakriti" [Post-Independence Odia

Literary Criticism], in *Adhunika Odia Sahityara Bhittibhumi*, Cuttack: Friends Publishers, 1964, p. 267.

60 Natabara Samantaray, "Swadhinata-para Odia Samalochana Sahitya: Samalochanara Parinam, Pattabhumi o Gati-prakriti" [Post-Independence Odia Literary Criticism], in *Adhunika Odia Sahityara Bhittibhumi*, Cuttack: Friends Publishers, 1964, p. 275.

61 A view on the negative consequences of the academization of Odia literary criticism has been pungently articulated by Mayadhar Manasinha in *Odia Sahityara Itihas*, Cuttack: Grantha Mandir, 1967, p. 411.

1 Mohini Mohan Senapati
Odia folktales

Introduction

Mohini Mohan Senapati (1881–1945) was a professor of philosophy, an essayist, a literary critic and an occasional poet. Son of the famous Odia writer Fakir Mohan Senapati, Mohini Mohan was a radical thinker who challenged established moral conventions, questioned the existence of god and attacked, in particular, the hallowed institution of marriage. He embraced Brahmoism as a young man but later mounted a trenchant critique of its practices and tenets. His disillusionment with religion and its institutions led him quite early in his life to espouse an atheistic outlook which shocked many people and was revolutionary for its time. His iconoclastic worldview was shaped by his intensive reading of western philosophers, especially Friedrich Nietzsche. He made a unique contribution to the essay as an emerging literary form in Odisha by lending it analytical rigour, logical precision and polemical energy. In his essays, he explored, with unrelenting clarity, contentious issues such as sexual liberation, emancipation of women and the possibility of an afterlife. In this respect, he was far ahead of his contemporaries. A skilled controversialist, he vigorously engaged in debates with his opponents. He himself published a selection of his own essays in 1939 under the title *Bibidha Prasanga* [A Miscellany]. He also edited his father's autobiography and short stories.

The essay "Odia Kahani" [Odia Folktales] was presented by Mohini Mohan at Cuttack Alochana Sabha [discussion forum] and was later serialized in *Utkal Sahitya* in 1902. This constitutes a pioneering attempt at developing a critical framework for a systematic study of the folktale, which was yet to gain the status of a respectable literary form. It may be mentioned here that the growing interest in the collection and publication of folktales becomes discernible in the late nineteenth century, especially in Bengal and later in Odisha. Notable among such early compilations of Odia folktales are Gopal Chandra Prahraj's *Utkalara Kahani* [Tales of Utkal] and Suchitra Devi's *Katha Lahari* [Wave of Tales], both published in 1901. The immediate provocation for Mohini Mohan's essay can be traced to Gopal Chandra Prahraj's "simplistic" account of the origin of folktales. Adopting an incisive

DOI: 10.4324/9781003224778-1

taxonomical approach, Mohini Mohan classifies folktales from Odisha into useful categories. This reminds one of and interestingly anticipates the Russian formalist Vladimir Propp's *Morphology of the Folktales* (1928) where he analyzes folktales in terms of stock characters and their clearly defined functions. Mohini Mohan undertakes close content analysis to reach insightful conclusions about the moral and emotional world portrayed in folktales. He pays particular attention to the role imagination plays in folktales and sharply contrasts it with the role realism plays in modern novels. He locates the former in the world of orality and memory, and the latter in a world governed by pen and paper. He dismisses the assumption that folktales are the products of naïve and unsophisticated ways of experiencing and understanding the world by focusing upon their layered richness and complexity. In doing so the essayist creates a valuable space where the folktale could be examined as a serious literary form deserving of nuanced critical analysis. This plea for enhancing the status of folktales as literature might have led to a renewed appreciation of Sarala Das's *Mahabharata* which had earlier been devalued by scholars for its intimate ties with the world of folklore.

*

Odia folktales[1]

Mohini Mohan Senapati

I

Everyone, even a child, knows what folktales are. But once we enter the world they conjure up we are captivated by their charm and simplicity, and feel nostalgic about our childhood. Memories of numerous incidents lit up by imagination come vividly alive in our minds. These lead us away from the complications, duplicity and cupidity of adult life back to our blissful childhood.

The inclusion of folktales in the literary domain of Odisha is an important event. It remains to be seen how far this small initiative to find access to the lost world of the distant past through the study of folktales will take us. In order to succeed, our effort must include profound reflection, penetrating analysis and hard work. It is not as if such attempts have not been made elsewhere. In Britain, a forum called Folklore Society has been created where members collect, discuss and compare folktales and aphorisms of different countries. Their study of ancient societies in terms of their history, traditions, behavioural patterns etc. has yielded fascinating results. Although we operate on a much smaller scale, we can reach similarly important conclusions if we follow their methods. I am not sure if folktales have been subjected to scientific study in India, but we should not feel disappointed if this has not been done yet. At least in this matter, Odisha can show the way to other regions. However, we have to analyze these tales in depth before we can hope to achieve deeper insights into our multi-layered past.

When we step into the realm of the folktales, four vast worlds unfold themselves before us and tell us their stories – *devlok*, or the world of gods; *pitrulok*, or the world of ancestors in the upper sphere; *naglok*, or the nether world, peopled by snakes; and *narlok*, or the world of human beings that exists on the earth.

(1) *Devlok*: It is lightyears above the earth and gods reside here. These gods have infinite powers and they are omniscient too. They appear before their devotees in response to their prayers. Among all the deities mentioned in folktales, Shiva and Parvati are the most prominent. In the dead of night when everyone is asleep, the divine couple take a tour of the world. They provide food to the starving, clothes to the naked, money to the destitute; they grant their devotees whatever they pray for and happily go away. Sometimes they even bring the dead back to life by throwing a handful of water and a flower on them. Of the two, Parvati is more kind-hearted and affectionate. Sometimes the wail of the wretched fails to move Shiva but it always succeeds in melting Parvati's heart.

(2) *Pitrulok*: It is situated neither in heaven nor on the earth. It is a separate world and is the abode of ancestors. However, ancestors do not figure very frequently in the tales, and not much is said of them. They are the progenitors of human beings. Hindus offer oblations to their forefathers in the dark fortnight of the month of *Ashwina*.

(3) *Naglok*: It is located many fathoms below the earth. Some of its denizens assume the form of serpents, others that of human beings, and yet others are shapeshifters. They sometimes mingle with human beings.

(4) *Narlok*: We shall discuss this world and its inhabitants later in some detail.

It is not as if faith in these four worlds forms the basis of folktales only in Odisha; people in every village and district in India believe in these. Besides, the Puranic worldview has been assimilated into folktales across the country. It is not just at the level of emotions and beliefs that folktales of different regions share deep affinities; their subjects are also often similar. For instance, in many tales we come across the following key motifs – a king going into the forest on a hunting expedition, the chief queen of a king being humiliated by his other queens, the prince and the minister's son undertaking a journey to a remote destination and being attacked by ogres on the way. We can now safely surmise that the origins of folktales can be traced to the time when the Aryans had just begun to settle in the western parts of India, and when the *Puranas* and other tantric texts were being composed. Subsequently when the Aryans moved into different regions of the country, they carried their folktales with them. The tales were then contextually adapted and moulded by various cultures using their knowledge and imagination.

One could explain the similarities between folk tales from different parts of India on the basis of their common origin. But how does one account for the similarities we find in folktales of the world? Be it India, Italy, France, Greece or the Arabian world, the youngest daughter or son of a father is often the victim of the worst kind of exploitation and discrimination, and in the end s/he triumphs over adversity and inherits the patrimony. There are other motifs which are common to folktales across cultures: a man is supposed to marry a woman but he is deceived into marrying another bride; a brave young man abducts a young maiden whose father then goes looking for her; a man who is married to a woman from another world, or a woman who is married to a man from another world, eventually has to part with her or him; certain chambers are never meant to be opened, but out of irresistible curiosity or simply by mistake, someone opens them at their own peril; a husband is forbidden to utter his wife's name and the wife has to refrain from uttering his; spirits from other worlds enter the bodies of animals; humans and animals become great friends and come to each other's rescue. Scholars in the West have arrived at varied conclusions after analyzing such incidents from multiple tales. Many scholars are of the view that the imaginative world and customs of the ancients found expression in works that originate not from different sources but from one fountainhead and flowed through different channels. Some scholars opine that the folktales were composed much later, first in India and that they then travelled to the western parts. Some others believe that Egypt was the cradle of human civilization, from where folktales came to India. The diversity of opinions on this matter makes it difficult to reach a definite conclusion.

The Scottish folklorist Andrew Lang's opinions on this matter appear the most convincing. Lang argues that although the imagination of people of different places works in different ways, the similarity in its ways of expression should not surprise us. For, like material objects, human imagination too obeys certain laws. It is governed both by natural laws and laws of the mind. If these two laws are the same across regions then it is possible for different people to imagine similar things. If an Indian poet and his Greek counterpart experience similar thought processes and the external conditions encompassing them happen to be more or less the same, the products of their imagination are likely to resemble each other. What are these external conditions? They are: fertility of land, climate, food and wealth. Moreover, different parts of the world exchange folktales with each other. Intrepid merchants travel to other countries. Men and women of one country are sold as slaves in another. Thus, it would be wrong to assume that tales did not accompany such people during their journeys to far-off places. It is precisely because of these reasons that we find similarities underlying tales told in diverse regions.

While analyzing tales we have made a tour of the world. Let us now get back to India. If we accept Lang's views, we would arrive at the following conclusions. It is patently obvious that tales in various regions of India have been crafted in different ways. The grandly elaborate accounts that we find in folktales are actually built out of minor incidents imaginatively recreated by the primitive man. Although these incidents unfold in different regions they undeniably share broad affinities. It is simply because, in a country like India, cultural exchanges have always taken place among different regions and provinces. For instance, many tales have travelled from Bengal to Odisha and viceversa. The story entitled "Dui Sangat" [Two Close Friends] which Gopal babu[2] has collected from Odisha resembles a story included in Lal Behari Dey's *Folk Tales of Bengal* (1883). Although we come across folktales of different provinces we cannot assert that they belong to or originated in these places. Suppose someone claims that Odia folktales are actually from Bengal, then how do we contest this avowal? We might say that hills, rivers, lakes and forests abound in Odisha. So, it is but natural to find a description of aquatic animals and wild beasts in the tales. Or, that Odisha is a coastal region and therefore, there are descriptions of uninhabited islands and the two-headed mythical bird *gandabhairav*. But seas, rivers and forests are not exclusive to Odisha; they are found all over India. Had the tales mentioned river Mahanadi or lake Chilika, we could have affirmed that they originated in Odisha. There is no dearth of treasures in Odisha that would stimulate one's imagination. These include the huge temples of Puri and Bhubaneswar, the natural beauty of the Khandagiri hills, the serene shores of the Salandi and the Baitarini, the awe-inspiring sight of the sea, and scenic sites of pilgrimage like Jajpur and Kendrapada. But we do not find any mention of these places in the tales.

Odisha has witnessed catastrophes such as devastating wars, calamitous famines, outbreaks of anarchy. But they have not cast even the faintest shadow on the folktales. The tales never tell us of pilgrims being looted and murdered by *Bargis* while on their way to Puri and that a woman from the group escapes the marauders and takes shelter at the palace of a local feudal lord; nor do they tell us of how King Purushottam Dev gets separated from his soldiers on his way to the battlefield and finds himself in the hut of a poor man who throws him out because he cannot recognize the king. Had such historical details found their way into the folktales we could have accepted that they originated in Odisha.

How do we convince ourselves that these tales have not been borrowed from elsewhere? The ancients knew how to separate knowledge from imagination. They believed that what is imagined should have nothing to do with the world of knowledge. To them imagination loses much of its power when it comes into contact with knowledge. For instance, if I say that in a certain land, people were forty-foot tall, their children were twenty or thirty-foot tall and that the trees there grew to a height of two hundred feet, you will be all ears. But if I say that people in Balasore or Cuttack stand forty-foot tall, you will turn away in disbelief. The farther removed a tale is from the real world in terms of space and time, the stronger will be its imaginative appeal. It is because of this reason that the writer of *Ramayana* ensured that Ravana was born in the far-off Lanka and the *asuras* lived in the *Treta* and *Dwapar* ages long ago. Had they not done so, Ravana would have been dwelling in the outskirts of Dandakaranya and the *asuras* would be oppressing us here in the *Kali Yuga* itself. For this very reason one does not find references to familiar places and contemporary times. Only recently have we made an attempt to integrate knowledge into the world of imagination. For example, in historical novels the grand edifice of imagination is made to rest on the foundation of facts. However, the ancients for their part chose to wrap imagination in the luminous cover of unknowingness.

Although it is not possible to determine exactly when folktales came to be composed, it could still be suggested that in Odisha they were produced not in the recent past but at least a few centuries ago. In the past four hundred years or so Odisha has been battered by several man-made and natural disasters. It is hard to believe that while battling such calamities, people in Odisha could create folktales imbued with joyful vitality. For, no one has seen a hungry man sing.

Gopal Chandra Praharaj has offered a rather strange account of the origin of folktales. He writes,

> There can be no doubt at all that these tales were composed for little kids. But everybody will agree that young children are certainly not the authors of these tales. These are surely the products of adult imagination. But usually these tales are recounted by old women. They are told to young children in order to hold their attention and keep them out of mischief. In our society this task falls to old women. Therefore, I strongly believe that old women are the inventors of these tales.

Using the logic Gopal Chandra employs to reach his conclusion can lead others to arrive at very different inferences. Some may suggest that idle women invent these tales to pass the time pleasantly when their men are away at work. Scholars can go on arguing in favour of one conclusion or the other according to their knowledge, taste or whims. But we are not at all in a position to say who is right and who is not simply because we cannot travel back in time to the remote past in order to adjudicate these rival accounts.

Events and their causes are inseparably linked to each other. If we consider an event to be important we have to regard its cause to be no less important. Folktales are fundamentally aesthetic creations; trivial matters such as attending to babies or whiling away time cannot be advanced as cogent reasons for the creation of tales. Aesthetic creations cannot be explained in terms of mere external factors; they have to be traced in the depths of the human heart. Humans have realized since time immemorial that nothing brings them greater pleasure than the experience of beauty. But not enough beauty can be enjoyed at one place in the external world. However, the powers of imagination can supply its deficiencies by visualizing what lies at a distant place and unifying diverse kinds of beauty. The desire for aesthetic experience is not only the creative source of folktales in Odisha but the wellspring of imaginative literature everywhere, be it Arabian novels or Persian romances. Thus, it would not be wrong to assert that the plays and novels of our times and the tales of ancient times have sprung from the same desire.

II

We have dwelt long enough on the origins of folktales. Now let us focus on their distinctive formal characteristics. If we compare tales from ancient times with modern novels, we can notice several crucial differences.

(1) Unlike novels, tales were not concerned with developing minute details. They focused rather on the broader picture. But in contemporary novels we witness just the opposite. Minor plots, when aided by imagination, expand and branch out in different directions. The plot engenders subplots as imagination works its way through fine details. It is not as if the ancients were incapable of detailing incidents. If we try to examine the aesthetic architecture of texts like *Hitopadesha,* we can see how it has produced innumerable sub-plots which are woven into each other. The lack of concern with developing details may be attributed to one of the two factors: first, the ancients not using ink and paper; and secondly, their not feeling the need to use these tools. But these days, no matter how short a piece of writing is, pen and paper are a must. You may ask how pen and paper are relevant in examining the strengths and weaknesses of a composition.

When we transfer the world we imagine to paper, it becomes available to us in a tangible form. Or, it gets imprisoned through being recorded in writing; no aspect of it can now escape the writer. Novelists first construct a draft-image (broad outline) and analyze every element in it and gradually develop them through writing. Each episode or chapter lends substance to the outline and fills it out. Let us suppose the outline imagined has not been recorded in writing. When the storyteller tries to develop one element in the outline, it is very likely that he would forget about the one he had worked upon earlier. As a result no matter however vast a canvas the storyteller spreads in his mind he will never be able to focus on details and lend many-layered complexity to the picture. It is just like the case of a mother who has many daughters. She fails to attend to the other daughters when she concentrates on looking after only one. Similarly, if the poet concentrates on the basic outline, he fails to pay adequate attention to the individual parts of the work.

This limited holding capacity of the mind is the reason why tales fail to do justice to the minute details of a narrative.

(2) The modern novel focuses more on cerebration. The tales of olden times concentrated on depicting flights of imagination. The novel is bound by certain conventions. It cannot breach the boundaries of the world of facts. That which is popularly known and accepted, and realistic constitutes the subject matter of a novel. When the novel delves into the domain of the preternatural and the improbable it ceases to qualify as a novel. However, the novel does not stop at reporting ordinary everyday events. Rather it traces the links between those events and man's moral destiny. The tasks of a novelist also include the portrayal of the beauty of external nature and the human soul, the exploration of the relationship between the individual and society, and the demonstration of inviolable laws governing society and individual life. Folktales, on the other hand, are bound only by a few fundamental laws of aesthetic enjoyment. They freely breach the barriers of naturalness and plausibility and uninhibitedly inhabit the world of the supernatural. However, these boundaries remain sacrosanct for the modern novelist. Nymphs flying across the sky using a tree as a carrier to watch a wedding, people travelling from one end of the universe to another wearing a pair of magic clogs, the presence of a fabulous palace for a beautiful damsel in the middle of a tank, a magic boat that takes the rider wherever they wish to go, winged horses, ghosts, ogres and witches have no place in a novel but are absolutely welcome in folktales. Both tales and novels create a sense of excitement and wonder in us and, satisfy our emotional needs. But there is yet another task that the novel has to accomplish; it seeks to help us uncover the laws underlying the workings of the real world.

If people of our times choose to write tales would they succeed as magnificently as the ancients? Conversely, if the ancients tried their hand at writing novels would they perform the task as effectively? It is difficult to find satisfactory answers to these questions for we cannot measure the potency of the human mind. However, at least our experience tells us that one cannot achieve what the other can accomplish. We may approach this issue in two ways.

Folktales demand the unfettered exercise of the imaginative faculty; novels on the other hand call for acute intellect and minute observation. People in modern times are undoubtedly superior to the ancients in terms of intellectual attainment. But should this lead us to believe that the moderns are deficient in terms of their imaginative faculty? According to the laws of evolution, the older faculties of our mind do not get replaced by newer ones. In light of this, one might say that modern novelists can compose folktales and can even surpass the ancients.

However, if we were to take into account one particular principle of the workings of the mind, we would arrive at a different conclusion. The early stages of the development of the intellectual world were dominated by imagination and faith. In these it was perhaps easy to imagine and lend credence to the improbable and the supernatural. But when the dominion of intellect expands, the emphasis on probability and naturalness grows stronger. An adult would not be able to repose as much faith in the improbable and the supernatural as a child can. If a four-year-old child and a ten-year-old are left in the same dark room, the latter will perhaps see one ghost, while the former will swear to have seen ten. As a human individual passes through periods of infancy and young days, the human race too has its own childhood and youth. The human race in ancient times can be compared with a child and in its present state it can be likened to a youth. Imagination was the defining characteristic of the ancient world whereas the modern is dominated by scientific knowledge. Therefore, by such a logic, the ancient authors would surpass their modern counterparts in crafting tales. If the creator of *Arabian Nights* were asked to write *Bisha Briksha* [The Poisoned Tree], he would be totally at a loss. Conversely, if Bankim Babu were asked to compose *Arabian Nights*, he would be completely bewildered.

From this it becomes clear that those endowed with a stronger imaginative faculty can appreciate and enjoy folktales fully. But in order to enjoy a tale one has to believe in it. If we are unable to suspend our disbelief we can never delight in it. The more credulous one is the more pleasure one derives from the tales. Children are not as sceptical as adults; their belief in the credibility of tales is stronger. And that is precisely the reason why tales absorb and entertain them so much. But does it imply that stories have nothing to offer to adults?

These days, quite a few people find it shocking that folktales are published as literature. They believe that since the tales are meant for children they have no value for adults. And even children lose interest in them when they grow up. Therefore, they are of the view that these tales should not be inflicted on readers. But do these tales really arouse aversion and disgust in adult readers? We have stated earlier that folktales are primarily enjoyed by children. Now, the question arises whether these can interest adults too? The answer is, adults do not belong to an entirely different species. There lives a child in every adult. If we so wish, the child lying dormant in us can be awakened and we can very well savour everything that a child takes delight in. You may ask, a child finds tales diverting because of ignorance but a grown-up endowed with knowledge, will he derive any pleasure from these tales? The answer is yes. Every human being is capable of surrendering himself to the wonderful and the fantastic by letting his imagination overpower his intellect. If man did not possess the faculty of imagination, he would not have been able to enjoy any aesthetic object, be it poetry, drama, fiction or visual arts. What after all is aesthetics? It is not the discovery of knowledge but imagination coming alive. It takes imagination to appreciate any aesthetic object; what has science to do with it? Those young men, who take pride in their knowledge and disparage imaginative tales, directly or indirectly denigrate and devalue their own powers of imagination. With this we come to the end of the second part of this essay. In the third part we shall briefly discuss the characters who appear in the tales and in the final part, we shall conclude by examining the potential of folktales as windows to their contemporary world.

III

In the previous sections we have spoken of four worlds – *devlok*, *pitrulok*, *naglok* and *narlok*. The prime concern of this essay is the fourth world, the world of men, which can further be divided into two realms, that of the sentient and that of the insentient. The first comprises humans, non-humans and animals. Humans are divided into men and women. In order to discuss the characters who inhabit the world of folktales, we have to divide them into five categories: (1) men, (2) women, (3) non-humans, (4) animals, and (5) insentient objects. One may find such classification funny, for we are familiar with only the analysis of the portrayal of human beings as characters in fiction. We rarely, if ever, come across any discussion of the characters of non-humans and never do we hear anyone analyzing the characters of animals and insentient objects. But in folktales each of these character types possesses language skills, emotions and souls. In the world of tales there is little difference between sentient beings and insentient objects. Therefore, each of these five broad types merit discussion.

(1) **Men:** Folktales feature relatively few male characters. Notable among them are kings, ministers, princes, sons of ministers, merchants and *kotwals* [police in modern-day parlance]. In the social order of those days, they occupied positions of power and that is why they are considered important in tales too. As in the present times, in the ancient days, ministers played key roles in the king's court. For example, the king sentences the queen to death and orders the minister to carry out the execution. He asks the minister to bring her blood from the place of execution, after seeing which he will have his food. This stuns the minister. The king adds, "if you don't do as I say, you and your family will be wiped out". This sums up the relationship between the king and the minister. Suppose today Edward VII gives a similar order to his minister Lord Salisbury, the world would turn upside down.

Of the prince and the minister's son, the former is generous and the latter, clever. Just as the minister helps the king, his son supports the prince. The two share strong bonds of intimacy. The minister's son accompanies the prince on his journey to distant lands. The inherent king-like qualities never desert a prince. Even if he is thrown into a forest, the prince eventually manages to marry a princess and gain the throne by virtue of his own abilities and luck.

(2) **Women:** In folktales, women appear as a strange lot; they strike one as a bundle of contradictions. They can be wise and silly, brave and

timid. When husbands face grave danger, their brilliantly resourceful wives often turn out to be their sole saviours. And yet a queen faints when she is informed that she has given birth not to a living baby but to a wooden doll. In the tale, every time she gives birth to a baby, her sisters bury it in a dung heap and place a wooden doll beside her. Even while going through terrible ordeals, women do not forget their bosom female friends for a moment, and yet a minor slip of memory makes them treat their husbands with atrocious harshness. Women are usually described as weak, helpless and dependant on others but in many stories we meet women who travel miles on horseback, climb trees, slay their enemies and commit many acts of daredevilry.

But there is one shortcoming which is repeatedly attributed to women in tales, i.e., their insatiable curiosity. Once their curiosity is aroused no power in the world can smother it. In a folktale, the son of a merchant tells his wife, "Open all doors, except this one". Saying so he goes away. The wife starts wondering, "Why did he forbid me from opening every room but one? He has definitely hidden some precious object in that room, but does not want me to see it." It is believed that on account of a woman's impatient curiosity that Lord Jagannath is bereft of his limbs. While the wooden images were being carved in a locked room, the queen[3] could not repress her curiosity and opened the door she was not meant to, and the divine sculptors left the images unfinished.

(3) **Non-humans**: In tales we find elaborate depictions of non-humans. Among the non-humans, the gods protect the humans and grant their prayers. But the non-humans we are about to discuss are the ones who cause dread and terror in human beings, and if a human ever falls into their clutches, they would find no escape. These non-humans may or may not have a physical form. The disembodied ones among them include *dahanis* [witches], *chirukunis* [witches of a lower order], *bhutas* [ghosts] and *brahmarakshasas* [ogres]. They wander around at night; sometimes human beings spot them in the dark but they return to their hiding places during the day. Among those who have bodies, *asuras* are the most important. They eat, sleep and move about just like human beings. But what they eat includes human beings. We shall discuss the disembodied creatures first.

Dahanis [witches] are the most important of the lot. They can spit fire through their mouths. When they open their mouths, their surroundings get lit up and when they close their mouths, these grow pitch dark. *Chirukunis* are witches' sisters but they belong to a lower order. Although there are instances of witches and *chirukunis* devouring children, they are less terrifying than ghosts. The souls of people who do not perform good deeds while alive do not reach heaven after death. They wander on earth as ghosts. They are usually very tall, so much so that when they sit atop a tree near a river bank, their feet touch the other bank across the river. They play dice with human bones. They snatch food from human beings and spread terror in the villages. The *brahmarakshasas* [ogres] are like ghosts but are far deadlier. Those young Brahmins who commit sins and other misdeeds when alive end up becoming *brahmarakshasas* after death.

One cannot be sure why these supernatural and unearthly creatures were created in the first place. But the ancients believed that human nature was incorrigible – those who were awful when they were alive would continue to torment people even after their death. Their souls are imperishable, and their next birth is decided on the basis of their good and bad deeds in this life. The belief in the indestructibility of souls, the incorrigibility of human nature, punishment for sins and rewards for virtues nourishes imagination and renders it vibrant.

But such forms of imagination, instead of leading us towards knowledge, drive us away from it. They enfeeble us. Listening to ghost stories in our childhood days has only made us shallow. Tormented by the glare of science, these ghosts and phantoms have retreated from our lives into the recesses of our minds where they survive as illusions. No one among us believes in these ghosts but sometimes our imagination so powerfully overwhelms our reason that ghosts appear vividly before us and we cannot but take illusion for reality. Sometimes we venture into the dark, steeling ourselves and lighting the way with the torch of scientific reason. But imagination like a gust of wind blows out the torch and we become incoherent with terror; our blood freezes and we faint. The imaginative faculty we feed with fantasy in our childhood returns to haunt and terrify us when we are adults.

Ghosts do not live in the open; they lie dormant in our minds. They may suddenly wake up and take us into their grip. We may exorcize them for a time through incantations and spells but we cannot permanently expel them by defying the laws of the mind. According to these laws, an image called up again and again crystallizes into a habit and will recur in response to the slightest stimulation. So, if right from our childhood ghosts are repeatedly invoked in our minds, it is not very hard to guess how brave we will turn out to be when we grow up! No wonder Odia men are so timid! In childhood, they are scared of ghosts. As they grow up, the ghosts enter the canes wielded by their teachers. When they receive higher education they are mortally afraid of their principals and professors. They fear that even the mildest criticism of the principal might lead to rustication and their career will be ruined. Subordinates do not wish to incur the wrath of their superiors, lest they should lose their job, and so on. Thus, we live dying every moment of our life. So, why did we digress so far while speaking of ghosts? In ghosts lie the origin of fear and fear stays with us until we die. If one wants to identify the shortcomings inherent in our community we should locate its source in fear. Just as modesty is considered a proper adornment for women, these days timidity has become an embellishment for men. The first has led to a loss of independence for women and the second results in the loss of independence of the whole community.

Enough has been said of the disembodied beings; it is time we turned to embodied non-humans. *Asuras* [demons] who belong to this category feature prominently in folktales. Often it is difficult to distinguish them from human beings, for even though they belong to a different category, their way of speaking and their manners are similar to those of humans. In some tales, *asuras* are presented as grotesque figures, and yet in others, they are mistaken for humans. Even though humans are the *asuras*' natural prey, sometimes these predators are seen helping human beings. *Asuras* have a few defining characteristics, such as:

i)   They are voracious eaters. We have heard stories of *asuras* devouring large quantities of rice, vegetables, drying an entire river to quench their thirst and so on. One may wonder if human beings cannot have a gargantuan appetite. But *asuras* have another defining characteristic, which human beings do not share.

ii) *Asuras* sometimes eat human beings. There are numerous folktales of humans being devoured by these demonic creatures. Take, for example, the famous tale of "Budhi Asuruni" in which an old demoness who invites some boys to her home offers them food, only to make a meal of them later.

iii) *Asuras* fear none, but someone wielding weapons terrifies them. In a tale, the son of a merchant goes to a village and finds it completely deserted. The *asura* who has devoured everyone in the village confronts him. When the young man brandishes his weapon, the *asura* falls at his feet and begs him to spare his life.

iv) *Asuras* can take any corporeal form they want or even vanish altogether. But not all among their species are capable of performing this trick.

(4) **Animals:** We shall now throw some light on animal characters in folktales. Animals might differ from humans in terms of physical appearance, but their ways and manners are not significantly different from those of human beings. But in one respect they are remarkably different from their human counterparts; gratitude is their defining trait. They are loyal to their benefactors and never fail to return a favour. In many tales, we come across animals who help their human benefactors when they are in grave danger. Among animals who feature in folktales, elephants and snakes deserve special attention.

i)   Elephants: It is said that when a king dies and his kingdom is left without a ruler, an elephant is made to carry a golden pitcher filled with water in its trunk. The person on whose head the elephant pours the water ascends the throne. Or when an ideal husband has to be chosen for a young princess, the elephant selects the intended one from among the suitors by pouring water from a pitcher thrice on his head. The elephant is tasked with bestow upon people what fate has in store for them. The elephant character in folktales reveals a deep-rooted belief of the ancients: "Na vidya na cha paurusham, bhagyam phalati sarvatra" [Neither learning nor valour matters; only what fate decrees comes to pass]. The elephant empties the pitcher of fortune on the head of one who does not have the ghost of a chance of becoming a king and on another who has not even dreamt of marrying a princess. The elephant functions as a figurative instrument of fate.

ii) Snakes: The ancients believed that there is a *mani* [gem] on the snake's hood. When the snake comes out, the glowing gemstone illuminates the area for miles around. Snakes give birth to snakes but also to human beings. They are shapeshifters too. There is the story of a *chakulia panda* [singing mendicant] and a prince of the *naglok* [kingdom of snakes]. The mendicant goes to a river to take bath. The young snake prince, who is eager to see the world, enters the mendicant's jug in the form of a snakelet. When the mendicant's wife empties the jug at home, she finds a handsome boy in it.

(5) **Insentient beings:** We shall now come to the last of the five types of creatures we encounter in folktales. In many tales, insentient beings act as if they are alive and conscious. But their actions are often driven by human needs. In many tales these function figuratively. Take, for example, the *gemstone* found on the snake's hood. Whoever has it in his possession can become rich by selling it. But once it passes into someone else's hands, it ceases to yield any benefit to its previous owner. The gemstone, therefore, is neutral; it brings happiness and prosperity only to the one who owns it. Let us now look at the role the gemstone plays in folktales. Here is one good example. In a tale, a merchant's son has a gemstone. He asks, "O *gemstone*, tell me, to whom you belong?" The gemstone replies, "I belong to the one who holds me in his hands". The merchant's son asks, "What can you do for me?" "Whatever you wish me to ...", comes the reply. The merchant's son commands the gemstone to build a magnificent jewelled palace with a beautiful pond bounded by marble embankments and a garden full of silver trees bearing golden fruits in front of the king's royal residence. The gemstone dutifully carries out the task in no time. However, when the king lays hold of the gemstone, it obeys the king with the same sincerity, and transports the merchant's son, now dressed in rags, to a doorless temple on a far-off island. Alas, the gemstone turns out to be entirely untrustworthy.

IV

We have spoken on so many issues pertaining to folktales but we have not touched upon a very crucial matter: what do folktales tell us about their contemporary world? Let us elaborate on this issue. We previously argued that folktales depict an imaginary world not rooted in a specific time and place. So, we cannot extract any verifiable historical information from these. Nevertheless, we must now ask, what can still be gleaned from folktales about the times and places in which they were created?

It is true that folktales have come from distant lands and are not related to contemporary times. But the characters featured in them, the way they express themselves and their manners do speak of the land of their origin. Folktales do not directly reveal any historical facts but it is possible for a perceptive reader to discover in them information on laws, customs, manners, knowledge systems, religion and so on. But if we were to discuss each of these topics in detail, it would require a book-length study. Therefore, we shall touch upon some of these issues and see what folktales reveal about knowledge systems, love, moral values, faith etc.

i) **Knowledge system:** Each folktale goes on to speak of the knowledge system prevalent in the period. We would be grossly mistaken if we thought that the ancients were constantly absorbed in a daydream; this daydream to which they then fixed wings has flown to us across the centuries and enraptures us with its sweet melodies. However short a tale might be, composing it demanded considerable skill and intellectual acuity. Had Gopal Chandra Prahraj taken this into account he would not have put forward the view that these were created by old women to divert restive children. If one accepts Gopal babu's view, we have to acknowledge that the ancient world was intellectually far more advanced than the world we live in today. It would be impossible to find a woman in the whole of Odisha in these days who could author such ingeniously crafted tales to put a child to bed. Have we then declined in terms of our imaginative powers? It would have been a golden age indeed if in every house there lived a woman of the calibre of Maria Edgeworth in Britain, Swarnakumari in Bengal or Reba Ray in Odisha. But there is no reason to accept Gopal babu's view.

In order to get a sense of how wise the ancients were, let us revisit the tale in which a king asks his minister to weigh his favourite elephant. The minister is warned that, if he fails to measure the weight of the elephant by the following day, he will be beheaded. A clever merchant's son promises to help the minister out of this crisis. He gets the elephant into a boat and marks with a piece of chalk the point to which water rises on the sides of the boat. After the elephant steps out, the boat is filled up with sand till it sinks to the marked point. The sand is removed from the boat and weighed, and thus the elephant's correct weight is ascertained. We can easily infer from this tale that knowledge and wisdom were valued in ancient times.

ii) **Love:** It is a matter of regret that the high ideals of love are not to be found in folktales. It is not as if people were strangers to the emotion of love in those days. But love is mostly defined in terms of physical desire. In a certain story, the prince and the minister's son feel attracted to the same girl, and decide among themselves that they would both marry her. But is the lady an object to be shared among men! It seems the experience of unconditional heartfelt love was absent in the world portrayed in folktales. We do not imply here that this experience is abundantly present in our time. Even now love is a matter of physical attraction; people look for fair-complexioned brides and shun dark-skinned ones. In folktales, one invariably comes across scenes of union; separation forms no part of their scheme.

iii) **Moral values:** Ambiguity characterizes the moral universe of folktales. On the one hand, a father heartlessly sends his little daughters into the jungle for having committed some trivial offence, a king orders the queen to be executed for the slightest lapse on her part, or a criminal is killed in the most unspeakably barbaric manner. On the other hand, characters display exemplary courage and loyalty under extreme circumstances. For instance, the minister's son smilingly lays down his own life in order to save the prince. Animals and birds also put their lives at risk to protect their benefactors. Some characters, to fulfil a vow, sacrifice everything including their wealth, honour and spouse. Do not these qualities indicate the existence of a noble moral order?

iv) **Faith:** Although a lot has already been written about the faith and belief systems of the ancients, we shall end this essay by briefly discussing this subject. The ancients were alien to both atheism or agnosticism. Our contemporaries recognize no world except the one experienced by humans and are convinced that the world exists solely for their benefit. The ancients, for their part, could not even imagine such a world and perceived a soul animating it. That is why in the Ganga they found a Ganga Mata, a god (Varuna) in the sea, a mother goddess (Vasumata) in the earth and a Lord (Indra) in the sky. They could recognize a living presence in every object of nature. They believed in life after death, and that consequences of actions in one life will be endured in another. They were also fatalists, who saw the working of fate in every event of life.

I had begun this essay with reminiscences of childhood experiences of listening to folktales and now I conclude by citing lines from a poem:

> After telling tales to each other, innocent young girls
> enthralled everyone with their playful laughter!
> The fair of merriment has come to a close and those
> Who delighted in it have gone no one knows where!
> ...
> Why did that enchanted world vanish,
> To me it seems as if it was all a dream!

Translation: Shaswat Panda

Notes

1 Mohini Mohan Senapati, "Odia Kahani", *Utkal Sahitya,* vol. 6, nos. 1, 2 & 4, ed. Biswanath Kar, Cuttack: Utkal Sahitya Press, 1902, pp. 13–19, 40–50, 85–88.
2 Gopal Chandra Praharaj is an eminent Odia lexicographer, literary critic, and public intellectual who collected and published a volume of Odia folktales titled *Utkalara Kahani* (1901).
3 [Translator] This is a reference to queen Gundicha, the wife of King Indradyumna. Legend has it that a divine sculptor came to King Indardyumna and assured him that he would carve the image of Jagannath out of the wooden log that the king had received. But he would do so only on the condition that he would be allowed to work behind closed doors and that the doors would not be opened without his permission. The only way of knowing that he was busy at work was the sound of the hammer and the chisel, which could be heard from outside. One day, when no sound is heard, the queen grows impatient and orders the doors to be opened. When the doors are finally thrown open, the sculptor is found missing and the construction of the images remain incomplete.

2   Chakradhar Mohapatra
Village songs in Odia

Introduction

Chakradhar Mohapatra (1908–1987) was an eminent creative writer, historian, biographer and folklorist. His novels *Duhkhini Gobar Gotei* [The Destitute Girl] (1930), *Khanjei Nahakani* (1932), *Balangi* (1932) and *Rodang Baxi* (1936) enjoyed pervasive popularity. The first two books received such readerly appreciation that they were given as gifts to brides at the time of wedding and the other two were based on episodes from the history of Odisha. Chakradhar's interest in history led him to explore incidents relating to Mughal rule in Odisha in *Utkal Itihasar Eka Ajnat Adhyay* [An Unknown Chapter in the History of Odisha] (1969) and speculate on the possibility of Gautam Buddha's birth in Odisha in a book written in English titled *The Real Birthplace of Buddha* (1977). His biography of the brief but eventful life of Kuntala Kumari Sabat (1901–1938), a legendary writer and public figure, is recognized as a classic. Chakradhar wrote poems and plays, edited the collected works of the poet and satirist Jadumani Mohapatra (1776–1866), and was closely associated with the project of compiling an Odia encyclopaedia executed by Utkal University. It is Chakradhar's thoroughgoing work as a folklorist which carved a niche for him in the cultural world of Odisha. In this endeavour, he was ably assisted by his wife Kanak Manjari Devi. He started assiduously collecting village songs in the 1930s and prepared a manuscript in 1947. The work involved extensive fieldwork carried out in different parts of Odisha. As institutional support was not forthcoming, it took him more than a decade to get it published. Building on Gopal Chandra Praharaj's pathbreaking work in this field, Chakradhar's ambitious book *Utkal Gaunli Gita* [Village Songs in Odia] (1959) expanded the scope of folklore studies in Odisha, and gave it a new direction.

The following has been excerpted from Chakradhar's exhaustive introduction to the book mentioned above. Here, Chakradhar takes exception to the expression *loka sahitya* [folk literature] and suggests a vital distinction between the terms *loka* [folk] and *gramya* or *gaunli* [relating to villages]. He is of the view that the term *loka* denotes people in general, city dwellers as well as villagers. He, therefore, argues that "folk literature" should be more

DOI: 10.4324/9781003224778-2

appropriately designated as "village literature". Chakradhar observes that urban literature tends to universalize and standardize expressions whereas village literature preserves the irreducible individuality of a language. He shows how translating a village song even into a cognate language is an extremely difficult undertaking. He then goes on to underscore the threats which the artificial Sanskritized idiom popularized by eminent modern writers like Radhanath Ray and Madhusudan Rao posed to the very survival of Odia language. He sees in Fakir Mohan Senapati's writings an attempt to retain and celebrate the vitality and distinctiveness of the language deeply rooted in a rural milieu. Recognizing women to be the authors of most of these songs, Chakradhar maintains that these have largely sprung from the lived experience of grief and loss. For their survival, village songs depended not on writing but on memory and transmission through performative practices. These belong to several types and are sung collectively and individually depending on the occasion. Chakradhar extends the scope of village songs by including songs written by city poets that achieved immense popularity among villagers through frequent recitation. In this excerpt, Chakradhar voices his anxiety about English education rapidly eroding literature created in the villages. Chakradhar's endeavour acquires significance when placed in the context of earlier attempts made by scholars like Shyam Sundar Rajguru and Mohini Mohan Senapati, who sought to locate the roots of Odia literature in its rich oral tradition. This contributed to the expansion of Odia literary canon and led eminent public figures such as Fakir Mohan, Gopabandhu Das and Nilakantha Das, who were engaged in bringing about a cultural renewal of Odisha, to find in the living idiom of the literature created in villages an alternative source of vitality.

*

Village songs in Odia[1]

Nomenclature

The widely-current colloquial alternative to the formal Sanskritized expression *gramya* [rural] is *gaunli* [relating to village life]. *Gaunli gita* or village songs may be defined as songs created by villagers themselves, which, having thoroughly grasped their meaning, they sing with great fervour and which spread from village to village.

These village songs, however, are our time being presented as *lokagita* [folk songs]. But the scope of the term is so broad that it cannot be made to refer to only men and women living in the village. One of the meanings of *loka* may be the general public. But *loka* usually means the whole world. A look at the word *lokantar* [another world] will make the meaning of the term *loka* clearer. Similarly, in Lokanath [god] and Lokamata [Lakshmi, the goddess of wealth] the prefix *loka* unequivocally means the whole of humanity. However, since long, humanity has comprised two distinct domains: *paura* [urban] and *gramya* [rural]. Literature created in the urban domain was usually written down whereas literature created in the village was oral in nature. The latter sometimes got merged into urban literature, and at others was lost without a trace. Urban literature placed a high value on devices of poetic embellishment and expression of emotions constituted the essence of village songs. Spontaneity characterizes village songs and they are usually rooted in the experience of sorrow. Other expressions or emotions also found expression in these.

Vedic incantations stemmed from the hopes and desires of simple, unpolluted hearts, were committed to memory, and orally transmitted from generation to generation. These originated in villages, not in urban spaces, for in those days the love for urban sophistication had not contaminated the human heart.

In *loka samasta sukhino bhavantu* [may everyone be happy], *loka* does not simply refer to people living in the countryside. Moreover, the prefix *lok* in Lok Sabha [Parliament] does not merely represent villagers but the entire population of India. By *loka* one chiefly understands people in general. One comes across the following line in our collection of village songs: "When people [loka] would ask me who I am, how could I tell them I am the daughter of the village headman?" Here too, the term *loka* encompasses people, ordinary as well as uncommon. Therefore, it is not correct to designate village songs as folk [*loka*] songs. However, they can appropriately be placed under the category of rural [*gramya* or *palli*] literature. In the line *janakirnam manye hutavah paritam grihamiva* [the crowded house appears to be consumed by fire], *janakirna* means "packed with people". Here city-dwellers are also referred to as *jana* or *loka*. Thus, the term *loka* includes all kinds of people such as city dwellers, refined ladies and gentlemen, aristocratic persons, and villagers. So, it would be convenient to consider songs current in rural areas as village songs [*gaunli gita*]. The volume is therefore entitled *Utkal Gaunli Gita* [Village Songs of Odisha]. Gopal Chandra Praharaj, the legendary compiler of *Purnachandra Odia Bhashakosha*, has used the expression *gaunli gita* several times in his discussion of proverbs and badinage.

Rural literature

From a linguistic point of view, a literature which has retained its distinctive individuality and not become standardized and universalized can be rightly called rural literature. The language of this literature, having escaped the uniformity brought about by standardization, has preserved its unaffected naturalness and spontaneity. It is but natural that the confined world in which this literature is rooted provides it with deep nourishment and protects it from contamination. But on account of its isolation, it lacks the energy to expand its scope of expression. Zealously guarding its separate sphere of existence, it often withers like a fragrant forest flower. Village songs are unadorned by any embellishment; they speak the language of the soil and share no similarities with flowers grown in a garden. These exude a sense of freedom one associates with birdsong and are completely devoid of deception. These are not fettered by the constrictive prescriptions of grammar. In these we hear the ancient Vedic chants recited with full-throated ease by *rishis* on the banks of river Saraswati. When a cuckoo sings, the sound of a resonating veena does not accompany its song. But its voice leaves the whole world enthralled and in it lies the soul of melody. Similarly, the language used in villages is the "essence" of language, and is the foundation on which all literature rests. All cultures owe their origin to the distinctive individuality of the language spoken by villagers. It is the mother of all civilizations.

One wonders if its insularity would endanger the language spoken in villages. Should one consider this undeveloped if the literature created in it does not get universalized? No, one should not. In fact, that which remains intensely rooted in the local constitutes the rural. If the literature of the village loses its singularity, in course of time, urban literature will perish, smothered by its own artificiality. When the latter faces a crisis of survival, it is the literature created in villages that comes to its rescue. The body of literature Radhanath Ray and Madhusudan Rao produced following Sanskrit models and employing an unnatural idiom would have made us forget how Odia was actually spoken or written, had Fakir Mohan Senapati not appeared on the literary scene. In fact, the dominance of the influence of Radhanath and Madhusudan for a few more years would have caused Odia language to die on its own. In their hands Odia language would have lost its cultural specificity as would be made clear by the following example:

> *Pahili pali bou delu pathai* [You sent me the first time, O Mother]
> *Sangare jaithile Sana Kakei.* [With me was father's youngest brother.]

This couplet does not easily translate into Bangla, which is a cognate language. The custom of *pahili pali* [sending a bride to her in-laws' place for the first time after she attains puberty] is not observed in Bengal. There, the groom takes the bride to his house two or three days after the wedding. The girl returns to her parental home ten days after the wedding to spend a few days there. The ceremony associated with her return to her in-laws' place resembles those connected with the *pahili pali* in Odisha. In Bengal this ceremony is known as *dwiragaman jatra* [the second journey]. A Bangla translation of the couplet will not be able to convey the cultural specificities inherent in the Odia couplet. However, similar challenges do not confront attempts to translate modern Odia poetry into Bangla. The following instance will illustrate this point. The line *bhadar nilakash badal rakhe aji ghodai* [the blue sky is covered by clouds in the month of Bhadrab] presents no difficulty when it is translated into Bangla. When a language finds itself on the verge of extinction, the literature of villages helps it retrieve its individuality. Thus, this literature is like a family heirloom of immeasurable value.

When we set out to write a history of language, village songs and stories prove to be extremely valuable sources of information. Moreover, they also help us trace the evolution of the rhythmic patterns of our poetry and identify the roots of our social practices and problems. In short, they are absolutely essential for getting to know our own culture intimately. Centuries of social and political subjugation rendered us timidly imitative. During such a crisis, the uninhibited expressiveness of literature of the village equipped us with cultural tools of self-protection. However, this crucial role of rural literature has been largely overlooked. A few notable exceptions come to mind in this regard: Shyam Sundar Rajguru, who authored a few original articles on Odia language and its rhythmic patterns; Gopinath Nanda Sarma, the philologist and critic; and Aparna Panda, who wrote articles on Odia proverbs. They have scrupulously examined the profoundly distinctive identity of Odia language. It should be noted that, afterwards, Gopabandhu Das and his associates, especially, Nilakantha Das and Godabarish Mishra, made vigorous efforts to employ living Odia speech in their writings. Gopal Chandra Praharaj's initiatives in this field also deserve special mention. The impactful contribution of these writers has led even those who trained their sensibility reading the works of Radhanath Ray and Madhusudan Rao to display in their own writings a deep affinity for the literature and language of villages. It is now widely accepted that enlarging the scope of collecting the literature of villages is a desirable undertaking.

Genesis of village songs

People living in villages far outnumber city dwellers. Urban literature was circulated among and carefully conserved by the ruling elite and the educated for they have material resources such as palm leaf, stylus, pen and paper, and institutions like the temple and the court at their disposal. However, the songs that expressed the hopes, joys, sorrows and festive ecstasy of innumerable villagers lacked this material means and institutional support. The songs found their vehicle in memory. And memory generated oral recitation. As civilization advanced, human memory grew less and less retentive and countless village songs sank into oblivion. English education erased these songs from the memory of the community. Things have now come to such a pass that when an elderly woman recited a beautiful song from memory to her daughter-in-law, she was laughed to scorn by an English-educated young man. The intensity of the ridicule wiped the song from her heart. One may thus conclude that the unimpeded flow of imaginative life in villages dried up under the scorching gaze of English education. Thousands of village songs, however, miraculously continue to survive. When one seeks to find out how these songs first came to be created and sung, one is filled with amazement. Oppressed by thirst while tilling a field far away from home, an unlettered and lonely ploughman sings in order to relieve the monotony and arduousness of his task. Some of his songs convey his feelings of joy and others a sense of deprivation. His joy knows no bounds when the seeds sprout, weeds are removed, and the time of harvest arrives. This is how songs of ploughmen were created and, later memorized and circulated orally. From time immemorial these songs have enlivened fields and groves in villages.

One day at hot noon, a young and slender daughter-in-law makes her way to a streamlet flowing at a distance from her house. As she trudges along, the sweet song of a cuckoo relieves her pain. Her heart overflows with feelings of a strange ecstasy without her knowing it. The cuckoo is joined by an oriole singing lustily "*Krishna koko ho*". Baby Krishna is restless when his mother Jashoda rubs turmeric paste on him. He calms down and sits still when this bird flies in and perches near him. Saying "You have done me a great favour", a grateful Jashoda lovingly puts a little turmeric paste on the bird. The daughter-in-law is familiar with this story. All these characters – Jashoda, Krishna and the oriole – flash before her eyes. The songs of *chasapua chahatia* birds come wafting from a distant forest and fill her heart with enchantment. The feelings these songs and stories stir in her heart find expression in sweet ditties. It seems as if her songs convey an extraordinary depth of pathos. The sweetness of her song seamlessly blends with the mellifluousness of the cuckoo's voice. It is neither fettered by the discipline of rhythmic patterns nor burdened by poetic embellishments. It is almost as if the distilled anguish women have experienced over the ages form the core of such songs.[2]

> *Shaga katibi boli paniki thoi* [While slicing greens for cooking]
> *Mana bikal hela padili soi lo.* [I felt sad and fell asleep.]
> *Hataru khaja muan ananti kini* [They would buy sweets from the market]
> *Bolanti tora bhai asichhi ani lo.* [And taunt me saying my brother has brought it]

What shame! What disgrace! And again,

> *Ghasidebaku gale se laganti gola* [He makes an issue of it when I go to press his legs]
> *Arakshit toki mora chhuanta goda je.* [Says, the orphan waif is touching my feet.]
> *Fingi je fopadi dyanti pahunda tala* [He throws me out of the room]
> *Kabata je kili dyanti andhar ghar je.* [And in my face, shuts the door.]
> *Pahundare thia hoi buhae luha* [I stand near the doorstead and shed tears]
> *Bou nana kale ia sahila diha je.* [My mother, my father did this to me and I have to suffer.]

The grief voiced here can melt even a stone. Renowned poets who are given to depicting women only as objects of lust and desire have much to learn from these songs. The sorrow of the daughter-in-law grieving by the stream-let echoes the agony of Sita, Janak's daughter.

A child is tormented by the humid heat of a summer afternoon and glimpses clouds in the sky. But it does not rain and the child, utterly disappointed, keeps waiting. Then suddenly one day drops of rain fall on the ground and the child excitedly sings out:

> *Megha barasila tupuru tapere* [Pit pat fell the rain]
>   *Keshur maila gaja* [Sprouts sprang from the seedling]
> *Sonepurthei tamak bajila* [Drums beat in Sonepur]
>   *Leuti aile raja.* [And back home came the king.]

He imagines that with the king, his father would also return home. With the advent of the rainy season, the child expects his warrior father would come back.

Village songs emerge from the matrices of such experience. Like *shlokas* originated in *shoka* [the emotion of grief], at the root of these village songs lies the shared sorrow of a community. Even joyful songs sung to the accompaniment of musical instruments become memorable only when they are instinct with ineffable sadness. All village songs in India, irrespective of their place of origin, share this characteristic. Their differences from each other can be accounted for in terms of the diversity of lifestyle. For this reason, the idea *vasudheiba kutumbakam* [the world as one family] owes it origin to this realization on the part of those who listened to these songs in many regions.

Performance of village songs

Most village songs are recited individually while some are sung collectively. A woman sings in the presence of her daughters and daughters-in-law in the rice-pounding shed. A mother also croons to her child in the evening or before dawn to divert her/him. These songs intimately embrace every aspect of daily life in a village. Village songs sung collectively include young girls singing together on certain occasions; *paiks* [peasant militia] singing and dancing on the village path to celebrate victory; dances in which the refrains of a song are repeated by a group of persons; daughters-in-law singing collectively on occasions such as marriage, birth and other ceremonies; and songs accompanied by musical instruments sung at festivals. In *Chandanjatra* celebrated in summer, villagers sing in unison:

> *Chandan ratire chaturi chuachandan basa* [In the fragrant chandan night she lies]
> *Aha prananath Bolina khare chhade nihswas.* [Mumbles 'lord of my life' and sighs.]

It can be seen that village songs reflect the hopes and aspirations, experiences of success and disappointments of the individual as well as the community.

Authors of village songs

It appears that most village songs have been authored by women. One gets the impression that the songs of parting and bereavement, songs young girls sing together on various occasions, songs of praise addressed to deities, songs sung by children in the village, and proverbs and badinage were composed by women. If one records the songs of lament voiced by a village woman even today, one would find out how an unlettered woman can express her agony in a coherent and powerfully expressive manner. Therefore, the claim that the songs mentioned above were composed by women cannot be dismissed. Other kinds of songs were created by men such as ploughmen and *paiks*. Again, some poets who are city dwellers compose poems using the language of villagers. Sometimes villagers also enjoy listening to these poems being recited. They get drawn to the poems for their beauty. Many such poems are recited not only by men but also by women. Countless villagers sing, "Says Balaram Das, I seek your protection". So, it would not be improper to accept such *pothi* songs [songs written in palm-leaf manuscripts] as village songs.

Translation: Animesh Mohapatra

Notes

1 Chakradhar Mohapatra, *Utkal Gaunli Gita*, Cuttack: Surama Mohanty, 2nd ed., 1971 [1959], pp. 1–9. The book has been reprinted by Bidya Prakashan, Cuttack in 2017.
2 [Editors' note] We thank J.P. Das, eminent author and scholar, for rendering these lines into English.

3 Debi Prasanna Pattanayak

Colophons of palm-leaf manuscripts in Odisha

Introduction

Debi Prasanna Pattanayak (b. 1931) is an eminent linguist and literary critic. Educated at Ravenshaw College, Deccan College and Cornell University, he was appointed the director of Central Institute of Indian Languages, Mysore in 1969. His books such as *A Controlled Historical Reconstruction of Oriya, Assamese, Bengali and Hindi* (1968), *Aspects of Applied Linguistics* (1969) and *Odia Bhasha o Bahshabigyan* (1985) made a seminal contribution to the field of linguistics. He reflected seriously on the language question in post-Independence India and passionately advocated the nurturing of a multilingual and multicultural ethos. He emphasized that promoting linguistic harmony in India is as important as maintaining communal amity in Independent India. He has consistently warned against the erosion of regional languages caused by the growing dominance of Hindi and English. These views were persuasively articulated by Debi Prasanna in books such as *Multilingualism and Mother-tongue Education* (1981), *Multilingualism and Multiculturalism: Britain and India* (1987) and *Orissa, Oriya and the Multilingual Context* (2003). The liveliness and originality of Debi Prasanna's critical sensibility is manifest in essays he wrote on various aspects of Odia literature. In his comprehensive introduction to *Kabilipi* [Letters of Poets] (1957), he shows how sources such as letters, diaries and journals lend depth, value and density to literary criticism. As a critic he casts his net wide and explores areas of study such as the production and circulation of *pothis*, medieval Odia literature, the historical novel, literary historiography, periodical literature in Odisha and the tradition of Odia devotional songs. His collected writings have been published in two volumes titled *Language and Cultural Diversity* by IGNCA and Orient Blackswan in 2014. His autobiography titled *Anek Jiban* [Many Lives] was published in 2001.

The essay titled "Pushpika" [Colophons of Palm-leaf Manuscripts in Odisha], published in *Jhankar* in 1957, focuses on the role of scribes in the dissemination of literary texts in Odisha. The production of literary manuscripts inscribed on palm leaves has a rich and long tradition. Well into the

DOI: 10.4324/9781003224778-3

nineteenth century, literary texts were produced, copied and circulated in the form of palm-leaf *pothis* and the scribes who copied these played a crucial role in disseminating literature. The scribes, however, did not confine themselves to merely copying the text; in the *pushpikas*, they recorded valuable information about their lives, social world and facts relating to their occupation. Debi Prasanna undertakes a close study of *pushpikas* from a comparative perspective by referring to *pothis* written in Bangla and Odia. He also points out the role played by monasteries as centres of culture where *pothis* were copied and preserved. Debi Prasanna carefully examines the conventions governing the task scribes engaged in and explains how they illuminate a fascinating world. Colophons enable a modern scholar to date a manuscript and reveal early attempts at using modes of punctuating the text. Some scribes give specific instructions as to how their *pothis* should be protected from damage and lay elaborate curses on potential thieves. Some of them also mention the time and trouble taken for copying a text and the remuneration received for their labours. Debi Prasanna shows how scribes on occasions lightened the tedium of their task through amusing wordplay. His insightful essay invites the reader's attention to a neglected but vitally important field of study in Odia criticism. His rigorous analysis of colophons of Odia *pothis* is a significant contribution to the history of the book before the advent of print culture in Odisha.

*

Colophons of palm-leaf manuscripts in Odisha[1]

Debi Prasanna Pattanayak

The analysis of *pushpikas*[2] [colophons], though not entirely unknown, is not quite common in Odia literary criticism. Therefore, one should grasp the exact meaning of colophon before discussing it. In a printed book, the name of the printer occurs either at the beginning or at the end of the book. But before the advent of printing in Odisha, hundreds of scribes painstakingly copied *pothis* [manuscripts], and in the process preserved the culture of the land. Few remember them today. Nevertheless, these scribes did not neglect to include information about themselves in the texts. The sentences which the scribe adds to introduce himself after he finishes copying a text are called the colophon. The Bengali scholar, Tapan Mohan Chattopadhyay says, "Having copied the text the scribe, so to speak, adds a tail to it. This consists in a brief note on the scribe, which is called *pushpika* or colophon" (*Manjari*, vol. 2, no. 2, 1359 [1952]). Sukumar Sen expresses the view that "the origin of the term *pushpika* may have something to do with the dry flowers that cling to fully-grown vegetables such as pumpkins or gourds" (*Bichitra Sahitya*, p. 226). According to Chintaharan Chakraborty, a colophon represents "a part of the text which brings it to a conclusion" (*Sahitya Parishad Patrika*, vol. 57, no. 3–4).

In Odisha, till today, the collection of palm-leaf manuscripts has not been undertaken very seriously. Of late, universities, museums and other institutions have taken some initiatives in this direction. Therefore, it is not surprising that the study of colophons has not received the attention it deserves. There is of course a need for discussing aspects of a manuscript such as its antiquity, subject matter, script, writing tools and materials used, shape, and illustrations. However, this essay chooses to study a relatively neglected subject such as *pushpika* from a comparative perspective.

Colophons in both Odia and Bengali manuscripts share remarkable similarities. Panchanan Mandal makes the following observation on the colophons of Bengali manuscripts preserved at Visva-Bharati:

> The autobiographical accounts of scribes included in colophons will provide all social science researchers with valuable source material. Colophons offer information on the following: the remuneration the scribe has received for copying manuscript in cash or kind; the owner of the manuscript and its readers; details concerning and eulogies addressed to them; site of work (the pargana, the revenue village, place of residence, and even the direction in which he turned his face while copying) and its duration (year and date, the quarter, the hour, minute and second). The scribe also mentions the religious sect he belongs to, his hopes and expectations, his concerns regarding fame or disgrace, and his family quarrels and financial difficulties etc.
>
> (*Punthi Parichaya*, vol. I, "Preface", p. 9)

However, there is more to colophons than what has been said above.

Odisha has been a site of different religions. Over the centuries, the fame of Lord Jagannath has drawn a large number of saints to Puri. Some of them have established *mathas* [monasteries] which carry traces of their religious faith. These monasteries evolved as centres of culture where discussions on religion were accompanied by activities such as writing and copying of religious texts, and their preservation. Besides, the *Bhagabat ghara* in every village where *pothis* were stored and worshipped became a hub of religious and literary discussion. Palm-leaf manuscripts were kept in the *pothi ghara* attached to the village temple just as *Madala Panji* manuscripts were preserved in the temple of Lord Jagannath. The crux of all that was said heretofore is that activities such as writing, collection, preservation and dissemination of *pothis* had a sacral function and significance. In the colophon of a Bengali manuscript, the scribe, even after dwelling on his poverty and distress, entreats God to grant him rebirth as a scribe. The accrual of merit through copying manuscripts is the chief objective of the scribe. It is then no wonder that the poverty-stricken scribe finds in copying manuscripts an easy way of earning merit. Religious scriptures emphasize the merit accumulated through the gift of books. A large number of scribes have also referred to this in their colophons. Many such statements made by scribes can be found in *Prashasti Sangraha*, published from Allahabad (see vol. 1, pp. 19, 27, 31, 38, 43, 46, 71). A list of specific rewards to be achieved through this activity is also included in the book. Although love of scholarship may be the obvious reason for collecting manuscripts, some rich people acquired these in order to flaunt their affluence and enhance their status. *Prashasti Sangraha* (vol. 2, pp. 375, 380, 737) and the Royal Asiatic Society of Bengal report on *pothis* (vol. 5, p. 3735) inform us that many of them took pride in donating manuscripts to scholars and temples. After the advent of print culture, rich and pious people donated religious texts in the form of books. For instance, *The Gita* translated by Biharilal and the same text translated by Jagabandhu Singh were published by the Raja of Darpani and the *mahant* of Emar Matha respectively and distributed by them for free.

One comes across instances of people selling manuscripts to overcome financial hardship and others purchasing them to build a collection. Let us look at the colophon of the manuscript *Itihas*, which is in my possession:

> Here ends chapter 41 of the text titled *Itihas*. Even Bhima fled ... forgive me. The copying of the text was completed on the fifth day of the solar month of Virgo in the 17th year of the king Ramachandra Deb's holy reign. The task was performed by the scribe Maguni Ratha, money-lender of Biseraipur village in Nuagarh. A vaishya of Rampur, money-lender to the village headman of Nilakanthpur, Gangadhar Mohapatra purchased this manuscript paying *dakshina* [cash or kind]. Learned readers are requested to ignore the errors committed by the scribe. May God forgive Maguni Ratha, the worthless scribe.

The verse "Even Bhima fled ... forgive me" in this colophon is discussed later in this chapter. It must be mentioned here that the scribe generally uses the word *dakshina* instead of citing the actual price of the manuscript. Let us now compare this with the colophons of two Bengali manuscripts.

> The *dakshina* for this [*pothi*] is two lengths of cloth and two rupees.
> (*Kalika Mangal*, Asiatic Society 9/322)

> The cash I received for copying this *pothi* is enough to support my family for which I am obliged. Besides, this has also enabled me to meet some of my daily needs.
> (Sukumar Sen, *Bangla Sahityer Itihas* [*History of Bengali Literature*], p. 465, footnote 4)

In this context, let me furnish an amusing example from another Odia manuscript – the 11th chapter of *Bhagabata*. The manuscript is in very bad condition and with great difficulty I managed to restore its last leaf. Let me present the colophon in its entirety:

32 | 32 | 32 | 32 | 32 | 32 | 32 | 32 | 32 | 32 | 32 | 32 | 32 | 32 | Sree | Sree | Sree | Sree | Sree | Sree | Sree | Sometimes even a mighty warrior like Bhima flees the battlefield. Even sages can commit errors. Therefore, please ignore the mistakes in the text I have copied. ° | ° | The copying of this manuscript was completed on Friday, an hour and a half into Maha Ashtami and the twenty-second day of the bright fortnight of the month of Virgo in the auspicious and glorious rule of Maharaj Sri Birakeswari Dev. ° | ° | Learned readers are requested to recite the text overlooking the mistakes of Gobindam, the scribe. May all be well. May all be well. May all be well. ∴ | ∴ | ∴ | ∴ | ∴ | ∴ | ∴ | ∴ |The fire of hunger is blazing in me so intensely that, like the great sage Agastya, I could consume the demon Vatapi and vanquish his brother and drink up the whole ocean 1 | 1 | 1 | 1 | 1 | 1 | 1 | 1 | 1 | 1 | 1 | 1 | 1 | 1 | 1 | 1 | 1 | 1 | 1 | 1 | 1 | 1 | 1 | 1 | 1 | 1 | 1 | 1 | 1 | 1 | 1 |

Let us focus on the last *shloka* of this colophon. This seems to have no connection with the rest of the colophon. One comes across many instances of scribes including their favourite *shlokas* or popular sayings which may not be relevant. I learnt from the historian Kedarnath Mohapatra that in the colophon of a Sanskrit manuscript in the Odisha State Museum, the scribe gives the lineage of the Bhoi dynasty in a *shloka*. But the *shloka* referred to earlier contains more information. However, it is presented in a modified form. The well-known *shloka* goes like this:

> *Atapirbhakshito yena batapishcha mahasurah,*
> *Samudrah shoshito yena samehgastyah prasidatu.*
> [May the great sage Agastya, who devoured Vatapi and vanquished the demon's brother,
> and drank the whole ocean up, bless me]

Generally, after a hearty meal, brahmin guests recite this *shloka*, caressing their bellies. Perhaps, after completing his task the scribe Gobinda was treated to a sumptuous meal and he added this *shloka* to express his satisfaction. The fact that the practice of selling *pothis* was quite common in the past is mentioned in *Prashasti Sangraha*, in which two *pothis* copied in the 12th century are referred to (1/161, 157). Of the remuneration received for copying *pothis*, Sri Chintaharan Chakraborty writes,

> The remuneration for scribes was quite high in the beginning of the nineteenth century, as Reverend Ward states in his famous book on the history, literature, religion of the Hindus. He notes that the price for copying thirty-two thousand words was twelve annas or one rupee [sixteen annas]. Given this rate of remuneration, copying an extremely large text like the *Mahabharata* must have involved vast expenses. The rate had increased fourfold by the end of the nineteenth century. Rajendra Lal Mitra notes in the 1869 *Proceedings of the Asiatic Society*

of Bengal that the remuneration for copying one thousand *shlokas* was four rupees around the same time.

(*Sahitya Parishad Patrika*, no. 3–4, Year 57, p. 57)

The date of composition of the *pothi* is generally specified in terms of the regnal year of the king of Odisha; however, on occasions, it is specified through Sal, Saka and the Christian eras. Some *pothis* mention both the Saka and the Christian eras. The scribe goes beyond mentioning the year of composition and refers to the lunar day, weekday, hour, minute and second. Details concerning the exact place of composition and place of residence are also added in *pothis*. Let me now cite a few more colophons:

1) The colophon of *Gita Govinda* which includes a commentary by Dharanidhar (Odisha State Museum) –

   Here ends the text. May all be well. It is the 1628th year of the Saka era, four years after the passing of Gajapati King Harekrushna Deb. The copying of the book has been completed. The name of this scribe is Krishnakinkar Deb Sharma; I belong to the family of Sri Basudev Sharma. This book has been copied in Srikhandi Bishe's village Faridpur. Om. May all be well.

2) The colophon of Juga Dasa's *Nrusimha Charita* (Odisha State Museum) –

   This is the end of Sri *Nrusimha Charita*. I copied what I saw. O learned readers, ignore my mistakes. Do not blame the scribe. It is the lunar month of Phalguna and four days into the solar month of Aquarius of the 11th–12th regnal year of the Great Sri Gajapati Gaudeshwar Nabakoti Karnat Kulabargeshwar Biradhi Biarabara Pratap Sri Mukunda Deb. The copying of this book is completed on Tuesday, around ten hours into the first day of the dark fortnight X X. May all be well.

3) The colophon of Kanhu Dasa's *Rama Rasamruta Sindhu*, vol. 1 (Odisha State Museum) –

   May all be well — O — Kiskindha Canto completed. ... The first volume comprises Kiskindha Canto, the others comprise the remaining cantos. ...
   Even Bhima fled ... forgive me. My back and waist are broken. ... Take good care of it. The copying of the first volume of *Rama Rasamruta* has come to an end and dusk has set in. I have completed the task, with the blessings of Sita's lord, Rama, on the first day of the week and sixth lunar day of the dark fortnight of Baishakh

in the year 1916. I have copied two volumes and I am now 15 years old. Let it be known that the scribe is Patahati Satpathy. The book also belongs to Patakaribara Satpathy. I seek the blessings of Rama and pray to Him, the slayer of Ravana to fulfil all my desires. I copied what I saw. Please overlook my mistakes. ...

4) The *pushpika* of one of the *pothis* in the Odia *pothi* collection at Visva–Bharati –

It is three hours past midday on Friday, the 12th day of the month of Taurus and fifteenth day of the bright fortnight of Jyeshtha in *san* 1316 of the reign of the great Sri Gajapati Gaudeswar Labakoti [sic] Kalyata [sic] Kalebar the fierce and brave Pratap Mukunda Deb. The scribe of this book is the *karana* of Nijigarh, Badamba, Chaitan Das. My waist is broken ... Take good care of the *pothi*. Let me tell you, O learned readers that the book can be found in the house of Natabar Pachhimira, which lies in the eastern part of Dahada Sahi in Badamba of Nijigarh. May all be well. O worthy and intelligent readers, while reciting the text take no notice of the scribe.

5) In this context attention may be paid to the colophon of *Abhinava Gitagovinda*, the oldest *pothi* in the collection of Odisha State Museum. It is perhaps the longest colophon. The lengthy eulogy of the king by the scribe is worth noticing. Equally noteworthy is the closing *shloka* on the sins one would incurr for stealing this manuscript. The colophon goes like this:

You, the beloved of the god of all gods, the supreme deity Sri Jagannath, you, who constantly protects his subjects and is the eliminator of all impediments, you, the son of Sri Durga, you, whose mind is as profligate as the bumble bee, is forever partaking of nectar at the lotus feet of Narayana like Sridhar who is constantly in Lakshmi's embrace; you, the devotee of Sri Nrusimha, look upon all with equanimity and are full of the qualities of forgiveness and kindness; you, the expert in Vedas and Vedanta, you of clear heart, are the supreme commander of Banga desha, the conqueror of Kulbarga-on-sea; you, who imprisoned the king of ancient Karnata and then freed him; you defeat enemies with the power of the sun; you are the great devotee of Shiva, Shakti and Vishnu; you are the victorious Sri Purushottam Dev and defeater of the prime enemy Todarmalla. On Sunday, the first day of the bright fortnight of Baishakha in the 34th regnal year of Sri Purushottam Dev, was this book completed. I seek protection at the feet of Sri Radhakrishna. Even Bhima. ... Please overlook my mistakes. May the lord of the world Sri Rama protect me. One who steals this book will suffer for life. He will find no place in heaven after death and his ancestors will go to hell. The copyist is Sridhar Sharma, who should not be held responsible for mistakes committed.

The above colophon mentions that the book was composed during the thirty-fourth *anka* or in the twenty-seventh year of the reign of Gajapati Purushottam Dev who ascended the throne in 1466.

Several examples may be cited to date the colophons precisely. All the Odia colophons cited above provide evidence relating to this. However, it may be in order to take a look at a couple of Bengali colophons here:

> Here ends [the copying of the book] on Thursday, the fourteenth day of the fortnight and 17th of Jyeshtha in the Saka year 1739, Bangla year 1224, English year 1827, Maghi year 1179 ...
>
> (*Bichitra Sahitya*, p. 218)

> Here ends [the copying of the book] in the year 1208 in the third watch of Thursday the 16th day of Jyeshtha. It is the Saka year of 1723 and the English year of 1801. The scribe is Sri Ram Prasad Choudhury who resides in Gudiyaghar in Habeli pargana.
>
> (*Bichitra Sahitya*, p. 218)

The scribe of Achyutanand Das's *Tattvabodhini Gita*, preserved in the Odisha State Museum, is Baidhar Mallick [a lower-caste surname in Odisha). Thus, it is clear that all the scribes engaged in copying manuscripts were not brahmans or members of the higher castes. The colophon of this manuscript is an amusing one; Malik seeks shelter at the feet of all deities, not excluding even a single one:

> Even Bhima .... My back and neck are broken. ... Take good care of it. O learned folks, recite the text overlooking the mistakes of this scribe. I have only copied from the source text. My guru shall save me from sins. Born, as I am, of low caste, my diction is impure, I am vile, wicked and stupid, and I do not follow the path of virtue. My mind is focused on the feet of my guru. I am but a minion of Lord Hari. Let Him grant me shelter at His lotus feet for ever. O virtuous men, bless me. I seek your protection. O learned souls, bless me morning, noon and evening. Ignore my mistakes. Copying of *Tattavabodhini Gita* was completed on Friday, the day Lord Hari was born. This humble and worthless Baidhar Mallick, who is at the mercy of Goddess Maa Sarala, is the copyist rendering service to zamindar Sri Sri Sri Babu Badyanath Pandit of *mouja* Korilo, *pargana* Tirana, *taluka* Srirampur, district Cuttack, police station Tritol. It is the sixth hour of the 15th day of the month of Leo, year 1314, Friday full moon 6 / 6 / 6 / 6.

Baidhar Mallick ... seeks shelter at the feet of Lord Jagannath. Seeks refuge at the feet of the goddess Maa Sarala. Seeks shelter at the feet of Sri Sri Sri Birjyai. Seeks refuge at the feet of Sri Sri Sri Chachakai. Seeks shelter at the glorious feet of the village goddess.

It is now time to clarify the words *adrusha* or *adrusya* (c.f. colophon of Juga Dasa's *Nrusimha Charita* above). This word is merely a modified form of 'adarsha', which refers to the source text of the scribe. Whenever a manuscript showed signs of decay or it was more than one hundred years old, it was usually copied and then either immersed in water or buried. That a lot of tantric manuscripts were buried is part of regional lore. Legend has it that in the Prachi valley a lot of manuscripts associated with the temple of a goddess were buried. However, as far as the scribes were concerned, they focused on copying the manuscripts word for word. In the colophons of many manuscripts, scribes seek to be excused by the readers saying that they copied the *adrusha* [verbatim] or that they copied what they saw. It is difficult to decide to what extent the scribes changed the language of the source text while copying it and whether they changed it for the better or worse. A scientific approach to preparing a critical edition of a *pothi* would therefore involve collation and comparison of several copies of the same.

Some scribes mention some contemporary events in their colophons. The colophon of an old manuscript of Sarala Das' *Mahabharata* in Gopinath Mohanty's collection constitutes a useful example:

The copying of the *Virat Parva* of *Mahabharata* has been carried out successfully. Even Bhima ... overlook my mistakes. My back and neck are aching. ... Take good care of the *pothi*. Copying of this canto was completed successfully on Friday, the third day of the bright fortnight of Jyeshtha, 73rd year of the ninth regnal year of King Dibyasingh Deb.

We are in the middle of a famine this year. 6 *gaunis* of paddy cost 1 rupee. The owner of this book is Bhabagrahi Nanda, *makadam* [head] of the brahman village of Prataprudrapur in Kothadesa. I seek shelter at the feet of Shri Om Akhandaleshwar Deb.

There is no dearth of similar accounts in Bengali *pothis*; the following may be taken as an example:

Last year, gods sent us drought, and now the price of paddy has soared to 24–25 pice. Can it get any costlier?

This year the harvest has been poor. Sugarcane harvest has been good. I earned nothing to meet my daily expenses. A piece of hand-woven cotton cloth costs 3/[missing in the orig.]; I haven't received the payment I had expected.

(*Bichitra Sahitya*, p. 224)

We have so far chosen not to include the formulaic utterance "Even Bhima …" in its entirety. In such utterances, the scribe begs to be excused for errors they might have committed out of misunderstanding or ignorance.

> O learned folks, recite this
> Overlooking the mistakes of the scribe.
> (*Bhagabata*, Canto 1, Visva-Bharati collection)

> Sometimes even a mighty warrior like Bhima flees the battlefield. Even sages can commit errors. Therefore, please ignore the mistakes in the text I have copied.
> (Sarala Das's *Mahabharata*, Gopinath Mohanty collection)

> I have copied what I saw in the original. No blame should attach to the copyist;
> Sometimes even a mighty warrior like Bhima flees the battlefield. Even sages can commit errors.
> (*Society*, 8/61[?]0)

> I merely copied what I found in the original,
> If you find mistakes in it, please do not blame me.
> (*Prashasti Sangraha*, 1/17, 18, 20, 22, 92, 111)

> I have copied this *pothi*, overlook my mistakes,
> Even sages can commit errors; I am but a worthless scribe.
> (*Bangiya Sahitya Parishad Pothi*, 70)

> Even a mighty warrior like Bhima flees the battlefield;
> Even sages can commit errors; I am but a mere insect.
> (*Bangiya Parishad Pothi*, 285)

One comes across everywhere the scribes' appeal for forgiveness for the mistakes made.

> Whatever errors you may find have been caused by
> My ignorance or weak memory.
> Take no notice of my mistakes and correct the errors as you read.
> Please do not be angry with this wicked writer.
> (*Prashasti Sangraha*, 2/525, 1261)

The scribes have also given various examples of the mistakes they themselves have committed. The colophon of *Gupta Bhagabata* in the Visva-Bharati collection of Odia manuscripts provides an example of this:

Even Ganesha, who wrote down the great epic as Vyasa dictated it,
Committed mistakes; I am but an insignificant man.

Here ends the copying of *Gupta Bhagabata* on the sixth hour of
Tuesday, the fourth day of the dark fortnight and eleventh day of
the month of Aquarius, san 1255 Sal. This has been copied by Shri
Lokanath Samal at Kimibar Bhandar.

Compare this with,

Goddess Saraswati is the source of all knowledge
Sometimes even she gabbles
On seeing a ferocious tiger
Even the elephant trembles.

(Calcutta University *Bengali Pothi Bibarana*
[A Report on Bengali Manuscripts], 3, pp. 644–652)

The following verse gives an idea of how difficult it is to copy a manuscript:

My back and neck hurt, there is pain in my waist
My sight has dimmed, poring over the leaves
So hard have I toiled to copy this book; please take loving care of it.

(*Society*, 8/6114; *Prashasti Sangraha*, 1/111, 2/666)

A vivid picture emerges here of an old scribe whose fingers hurt from wielding an iron stylus, whose sight fails, poring over the manuscript for long hours, and whose back and neck ache, bending continuously over the manuscript while copying. In some Odia colophons, slightly different versions of this shloka obtain. The colophon of the aforementioned Sarala Das' *Mahabharata* features the following:

My sight has dimmed, my back and neck are bent,
I have taken great pains to copy this book; take loving care of it as if it
is your son.

The colophon of *Tattvabodhini Gita* contains the following:

My sight has dimmed, my neck and back are bent,
I have taken great pains to copy this book; take care of it as if it were
your son or grandson.

And the following lines occur in the colophon of a *pothi* in Visva-Bharati
Museum:

My sight has dimmed, my neck and back are bent,
I have painstakingly copied this book; take care of it as if it were your
own child.

These examples show how a word/phrase has been modified in order to extend its meaning. For example, "take loving care of it as if it is your son" has been changed over time to "take care of it as if it were your son or grandson". This may be understood as a request to preserve the *pothi* for a longer period. One finds in some colophons specific instruction as to how the reader should protect the *pothi* from possible damage.

> This book faces threats from mice, thieves and water
> Take loving care for I have taken great pains to copy it.
>
> (*Prashasti Sangraha* 1/108, 142)

> Keep the book away from oil and water and keep it well-bound
> Make sure it does not fall into the hands of a fool.
>
> (*Prashasti Sangraha* 1/154, 200, 637, 666, 740)

In several colophons, the scribes include precautions against the possibility of the *pothi* getting stolen. The scribes also shower curses on potential thieves. Two examples may be cited here. The colophon of the *pothi* of *Gita Govinda* in Gopinath Mohanty's collection which includes a commentary by Dharanidhara reads thus:

> Even Bhima. ... Whoever steals this book will suffer grievously. He will not go to heaven after death. His ancestors will be expelled from heaven and consigned to hell.

The second example is found in the colophon of the first Canto of *Bhagabata* which is in the collection of Visva-Bharati Museum.

> I pay obeisance to Brahma and all the gods who are the protectors of brahmans and cows. ... The scribe is Chandra Prasad Datta of Barada, pargana Painda, police station Salepur outpost, Keshnagar area. This book belongs to Babu Bharatchandra Datta of Barada. Whosoever steals this *pothi* will be caught. He who borrows the book and returns it not will earn hell for his ancestors across seven generations. The sun, the moon and the guardians of the eight directions bear witness to this.

Compare this with the following examples:

> Steal this book and you are doomed
> You will not find your way to heaven after death
> Your ancestors will be consigned to hell.
>
> (*Pothibibarana* of Calcutta Sanskrit College, 5/76)

> If you steal this book copied with great care
> Your mother is a pig and your father, a donkey.

Whosoever steals this book
Shall one day sleep with his mother-in-law
Or bed his daughter-in-law.

(Parishad pothi, 285)

The above examples may be compared with "Book Rhyme" published in
Wilson Bulletin for Books and cited by Chintaharan Chakraborty:

Steal not this book, my honest friend
For fear the gallows should be your end.
And when you die the lord will say
And where's that book you stole away?
Look ye, my friend,
If this book I lend,
Be sure to return,
Or in hell you will burn.
Remember, books in my cozy shelves
From which my friends help themselves.
And like a dove with wings unloosed
Return, come back, fly home to roost.

The colophons contain many spelling mistakes resulting from the scribe's
ignorance or inattentiveness. One is therefore advised to correct them while
reading the text. In many *pothis* the punctuation mark, full stop, is conspicuous by its absence. Whenever the scribe felt the need for a pause in the
course of copying, he introduced a stroke mark. Words such as 'shuddha',
'ashuddha', 'pustaka', 'adarsha' have been changed to 'shudhya', 'ashud-
hya', 'postaka' or 'posteka' and 'adrusha' etc. in an attempt, perhaps, to
Sanskritize the language. However, one need not make fun of these words
for they occur due to the influence of the spoken idiom. Some scribes display
lively playfulness. For instance, 'Patahati Satpathy' has been changed to
'Pata Karibar Satpathy' in the colophon of Kanhu Das's *Rama Rasamruta
Sindhu*. (Patahati [the best royal elephant] rewritten as Pata Karibara adds
another layer of meaning to the proper name; Kari means an elephant as
well as bamboo shoot.)

The above discussion makes it clear that although colophons do not
occupy much space in *pothis,* they should not be neglected by scholars.
These could be productively analyzed from various perspectives. However,
not much attention has been paid to the study of colophons. Here, I have
discussed only a few colophons from the *pothis* I have studied. I hope this
essay will encourage future scholars to study colophons extensively and in
greater depth.

[Author's] Acknowledgement: I am indebted to all those who gave me
access to their manuscript collections.

Translation: Urmishree Bedamatta

Notes

1 Debi Prasanna Pattanayak, "Pushpika" [Colophons of Palm-leaf Manuscripts in Odisha], *Jhankar*, vol. 9 no. 5, 1957, pp. 492–499. Reproduced in Debi Prasanna Pattanayak, *Sahitya Beeksha* [An Analytical Study of Literature], Cuttack: Grantha Mandir, 1965, pp. 131–149.
2 *Pushipka* is etymologically linked to *pushpa* or flower.

4 Shyam Sundar Rajguru

Sudramuni Sarala Das: author of the Odia *Mahabharata*

Introduction

Shyam Sundar Rajguru (1866–1909) was an essayist, grammarian, language activist and a leading public figure. Born into the family of royal preceptors in Paralakhemundi, then part of the Madras Presidency, he acquired a fine command of Sanskrit very early in life. Later, he received English education at Rajahmundry college. In due course, he served as tutor to the prince of Paralakhemundi and involved himself in a series of public activities. Through his initiatives a printing press and a library came to be set up in Paralakhemundi; he was also instrumental in establishing Padmanabh Rangalaya, then the only proscenium theatre in southern Odisha. He spearheaded a movement to introduce Odia in the offices, courts and schools in Ganjam where Telugu until then was the only language used. His early efforts at mobilizing popular support for the unification of Odia-speaking regions helped lay the foundation of *Utkal Sammilani* [Utkal Union Conference] in 1903. For fifteen years he helmed the Paralakhemundi Municipality and served as a member of the Ganjam and Srikakulam district boards. He edited *The Ganjam News*, a weekly that aimed to acquaint British authorities with the problems facing Odias. His keen interest in promoting Odia led him to undertake an intensive study of its grammar. This is reflected in a series of essays on pronouns, prepositions and rules of composition in Odia. He acutely felt the absence of literary historiography of Odisha at the time and wrote brief accounts of the lives and works of fourteen neglected but important authors. His pioneering essays which undertook an objective evaluation of literary works and issues paved the way for writing histories of Odia literature in future.

This essay has the distinction of being the first ever critical essay on the monumental Odia epic, the *Mahabharata* composed by Sarala Das. The essay was published in the October 1903 issue of *Utkal Sahitya*. It may be mentioned here that the attempt to assign Odia poets and their works to a specific period in history began to be made only after the advent of colonial modernity. In 1872, W.W. Hunter published a list of Odia authors and sought to arrange them in a chronological order. Krushna Prasad Choudhary

DOI: 10.4324/9781003224778-4

drew up a list of living Odia authors and emphasized the need for writing
a history of Odia literature in 1896. A brief narrative history of Odia language and literature by Monmohan Chakravarti was published in *Journal
of the Asiatic Society of Bengal* (1897–1898). Shyam Sundar Rajguru's
essay on Sarala Das (and other writers) may be seen as a major contribution
to this ongoing initiative to construct a historical account of Odia literature.
To Shyam Sundar goes the credit of recognizing Sarala Das as the first major
poet in Odia literature and this soon led to Sarala Das being universally celebrated as the *adikavi* [the first poet] of Odisha. Subjecting available evidence
to diligent scrutiny, Shyam Sundar comes to the conclusion that Sarala Das
was a contemporary of the king Kapilendra Dev and that his epic was composed in the fifteenth century CE. Although for centuries Sarala's version of
the epic had enjoyed wide circulation among common readers it was looked
down upon by the Sankrit-educated literati as rustic and lacking in aesthetic
refinement. Shyam Sundar carefully examines the language Sarala employs,
identifies its defining characteristics and goes on to show how it draws its
vitality from folk sayings and popular proverbs. He convincingly defends
the absence of any discernible metrical pattern in Sarala Das's composition
and celebrates the unfettered freedom of his lines. He insightfully adds that
Sarala Das's deviations from the Sanskrit original are not to be viewed as
deficiencies but as sources of imaginative felicity.

*

Sudramuni Sarala Das: author of the Odia *Mahabharata*[1]

Shyam Sundar Rajguru

I

Sudramuni Sarala Das is the earliest among the poets who wrote in the vernacular in Odisha. It is possible that he might have been preceded by poets
writing in the vernacular but none composed a text on such a grand scale
like the Odia *Mahabharata*. Sarala Das was born in a village near the shrine
of goddess Sarala in the *pargana* of Jhankad. He assumed the name "Sarala
Das" on account of his profound devotion to goddess Sarala.

> The name of the goddess is Sarala Chandi.
> And I, poet Sarala Das, am her servant.
>
> (*Adi Parva*)

Some are of the view that calling oneself a *muni* [sage] would smack of
pride; the poet has therefore added the prefix "Sudra" to *muni* in order to
express his humility.

The *brahma* manifests itself in this sudra
I am to carry out the command of the goddess.
....
I added sudra to my name in obedience to your command
So, give me the mental strength to compose the verses.

(*Adi Parva*)

But in fact, the poet is a sudra by caste and muni by subcaste. (There is a subcaste called muni in our part of the country;[2] so, it is possible that such a subcaste also exists in Odisha. Like people belonging to the Raul subcaste, their main occupation is to offer worship to the local goddess.) The author of the Sanskrit *Mahabharata* was known as Brahmamuni; to confer on himself the same kind of dignity the author of the Prakrit *Mahabharata* combined the name of his caste and the name of his subcaste and called himself Sudramuni. One comes across several instances in his epic where the poet presents himself in a dignified manner. In the canto titled "Swargarohana" [Ascent to Heaven] the poet writes:

I was born as poet Kalidasa in my first birth
In the second, I was the great destroyer.
In the third birth, I am poet Sarala Das,
I will appear on this earth once more.
In every birth, I think of fifteen lakh things,
In four births, I will speak of sixty lakh things.
Having said all these things on this earth,
I will go and guard the doors of Lord Shiva.

What is wrong if the poet calls himself "Kalidasa", "Sudramuni" or even "Brahmamuni", when there are gentlemen who consider themselves great poets after publishing a mere four-page booklet?

Sarala Das composed the *Mahabharata* during the reign of Kapilendra Dev, King of Odisha. In *Adi Parva*, after describing Nilachala [the seat of Lord Jagannath] the poet writes, "I humbly serve King Kapileshwar, who offers worship at the feet of thirty-three crore deities". According to W.W. Hunter, Kapilendra Dev reigned from 1452 AD to 1479 AD. This means Sarala Das is a 15th-century poet. It is impossible to say with certainty in which year he was born. But he himself has claimed that he composed the *Mahabharata* when he was very young:

Never did I have the company of learned brahmans,
I was very young and knew as much as a child did.

(*Madhya Parva*)

Even though the poet says of himself, "No erudition can I boast of, I am but a simple person full of ignorance" (*Adi Parva*); and "An unlettered person, I am not versed in the scriptures" (*Madhya Parva*), it becomes clear when one reads his *Mahabharata* that the poet possessed fairly good knowledge of Sanskrit. Otherwise it would not have been possible for someone who knew no Sanskrit to expertly use Sanskritized expressions such as "dasakruta aparadh", "patim dehi patim dehi", "sabhasthita dwijbara", "bhikhyashi Brahamana", "badati Agasti", "baschatari sodhana", "na cha stree na cha punsa". Without some knowledge of Sanskrit, he would simply not have been able to translate not one or two but all the eighteen books of the *Mahabharata*. In order to demonstrate their humility poets often describe themselves as "illiterate", "destitute", "lowly", and "ignorant". In illustration, the following instances may be cited:

Krushna Singh in his version of the *Mahabharata* says this of himself —

Distracted by worldly affairs
I forgot to pay worship to gods and brahmans.
From learned saints I never absorbed knowledge of the scriptures,
Although an ignoramus, I embarked on the task of composing the *Mahabharata*.

Similarly, Balaram Das offers the following description of himself —

I, Balaram Das, am an utterly ignorant person
I implore the learned to overlook my mistakes.

And, the poet Surayamani Chyaupattanaik introduces himself thus —

Since my birth I have never listened to the scriptures being recited,
So how could I learn to read?
The company of the learned never did I keep
I spent my days among the unlettered.

Although Sarala Das was not averse to self-promotion, he followed the poetic convention of expressing self-deprecating modesty.

Sarala Das also possessed knowledge of astrology and it seems he had tremendous faith in this field of study. Whichever book of his epic you look at, you would never find him describe an event without mentioning the relevant astrological systems of reference such as lunar day, stellar day, *karana*[3] and *lagna*.[4]

The last part of the ninth day of the bright fortnight of the month of Mesha[5]
Then approaches the tenth day
It's the third watch of Saturday
After this comes the hour of planet Brihaspati.
Balaba, the ceremony of giving name to a child is Yogalila

....
Yudhusthir assumed the throne when planets were aligned
auspiciously.

(*Adi Parva*)

On Tropic of Capricorn, solar month of Magha,[6] eleventh day of
bright lunar fortnight
Wednesday, on the tenth constellation
That day Draupadi performed the ritual of purification
And offered obeisance in the presence of holy men.

(*Madhya Parva*)

Fifth day, the solar month of *Ashadha*,[7] Thursday
It is a day of *Shrabana*, the twenty-second asterism.
An auspicious moment when a woman prays to deities
to extend her husband's lifespan.

(*Musali Parva*)

II

Sarala Das's *Mahabharata* does not follow the Sanskrit source closely. Many
elements in the Sanskrit original have been discarded and new elements are
introduced. The poet for his part admits to having done so:

The *Mahabharata* is an unfathomable ocean,
If I seek to include everything in my story, it will be an endless one.
I therefore decided to choose from it what I need
With the blessings of goddess Paramamaheshwari.

(*Adi Parva*)

The language of Sarala Das's epic is simple and elegant, and his descriptions of events and people are distinguished by an unaffected naturalness.
Yet, they successfully evoke powerful emotions. Consider the way he
depicts the loveliness of Draupadi in the "Lakhabindha" [Shooting the
Target] scene:

Kaladamana said in the royal assembly
No ornaments adorn this girl's body.
Duryodhan said, "Have you gone mad?"
Don't you see a body so delicate cannot support ornaments.
....
One glance from her would slice through the bodies of many here.
So, lowering her eyes, she spared them.
If she casts even a furtive glance at the suitors,

She would be guilty of many a murder.
Wary of committing a crime, the virtuous and wise woman
Refrained from glancing at the assembled suitors.
....
Her very breath would transform
Even *neem* and *shahada* trees into sandalwood.
Not reddened by betel juice her lips are so crimson
They surpass the radiance of the rising sun.
....
Petals of jasmine pale beside your shining nails,
So, out of shame they drop to the ground.
....
Like a flock of swans gracefully swimming on water
Move the feet of the enchantingly lovely Draupadi.

Let us consider the example of Arjun taking a vow:

A very chaste and devoted wife's curse cannot be evaded.
Arjun said, Devi, listen to what I say.
Only Drupad can now help me.
Hanumant alone could destroy Lanka.
The whole ocean was churned with only one mountain, Mandara
With the supreme power of Lord Narayan.
Garuda, the son of Vinata single-handedly
Wiped out the clan of serpents.
All by himself, Bhagirath of the Ikshaku clan
Brought the Ganga from heaven to earth.
Ananta, the king of cobras, alone
Holds aloft on his hood the earth and seven oceans.
Single-handedly did Parshurama, the supreme warrior
Eliminate the race of Kshatriyas twenty-one times.
All by himself, our ancestor, King Jajati
Brought into being nine worlds.
When only a young boy, Sage Agasti
Drank up seven oceans in one gulp.

Wherever the poet has allowed his imagination unfettered freedom, he has succeeded in creating evocatively beautiful descriptions presented in mellifluous diction.

One comes across in Sarala Das's *Mahabharata* many words and expressions which have fallen into disuse. These include, *muku* (mate) [me], *tuku* (tate) [to you], *putranta* (putramananku) [to the sons], *jibante* (ji thau thau) [when alive], and so on.

Except for the employment of rhyming words at the end of a couplet, Sarala Das follows no other rule. There is no uniformity in the number of letters used in a line; they may range from twelve to twenty-four. However, now and then one comes across instances where the number of letters in the lines of a couplet is the same. One cannot reach definite conclusions regarding this. Close scrutiny, however, leads one to surmise that Odia proverbs and folk sayings constituted his most significant model. Many Odia proverbs do not follow any prosodic rules other than end rhyme. Given below are a few illustrative examples:[8]

(1) When angry, the husband gives her a beatin'
     And she throws her earrings at his kin.
(2) You wanton gourd!
     To go to the rooftop you want a coaxing word.
(3) A man with small worries, a nagging wife, and a bullock that is indolent
     Need not seek Yama's abode for he dies every moment.
(4) Wealth is glory, wealth is eminence, wealth is supreme power;
     It makes a hunchback handsome, and makes the enemy cower.
(5) A bigamous man better make bold
     To tell his wives in advance, if he wants his meal hot or cold.

Some proverbs also contain the same number of letters in each of the two lines.

(1) Fancy drinking milk, keep a bovine mother.
     Feel like a squabble, summon your brother.
(2) I thought auntie's place will be good for hiding
     But all I got from her was some nasty beating.

These *dhagas* [folk sayings] are not sung following any melodic modes. Readers know that Sarala Das's *Mahabharata* and Balaram Das's *Ramayana* are recited without following any prescribed melodic modes. In other words, these are read out and not sung. *Dhagabrutta* [the tune to which proverbs are recited] should not be dismissed as inferior. One finds instances of other famous poets composing *chhandas* and *chaupadis* employing *dhagabrutta*. Even a highly ornate *kavya* like Upendra Bhanja's *Labanyabati* furnishes instances of lively *dhagabrutta*.

How did Sarala Das come to compose *Bharata*? A hand-written text provides us with the following fascinating account of a miracle:

The resident of Mount Kailas took birth as Sarala Das.
He was born an ignoramus in a sudra's family.
And tilling the land, he made a living.
One day, the first lines of a song, he sang.

Turning around he saw me, Goddess Sarala who had assumed the
form of an old woman.
Startled, he stopped singing his song.
And went on ploughing the field.
Then he smiled and resumed his song.
I, who appeared very old and frail
Approached the farmer busy ploughing.
I tottered as I walked
And the ridge I could not climb.
The farmer rushed to my help
When I stumbled and fell to the ground.
He raised me with his hands
And gently made me sit down.
Whose mother are you and where are you going?
Why is no one accompanying you?
I have no kith and kin.
So, I am on my way, alone.
In village Jakshpur I live
But I have somehow lost my way.
Ferry this old woman across the river
And may God grant you the years that are left to me.
Old and unwell I am
I'll fall ill if the water soaks me.
O farmer, take me to the other side of the river.
I am in a hurry to reach Jakshpur.
Hearing this, the farmer laid down his plough
And held me in his arms.
When he reached the bank
The swelling river filled him with fear.
He thought to himself
How can I ever cross this river?
I said, let us cross this river son
For I can't brook any delay.
Hearing this, he quickly stepped into the water
His left arm supporting me.
In his right hand he held the long stick [with which he prodded his
bullocks]
And gingerly proceeded feeling the river bed with it.
Slowly, the water rose to his waist
And he raised me to his shoulder.
When the river reached his shoulder
He placed me on his head.
I knew his heart was full of fear
And asked him to sing a song.

To this he said, an unlettered fool I am, o mother
How can I sing a song that would please you?
I told him, my son, I have blessed you with learning
Go on and write Shri *Mahabharata.*

In the manuscript it is mentioned that Goddess Sarala had narrated this to some brahmans in a dream. However, the diction used here differs from that of Sarala Das. Another manuscript of Sarala Das's *Mahabharata* which was copied eighty-two years ago does not feature this story. Some forger must have inserted this into the narrative. Whether it is written by Sarala Das or someone else, its indebtedness to the rhythmic pattern of folk sayings is patently obvious.

Chandipurana is another work composed by Sarala Das. W.W. Hunter has wrongly attributed the authorship of this text to Balaram Das. One hopes to find out what other works Sarala Das authored.

Translation: Niroj Kumar Sethi

Notes

1 Shyam Sundar Rajguru, "Sudramuni Sarala Das: *Mahabharata* Rachayita" [Sudramuni Sarala Das: The Author of Odia *Mahabharata*], *Utkal Sahitya*, vol. 7, no. 4, Cuttack, 1903, pp. 114–119.
2 Rajguru hails from Paralakhemundi which then was part of the Madras Presidency and now in southern Odisha. The village of Sarala Das as identified by Rajguru was then part of the Orissa Division of the Bengal presidency.
3 One of the eleven divisions of the time of the day according to Hindu astrology
4 The time of rising of any of the zodiacal signs
5 *Mesha* refers to the month April–May and is named after one of the zodiacal signs (Aries).
6 *Magha* refers to the month January–February and is named after one of the zodiacal signs (Capricorn).
7 *Asadh* refers to the month June–July and is named after one of the zodiacal signs (Gemini).
8 We are grateful to J.P. Das for translating these couplets.

5 Gopinath Nanda Sarma

Reflections on Sarala Das's *Mahabharata*: excerpts from *Sree Bharata Darpan*

Introduction

A man of vast erudition and a polyglot, Gopinath Nanda Sarma (1869–1924) significantly contributed to the shaping of modern Odia critical discourse in its formative phase writing pioneering scholarly works on Odia language and literature, and compiling a remarkable Odia lexicon. Closely associated with the royal court of Paralakhemundi, which was then a vibrant centre of scholarly discussion on Sanskrit, Odia and Telugu literatures, Gopinath actively engaged in writing creative and critical works. Several of his plays which he wrote following Sanskrit models were staged at Padmanabh Rangalaya in Paralakhemundi. He also translated into Odia classics such as Valmiki's *Ramayana* and Kalidasa's *Kumarasambhava* for students. In spite of having received very little formal education, he was appointed as a lecturer at Paralakehmundi Maharaja Mahavidyalaya in recognition of his impressive scholarly credentials. The increasing awareness of the need to assert Odia identity in the closing decades of the nineteenth century led Gopinath to rival in his own writings in Odia the rhetorical sophistication distinguishing Telugu literature. He also got passionately involved in realizing the three key projects envisaged by the Utkal Sahitya Samaj, founded in 1903 to promote and revitalize Odia literature. These projects included a comprehensive dictionary, a definitive grammar and a history of literature. Gopinath contributed numerous articles to the major literary periodicals of the time such as *Utkal Sahitya*, *Mukur* and *Satyabadi*, which provoked lively debates among scholars and sometimes aroused considerable hostility.

The present essay comprises multiple excerpts from Gopinath Nanda Sarma's *Sree Bharata Darpan* which was published posthumously in 1928. Its manuscript was completed in 1909 and it was serialized in *Utkal Sahitya* between 1911 and 1915. It may be mentioned here that this is the first book-length study of Sarala Das's *Mahabharata*. Before this, in one of the earliest articles on Sarala Das (included in this volume) Shyam Sundar Rajguru, also from Paralakhemundi and Gopintha's senior contemporary and mentor, had discussed the epic and referred to its author as the first major poet of Odisha. Gopinath's intensive study of Sarala Das's *Mahabharata* assumes

DOI: 10.4324/9781003224778-5

crucial significance in the context of the contempt with which Sanskrit pandits looked upon the Odia epic and the hostile indifference with which western-educated literati treated it after the advent of print culture. This unsympathetic attitude stemmed from two major sources: Sarala Das's spirited deviations from the revered Sanskrit text, and his exuberant incorporation of folk elements in the epic. In his groundbreaking work, Gopinath perceptively compares Sarala Das's *Mahabharata* with Vyasa's epic, studies in depth its language and literary quality, and reconstructs the life of the author from information available in the text and local legends. As one of the earliest comparatists, he extends his critical enquiry beyond Sanskrit sources and brings his knowledge of Telugu, Bangla and Hindi versions of the *Mahabharata*, wherever necessary, to bear upon his study of Sarala's epic and conveys its singularity. He pays particular attention to the text getting corrupted through its scribal reproduction over centuries. His celebration of Sarala Das's *Mahabharata* as a national treasure can be seen as part of an initiative to give Odia identity a firm cultural foundation by tracing its magnificent genealogy. He singles out the energetic simplicity of Sarala Das's poetic idiom for praise which the author inventively shaped when Odia language was in its infancy. However, Gopinath's assessment of Sarala Das's *Mahabharata* is not entirely laudatory; he painstakingly points out several inconsistencies in the epic which can diminish the reader's enjoyment. Gopinath's work contributes immensely to the evolving critical discourse in early twentieth-century Odisha by ingeniously combining traditional modes of aesthetic interpretation with emerging modern methods of evaluating a text.

*

Reflections on Sarala Das's *Mahabharata*: excerpts from *Sree Bharata Darpan*[1]

Gopinath Nanda Sarma

Introductory Remarks
(pp. 85–86)

Wise, knowledgeable readers! After duly bowing to the *shastrakara* [author], Srikrushna Dwaipayana, and having mustered up the courage and patience, we have embarked on this onerous task of presenting before you an extensive critical analysis of the exceedingly complex text of the *Mahabharata* by Sarala Das. We implore you to take the trouble of offering your invaluable opinion on the relative merits and flaws of our effort without getting exasperated at the prospect of the treatise trying your patience and prompting you, as it inevitably might, to postpone reading it. Do not suppose that reading and evaluating this work will amount to

a waste of your time. There is nothing unusual about anyone perpetually postponing the reading of the myriad-featured, unboundedly-oceanic
Mahabharata that is also beyond a common reader's comprehension. Even
so, we are not at all interested in embellishing our work with scattered,
unnecessary, meaningless and incongruous sentences that are imported
from *Vilat* [England]. In this context, the advice offered by the author
of the great Sanskrit *kavya Naishadha Charita*, Sriharsha, "*mitam cha
sraram cha vachohi bagmita*" [true eloquence consists in expressing a lot
using only a few words] seems apt because of which we shall try, to the
extent possible, to write with precision only about the worthy and essential subjects.

It might be necessary for us to clarify here that this essay in criticism
will appear in four parts: (i) analysis of similarities and differences (between
the Sanskrit and Odia *Mahabharatas*); (ii) study of its language and literary quality; (iii) introduction to the poet; (iv) concluding remarks. However,
before proceeding to analyze Sarala Das's *Mahabharata*, the reader may be
informed that much of its divine beauty, sweetness of versification and exquisite craftsmanship has been lost through scribal reproduction of the text. At
places, the fascinating poetic images of the original have been thoughtlessly
defaced. Not all the flaws that we now come across in Sarala Das's text are
his. It is true that the poet's work is not flawless from a modern point of
view but his text got corrupted by the errors introduced by incompetent and
ignorant scribes. This epic is at least five hundred years old and has been at
the disposal of succeeding generations of undeserving people. The text has
suffered the fate of a *shalgram* [a geode stone worshipped as Vishnu] which
has fallen into the hands of a stupid monkey. Sanskritic discourses were
overwhelmingly dominant when the Odia epic came to be composed. Almost
everyone in the elite sections of society placed a high value only on texts
written in Sanskrit. At that time, Odia, which originated from a combination of several *prakrit* languages, was in its infancy. It had not gained wide
currency yet and its use was confined to the lower classes. Some of you might
have come across Sanskrit pandits in Odisha, whose scholarship is based
on mindless rote-learning, expressing utter contempt for anything written in
their mother tongue. If they run into another pandit of their calibre reading a
book in Odia, they tell him derisively, "how can you waste your time reading
a book written in *bhasha*?" Such an attitude is a sign of their perverse stupid-
ity. A sensible reader will deeply appreciate the deft arrangement of incidents
delineated, imaginative richness of narration and description, and the virtuosity displayed in any *kavya* written in any language. Pandits who are complete strangers to these express an absolute indifference to literature written
in their mother tongue. Looking at such pandits of our time, we can easily
imagine how, five centuries ago, Sanskrit pandits would not condescend to
touch Sarala Das's *Mahabahrata,* let alone read it. As a consequence, this
wonderfully delicate poem came to be copied by semi-literate scribes and
copies made by them were subsequently further corrupted by ignoramuses.

The Sanskrit *Mahbharata* and Sarala's Odia version
(pp. 109–110)

That Sarala Das achieved intimate familiarity with the Sanskrit *Mahabharata* becomes evident in the minutest of details in the original found in his version. At the same time, he brilliantly succeeded in imaginatively transforming some of the major events featured in the original. Vyasa's epic mentions that the Pandavas stayed incognito in a potter's cottage in Drupada's kingdom around the time Draupadi's *swayamvar* was held. Sarala Das closely followed Vyasa in depicting this episode. In Vyasa's epic, festivities are observed for fifteen days preceding the event of the *swayamvar* and on the sixteenth, a properly bedecked Draupadi appears before the congregation of her suitors. This detail is also found in Sarala's version. However, whereas in the Sanskrit original, it is Draupadi's brother, Dhrustadyumna who briefly introduces the royal suitors present, in Sarala's version, it is Draupadi's companion Keshini who introduces them elaborately giving them names that do not figure in Vyasa's text. Sarala Das's description of the suitors' attempts to hit the target during the *swayamvar* is also highly exaggerated. In Vyasa's epic, Karna is infuriated when Draupadi bars him from participating in the competition, saying that she would not accept him as her husband even if he succeeds in hitting the target because he is the son of a *suta* [a charioteer]. Sarala Das strikingly departed from this version. In his version, it is Sri Krishna who realizes that Karna would surely succeed in hitting the target; so, he surreptitiously used his discus to prevent his arrow from hitting it. Although, in this instance, Sarala has deviated from the original, he did not violate the essence of the original in any way.

(pp. 115–117)

It is but natural that an author would stay close to the train of main events while rewriting a text written in one language in another. However, it needs to be pointed out that even while representing the main events of the original, Sarala Das allows them to ramify. Many of Sarala's characters are different from and opposite of their counterparts in the original; some of them are also exaggerated. These sections do not exactly match those in the original text, no doubt; but the combination of the genius of the poet and his extraordinary art of composition is so compelling as to move the reader's heart, inspiring awe and ensuring enjoyment. At places, however, the poet is caught in the trap of his own ability to compose poetry impromptu, because of which he could not perceive the contradiction between earlier and later passages. We furnish a few instances below to illustrate such inconsistencies. For example, he said at the beginning of the *Udyog Parva* that, after their exile, the Pandavas left Virat's kingdom and stayed at Indraprastha (or Varunavanta). On being asked by Dhritarastra, whether the Pandavas had anyone accompanying them, the messenger mentioned princess Uttara, Virat's daughter. A few days later, in the same text, it is mentioned that the Pandavas with Krishna and Abhimanyu journeyed to Virat's kingdom to perform rituals associated with Uttara's coming of age. First of all, he writes that Uttara lived with the Pandavas at Indraprastha; and then he says she was at Virat Desha; and then, again, he says that she reached puberty at her father's palace. Even so, nowhere does he indicate that Uttara had returned to Virat's kingdom from Indraprashtha. Again, in the selfsame *Udyog Parva*, Sri Krishna goes to Hastinapur as the emissary of Pandavas. Upon his arrival there, Krishna informs Kunti that Pandavas are now living in Varunabanta after leaving Virat's kingdom. The poet, however, gives no hint of the Pandavas having shifted to Varunavanta. Sarala Das's earlier statement is in accordance with Vyasa's account of the event in the source text; Pandavas were living in Virat's kingdom when Krishna came to Hastinapur as an emissary. Now, to say that they were in Varunavanta is an anomaly.

(pp. 210–211)

Like Sarala Das, the Bangla *Bharata* writer Kashiram Das, Hindi *Bharata* writer Sabala Singh and Trailanga *Bharata* writer Tikanna Somajaji do not include a translation of the *Bhagavad Gita* in their versions of the epic. But they explain the whole of it in one or two pages coherently; Sarala Das's discussion of this episode in the battlefield is rather negligible. True, Sarala follows the original in making the pious Yudhisthira approach his enemies before the battle, but he introduces many irrelevant issues and intentions into his conversation with Bhishma and others. Sarala also interferes with the sequence of events.

This is followed by the episode depicting the death of Bhishma. Here, as in the original, there are detailed descriptions of combats involving charioteers and between wrestlers. But it can be safely said that Sarala Das's accounts differ significantly from those provided in the original.

Dating the Mahabharata War
(pp. 195–198)

We feel that there is a need to date the Mahabharata war. To do so, we shall first try to ascertain how many years ago this cataclysmic event took place. After collecting evidence pertaining to the year of the war, we will get down to details concerning the month and days. Neither in Vyasa's epic, nor in its numerous vernacular versions does one come across any conclusive proof based on accurate calculations. The pieces of evidence available in *Srimad Bhagavat* and *Sri Vishnu Purana* do not match each other. It is quite possible that their inner meanings are beyond our comprehension. So, many take recourse to changing words in relevant lines to suit their own interpretations. Let alone smoothening our task, the essay would become complicated and unnecessarily lengthy if we seek to harmonize these divergent views. We have seen how, in using the time of the Buddha or the reign of king Chandragupta as reference points, many scholars have come up with completely unconvincing interpretations. The opinion of one does not square with that of another. The evidence found in the original has been stretched, altered, edited or trimmed by different scholars to fit them into their own schemes of conjecture. The dates they suggest are separated by centuries or by even a millennium. This is the reason we did not feel like needlessly increasing the length of the essay by taking into account all these diverse interpretations. So we have followed the well-considered view advanced by Kalhan in his treatise, *Rajatarangini* in order to offer proof of the time of the Mahabharata war. We believe knowledgeable readers would find it acceptable.

Sage Garg says:

> Kali Yuga was into its
> Six hundred and fifty-third year
> When Nrupati Yudhisthira ruled his kingdom.

Kalhan, based on sage Garg's opinion, has come to the conclusion that the war between the Pandavas and Kauravas was fought 653 years after the advent of the Kali Yuga. Those who still hold the view that this war was fought towards the end of the Dwapara Yuga, realized that their calculations were erroneous, and tried to prove through devious means that their calculations were correct. Kalhan avers that *Rajatarangini* was composed in the year 1070 according to the Shalibahana Shaka Calendar [or the Indian national calendar]. 2,330 years had elapsed by this time (1070) from the time of Gonarda the Third (aka, Gonanda), the King of Kashmir. Between the time of Gonarda the First (a contemporary of the Pandavas) and Gonarda the Third, fifty-two kings had reigned for 1,266 years. So, we add 1,266 (the years between the first and third Gonardas) and 2,330 (the years between Gonarda the Third and the time of the composition of *Rajatarangini*) to reach the figures 3,596 years. This is the period between the Mahabharata war and the time of the composition of *Rajatarangini*. Presently, it is 1912 CE, which according to the Shalibahana Shaka Calendar is 1834. We subtract 1,070 from 1,834, and we get the year of the composition of *Rajatarangini*, which is 764 CE. Now, adding 3,596 and 764, we get 4,360. That is, the Mahabharata war was fought 4,360 years ago. By subtracting it from the present epoch of Kali, 5,013 years, we get 653 years, which is what was computed by Sage Garg as per the gentleman quoted above. As per this deduction, one can conclusively say that the Mahabharata war was fought 4,360 years back from now, i.e., in the year 2448 BC.

From now on, it becomes increasingly difficult to compute and ascertain the exact months when the Mahabharata war was fought. One does not come across any definite information regarding this even in the original. The evidence available in the vernacular translations of the original is quite mis-leading. It will, therefore, be necessary to arrive at conclusions by consulting the original passages along with the relevant lines in the other versions.

Sarala Das initially mentions quite erroneously, though, that the corona-tion of the Pandavas took place in the kingdom of Virat on the fourth day in the bright fortnight in the month of Makara [January–February]. And then, later, he says that the Mahabharata war also began on the same *tithi* [lunar day]. It is also possible that scribes subsequently added this error.

But the date Sarala Das mentions as regards the commencement of the Mahabharata war is completely untrustworthy, flawed and unfounded. Considering all this, it is impossible for us to believe that Sarala Das had a proper understanding of the sequence of events involving the Pandavas. Otherwise, he would not have presented Bhishma lying on the bed of arrows for more than a month, and leaving his mortal body during the *uttarayana* [northward movement of the earth].

Kashiramdas, the author of the Bangla *Mahabharata* says in the *Udyog Parva* that the Pandavas emerged from their exile on the fifth day (there is no mention here of the month) with all their soldiers and reached Kurukshetra in the space of three days. He has also mentioned that Duryodhan, on hear-ing from the messenger that the Pandavas had reached the battlefield, began preparing for the war. Yet, in *Bhisma Parva*, he indicates that the Kauravas set out on the fifth day in the dark fortnight in the month of Margashira [November–December]. This day cannot be accepted as the one on which the war commenced.

A note on its literary quality and its use of language
(pp. 267–268)

In his version of the *Mahabharata*, Sarala Das employs an idiom which is uniquely lucid and admirably accessible. Every section is replete with evocative descriptions of natural beauty. Needless to say, such beauty and expressiveness which he infuses into Odia language in its infancy was pos-sible owing to Sarala's astounding intelligence and profound empathy. If the language of this work is compared with that of the carved inscriptions and royal decrees contemporaneous with it, it must be accepted that the poet has raised it to a level of amazing refinement exercising his extraordinary creative talent. While fashioning his monumental work, the *Mahabharata*, this great poet did not have the luxury of building on any model available in Odia, with the help of which he could have enriched and bedecked his impoverished mother tongue, an object of worship for him. By trusting his own genius and breadth of sympathy, he was able to enrich his mother tongue to such an extent that, even after five hundred years, his work is in no way inferior to anything written in modern Odia, a language which now can hold its head high among its sister languages. Leaving aside a few blemishes here and there in the voluminous work, the elemental freshness

of Sarala Das's simple language conveys more brilliantly the national character than does modern Odia. It took a genius of Sarala Das's stature to
transform Odia language into a priceless national treasure, by writing in it a
literary work on such a grand scale. All that Odia literature could boast of
till Sarala's time comprised only a handful of minor works such as "Keshab
Koili" and "Gopi Bhasa".

(pp. 301–305)

Generally speaking, Sarala Das's description of female beauty is extraordinarily skillful. Likewise, he excelled in the depiction of male beauty, in the
sense that it is in keeping with the guidelines unanimously laid down by
master poets. If the reader has any doubts on this score, they can look up
Sarala Das's portrayal of Karna's childhood in the *Adi Parva*.

Our ancient poet is brilliant in dealing with *sringara rasa* [the erotic senti-
ment], no doubt; but he is no less adept at the delineation of *veera rasa* [the
heroic sentiment] and, for that matter, the other *rasas*. When the reader goes
through Sarala Das's depiction of any *rasa*, the feeling of the same *rasa* is
aroused in them. We shall desist from describing these in our own words; it
would be prudent to quote passages extensively from the text. Let us look at
the passages dealing with the mace fight and wrestling between Bhima and
Duryodhan to see how Sarala arouses the heroic *rasa*:

> Roaring, they call out each other's names
> Sounding like the thunder in clouds that spells catastrophe.
> They loudly smite one hand with another,
> Their bodies glow like flaming fire.

The passages from the "faithful" translation by a more recent Odia poet,
Krushna Singh, may be compared to similar passages in Sarala's epic. We
see that even after centuries, Krushna Singh's version has not been able to
match the supple lucidity of Sarala Das's language and the rhythmic energy
of his lines.

Depiction of *bibhatsa rasa*:

> Rat-tat; boom-clang, sounds infernal
> As if fireballs are hurtling down on the roofs
> …
> Deadly deities excitedly devour blood and flesh
> Lying naked flat on the ground
> Some wearing skull garlands around their breasts
> Dancing their macabre dances with laughter on their lips
> Their lips are in the skies and mouths in hell
> At one go they devour a myriad bodies …

Here, as elsewhere, Sarala Das is able to depict *bibhatsa rasa* [the odious sentiment] quite vividly in his *Mahabharata* using his own imaginative resources. One gets the flavour of the *bibhatsa rasa* that one encounters in the fifth act of the great poet Bhabavuti's play, *Malatimadhav*, in which the demons are shown as indulging in bizarre acts such as gleefully devouring the flesh, bone and sucking out the bone marrow of cadavers.

These passages are illustrative of Sarala Das's familiarity with the prescriptions and laws laid down by prominent aestheticians.

Translation: Sumanyu Satpathy

Note

1 Gopinath Nanda Sarma, *Sree Bharata Darpan*, in *Pandit Gopinath Nanda Granthabali*, vol. 1, ed. Sudarsan Acharya, Cuttack: Prachi Sahitya Pratisthan, 2011.

6 Sarala Devi

Portrayal of women in Sarala Das's *Mahabharata*

Introduction

Sarala Devi (1904–86) was a renowned freedom fighter, social activist and writer. At a very young age, she joined the freedom struggle led by Mahatma Gandhi. She played an active role in the Non-Cooperation Movement in Odisha and was imprisoned. In 1936, when Odisha became a separate province, she was elected to the Legislative Assembly as its first woman member. In the Assembly, she was instrumental in getting bills relating to women's education and welfare enacted. She stressed the importance of making primary education free and universal, and raised her voice against the practice of dowry. She was a prolific writer who contributed significantly to several branches of literature. She wrote poetry, short stories, plays, biographies, books for children, literary criticism and essays. Her essays constitute a pioneering achievement in that they reflect a potent political awareness which was rare in women's writing of the time. Many of her essays incisively explored the place of women in society, past and present, and mounted a trenchant attack on the patriarchal social fabric. Her writings were animated by the passion of a social and political activist, and exhorted women to step out of the confines of domesticity and realise their full potential in the public sphere. Although she had not received much formal education, her essays display a cosmopolitan outlook and a lively awareness of international issues. Her major works include *Narira Dabi* [The Rights of Women] (1934), *Nari Jagat* [The World of Women] (1935), *Bharatiya Mahila Prasang* [Matters Concerning Indian Women] (1935), *Rabindra Puja* [A Tribute to Rabindranath Tagore] (1941), *Utkal Bharati Kabi Pratibha* [The Poetic Achievement of Kuntala Kumari Sabat] (1948), *Biswa Biplabini* [Revolutionary Women of the World] (1958, 2nd ed.) and *Raya Ramanand* (1963). A selection of her writings in English translation has been edited by Sachidananda Mohanty and published under the title *The Lost World of Sarala Devi* (2016).

The essay given below consists of selected excerpts from Sarala Devi's book *Sarala Mahabharatiya Narichitra* [Portrayal of Women in Sarala Das's *Mahabharata*] (1952). She had earlier published a series of eight essays on this subject in the monthly literary magazine *Sahakar* in 1938–39. The book

DOI: 10.4324/9781003224778-6

brought together revised versions of these essays. In the preface to her book Sarala Devi says that she undertook the task in view of the near absence of works of criticism focusing on a single aspect of a specific literary text. Her lifelong interest in the woman question led her to concentrate on exploring the depiction of women in Sarala Das's monumental fifteenth-century Odia epic. She believes that women in the modern world have a lot to learn from the lively and vivid portraits of women presented in Sarala Das's epic. Women in Sarala Das's *Mahabharata*, Sarala Devi argues, differ fundamentally from their counterparts in Vyasa's epic in being endowed with intensely human attributes and not divine qualities. Even when presented as unmistakably human, they are not always portrayed as likeable and reasonable. Sarala Devi's work represents an early attempt at applying a sociological analysis to a foundational text. She meticulously maps the social world of fifteenth-century Odisha as depicted in Sarala Das's *Mahabharata* and locates women in it. An interesting aspect of her analysis is the way she presents points of contact between the past and the present. The book derives its significance in the evolving Odia critical discourse from its developing a proto-feminist approach to a literary classic.

*

Portrayal of women in Sarala Das's *Mahabharata*[1]

Sarala Devi

Sarala Das's *Mahabharata* occupies a unique place among texts written in Prakrit in terms of the vastness of its imaginative universe and the bold originality displayed in its portrayal of characters and incidents. One rarely comes across Prakrit texts composed on such a massive scale in the fifteenth century. In fact, the greatness of Sarala's epic derives from its not being a direct translation of Vyasa's *Mahabharata* and from being peopled with hundreds of characters who are vibrantly alive. If we regard Vyasa's epic as a treatise on social mores and political codes prevalent in his time, Sarala's epic may well be seen as a mirror reflecting the social and political realities of Odisha in particular and India in general of the century he lived in.

The fifteenth century in the history of Odisha was a period of crisis. The kings of the Ganga dynasty who ruled Odisha in the early part of the fifteenth century were weak and the kingdom was attacked and plundered by invaders from outside. Some bigoted Muslim kings destroyed and defiled the temples and images of the Hindu deities. Firoz Shah had invaded Odisha a few years before Kapilendra Dev ascended the throne. He proceeded towards Puri and destroyed many a temple on the way, and even the Jagannath Temple was not spared. Even after Kapilendra was enthroned, unrest continued to plague Odisha. In fact, it took him quite some time to restore order in the kingdom by repelling external invaders and suppressing resistance from rebels within. Sarala Das who composed the *Mahabharata* during this period must have been a witness to the turbulence and uncertainty of the time. We get some hints about this in his depiction of characters and incidents.

It seems Sarala Das described in his epic the general condition of Odisha during the period, and its traditions and rituals. There is something innovative about the ways in which he portrayed women in the epic. Many of his characters remind one of typical Odia women of his time. Sarala did not closely follow the Sanskrit *Mahabharata*; he drew upon the local customs and conventions. It is not within the power of any ordinary poet to create a new and multifarious imaginative world.

In his portrayal of women Sarala Das displays exemplary artistic skill. His women characters present a blend of good and evil, and embody a conflict between divine attributes and human qualities. For this reason, Sarala Das's *Mahabharata* not only provides readers with moral lessons like a *purana* but also entertains them like a novel.

In those days men and women followed customs such as fasting, goddess worship and other social sanctions and restrictions. People engaged in activities like offering oblations to ancestors, charitable deeds, worshipping deities, and valued qualities such as devoutness, humility, kindness, bravery and reverence for teachers. Nobody deviated from the norms relating to everyday life prescribed by scriptures and society. People had faith in astrology and they sought and followed the advice of pandits and astrologers. Sarala Das dramatizes the sad and disastrous consequences of the evil deeds done by bad people. A discussion of the characters of the *Mahabharata* reveals that life becomes miserable for people who stray from the path of virtue, and follow the devious path of the unjust and the hypocrite, the shrewd and the wrongdoer.

In *Sarala Das's Mahabharata*, we find many instances of abduction of women. Young maidens valued the prowess and bravery of their suitors more than their material prosperity; they spurned men who were cowardly, weak and ugly. Love formed the basis of marriage, but since women attached more importance to valour and physical strength in men, they considered *rakshasa vivah* [a form of marriage where the man abducts the woman against her and her family's will] as acceptable as *gandharva vivah* [a marriage based on mutual attraction and without involving any witnesses, rituals or family participation]. They had access to general education, knowledge of art, statecraft and war; and they performed all sorts of social duties using their intuition.

Rules of marriage

Sarala Das's elaborate discussions of marriage include the following details many of which remind one of the prevalent rituals and customs associated with a typical Odia wedding: *dianmangala* [seeking the local deity's blessings]; the ritual involving anointing the couple with *kumkum* [vermillion], oil, turmeric etc.; the bride and groom's play with cowries after the wedding; the blessings bestowed on the couple by seven married women; joining the hands of the groom and the bride with the sacred *kusa* grass; the washing of the groom's feet by the bride's brother; the bride's father ceremonially offering his daughter; the bride and groom made to sit ritually on a newly woven reed-mat; the collection of seven water-filled pitchers from seven different houses in the village; the ritual bath and decking up of the groom and the bride; seating the bride and groom on a stone; the chanting of the Brahman invoking the gods and the Veda mantras; and the request by the father of the bride to forgive her ten faults, etc. The musical instruments played during the ceremony include conch shells, trumpets, pakhavaj, pipes, veenas, etc. The custom of inviting kinspeople by sending them areca nuts is also mentioned in the epic. The father of the bride gave her cows, horses, elephants, utensils, palanquins, gems and precious stones, and attendants and maidservants in the form of dowry. Sarala Das also shows how married women poked fun at the groom near the marriage altar. Women in those days wore tattoos on their bodies.

The kind saris and ornaments which women wore in Sarala Das's *Mahabharata* were used even in the early decades of the twentieth century. These include pearl necklaces, diamond-studded gold necklaces, earrings, bracelets, bangles, etc. Sarala Das also wrote about the duties a woman had to perform.

Young maidens were considered fit for marriage after attaining puberty, and to keep such maidens at home without getting them married was regarded a sin and the parents of such maidens had the fear of displeasing the souls of their ancestors who would not even receive oblations from them. Sarala Das introduced the figure of the matchmaker who helped fathers find a groom for their daughters. He even brought in Sage Narada to mediate in some cases of *rakshasa* marriage which often resulted in violent conflicts before leading to a settlement.

Sarala Das shows the father of the bride breaking down and weeping at the time of her departure for her in-laws' house. The poet also refers to the parting-songs mothers sang when the daughter left home:

> So lamented the queen and her companions
> Everyone wailed taking the name of the daughter.
>
> (*Madhya Parva*)

This tradition of singing wailing-songs for the daughter is still prevalent in Odisha.

Gandharva and Vedic marriages

Sarala Das writes how a relationship formed according to the *gandharva* mode would later be solemnized following Vedic rituals. It seems, in the puranic era, considerations of convenience, not rigid moral principles, guided most activities. This is true of Sarala Das's *Mahabharata* as well. Under the pressure of deeply-felt social needs, many rituals and customs were changed, and the changed ones were treated as norms. But it is true that humanity transcended all other values. This explains how a strange social discipline regulated evolving social rules and customs, and allowed space for human values to flourish. It would not be an exaggeration to claim that Indian civilization took shape during the age of the *Mahabharata*. Although Hindus adhered to *varnashrama* [duties performed according to the system of four castes], they also felt free to violate its prescriptions when necessary. On occasion, a brahman could marry the daughter of a sudra and his action could be accommodated within the liberal Vedic society. This flexibility allowed an otherwise rule-bound society to emerge robust and resilient. Society in the *Mahabharata* era did not stagnate because it struck a fine balance between the individual and the collective.

Scandals in marriage

In Sarala's time, people were very much afraid of scandals, and if the girl lost her chastity, the family of the girl would suffer humiliation and shame. On getting to know of Samba secretly seducing Chandrabati, Yudhisthir told Duryodhan,

> This brings disgrace upon King Managovind [Duryodhan]
> And shames our clan in Hastinapur.

To find a way out, Duryodhan asked Sahadev to tell Samba that he should abduct Chandrabati at a *swayamvar* attended by one lakh kings. At that time, shame and humiliation could be erased through a daunting show of prowess. Sarala Das writes,

> If the girl comes of age in her father's house
> Would the ancestors accept oblation from her father?
> The clan can never have a bright future
> And the Vedic pandits declare,
> "Never ever keep nubile daughters at home,
> Their presence brings misfortune to the family."
>
> You, Indra, let an unmarried daughter remain at home
> And earned wrath and displeasure
> The son is not to be blamed in all this
> If you are a virile man, you cannot resist a young woman
> ...
> Slur and scandal have polluted your daughter
> And it is not possible to betroth her to another person.
>
> (*Madhya Parva*)

After the abduction of Chandravati, Yudhisthir, fearing humiliation and ostracization, says,

> Such a bad thing happened without our knowledge.
> And it is not desirable to hide a sin
> As in this world infamy dies on its own.
> No one would blame the girl for what she did
> And some shall hold us responsible.

From the above lines, we can infer that everyone, from the king to his subjects, was afraid of social ostracism and public humiliation. And as people placed the community above the individual, respect for public opinion regulated social behaviour.

Women's Education

In those days women were imparted education. If women were uneducated, Sarala would not have shown even the maids of the princess singing songs at the marriage altar. In the *Virat Parva*, we find Arjun, disguised as a woman named Brihannala, teaching the princess Uttara the art of dancing and singing when the Pandavas were living incognito in the palace of King Virat. Though, unlike Vyasa, Sarala did not refer to Draupadi as a *vidusi* [a learned woman] one could infer from her actions that she was quite accomplished. During the abduction of Subhadra, when the kings supporting the Kaurav brothers waged war against Arjun, the abductor, Subhadra served Arjun as his charioteer; similarly, Sataybhama, Krishna's spouse, acted as his charioteer. These examples indicate that women from aristocratic families were adept at horse riding, charioteering, and archery. Those days, women learnt how to promote harmony and stability in the extended family and community by grasping rules governing social practices. The art of wielding weapons, and learning the *Vedas* and scriptures formed key aspects of women's education.

It has already been mentioned that women used to read and write in Sarala's time. In the episode where Bhima killed Kichaka, Sudeshna, the queen of Virat and Kichaka's sister, sent a letter to her brother through Draupadi who served her as a maidservant. Given the situation in which she found herself, it is quite possible that Draupadi went through the contents of the letter before delivering it. That Draupadi was highly educated becomes evident when she consoled Kichaka's widows and mistresses referring to the transience of human life and futility of material possessions like a philosopher. Apart from acquiring reading and writing skills, women in this era also learnt to draw. Arjuna, shortly after marrying Chitrangada, proceeded to the forest to do penance for twelve years. He asked a disconsolate Chitrangada to draw his portrait and keep it as a souvenir.

Avoidance relationships

Women of ancient times would avoid appearing before their brothers-in-law; they would take care not to be seen by their husbands' elder brothers, and her by their maternal uncles, her sons-in-law, and their sisters' husbands. These rules governing relationships were meant to make joint families function smoothly. In *Adi Parva*, when Pandu approached Dhritarastra, who was engaged in a conversation with his queen Gandhari, she left the place.

Casting a spell on the husband to ensure his fidelity

Women in Sarala Das's *Mahabharata*, especially young unmarried ones, sought to learn *mantras* which had the power to enchant future husbands. Sarala mentions women trying to master forms of tantric knowledge such as *ulluka vidya* [a magical art which enables a person to see in the dark], *naganta vidya* [black magic], *stambhan* [a kind of magic used to benumb someone], *mohan* [enchanting a person by employing *tantric* charms] and use of medicinal plants.

During the years Pandavas spent in the forest as exiles, Sri Krishna accompanied by his wife Sataybhama visited them. Satyabhama asked Draupadi how she could make her five husbands remain loyal and attached to her when she and numerous other wives of Krishna had failed to win his heart. She enquired if Draupadi was adopting some *tantric* tricks. Draupadi replied that she received the unwavering love of her husbands not through black magic but on account of her devoted service to them. Since men took many wives, rivalry among co-wives was common and each tried to draw the husband's attention to herself. For this reason, many of them had to learn *tantric* practices. Draupadi gave Satyabhama the instance of a woman who gave her husband food mixed with magic potions to win his love. But the woman ended up losing her husband and she became a widow.

Images of domestic life

Sarala Das implanted some divine traits into the characters of Kunti and Gandhari, yet at the same time, he presented them as unmistakably human by highlighting their rivalry as the wives of two brothers in the same family. The following amusing incident, which does not occur in the Sanskrit *Mahabharata*, maybe recounted here.

Gandhari and Kunti offered worship to Lord Shiva in the morning every day. One day, when Kunti reached earlier for the *pooja*, Gandhari said in anger,

> Your turn to worship Shiva comes after me
> How dare you pay worship to the Lord before me …!

Many a harsh word did Gandahri utter
Feeling deeply insulted Kunti replied
I worship the Lord every day
How come this appears improper to you?

Hearing them quarrel, Lord Shiva appeared in the guise of a brahman and told them that it was unbecoming of two royal ladies to fight in that manner. He added that one who would bring a thousand golden champak flowers in the morning of the following day would have the right to worship the Lord.

Gandhari and Kunti returned home. Deeply worried, Kunti went to bed without taking food. She was scared that Gandhari's hundred sons would be able to arrange those thousand flowers. Seeing her mother upset, Arjun promised that he would fill the temple of Shiva with golden champaks. Then Kunti got up and ate. But she was so anxious that she could not sleep. When she reached the temple before daybreak, she found a massive heap of golden champaks near the temple. And then she offered worship to the Lord with those flowers. When Gandhari reached the temple, she found the entrance blocked with flowers and crestfallen, she went back home. Summing up the episode, the poet writes,

Kunti triumphed because she was the mother of worthy sons
Crushed by shame, Gandhari made her way to the palace.

Sarala Das shows that in worthy sons a woman finds a source of happiness and likewise, worthless sons bring terrible unhappiness to a mother.

Moreover, in Sarala's epic, we get to know of the place women occupied in the Pandava household. One day, Krishna visited Kunti at her palace. When Sri Krishna bowed before Kunti, she blessed him and asked after his family. Yudhisthir requested his mother to prepare food for the guest and Kunti walked into the inner wing of the palace:

Kunti went inside and said
Krishna has come,
Draupadi felt overjoyed
And prepared dishes having six flavours
She prepared food of different colours
And prepared the *payas* [dessert] in *panchamruta* [the elixir of gods prepared out of five ingredients]
And five cakes in five different colours
Which Lord Janardan [Krishna] would relish.
After the cooking was finished, Drupada's daughter
Informed Queen Kunti quickly.

Sri Krishna and the Pandava brothers sat down to eat together. Kunti served the food to Krishna and her sons.

It is clear from the above that it was the duty of the daughter-in-law to cook and it fell to the mother-in-law to serve. Those days, mothers-in-law were not expected to do the cooking.

This practice is prevalent in many places even today, which is getting eroded under the influence of western culture. Joint families are disintegrating under the pressure of changing economic conditions.

Dowry system

Kings used to give dowry when they got their daughters married and Sarala Das mentions it at many places in his epic. When Bhumanu offered his daughter Bhanumati in marriage to Duryodhan, he lavished many gifts on him which included thousands of servants, and many courtesans and dancers.

A daughter's say in her marriage

It becomes clear from Bhanumati's *swayamvar* that fathers valued the opinion of their daughters. Bhumanu invited a lot of kings to the *swayamvar*, but his daughter Bhanumati laid down the conditions for choosing her husband. She insisted that she would marry the person whose hand would bear the signs of the lotus and conch shell. And, eventually, she married Duryodhan because he bore those signs.

Marriage without consent

Sarala Das's *Mahabharata* features many elaborate descriptions of *swayamvars* organized for maidens, celestial as well as human. He also offers instances of girls selecting their spouses exercising their free will even before the *swayamvar* takes place. On many occasions, he gives detailed descriptions of wars resulting from *swayamvars*. And many maidens expressed their unwillingness to take part in *swayamavars*. Ganga had resolved to take Lord Shiva as her husband; she was against marrying Shantanu whom her father had chosen as her groom. Sarala Das vividly describes how marrying against her will ruined her conjugal life. From an ethical point of view, the picture presented may look unacceptable, but as a psychological portrait, the character of Ganga appears quite convincing.

Wives as advisors

In both prosperity and adversity, wives offered their husbands advice and suggestions. Their counsel was sometimes as valuable as that of sagacious ministers. The advice Gandhari gave Dhritarastra when he felt depressed after relinquishing the throne in favour of his younger brother Pandu provides an excellent example. Had Dhritarastra continued to occupy the throne, Gandhari would have enjoyed the elevated status of the queen. But she advised her husband to calmly accept his lot as a blind person because everything in the world is transient. No one is great or small in the eyes of God who alone is supreme. Thus, ascending the throne, Pandu did not achieve greatness nor did Dhritarastra become small by giving it up. Bhanumati and Draupadi too gave similarly wise advice to their consorts.

Prominent women characters in the *Mahabharata*

In the ancient era, Draupadi became the wife of five husbands. Sarala Das says that this happened because all five brothers wanted to marry her. This was in Yudhisthir's mind when he called out to his mother from a distance, "We have brought a fruit today". To this Kunti replied, "The five of you should share it". In obedience to their mother's command, the five brothers took Draupadi as their wife. In those days the practice of polygyny and polyandry was acceptable. Men and women were dubbed unchaste if they indulged in mere physical pleasure. They were considered sinners adulterous acts. The liberal attitude towards polygamy was prevalent not only in human society but also in the celestial world. The society of those times did not victimize common people who were usually morally upright and religious. However, this does not mean there was any dearth of fallen and despised people. There was indeed a subtle distinction in society between what was moral and what was immoral. But the entire societal perspective was accommodating and liberal. Such an outlook allowed women like Draupadi, Kunti, Tara, Mandodari to be admired and worshipped as goddesses.

Draupadi was a strong woman who bravely faced life's many crises. Her harsh words towards her husbands did not spring from her selfish motives. When the need arose, Draupadi also served as a wise counsellor to her husbands. Considered as husbands, the Pandavas may strike one as weak and cowardly. However weighty the principles of justness and morality may be for men, they should count less than the need to help a woman who depended on them for her protection. This was the true definition of manliness.

After the game of dice, when the Pandavas went into the forest, Dhritarastra asked Sanjay about the expressions they wore on their faces. Sanjay replied that Draupadi ignoring the advice of everyone to tie her hair, wore it loose.

> Draupadi has kept her hair untied
> Chaste she is, devoted to her husbands
> Bhima would rip up Duhsasan's right hand
> To fulfil his oath
> Deeply concerned, everyone asked Draupadi
> ...
> Why have you kept your hair untied?
> Now you tie it, dear princess

Vyasa and others requested her, yet she paid no heed
You are wise, do as you please.

Pandavas, for their part, set a high value on truth, ethical principles and honour.

Dhritarastra says, listen to me O Bidura
Wealth the Pandava brothers never cherished
And so they can't be destroyed
But if they fail to honour a vow, they face disgrace.

For a woman, manliness consisted in protecting a woman's honour but men did not understand manliness in this way. Men attached more importance to the performance of great deeds and fulfilment of vows than to defending women from disgrace. Thus, from philosophical and psychological points of view, the way men looked at life diverged radically from that of women.

Ganga

In Sarala Das's Ganga, one finds a gripping portrait of a woman. In Vyasa's epic, Ganga is delineated as a goddess and noble qualities are attributed to her. Sarala Das's Ganga sharply contrasts with Vyasa's; she is an ordinary, ill-tempered woman like Gangi. Even today "Gangi" refers to a stridently assertive wife. A woman is called "Gangi" when she is quarrelsome and ill-treats her docile husband. She Says, "I'll stay with you so long as you call me Ganga but I'll leave the moment you address me as Gangi".

When Ganga turned thirteen, her father, King Nirghat planned to organize a *swayamvar* for her. But when Ganga said she had set her heart on marrying Lord Rudra [Shiva], the king was forced to wait. Later, Nirghat reasoned with her saying,

Listen to me O daughter
If you do not marry, the world will blame me
If I keep you at home after you reach puberty
Twenty-one generations of our ancestors will be consigned to hell
Ganga said many aeons will pass
I'll not come of age.

While Ganga was deep in meditation, Shantanu saw her and was irresistibly drawn to her. This made King Nirghat give Shantanu his word of honour at an auspicious moment that he would give his daughter in marriage to him. With great reluctance Ganga agreed to marry Shantanu laying down stringent conditions:

O Shantanu, you'll keep quiet even if I commit innumerable offences
When I destroy something, don't you utter a word

Never ever dare to scold or admonish me
And you'll always take excellent care of me.
Always address me as Ganga with respec
Call me Gangi, and I will leave you forthwith.

Ganga's arguments with her father and the conditions she laid down before her would-be husband reveal that women in Sarala's time were not timid, cowardly or docile.

Translation: Kalidas Misra

Note

1 Sarala Devi, *Sarala Mahabharatiya Narichitra* [Portrayal of Women in Sarala Das's *Mahabharata*], Cuttack: Utkal University, 1952, pp. 1–31.

7 Gaganendra Nath Dash

Representations of the conflict between people living in cities and forest dwellers in Odia literature

Introduction

An eminent literary critic and linguist, Gaganendra Nath Dash (b. 1940) has written extensively on Odishan culture, history and religious traditions. Relying extensively on archival sources and drawing on modern western scholarship in the fields of linguistics, history and anthropology he has offered new interpretations of canonical literary texts and popular legends. His writings are distinguished by polemical rigour and unsentimental assessment of texts and issues. He has built on the foundations laid by eminent critics such as Nilakantha Das and Natabara Samantaray. He was closely associated with the Harvard-Bhubaneswar, India Project (1961–73) and was the Field Director of the Orissa Research Project (1970–75) launched by Heidelberg University, Germany, and worked with several acclaimed scholars like Cora Du Bois, H. von Stietencron, Hermann Kulke, Anncharlott Eschmann, Gaya Charan Tripathi and Akio Tanabe. His major works, which straddle several disciplines, include *Janashruti Kanchikaveri* [The Legend of Kanchikaveri] (1979), *Odia Bhasha Chacrchara Parampara* [Tradition of Enquiries into Odia Language] (1983), *Descriptive Morphology of Odia* (1982), *Odia Bhasha Suraksha Andolana* [Save Odia Language Movement] (1993), *Hindus and Tribals* [1998], and *Saraswati Fakir Mohan: Sahitya o Byaktitva* [Fakir Mohan Senapati: A Critical Study] (2006). In collaboration with Ranjan Kumar Das, he edited *Jagannatha and Gajapati Kings of Orissa: A Compendium of Late Medieval Texts* (2010). Besides, he published *Conversational Oriya* (1972) with D.P. Pattanayak, and collaborated with Hermann Kulke and others in the compilation of *Orissa Bibliography* (1981).

The present essay, chosen from the volume titled *Naba Digantara Sandhanare* [In Search of a New Horizon] (2016) insightfully examines aspects of contact and conflict between forest dwellers and city dwellers. He undertakes a comparison of the portrayal of the Ekalavya episode in the Vyasa *Mahabharata* with its presentation in Sarala Das's fifteenth-century Odia *Mahabharata*. The minor episode in Vyasa's epic has been considerably expanded by Sarala Das who adds complex new dimensions

DOI: 10.4324/9781003224778-7

to it. Gaganendra Nath argues that Sarala Das underscores the forest-city conflict and links it to the changes he must have witnessed in his own world. Moreover, he also strongly advocates the need for social justice for the forest dwellers. Gaganendra Nath perceptively identifies the contours of the pattern underlying the conflict dramatized by Sarala Das in the Ekalavya episode: city dwellers' aggressive intrusion into the forest, their treatment of women forest dwellers as rightful of objects of desire, the resistance of the forest dwellers to such aggression and their eventual defeat. The essay goes on to show how the conflict continues to be enacted in the modern world and follows almost the same pattern. Godabarish Mishra's narrative poem "Arjun Singh", Bhagabati Charan Panigrahi's short story "Shikar" [The Hunt] and Gopinath Mohanty's novel *Paraja* illuminate forest dwellers' vulnerability in the face of the city dwellers' exploitative machinations. These, therefore, echo Sarala Das's prophetic depiction of Ekalavya's predicament. Gaganendra Nath has placed his central argument in the context of scholarship on state formation, theories of racial superiority, the accounts of royal lineage in Odisha, and the increasing marginalization and displacement of the tribal population in coastal Odisha over the centuries. Such an interdisciplinary approach and the adoption of a comparative perspective lend richness and depth to the essay.

*

Representations of the conflict between people living in cities and forest dwellers in Odia literature[1]

Gaganendra Nath Dash

I

One should not equate contemporaneity with modernity. Modern sensibility constitutes a certain outlook on life and the world and is not defined by temporal boundaries. One might find traces of traditional thinking in contemporary (or the so-called modern) times. Similarly, it is possible to find a semblance of modern sensibility in the so-called medieval ages. This is because many litterateurs of the past reveal certain prophetic elements in their writing. The famous Bangla verse "Hear O fellow humans! Man is above everything else and there is no other truth", which is often attributed to the medieval Bangla poet Chandi Das, also carries the resonance of modern thinking, for humanism is not only one of the fundamental features of modernity but is also its foundational principle. This is particularly important because it tells us that modern ways of thought are not the result of the influence of the western world on us; we have inherited these from our own tradition. The following is a brief account and analysis of Sarala Das's *Mahabharata* and his reflections on the struggle between socio-economic forces and counter-forces.

It is only in recent times that we have developed an awareness of the rights of indigenous groups and forest dwellers. Of course, it is true that their lifestyles, manners, food and clothing habits and outlook towards society are different from ours but they are entitled to equal rights because, like us, they too are human beings. So, of late, we have come to the realization that, like us, they also have a right to social justice. But not so long ago, they were considered uncivilized and savage. It may be mentioned here that, although humanism was considered the cornerstone of the Renaissance, slavery was an accepted practice in America in the so-called modern age. Even in the first half of the twentieth century, the dictator of a prosperous and scientifically advanced Germany, Adolf Hitler stated unhesitatingly that some humans are racially inferior (the non-Aryan or *untermenschen* or sub-humans) in his autobiography *Mein Kampf*. As William Shirer quotes Hitler in *The Rise and Fall of the Third Reich*,

> Thus, for the formation of the higher cultures the existence of lower human types was one of the essential preconditions … it is certain that the first culture of humanity was based less on the tamed animal than on the use of lower human beings. Only after the enslavement of the subject races did the same fate strike beasts. For first the conquered warrior drew the plough … and only after him the horse. Hence it is no accident that the first cultures arose in places where the Aryan, in his encounters with lower peoples subjugated them and bent them to his will. … As long as he ruthlessly upheld the master attitude, not only did he remain master but preserver and increaser of culture.[2]

Hitler spoke of non-Aryan races adopting a similar tone in other contexts as well. Racial anthropology as a discipline could emerge because of the respectability which was accorded to statements like the one made by Hitler. Besides, Malinowski, like many other western intellectuals, categorized many aboriginal tribes as savage. Writing under the influence of such intellectuals, celebrated Odia author Fakir Mohan Senapati, who was otherwise a humanist, called the *Bhuyans* of Keonjhar an uncivilized *jati*. In a nutshell, it is rather a very recent realization that all human beings are equal and tribal people should be treated with dignity.

The forest and the city

The conflict between city dwellers and forest dwellers has gone on for ages. A city dweller could live away from the forest and the city could fulfil all his worldly needs. But the hunger of the city dweller is insatiable and recognizes no limits. His wants and needs can be defined in conventional philosophical terms as *bhoga*[3] because these are not his essential needs. Moreover, to meet these, he relies heavily on the forest and its inhabitants. In addition, he assumes that depending on the forest and forest dwellers is his fundamental right and they have been created in order to be of use to him. He justifies his avarice under the pretext of science. They ruled over us only with the intention of civilizing and educating us; we the browns and the blacks were the "white man's burden"– such was the claim made by colonizers to legitimize their power. The truth, however, is that it is city dwellers who are a burden on the forest dwellers. The city dweller trespasses into the jungle for his so-called noble purpose and assaults the forest and its inhabitants. The forest dweller resists him and protests, and as a result a conflict between the two ensues. Even though forest dwellers manage to resist the onslaught of the city dwellers for a while, ultimately the latter prevail. As a result, across ages and countries, forest dwellers live as minorities in cities following their defeat or as a defence mechanism they have moved further away from cities. As a result, cities have been expanding and forest lands have been shrinking. This is true not only of Odisha or India but of the world as a whole. That the consequence of this phenomenon can be dangerous has only recently been realized by environmentalists.

It may be observed here that among the people of northern Odisha belonging to the Austro-Asiatic or *Munda* linguistic family, the word *diku* and its variations are used widely. Social scientists have also extensively employed the word. In my humble opinion, this word refers to city dwellers who exploit forest dwellers and trespass into their world. Seen from such a perspective, the "political other" which political scientists refer to in the context of identity can be understood using this term. The animosity towards *diku* is so intense that the term has become part of religious discourse. For instance, in *oteuli* – a ritual related to land – the priest of the Hos chants, "We shall kill snakes, witches and *dikus*". Such *mantras* not only indicate the tense and uneasy relationship between forest dwellers and city dwellers but also tell us about the bitter hostility between the two. Of course, Sitakant Mahapatra, based only on the comments and reports of the British officials, says, "but the hatred, distrust and resentment against the outside world and the *diku* had its beginning in the nineteenth century".[4] But the foundation of such an argument is weak because it does not take into account the linguistic constraints and cultural limitations of the British. I am of the opinion that the word *diku* was coined and used before the nineteenth century even though no written evidence supporting this claim is available, which is understandable.

It may be relevant here to discuss the views of researchers on state-formation in postmodern India. It is generally assumed that state-formation is more often than not synonymous with the building of cities. Of course, thinkers and experts disagree with each other so far as their analyses of state-formation are concerned and the premises of their arguments diverge. A thorough discussion of the same is beyond the scope of this paper and is not immediately relevant. However, it is important to briefly mention their opinions on Odisha since they lend support to the main argument of this essay. For instance, Burton Stein and Hermann Kulke hold different views on this issue in the context of Southern India; both can nonetheless prove useful for the discussion of state-formation in postmodern Odisha. Kulke, in 1978, following Stein, wrote,

> The spatial distribution of these nuclear areas of well organised and integrated areas of settled, agricultural villages coincided in South India with the lower courses of three major rivers at the Coromandel coast and their gradual extension caused a 'sustained displacement of tribally organized, pastoral and hunting society of forest and upland areas by caste-organized village-based societies'.[5]

Kulke offered a slightly different analysis of Odisha's social milieu:

> Although the relationship between the Hindu society and the tribals was never without tensions, its generally peaceful character – especially if we compare it with the annexation of northern America by the European settlers – was certainly one of the greatest achievements of Indian history. Generally speaking, in Orissa it was more a continuous process of indoctrination and partial integration than a process of "sustained displacement".
>
> During this gradual development the Brahmins played a prominent role. They defined and codified the duties of the tribes, which, as the *Mahabharata* puts it, "reside in the dominion of the (Aryan) kings". According to the *Mahabharata* they should be a "recluse living in the forest ... and serve their kings, ... dig wells, give water to the thirsty travellers, give away beds, and make other reasonable presents upon Brahmins". And it was again the task of those Brahmins to whom villages in remote areas had been allotted to propagate this ideal for their own and for their kings' sake.[6]

This long excerpt is relevant to the analysis of the story of Ekalavya from the *Mahabharata*. It is worth noting here that Kulke seems to suggest that the intensity of rivalry between city dwellers and forest dwellers was less in Odisha. Later, in 1995, Kulke revised and expanded his views.[7] Prior to and after Kulke the same issue was explored by Surajit Sinha and Akio Tanabe.[8]

In Odisha, state-formation is usually accompanied by another practice. Kulke, in "Tribal Deities at Princely Courts: The Feudatory Rajas of Central Orissa and their Tutelary Deities (*ishtadevatas*)", draws researchers' attention to this. A few lines from the same may be quoted here:

> According to the legendary accounts, several founders of Raj families entered their future realms as strangers ... Several of the *rajvamsabalis*

relate their first act of the future raja the "ritual killing" of a member of a tribe of that region. His ritual killing usually took place after he himself had told the founder of the dynasty about some miracles which had occurred in this place and after advising to construct his new fort at this spot. In all cases the victim, before being killed, requested the future rajas to worship his head as the *ishtadevata* of his family. These heads of the victims – usually in the form of an iconic stone – have been worshipped till recently in minor shrines near the places.[9]

The local legends or traditional accounts that Kulke refers to are related to the process of state-formation and royal dynasties. The accounts that they provide can be summarized as follows: the chieftain of a forest or tribal clan of a certain region provides help and shelter to a city dweller (*kshatriya*) who happens to be either on a pilgrimage or has possibly been ousted from his homeland. Strange incidents like a dove combating a hawk or a mouse/frog killing a snake make the city dweller aware of the potential of the place and he decides to build his fort there (a metaphor for state). The guest, then, resorting to deceit disguised as entreaty kills his host and consecrates his severed head as a deity and starts worshipping it thereby securing the allegiance of the community. For instance, commenting on the establishment of Khordha and Barunei fort by Ram Chandra I, *Chakada Pothi* says,

> Midway between Purushottam and Cuttack, *Shudha Shouri* Bali Vikram Singh ruled over a village called Khordha. The King took it from Vikram Singh and rechristened it Jagannathpur Cuttack. He beheaded Vikram Singh and buried his head at the holy point of the (future) fort.[10]
>
> (Pattanayak 6)

It is important to note here that the term *Shudha Shouri* is a Sanskritized version of the name of a *Sabara* clan *Sudha Saura*.[11] One comes across a similar story relating to Dhenkanal:

> The state is said to derive its name from an aborigine of Savar Caste, named Dhenka Sawara, who was in possession of a strip of land, about a couple of miles in area, upon which the present residence of the chief stands. There still exists to the west of the Chief's residence a stone, commonly known as the *Dhenka Sawara Munda* (head), to which worship is rendered once or twice a year. About the middle of the seventeenth century, one Singha Bidyadhar, a scion of the Khurda (Puri) Raj family, is said to have conquered the country and founded the State. Legend relates that the conquered Savar, when put to death, prayed that his head should always be worshipped.[12]

All these legends are relevant to our discussion. They not only tell us about the age-old battle between forest dwellers and city dwellers but about the selfishness and hypocrisy of city dwellers. By consecrating the head of the dead host, the city dwellers manage to secure the allegiance, devotion and loyalty of the forest dwellers, which is essential for them. As a result, the conflict comes to an end or its intensity gets attenuated. This has been noted by Kulke. Burkhard Schnepel voices a similar view in the context of Southern Odisha:

> Most if not all the south Orissan jungle kings sought to gain legitimacy in the eyes of the tribal population of their various realms, winning their loyalty and integrating them into the Hindu fold of power by patron- izing tribal goddesses and establishing them as their tutelary deities (*ishtadevata*).[13]

The following are some reasons why the battles' intensity abated: (a) the population of aboriginals or tribals was far larger compared to other com- munities; (b) the tribals, initially, were not considered minorities and could directly become Kshatriyas; (c) the "Jungle King" looked up to the tribals for military support and the Gajapati of the central province for territorial security; and (d) along with the Aryanization of their deities (here Lord Jagannath is not the only case, deities like Goddess Bhattarika of Badamba and Goddess Khilamunda of Ranpur furnish other examples) their tribal priests were also conferred to some extent status equivalent to that of Hindu priests. In Odisha, the conflicts became less intense but it cannot be denied that they continued. Such a view finds support from a careful scrutiny of the Ekalavya episode from Sarala Das's fifteenth-century Odia *Mahabharata* (henceforth *Sarala Mahabharata*).

II

The Ekalavya episode in *Sarala Mahabharata* bears testimony to the fact that, as early as the fifteenth century, the prophet-poet Sarala Das was not unaware of the conflict between forest dwellers and city dwellers. He has sketched the complex contours of the conflict.

Here one should compare the Ekalavya episode in *Sarala Mahabharata* with the version narrated in Vyasa's Sanskrit *Mahabharata*. The Ekalavya episode in the *Adi Parva* of the Vyasa *Mahabharata* is rather brief, compris- ing only thirty *shlokas* or stanzas. The discussion that follows relies on the critical edition of the epic.

A few other incidents from the Vyasa *Mahabharata* need to be referred to here in order to understand the Ekalavya episode more fully. Acharya Drona, guru of the princes (Pandavas and Kauravas) of Hastinapur king- dom vowed to take revenge upon King Drupada with the help of his pupils. When his royal pupils completed their training under his tutelage, Drona asked them if they would help him take revenge on his enemy. Of them only Arjun came forward to fulfil his vow. From that very day, Arjun became

Drona's dearest pupil and at that very moment, Drona pledged to make him the greatest archer of the world.[14]

Now let us undertake a brief analysis of the Ekalavya episode from the Sanskrit *Mahabharata*. The fame of Drona, the guru of the Hastinapur princes, spread far and wide. As a result princes from other kingdoms thronged to him to learn the art of warfare. Prince Ekalavya, the son of the tribal king Hiranyadhanu, also approached Drona with a request to teach him archery but Drona refused to oblige him because he was a tribal. This incident, however, should not be generalized as a Brahman's usual response to someone from a lower order; this merely reflects Drona's lack of ethical values. As the narrator of the *Mahabharata* observes, Drona, despite being aware of *dharma*, clearly violated its principles and ethics (*Adi Parva*, 1/123/11). Commentators have observed that Drona's conduct was not in consonance with those prescribed under the code of Brahmanical conduct. Drona's bias, which works in favour of Arjun, his favourite pupil, was the real reason behind his conduct. So, Drona refused to take Ekalavya under his tutelage fearing that he might gradually surpass Arjun whom Drona had intended to groom as the world's greatest archer. It may be mentioned here that Drona violated ethical principles out of gratitude to Arjun. Despite being rejected, Ekalavya sought Drona's blessings and returned to the forest. He made a clay image of Drona and started practising archery before it. And in no time, he mastered the art of archery.

One day, with Drona's permission, the Pandavas went into the forest on a hunting expedition, accompanied by a servant and a dog. The dog strayed away from the group and barked at Ekalavya, who was dressed in unusual attire. Finding the dog's constant barking an irritating distraction, Ekalavya silenced it by shooting seven arrows into its mouth. The dog came running back to the Pandavas, who were stunned to see the dog in this condition and became aware of their own limitations as archers. They started praising the archer who, with incredible swiftness and precision, could pierce unerringly his target. They traced the great archer and introduced themselves to him. Ekalavya introduced himself as the son of the tribal king Hiranyadhanu and informed them that he had learnt the art of archery from his guru Drona. Pandavas returned and narrated the rather strange incident to Drona. Thinking of Ekalavya (or stung by jealousy), Arjun complained to Drona, "You had promised to make me the world's greatest archer. How come Ekalavya, the son of a tribal king, is a far more skilful archer than I am and he claims that he is your student?"[15]

On hearing this, Drona thought for a moment and went to Ekalavya, taking Arjun with him. He saw Ekalavya assiduously practising archery. Seeing Drona approach him, Ekalavya reverentially touched his feet. He then performed the rituals of teacher worship and stood before him with folded hands. Drona said, "If you consider me your guru pay me my wages" (*Adi Parva*, 1/123/35). In response to this, Ekalavya said that there was nothing in his possession that he would not like to offer to Drona. Then Drona asked Ekalavya to offer the thumb of his right hand to him. In response to this inhuman demand, Ekalavya obediently chopped off his thumb and smilingly offered it to Drona. After this incident, Ekalavya tried to practise archery with his index and middle fingers but lost his swiftness. Thus Drona kept his promise of making Arjun the greatest archer of the world.

Now let us examine the implications of the story. The fact that Drona asks for Ekalavya's thumb as wages and not *gurudakshina* [preceptorial fees] reveals that, contrary to popular belief, this incident does not involve a Brahman looking down upon someone from the lower rung of the social ladder. If one analyses the story carefully, one would come to the conclusion that, had Ekalavya not been a tribal but a Brahman or kshatriya or instead of belonging to the forest, had he been a city dweller, Drona would have still done the same injustice to him. The story, instead, shows the jealousy and animosity that Arjun feels towards someone who practises the same profession (*samadharma*) but is better skilled and it also reveals Drona's favouritism and his blind commitment to making Arjun the greatest archer of the world. In everyone's mind, there are recesses where dark emotions such as lust, avarice, malice, bias and, worst of all, vindictiveness reside; even the so-called noble individuals and incarnations of gods are susceptible to these evil propensities. These always seek outlets and manifest themselves in the form of dereliction of duty. Demonstrating this was either 'the' or 'one of the' main aims of the Vyasa *Mahabharata*. The fear of people becoming vulnerable to such dark propensities led to their being discouraged from reading the *Mahabharata* at home lest it should lead to family squabbles. Therefore, in my humble opinion, in the Vyasa *Mahabharata*, there is hardly any mention of the conflict between the city dwellers and the forest dwellers and if at all there is any, it has not been accorded much importance. It is to be noted that the story of Ekalavya as presented in the Vyasa *Mahabahrata* does not mention the Kauravas.

In *Sarala Mahabharata*, the story of Ekalavya is narrated in two separate sections: in the fifty-second chapter titled "The Story of Jara Sabara",[16] and the sixty-eighth chapter titled "The Story of Ekalavya" (p. 3331–3339). However, it is difficult to believe that Sarala Das himself did the chapterization and provided the chapter titles. Similarly, in the Dharmagranth Store edition, these stories can be found in pages 100–101 and 103–106.[17] Besides, it is more descriptive than, and different from, the account offered in the Vyasa *Mahabahrata*. In *Sarala Mahabharata*, nowhere does one find the name Ekalavya; he is referred to as Jara. It seems Sarala was fond of this name as he used it for many of his tribal characters. But to avoid confusion, this essay refers to the story as the story of Ekalavya. His father is Ajapati, not Hiranyadhanu. Moreover, there is a mention of his wife in the 52nd chapter as Tara and as Siria in the 68th chapter. In the Vyasa *Mahabharata* he is shown to belong to a tribal community whereas in Sarala's version he belongs to the Kirata tribe and its principal deity is named *Panthai*.[18] Odisha is home to a large tribal population. So, in frequently using the term *Sabara* with regard to the forest dwellers, it seems, he lays greater emphasis on the *Sabara*[19] tribe. Many villages and *sahis* in southern and coastal Odisha are called *Sabara Palli* and *Saara Sahi* which are inhabited by *Sabaras* or *Saaras*. Although at present, these communities speak Odia, previously their language belonged to the Austro-Asiatic or *Munda* linguistic family. Sarala uses the word *Kirata* interchangeably with *Sabara* (particularly in *Musali Parva*). At other instances in the text, he uses the word *banachara* or wanderers of the forest for *Jara*.[20] Further, Jara's spouse also identifies herself as,

We the forest wanderers feed on wild animals.[21]

Again addressing Jara, she says,

O, ignorant fool, you are born of a forest wanderer.[22]

It is important to notice that Jara identifies himself as a forest wanderer and introduces himself to Arjun thus:

I am a forest wanderer, why have you come to my hut?[23]

It seems his primary identity is that of a forest wanderer or that of a forest dweller and *Sabara* or *Kirata*, his second.

Let us now take a close look at the story of Ekalavya as it unfolds in Sarala Das's *Mahabharata*. More elaborate, it has many complex dimensions, which have been rendered realistic by adding to it elements of contemporary experience. Among other things, the conflict between the city and the forest finds a prominent place in the text. The narrative also clearly reflects Sarala Das's feeling of love and compassion for forest dwellers (who were thought of as belonging to a lower order) and his awareness of their problems. The story of Ekalavya indicates that Sarala was both aware of and championed the need for social justice for tribal people. So, Sarala Das introduced changes in the narrative and imaginatively reworked Vyasa's version. How Sarala imaginatively reworked the Ekalavya episode narrated in the Vyasa *Mahabharata* will be discussed below. It may be mentioned here that most of the characters in *Sarala Mahabharata* represent different social classes of contemporary Odisha. Jara and his wife Tara alias Siria represent forest dwellers; Duryodhan and the Kaurava brethren are powerful leaders of city dwellers; Drona is the representative of opportunistic intellectuals from the metropolis and Pandavas can be seen as the powerless commoners of the city.

Drona accepting Jara as a pupil with the consent of Arjun and Yudhistira, and his expulsion from his academy at Duryodhan's bidding do not find a mention in Vyasa's *Mahabharata*. This story is an example of the powerful leaders of city dwellers depriving forest dwellers of education and scientific knowledge because that would render the latter perpetually powerless. Here, one must keep in mind the adage "knowledge is power". So, depriving them of knowledge equals depriving them of power. Drona's predicament vividly illustrates the helplessness and opportunism of the metropolitan intellectual. In *Sarala Mahabharata*, Drona does not bear any animosity towards forest dwellers; in fact, he is shown to be sympathetic towards them. Despite this, Drona is portrayed as a powerless intellectual compelled to sell his knowledge to the powerful for survival. Sarala renders the character of Drona complex and multi-dimensional by making him embrace two conflicting tendencies.

Vyasa's *Mahabharata* does not mention anything about the need for rhinoceros meat on the occasion of the death anniversary of Drona's wife Krupi. It only speaks of the Pandavas and the Kauravas entering the forest to hunt deer, that is to say, city dwellers trespassing into the land of tribals. In other words, city dwellers have assumed that they have the right to do so. Sarala's depiction of this incident is marked by depth and sophistication. The act of trespassing is justified under the pretext of performing a rite, and here the rite involves procuring rhinoceros meat for the observance of Krupi's death anniversary. This has been designed to highlight a strategy employed by city dwellers. In *Sarala Mahabharata*, it is only to collect materials for a ritual that a city dweller is compelled to enter the forest and in doing so asserts his right over it.

The Sanskrit *Mahabharata* does not feature the female character Tara or Siria, nor does it mention her molestation by the Kauravas, as *Sarala Mahabharata* does. The so-called need of the city dwellers has been termed pleasure in traditional accounts. One wonders if there is an end to this lust. Women have been among the greatest sources of pleasure for men from cities. Just like the forest, its inhabitants are assumed to have been created for the benefit of city dwellers; women from the forest are considered objects of pleasure by the powerful lords of the city. Social scientists have established that the desire for women is not just about satiating one's lust; "rape of women" is also a display of power by the victor over the vanquished. Duhshasana's real intention behind his attempt to rape Jara's wife is revealed in the following lines:

> How come you, a forest dweller, have a wife
> That is worthy of a king?
> We, the scions of the *Som* clan, the rulers of the earth
> Shall make you pay through your life.[24]

Here it is worth noting that Duhshasana addresses Jara as a forest dweller and, expressing contempt for him as someone different from and inferior to his kind, tries to legitimize his claim on Jara's wife. The forest dweller always resisted these claims of the city dweller and hence the never-ending conflict between the two. This conflict is vividly dramatized by Sarala Das.

The following sequence of incidents does not find a place in the Vyasa *Mahabharata*: the attempted rape of Tara by Duhshasana and other Kauravas; Jara's arrival on the scene on hearing his wife's cry for help; the ensuing fight between Jara and Duhshasana; the death of Duhshasana and other Kauravas at Jara's hands; Drona's discovery of the dead bodies after twelve days; Arjun's meeting with Jara after trying to find out the brave fighter who could kill such skilled warriors; and his battle with Jara. The fight between the Kauravas and Jara can be seen as an unending conflict between those from the city and those from the forest.

No one emerges victorious in the battle between Arjun and Jara. On hearing the din of the battle, Drona, Bhima and Karna rush to the spot. On being questioned by a surprised Drona who was his guru, Jara replies, "You, Drona are my guru". Consider the lines that follow:

> The guru is left astounded.
> O learner, I'm that Drona.
> How can Drona be your guru?
> Tell me, who is it that you really learnt archery from?[25]

Jara recounts his journey to Barunabanta, his imploring Drona to take him as a pupil, the humiliation Duryodhan subjects him to, then his making of an image of Drona and practising archery before it following his wife's advice. Then, obeying Drona, he brings the dead Kauravas back to life shooting the *jivanyas* arrow. This incident full of theatricality is absent in the Vyasa *Mahabharata*.

Drona then blesses him with invincibility. This means he did not harbour any ill-feeling towards him.

> Live in this forest, o Jara, says Drona.[26]
> ...
> May you get all that I bless you with
> May no one ever defeat you in a battle.[27]

Jara prostrated himself at his guru's feet saying, "Do ask for your *gurudak-shina*, this very moment".[28] Therefore, unlike in the Vyasa *Mahabharata*, Drona does not ask for "wages". In Sarala Das's *Mahabharata* it is Jara who volunteers to offer him *gurudakshina*.[29]

Since he makes a promise which he cannot retract, Drona asks for the thumb of his right hand. Jara cuts his thumb off and gives it to his guru. Although Sarala Das borrowed the story from the Vyasa *Mahabharata*, he significantly transformed certain aspects of it. The usual interpretation of this incident emphasizing the Brahman's malice towards the tribal folks or lower orders is rather simplistic. It reveals the keenness of the metropolitan intellectuals to act at the behest of their city overlords and deny knowledge to forest dwellers. The story makes no mention of Arjun's envy towards Jara nor of Drona's bias towards Arjun. Jara understands that it is not merely a question of favouritism on the part of Drona; it is about serving the larger interest of the mighty Duryodhan and his brothers. Sarala Das writes,

> O, guru since you feared me,
> You ruined me to rescue these men.
> When at Barunabanta I suffered indignity at Duryodhan's hands
> I resolved to
> Decimate Duryodhan's army
> And destroy his clan.
> You understood it well, o guru
> O great soul, your heart was full of apprehension.[30]

Here, Sarala Das powerfully depicts the conflict between the inhabitants of the city and those of the forest and displays his dexterity as a narrator. The incident also demonstrates the extent to which city lords can go to exploit tribals, violating ethical principles and taking advantage of the generosity of forest dwellers, if necessary. In the Vyasa *Mahabharata* Drona serves the interests of Arjun while in the Sarala *Mahabharata* he acts at the behest of the powerful Duryodhan. The otherwise venerable Drona, who acts like a stooge of the powerful city lords, appears mean when compared with the generous and magnanimous forest dweller, Jara. One might mention here that in the third volume of *Purnachandra Bhashakosha* (1933), the word *Choharda* has been defined as,

> The *dhangad jati* found in Hazaribagh etc. is like the *hadi jati*[31] of our land. These people are of the same *jati* as Ekalavya from *Mahabharata* and carry the bow and arrow. It is a common ritual amongst people of certain sub groups of this *jati* to cut their own thumb. Those who do not observe that ritual, operate the bow and arrow without using their thumb.[32]

The persistence of this tradition over the years, following Ekalavya, is symbolic of the silent protest (or *satyagraha* in contemporary terms) by the tribal folk against the gross injustice of city dwellers. The *Chohardas* have been described as uncivilized and barbaric and belonging to a lower order. This shows city dwellers' contempt for tribals.

Sarala Das has rendered the story of Ekalavya more fascinating than the one we come across in the Vyasa *Mahabharata* by incorporating into it the attempt to violate Tara, her husband's revenge and the events that ensue. In fact, this particular episode anticipates what is to happen later in the narrative, because another woman, Draupadi suffers ignominy at the hands of the Kauravas which leads to the epic war.

The Ekalavya episode in Sarala Das's rendition of the Sanskrit epic is lent greater richness by linking it to the consolidation of the Odia identity in the text. One may call it a continuation of *Skanda Purana*.[33] Lord Jagannath appears as Lord Nilamadhava (a tribal deity worshipped by Sabaras) in *Musali Parva* in Sarala Das's *Mahabharata*. This particular issue deserves close attention because this episode does not occur in Vyasa's version. By including it in his narrative, Sarala has again shown his deep awareness of the world of forest dwellers.

The story of Nilamadhava drawn from the Sanskrit *Skanda Purana* is partly a new addition and certain instances from the same echo Sarala's sympathy for forest dwellers. In King Indradyumna's dream, Lord Nilamadhava appears and shows his displeasure over the king's killing of the *Sabaras* and identifies the slain as his sons in the following couplet:

> Said Madhava, O King what an evil deed have you done?
> Why did you kill these *Sabaras*, my sons.[34]

Similarly, it has been said that when the entire army of the king failed to lift the *daru*[35] floating in the sea, the Brahman Basu and the *Sabara* Biswabasu were able to lift it, and it was the latter who was able to do this with ease. Sarala says,

> Pushing aside the Brahman, it [the *daru*] approaches the *Sabara*
> Krishna's will prevails and he lifts it up[36].

These lines make it amply clear that the *Sabaras* were Nilamadhava's favourite; people just like them have Sarala Das's sympathy. Besides, in *Musali Parva*, Sarala Das describes *Sabaras* as wanderers in the forest[37]. It can thus be argued that the story of Ekalavya presented in *Sarala Mahabharata* is an eloquent plea for social justice for tribals.

Moreover, affirmation of the interpretation of the Ekalavya episode made above also comes from a few instances from modern Odia literature. We can find parallels between Sarala's account of the conflict between city dwellers and forest dwellers and those found in a few modern literary works in Odia. In other words, from medieval times to the modern, the same issue has drawn to itself the attention of some of the most gifted writers and has found a place in their writings. These therefore deserve close critical scrutiny.

Before delving deeper into the matter, it is important to mention that, in the past five decades, under the influence of Krishna Chandra Panigrahi, an eminent historian, the interpretation of *Sarala Mahabharata* has been slightly skewed. Panigrahi's major contribution was his reading of the text in terms of Sarala's contemporary and earlier political and military conflicts. He did so by picking out elements from *puranas* in the text.[38] If real history is to be discovered from *Sarala Mahabharata*, it is necessary to analyze the history of socio-economic conflicts in the writer's time. Panigrahi, however, does not seem to have paid enough attention to this. The present author has tried to show on several occasions that his analysis is misleading.[39] Sachidananda Mishra has also tried to make a similar point.[40] Besides, the present author has also pointed out how socio-economic conflicts are implicit in the account of the worship of Lord Jagannath in Puri.[41] Despite all these efforts, Odia intellectuals have not succeeded in freeing themselves of Panigrahi's influence. To get rid of this influence is the need of the hour.

III

Instances of three different literary genres – a ballad, a short story and a novel – from contemporary Odia literature may be cited to show that the writers present the conflict between the two forces as their major theme and demand social justice for tribal communities. That is because at present this conflict has grown even more intense. For instance, Godabarish Mishra in his ballad "Arjun Singh",[42] Bhagabati Charan Panigrahi in his short story "Shikar" [The Hunt] and Gopinath Mohanty in his novel *Paraja* have directly or indirectly explored this issue.

"Arjun Singh", a ballad based on a local legend published in his anthology of narrative verses *Alekhika*, centres on the same age-old conflict. Arjun Singh, the nineteenth-century ruler of Singhbhumi (now Singhbhum) is the central character of the poem. The legend behind the story is embedded in a historical context. It is believed that Godabarish came across the legend during his stay at Singhbhumi between 1921 and 1924. It is a lesser known text as compared with the ones written by Bhagabati and Gopinath. It is therefore necessary to provide a few details from the ballad.

The text, right at its very beginning, shows how the city dweller coercively asserts his rights over the forest dwellers. The king had managed to establish his kingdom in Singhbhumi with the help of a tribal community named *Surakh*. Subsequently, with their help he also brought *Kolhas* under his rule. The *Kolhas*, however, could not be completely subdued. In the words of the poet,

> The King of Singhbhumi, Arjun Singh's rule is just,
> He fought the lion and earned his fame on earth.
> Singhbhumi is known in Odisha since time immemorial,
> The mighty army of *Surakhs* kept the banner of the king flying high.
> ....
> That which the world calls defeat was unknown to *Surakhs*;
> They would rather get beheaded than bear the shame of defeat.
> The mighty hold the reins of power on this earth,

Surakhs obeyed Arjun Singh ardently, who was a father figure for all
of them.
Conquering the *Kolha* land, he annexed it to his kingdom;
The *Kolhas* therefore prepared to rise against the king.
....
Alas! Their plan for uprising came to naught for Arjun Singh was
mighty;
He assembled his forces and subdued the *Kolhas*.
Only once a year did they come to pay their taxes,
Wiping their tears, they said, "What grief have you brought upon us!"

Here, the plight of the freedom-loving Kolhas has been described vividly.
    Then further in the narrative, Arjun Singh's tyrannical ways are shown
through his treatment of women on whom he exercised his rights and whom
he considered objects of pleasure. The poet says:

The army of *Surakhs* was huge and Bhujendra Jani was its commander
His fame spread across the land, he was a jewel in the crown.
....
The girl named Sinhasini was his only child
Born at the 'Entrance to Lion's Den', she was about sixteen.
Once out on a hunt, the king came to the Surakh land,
He saw Sinhasini and charmed by her beauty exclaimed,
"O Lord how could you be so unfair? In a *Surakh*'s miserable house
How such a heavenly beauty could take birth!
This maiden is meant for palaces; come what may,
She shall be the queen of Singhbhumi."

Arjun Singh's desire for the girl can be compared to the Kauravas' lust for
Jara's wife, Siria. Arjun Singh abducted Sinhasini against her will.
    Protesting against the injustice, the oppression of the king, symbolizing
the almighty city dweller, the *Surakhs* in unison cry:

Seated on his throne, he is hailed as "the king of the world"
Dharma has deserted him, let us snatch his royal insignia.
....
Let us all go O soldiers and crush the king's pride;
Let us remove each brick from his bastion.
Asking them to restrain themselves, one of their old men said,
He is like our father and we are his sons.
We are beholden to him for food and drink he provides.
....
But there is no *dharma* left in this land;
Let us move to another land and let the king rot in shame.

It is worth noting that although the king enjoys certain rights, the unwritten pact between him and his subjects requires the king to act like a benevolent patriarchal figure and protect the tribal communities, safeguard their interests and respect their rights and customs. In other words, the lines for both have been clearly drawn, in terms of their duties and obligations towards each other. This is what the old man defines as dharma. Neither of them is supposed to overstep that mark. So, acting on the old man's advice, they all migrated from their homeland. Just like Jara's, the generosity shown by *Surakhs* is worth paying attention to. The silent protest, the ahimsa practised by the tribal communities, are exemplified by this incident.

After the *Surakhs*, who formed the strongest unit in Arjun Singh's army, left the kingdom, the recalcitrant *Kolhas* who were anyway hostile to the king, united and mobilized themselves to regain their lost liberty. Having lost their faith in the people of the city, the *Kolhas* turned vengeful. Eventually, when Arjun Singh failed to defeat the *Kolhas*, he sought help from his arch enemy, the king of Banei, who in turn sent only one man named Sripati Ota. He was sent with the instruction,

> Rush Ota, the king of Singhbhumi has sought our help;
> The Kolhas have rebelled; do not come back without defeating them.

Sripati Ota can be compared to Drona because of his opportunistic nature. The poet introduces him as follows:

> This son of Ota is equally skilled in his use of force, wisdom and strategy
> Known he is in Banei as "divisive Sripati"
> He can separate a cow from her calf and a father from his son,
> And can make a cat and a mouse, and a tiger and a deer befriend each other.

By referring to him as one who engineers rift and informing the reader about his special skills, the poet draws a clear picture of the character. Sripati Ota entered the *Kolha* quarters in the guise of one of their men. The naïve and gullible tribal men failed to recognise him. Sympathizing with the tribals, the poet writes,

> The *Kolhas* are naïve like kids
> How can they possibly understand deceit and conspiracy?

Making use of their innocence and vulnerability, Ota guided Arjun Singh's soldiers to that place. After a fierce battle, the *Kolhas* lost and the rebellion was quelled.

The rest of the narrative can be briefly told. Since he did not enjoy the support of either the *Surakhs* or the *Kolhas*, the British army defeated the king and deported him to Kashi. Even if Arjun Singh had enjoyed the support of the *Kolhas*, the result would not have been different. The opinion of the writer and that of the public gets reflected here and it is of some importance to our discussion.

Even though this ballad may be read as a narrative of poetic justice, at its very core lies the protest against the injustice meted out to the tribal people. Arjun Singh and Sripati Ota, who represent the city dwellers, are exploitative and full of lust, avarice, and malice. On the other hand, the *Kolhas* and *Surakhs*, who are prototypes of forest dwellers, are simple folk who love freedom, follow ethical principles and are courageous. The poet's sympathy for the tribal community is vividly revealed at several points in the narrative. For instance, there is a moving account of the plight of the *Kolhas* following the failure of their rebellion.[43] However, Krishna Chandra Panigrahi does not wholly accept Godabarish's version of the story relating to Arjun Singh. He lays emphasis on Arjun Singh's fierce resistance to British rule and is reluctant to see any flaws in his character. It must be remembered that Godabarish himself was a nationalist; despite this, his portrayal of Arjun Singh was based on public perception.

Bhagabati Charan Panigrahi's celebrated short story "Shikar" [The Hunt] (1936) explores a conflict of a similar nature. In it, Ghinua, a *Santal* boy stands for tribal people. The narrator calls him 'junglee' or forest dweller. The protagonist retains his simplicity, which is characteristic of people from the jungles. He, therefore, failed to understand the complicated ways of men from the city even until the end. Characters such as Gobind Sardar, the British deputy commissioner George sahib, the public prosecutor, and the deputy commissioner's orderly embody the values of the urban world. Gobind Sardar is one of those typical car-driving and gun-brandishing city lords, who considers lusting after women of the forest his birthright. Consequently, forest dwellers opposed his oppressive ways. Ghinua did what Jara had done. Even though the outcomes of their respective actions are different, the similarities between the two characters cannot be overlooked. The differences between the complex laws of the city and the simple values of the forest folk have been highlighted. The deed, which, in the eyes of forest dwellers deserves a reward, condemns the doer to capital punishment according to the law of the city. Thus, the story dramatizes the clash of two systems of justice.

The action of Gopinath Mohanty's *Paraja* (1945), an iconic Odia novel which was translated into English in 1986, also revolves around this conflict. One finds a remarkable similarity between it and the Ekalavya episode depicted in the Sarala *Mahabharata* though the two texts are separated by five centuries. It is obvious that both the texts bear the imprint of their milieux. In Sarala Das's time, forests in Odisha were denser and vaster, and cities were comparatively less powerful. With the passage of time, powerful people from the city institutionalized their control over the forest in the name of political and administrative necessity, and securing the welfare of forest dwellers. The danger that threatened the existence of forest dwellers was grasped by a few visionary writers. Under the impact of the city dweller, and for political, social, economic, and religious reasons, many forest dwellers drifted away from their value system. The extent to which this influence worked varied. Those who stuck to the ethos of the jungle, their number was on the decline.

The city declared everything illegal that the people of the forest did to earn a living (cow herding, collecting honey, cultivating unclaimed lands, practising stepped farming, preparing liquor etc.) under the pretext of welfare. It introduced laws which did more harm than good and no one spared a thought for tribal people. The reason was the city dwellers' unquenchable desire to usurp their rights. Similarly, for making inroads into the jungle in the name of welfare, they did not hesitate to scapegoat forest dwellers, assault their dignity and the modesty of their women. All these issues have been explored thoroughly in *Paraja*.

A guard employed by the government entered the forest disguised as a hunter, saw a girl of Paraja tribe Jili bathing in a stream and was aroused by her beauty. This is how Gopinath Mohanty's *Paraja* opens and five centuries ago Sarala Das had painted a similar picture showing Duhshshana and his brothers lusting after Siria. Of course, in *Paraja* it was not just the guard but also the *gumasta* and the moneylender who entered the jungle in disguise. Given the temporal difference and the different contexts, the narrative technique in both the texts differ. What was expressed through the use of suggestive irony in the short story "Shikar" is described in great detail in the novel *Paraja*. Despite all the differences, the car-driving Gobind in "Shikar" is very similar to the horse-riding Ramchandra Sahukar in *Paraja*. Similarly, Ghinua from the short story is reincarnated as the trinity of Sukru, Mandia and Tikra.

The guard in *Paraja* exclaimed the moment he set his eyes on Jili and Bili, "Ah, the skin on her limbs is as smooth as butter, her breasts are like mountains and her complexion resembles lightning. I have not seen anything like this among the Parajas."[44] These lines echo what Duhshashan says when he catches sight of Siria.

The action of *Paraja* opens with this scene and all the significant incidents follow the way a spreading banyan tree grows from a tiny seed. A minor incident like the one mentioned above casts its shadow over the family of the poor Sukru Jani and its consequences are felt when the novel ends. Both Jili and her father declined the proposal made by the lecherous guard and in a way protested against it. The man from the city felt deprived when he failed to satiate his lust and turned vindictive. The poor Sukru Jani and his family were made to suffer at the hands of the 'law' for their protest. Here, one may recall the line "the fine trap of law" from "Shikar". Sukru and his younger son Tikra were made to work as bonded labourers for the moneylender Ram Bisoi for committing the "crime", or rather "sin", of protesting.

The guard is not the only prototype of a city-based character who encroaches on the forest land. There are others like *rebini* [the revenue official], the *amin* [land surveyor], Rout, *gumasta* [record keeper], Saltu, too. Directly or indirectly they seek to establish their authority over the tribal folk. They use every means at their disposal to snatch what rightfully belongs to the folks of the forest since time immemorial. It is precisely because of this reason that Mandia Jani, who was accused of brewing liquor, was forced to work as a bonded labourer for Bisoi in return for the fine paid to bail him out.

When such a situation arose, both Jili and Mandia's respective lovers (Bagla and Kajodi) deserted them and married each other. This incident was unbearable for everyone in the family but particularly for the two siblings. The departure of their father and brother, and unrequited love and pangs of hunger compelled Jili and, under her influence, Bili to work as labourers in a road construction project. They did so without informing anyone in the family and without seeking their permission.

To come to the rescue of his children, Sukru mortgaged his land to the moneylender much against his will. But he only succeeded in freeing himself. So he mortgaged his land on the condition that "the land could be redeemed if Sukru Jani paid twenty-five rupees to Sahukar but until then it was his". The witnesses to this transaction were "*Dharmu*, the Just One", "the Earth goddess Dharatini" and the bonded labourers of Sahukar.[45]

The powerful city lords who usurp the forest land also consider its women their possession. It is this lust for the labouring Jili and Bili which drew the *gumasta*, the lecherous city dweller, into the forest. After freeing himself, Sukru Jani managed to rescue his daughters like a brave man. The sacrifices he made for his daughters is remarkable. But later it became difficult for him to rescue Jili from the clutches of the moneylender, Rama Bisoi. Although Sukru cleared the debt with interest, the moneylender, employing his cunning, grabbed his land. The law, which belongs to the city, predictably failed to come to Sukru's rescue and he ended up losing both his land and his daughter.

When Sukru and both his sons visited the moneylender to plead for the release of his land, the moneylender kicked Sukru. At that very moment, Sukru and his sons were shocked to see Jili approaching the room and, stupefied, they exclaimed "Is it you Jili?", to which the moneylender replied,

> Yes, Jili. And isn't there another called Bili at home still? Bring her to me. I've taken the land; I've taken one sister; and I shall take the other too. I shall take your wives; I shall drive you from court to court through the length of the country. I shall make you sweat your lives as *gotis*.[46]

They cried out in protest, "You've cheated us out of the land, Sahukar, but you won't enjoy it!"[47] In the end, the cries were followed by blows from Mandia Jani, his father and his brother. The moneylender succumbed to their attack just like Duhshasan and his brothers who had been put to death by Jara's unfailing arrows.

The same afternoon, Sukru and his sons went to the police station and told the inspector, "We have killed a man. Give us whatever punishment we deserve".[48] Such a bold pronouncement mocked the law of the city, which in their view was an infringement of *dharma*. The law that they chose to bow before was not that of the city but of the forest because it did not hold them guilty; it was the moneylender who was culpable. This is where the novel comes to an end.

Drona had denied justice to his devoted pupil Jara. So, although Gopinath Mohanty does not mention it, the discerning reader knows what fate Sukru and his sons would meet at the court of law. Be it in the *Sarala Mahabharata* or in *Paraja*, the forest dweller is always denied social justice. The village headman said, "You see, he is a big man, and he can always do what he wants to do".[49] Sukru, acting like the true protagonist of a successful literary creation, was not convinced by this argument even though others accepted it.

Sukru Jani is one of those naïve yet brave men who firmly believed in the age-old ethos of the forest. He is "a lonely old man, helpless and drained of all strength".[50] Although extremely vulnerable and weak, Sukru Jani finally emerges as the symbol of unflinching courage and resilience.

The conflict between Sukru Jani's family, and the moneylender, *gumasta* and the guard is by no means a personal one; it is, in many ways, an administrative, social and economic conflict between the city and the forest. The defeat of the naïve tribals at the hands of the conniving men of the city is inevitable. In the novel while some forest dwellers submit to the power of the city, Sukru Jani and his sons do not.

IV

Scholars emphasize the importance of comparative analysis in literary criticism. So the point need not be laboured. However, it may be said that, while undertaking a comparative analysis it is desirable to go beyond categories of time, language and form. Comparing Sarala's *Mahabharata* with Vyasa's on the one hand and with works of modern Odia literature on the other illuminates unexplored aspects of the Ekalavya episode. Like a stream which changes its course on encountering hills or sand dunes, the message(s) transmitted by the story of Ekalavya changes from one text to another. However, despite differences in temporal and spatial contexts, *Sarala Mahabharata*, "Arjun Singh", "Shikar" and *Paraja* show structural similarities which deserve close scrutiny. Some of the constituents of the structure are as follows: (1) the prototype of the man from the city trespassing into the forest and lusting after women; (2) the forest dweller getting into a conflict with the city dweller and the former almost killing the latter; (3) early victory of the forest dweller followed by his eventual defeat. Despite all setbacks, the protagonist from the forest emerges as a brave hero. Perhaps, this is why all the four Odia texts convey more or less the same message.

So, seen from a comparative perspective, Sarala Das's story of Ekalavya (Jara) provided the basis for all the three modern Odia texts. In describing the conflict between the city and the forest, and voicing an impassioned plea for social justice for people of the forest, all these texts can be placed in a straight line. Although the Ekalavya story has puranic roots, "Arjun Singh" is based on popular legends, their historical claims cannot be dismissed. "Shikar" seems to be entirely a work of imagination. But *Paraja*, as one learns from Gopinath Mohanty's autobiography, has its roots in the real world.[51]

It seems that, in comparison with "Arjun Singh" and "Shikar", *Sarala Mahabharata* and *Paraja* present the conflict between the city and the forest in more complicated ways and in greater depth, and are therefore more successful creations of art. For instance, Yudhisthira, Bhima and Arjun are those powerless men from the city who are sympathetic towards people of the forest. This kind of nuanced characterization is difficult to find in all the other texts discussed here. Similarly, the story of Ekalavya features a character like Drona who acts like an opportunist metropolitan intellectual. One does not come across such a character in "Shikar" or *Paraja*. The critique of the opportunist intellectual from the city can be found in the story of Ekalavya and "Arjun Singh". In *Paraja* and "Shikar", the struggle between the city and the jungle has been presented directly. In *Sarala Mahabharata*, the same issue has been dealt with indirectly through the use of irony and allegory, which makes it artistically richer. So the advocacy for social justice for forest dwellers is more richly nuanced.

Again, in all the three modern texts there is a hint of the irony of defeat concealed in a temporary victory. In "Shikar" and *Paraja*, the same is presented as an inevitable outcome of British rule. On closer observation, it can be seen that in *Sarala Mahabharata*, this defeat is presented in a more interesting way than in the other three texts.

The three modern Odia texts – "Arjun Singh", "Shikar" and *Paraja* (especially the last two) – convey a humane sensibility in being sympathetic towards tribal communities, which is why they have found a wide acceptance. Closer scrutiny, however, would reveal that *Sarala Mahabharata* is no less sympathetic to the cause of tribal people. In fact, the argument in favour of social justice for forest dwellers is more powerfully articulated in *Sarala Mahbharata* which was written five centuries ago. This is why the text has assumed a national character and become the narrative of the formation of a community's identity.

Translation: Shaswat Panda

Notes

1 Gaganendra Nath Dash, "Bikalpa Adhunikata: Sarala Mahabharata ra Ekalabya Upakhyan (Janapada o Jungle Madhyare Sangharsha ra Chitra: Ekalabya Upakhyan ru *Paraja* Parjyanta)", *Naba Digantara Sandhanare* [In Search of a New Horizon], Bhubaneswar: Rama Devi, 2016, pp. 17–69.

2 William L Shirer, *The Rise and Fall of the Third Reich,* New York: Fifth Crest Printing, 1963, p. 169.
3 It could mean pleasure or enjoyment or indulgence.
4 Sitakant Mahapatra, *Modernization and Ritual: Identity and Change in Santal Society,* New Delhi: OUP, 1986.
5 Anncharlott Eschmann, ed, *The Cult of Jagannath and the Regional Tradition of Orissa,* New Delhi: Manohar, 1978, pp. 126–130.
6 Ibid., p. 128.
7 Hermann Kulke, *The State in India: 1000–1700,* New Delhi: OUP, 1995.
8 Akio Tanabe, "Early Modernity and Colonial Transformation: Rethinking the Role of King in Eighteenth and Nineteenth Century Orissa, India", in Masaaki Kimura and Akio Tanabe, eds, *The State in India: Past and Present,* New Delhi: OUP, 2006.
9 Hermann Kulke, *Kings and Cults: State Formation and Legitimation in India and Southeast Asia,* New Delhi: Manohar, 1993, p. 117.
10 Sudhakar Pattanayak, *Chakada Pothi O Chakada Basana ba Chayani Chakada,* 1959.
11 Gaganendra Nath Dash, *Hindus and Tribals,* New Delhi: Decent Books, 1998, pp. 43–70.
12 Cobden Ramsay, L.E.B., *The Feudatory States of Orissa,* Kolkata: Firma KLM, 1910/1982, p.164.
13 Buckhart Schnepel, *Die Dschungelkoengie: EthnohistorischeAspekte Von Politick und Ritual in Sudorissa/Indiene,* Sturtgart: Franz Stenier, 1997, p.271.
14 Sarala Das, *Adi Parva,* 1/123/6, Bhubaneswar, Department of Culture, Government of Orissa, 1965.
15 Ibid.
16 Ibid., pp. 308–311.
17 Sarala Das, *Sarala Mahabharata,* Cuttack: Dharma Grantha Store.
18 Sarala Das, "Adi Parva", Canto I, 68/47, Bhubaneswar, Department of Culture, Government of Orissa, 1965.
19 Spelled variously as Savara, Saara, Swara, Saura and Sora.
20 Sarala Das, "Adi Parva", 1st canto, 52/7, 52/9, 52/21, 52/25, 68/25 and 68/46, Bhubaneswar, Department of Culture, Government of Orissa, 1965.
21 Ibid., p. 310.
22 Ibid., p. 310.
23 Ibid., p. 335.
24 Ibid., p. 333.
25 Ibid., p.336.
26 Ibid.
27 Ibid.
28 Ibid.
29 Presents offered to a guru on completion of training.
30 Sarala Das, *Adi Parva,* Canto I, 68/102, Bhubaneswar, Department of Culture, Government of Orissa, 1965, p. 339.
31 A community engaged in scavenging.
32 Gopal Chandra Praharaj, *Purnachandra Bhashakosha, vol. 3,* Cuttack: Utkal Sahitya Press, 1933, p. 2742.
33 Sarala Das draws heavily in his *Musali Parva* upon *Skanda Purana* for the construction of the Jagannath Temple and the carving of Jagannath's image out of the *pinda* of Lord Krishna which could not be reduced to ashes during cremation.
34 Sarala Das, *Musali Parva,* 9/63, Bhubaneswar, Department of Culture, Government of Orissa, 1965.
35 Logs of wood from supposedly sacred trees bearing symbols associated with the deities of the Jagannath temple at Puri. The wooden images of the deities are

carved out from these logs once every nineteen years when the lunar month of Asadha (roughly June-July) occurs consecutively twice in a year in a ritual titled *Nabakalebar* or the new body.

36 Sarala Das, *Musali Parva*, 9/93, Bhubaneswar, Department of Culture, Government of Orissa, 1965.
37 Sarala Das, *Musali Parva*, 5/12 (46), 6/27 (52) and 6/33 (53) Bhubaneswar, Department of Culture, Government of Orissa, 1965.
38 Krishna Chandra Panigrahi, "Sarala Sahitya ra Aitihasika Upadan" [Historical References in the Works of Sarala Das", Cuttack: Prajatantra Prachar Samiti, 1954.
39 For more on this topic see the following works by the author:
    Gaganendranath Dash, "Janashruti Kanchikaveri" [Kanchikaveri and Popular Imagination], Berhampur: Pustak Bhandar, 1979.
    Gaganendranath Dash, "*Sarala Mahabharata* o Itihasa" [*Sarala Mahabharata* and History], Eshana, No. 17, 1988.
    Gaganendranath Dash, *Nirbachita Prabandha Sankalan* [Collection of Selected Essays], Cuttack: Vidyapuri, 2005, pp.1–31.
    Gaganendranath Dash, "Soma-Vamsi Yayati in Tradition and Medieval Odia Literature", *Studies in History*, Vol 28, No 2, 2012, pp. 171–174.
40 Sachidananda Mishra, *Sarala Mahabharata: Eka Adhyayana* [Sarala Das: A Study], Cuttack: Grantha Mandir, 2006, pp. 270–278.
41 For more on this topic by the present author see, Gaganendranth Dash, *Hindus and Tribals*, New Delhi: Decent Books, 1998.
    Gaganendranath Dash, *Nirbachita Prabandha Sankalan* [Collection of Selected Essays], Cuttack: Vidyapuri, 2005, pp. 32–51.
42 Godabarish Mishra, "Arjun Singh", *Alekhika* [Writings], Cuttack: New Students Store, 1955, fifth edition.
43 For a detailed account of Arjun Singh's life, see Krishna Chandra Panigrahi, *Sahitya o Sanskruti* [Literature and Culture], Cuttack: Prajatantra Prachar Samiti, 1994, pp. 77–93.
44 Gopinath Mohanty, *Paraja,* 1945, Tr. Bikram K Das, New Delhi: Oxford UP, 1987, p. 30.
45 Ibid., p.233.
46 Ibid., p. 372.
47 Ibid., p. 373.
48 Ibid.
49 Ibid., p. 354.
50 Ibid., p. 233.
51 Rajkishore Mishra, *Gopinath nka Upanyasa ra Marama Katha* [The Story behind Gopinath Mohanty's Novels], Cuttack: Vidyapuri, 2007, pp. 23–25.

8   Mrutyunjay Ratha

An essay on Dinakrushna Das's *Rasakallola*

Introduction

Mrutyunjay Ratha (1882–1924) was an eminent biographer, essayist, translator and creative writer. Although a few attempts had been made at writing biographies in the latter half of the nineteenth century in Odisha, it was Mrutyunjay who brought a degree of sophistication and professionalism to life-writing. He wrote biographies of Sarala Das (the author of the fifteenth-century Odia *Mahabharata*), Gourisankar Ray (one of the architects of modern Odisha) and Madhusudan Rao (a famous poet and a leading Brahmo). In *Sarala Charita* (1911), he addresses the problem of retrieving facts about a life lying buried under layers of hearsay, legends and unverified information. He speaks of historians' tendency to rely on guesswork when they encounter absence of evidence and finds western historians of India particularly guilty of this practice. In his biographies of Gourisankar (1838–1917) and Madhusudan (1853–1912), Mrutyunjay seeks to construct coherent narratives of their lives supported by documentary evidence. The lack of stageable plays in Odia prompted Mrutyunjay to translate Sanskrit classics, Kalidasa's *Vikramorvasiya* (1909) and Vishakhadatta's *Mudrarakshasa* (1910). Mrutyunjay's essays reflect the wide range of his scholarly and critical interests and were published in major literary periodicals of the time such as *Utkal Sahitya* and *Mukura*. In some essays he traces the origin of Odia language and in some others, he writes on the impact of technology on life. A few other essays are devoted to a study of rock edicts and Odia *pothis*, and in yet others, moral issues are explored. Mrutyunjay published a novel titled *Adbhut Parinam* [Strange Consequences] (1915) and a long poem titled "Naraj" (1915). He also authored a number of textbooks and stories for children.

Mrutyunjay Ratha's essay on Dinakrushna Das, which had won the Talcher Medal, was published in *Utkal Sahitya* in 1910. This medal had been instituted by the king of Talcher to promote critical appreciation of Odia literature. The rules governing the award of the medal required the contestants to answer a set of questions relating to a particular *kavya* and its author, and these questions were published in reputed periodicals well in

DOI: 10.4324/9781003224778-8

advance. The questions asked assume particular significance as they prepared the ground for a new approach to understanding and evaluating literature. The essay was published in two parts and the translation of its first part is given below where Mrutyunjay answered two of the five questions. The first sought information on the biography of the author citing internal textual evidence and the other required the contestant to discuss formal and contentual aspects of the text. Mrutyunjay carefully sifts through and weighs evidence and scrupulously distinguishes verifiable facts from popular legends. In his biographical sketch, Mrutyunjay strives to locate the poet not in a hazy or hallowed past but in an identifiable social world established through spatial and temporal specificities. Mrutyunjay draws one's attention to the innovations Dinakrushna's *Rasakallola* introduces at the level of both form and technique, and examines their aesthetic effectiveness. However, Mrutyunjay's assessment of *Rasakallola* is not entirely adulatory; he takes the poet to task for the presence of obscene elements in his *kavya*. Mrutyunjay's response can be explained with reference to his absorption of puritanical Brahmo attitudes, and echoes the *Indradhanu-Bijuli* controversy which raged in the 1890s. The essay shows how, in the early part of the twentieth century, institutional interventions gave critical discourse a new orientation and method.

*

An Essay on Dinakrushna Das's *Rasakallola*[1]

Mrutyunjay Ratha

Question 1

Show that the author of *Rasakallola* was a resident of Puri by citing internal evidence available in the text, and give an account of the poet's life based on legends and facts collected through research.

Answer

After the death of Chaitanya, there was a proliferation of Vaishnavite literature in Odia language. Gradually, several poets, focusing upon the passionate love between Radha and Krushna, went on to compose *kavyas* and songs. In the history of Odia literature, this period is worthy of being regarded as the age of love poetry. Among the gifted poets who lived and wrote in this age, 'the devout' Dinakrushna is the most important.

Year of birth

It is not possible to know with certainty when and where Dinakrushna took birth. However, it may be inferred from legends that Dinakrushna was a contemporary of the famous poet, Upendra Bhanja. The noted historian of India, W.W. Hunter expressed the view that the poets Upendra Bhanja and Dinakrushna lived more than three hundred years ago. No other sources than legends indicate that Dinakrushna and Upendra were contemporaries. It is believed that Dinakrushna, after composing *Rasakallola*, each line of which began with the letter "ka", once presented it to Upendra and sought his opinion. After going through the text, Upendra observed that the principles of composition followed in the first section of the text should have been adhered to in the succeeding sections. Moreover, Dinakrushna had not followed the example of Upendra's *kavya Baidehisha Bilasa* in this regard. For these reasons, the poem was flawed. Upendra's criticism stung Dinakrushna who accused the senior poet of being conceited. To avenge this insult, Upendra ended up composing "Kalakautuka", each line of which began with the letter "ka".

> Ka-initial is the rule,
> The holy or the ordinary, matters not.
> It is filled with so much delight [*kautuka*].
> Obtain rasa, churning the ocean of milk.
> Make intellect soar like Mandara mountain.

(p. 141)

It seems that these lines from the last section of *Rasakallola* targeted Upendra's "Kalakautuka"; however, from the manner in which the poet of *Rasakallola* has used the word *kautuka* [used in the sense of "delight" in the given lines], it cannot be inferred that the lines were aimed at "Kalakautuka". Probably, *kautuka* was a favourite word of the poet. However, at this point, it is difficult to ascertain if these poets ever met and traded insults. But a few stanzas in *Rasakallola* point to the possibility of a rift between the two poets. As the poet says in the sixteenth canto of *Rasakallola*,

> I created the song with the ka-initial,
> Never ever censure me for this.
> Only if you yourself are a poet
> You would realize the hard work it entails.

(p. 20)

> If you practise deceit
> Lord Krishna will punish you
> When He engages in His divine sport in Vrindavan.

(p. 72)

This sarcastic remark does not seem to be aimed at Upendra. The poet, in several places, used such denunciatory expressions for people who were wicked and hostile to talent. However, one may observe in this context that

Upendra, while following the principle of beginning each line with the letter "ka", wrote a better-crafted poem like "Kalakautuka". Therefore, Upendra may be considered a younger contemporary of Dinakrushna in the absence of any proof to the contrary. If one examines the language, emotions expressed and standards of taste in the *kavyas* written by both poets, it becomes clear that one preceded the other by a few years. But a close look at the history of Odisha reveals that its celebrated poets who infused vigour and vitality into Odia language were separated by almost a century. Among them Sudramuni Sarala Das is the foremost path-finder. He appeared around the early fifteenth century. Almost one hundred years later, that is, at the beginning of the sixteenth century, the author of *Bhagabata*, Jagannath Das appeared on the literary scene. It is most probable that the poet of *Rasakallola* lived and wrote almost a century after Jagannath or in the early part of the seventeenth century. He was closely followed by Upendra Bhanja. Each of these poets blazed a new trail in Odia language and literature.

Till now we have referred to the author of *Rasakallola* as Dinakrushna, based on prevailing legends. But at times doubts arise whether the author's name really was Dinakrushna. The main source of such uncertainty lies in the fact that in most places in several other texts composed by him, the poet has presented himself as 'Krushna Das'. The following are the concluding lines of *Rasakallola*:

(1) The mind of Krushna Das is like a lotus awakened by the rays of the sun.

(p. 141)

(2) Remembering this moment, the poet Krushna Das has achieved glory.

(p. 141)

(3) Krushna Das unwaveringly meditates on His form.

(p. 67)

(4) He strikes enthrallingly playful poses, which charm the poet Krushna Das.

(p. 119)

(5) Krushna, the poet deeply longs for Lord Krishna.

(p. 14)

(6) Overhearing what Uddhaba and Gopis tell each other will fill the heart of the poet Krushna with bliss.

(p. 131)

The poet expressed similar sentiments at several places in *Namaratna Gita*. This makes it clear that the poet's real name is "Krushna Das". The word *dina* [poor] has been applied only as an adjective in certain places. Therefore, it would not be wrong to refer to the poet as Krushna Das. Such names were often adopted by poets who were devotees of Lord Krishna. It is difficult to determine if he was given this name by his Brahman teacher or if it was a name given to him at birth. One may suggest that, just as the devotee of Goddess Sarala came to be known as Sarala Das and the devotee of Jagannath was celebrated as Jagannath Das, the devotee of Lord Krishna achieved fame as Krushna Das. Of course, such names supersede the names given to them by their families and find wide acceptance in society. Such a convention allowed names such as Siddharth, Ratnakar and Srikant to be superseded by Buddha Dev, Valmiki and Bhavabhuti. If one analyzes the list of names of the noble authors of ancient texts, it is seen that their names denoted what they achieved in life. The names of most great men were changed later in the light of their character traits. The names of the disciples or preachers of Acharya Shankar are different from their names cited in *shastras*. With all this, it seems clear that their names were given in the light of their natures and gained popular currency through *shastras*. The names and surnames of our ancient poets Sarala Das and Jagannath Das were not such. Although their original first names are not known, there is evidence that Das replaced Parida and Badapanda. The name of the poet of *Rasakallola* also underwent a similar change. That the poet was a supreme devotee of Krishna the text makes abundantly clear. There is no need for further discussion; one gets an indication of this in the following lines:

(1) Keep meditating on Krishna's form
     Keep reciting Krishna *charita*.

     Keep listening to Krishna *katha*,
     The world is Krishna, know this.

     In the service of Krishna, show readiness,
     Dedicate all good things to Krishna.

     Blissfully sing the songs of Krishna
     And Krishna will bless you.

                                                            (p. 46)

(2) Think of Krishna.
     Savour the tales of Krishna.

                                                            (p. 142)

(3) The poet feels blessed when
     The word Krishna resonates in his ears.

                                                            (p. 13)

(4) Chant the names Krishna, O folks!
     Listen to the tales of Krishna.
     One who is not drawn to stories about Krishna
     Will be destroyed in no time.

(p. 19)

So far, we have dwelt on debates over the poet's name. Let us now turn to the question of the poet's place of residence. On the basis of internal textual evidence, scholars have reached the conclusion that the poet was a resident of Puri. We shall now examine various excerpts from *Rasakallola* and seek to establish with proof that the poet was a resident of Puri.

Place of birth

A red glow in the eastern sky at dawn, the chirping of birds, and the crowing of the rooster etc. are natural phenomena. To the description of the breaking of dawn in *Rasakallola*, the poet, ignoring the natural phenomena mentioned above, provides the following details:

The **morning conch sounds** in Niladri (the abode of Jagannath).
He who wields the discus, the God of gods, is roused from slumber.
Discarding garlands, the Lord **puts on fine clothes**,
And sits on a chair to **brush his teeth**.
He rinses His mouth with **water in which** *triphala* is soaked and takes a bath.
Donning a nice-looking attire, the King of Niladri is ready for the day.

(p. 103)

It is possible for none other but a resident of Puri to have a glimpse of the highlighted special rituals of Lord Jagannath. Moreover, it is highly unlikely for many to even have heard of these rituals. Lots of people often visit Jagannath Temple, but only the temple servitors and some residents of Puri would be familiar with these morning rituals. One comes across such references at several places in *Rasakallola*. It is very likely that the poet associated the break of dawn with memories of morning rituals performed at the temple of his beloved Lord. This is a vivid example supporting the claim that he was a resident of Puri:

The cocks heralded the break of dawn,
the sound of conches filled the abode of gods,
the parade of guards and thieves shrank,
the moles who love the moonlit darkness fell into a hush,
the heavy wooden doors of Niladri were flung wide open,
and, *Kripasindhu* awoke from sleep hurriedly.

(p. 119)

Puri was once the capital of Odisha. Kotwals used to guard the town through the night. In the third and fourth lines, the poet, who was a resident of Puri, narrates his experience. Yet, this alone may not suffice as reliable evidence of the poet's residence in Puri. One may support this evidence further by citing the poet's description of the clothes worn by men and women.

> Their ears are adorned with rings which look like *bhramari* flowers,
> their necks bear many ornaments.
> **Dyeing their lips betel-red,**
> They try men's patience.
> Their nose is decked with rings, pins and studs,
> The thick lines of collyrium adorning their eyes,
> Stretch **up to their ears.**
> ....
> Armbands, bangles and *kaḷiari* **[bracelets]** deck their hands,
> Their anklets tinkle when they walk.
> Wearing **beaded talismans** around their waists
> They drape themselves with sarees, the colour of sable clouds.
>
> (pp. 10–11)

Such distinctiveness of dress and ornaments is visible even now among the women of Puri. Bracelets, waist-chains and such ornaments are used in Puri in a way which one does not find in any other region of Odisha. For instance, *kaḷiari* is not worn as an ornament in any other part of Odisha. Besides, no pre-modern Odia poet mentioned *kaḷiari* while describing female dress and ornaments. Just as the use of *kaḷiari* as an ornament is associated with Puri, the frequent use of the word *kākusta* [earnest entreaty, supplication] is a distinctive marker of his poetic diction. "**In supplication [*kākusta hoi*],** they, with tear-filled eyes say softly, O Kripanidhi" (p. 109). "Distressed, they join their hands in prayer near the Garuda pillar" ("Artatrana"). No other poet is known to have used *kākusta* which is a favourite word of Dinakrushna. Secondly, the poet's references to the aspects of the summer season evoke experiences peculiar to Puri. Consider these lines and see for yourself. In the following highlighted expressions, is not there an indication of *Chandan Jatra* of Puri?

(1) Like the black bee, **a skilled dancer**
    the *bātachakra* [a wheel propelled by wind] begins to whirl.
    Fish, tortoises and frogs look thin and weak
    Like fasting devotees.
    Some engage brahmins **to give water**
    to thirsty wayfarers.
    While some, when the day ends,
    take a dip to escape the heat.

(p. 63)

(2) The **dot of sandal paste** on Keshava's forehead
  Looks like the Moon emerging from the clouds.

(p. 108)

People who have seen the Brahmans of Puri would be able to appreciate how the simile mentioned above reminds the poet of the sandal paste mark on Brahmans' foreheads. Elsewhere, the poet writes,

The Lord sometimes appears in the guise of a bangle-seller
And at others, of a fisherman, a gardener, a ghost, or
A boatman waiting to ferry beautiful women, pestering them for
a fee.

(p. 77)

Women endlessly bargain with bangle-sellers. Bangle-sellers in Odisha came from its southern part and settled in Puri; their settlements are found nowhere else in the province. Other devotees of Krishna represented Him as a fisherman, a boatman, and a cowherd with a flute. But almost no one has portrayed Him as a bangle-seller. Therefore, such a portrayal is possible for a poet who was an inhabitant of Puri. Also, words such as scarecrow [*kaḷ ābhūta* or *pāḷabhūta*] have wide currency in Puri. In the invocatory part of *Rasakallola* the poet hints at Puri being his place of residence:

Gather your thoughts, O pious ones,
Fix your mind on the Lord of the Blue Hill,
His lotus eyes give immense happiness,
His irises look as if kissed by large black bees.
When the gold chain on His forehead sparkles,
There is none whose body does not tingle with pleasure.
One cannot praise enough the beauty of His red lips,
Which fills this poet with wonder.

Other famous poets of Odisha also composed invocations addressed to Lord Jagannath, but the depth of Dinakrushna's experience as evident in the invocation of *Rasakallola* has no parallel elsewhere. The third and fourth lines clearly suggest that the poet had a daily *darshan* of Jagannath. Elsewhere, the poet writes,

One who bathes in the sacred waters of this holy land,
And chants the holy name is absolved of all sins.
One who partakes of *kaibalya* does not suffer from hunger ever.
And finds for himself a place in heaven.
With this in mind
Dinakrushna lives out his days.

(p. 6)

From this, it becomes clear that the poet was a permanent resident of Puri. Similarly, stronger evidence in this respect may be obtained from texts such as "Artatrana Chautisha", but this lies outside the scope of the present essay.

One would now like to learn about the poet's family and lineage; but reliable information on this is difficult to come by. However, employing methods used in the previous sections, we would try to shed some light on the poet's life.

A biographical sketch

It is well known that the poet was born in a *Karaṇa* [a writing caste] family in Puri. Some say that he was the son of a courtesan but there is no firm evidence to support this claim. Whatever caste he might have been born into, it ceased to matter when he embraced Vaishnavism. If the above statement is true, then the saying "A Vaishnava has no caste" owes its origin to such a context. Although there is no way one can find out what kind of education he received as a child, there is no doubt that he acquired some knowledge of Sanskrit. The feelings and sentiments expressed in Dinakrushna's poetry echo those which one comes across in Sanskrit poetry, and many of the figures of speech he employs are similar to those found in ancient poetry.

It may be mentioned that the poet's early education was impeded by poverty. The lines given below show how, oppressed by poverty and hunger, the poet strayed from his chosen path:

> O Lord! Why did you entangle me in worldly cares?
> Why didn't you make me a bee hovering over the flowers at your lotus feet?
> Would I have forsaken the path of devotion?
> Would I not have danced around in joy?
> The despicable cravings of hunger have led me down paths unholy,
> I am weary of bearing the burden of worldly cares.

(1) At times I am a dishonest stupid scholar
(2) At times I am a worthless actor
(3) At times I am a deaf bard
(4) At times I am a monkey hoping to drink from an empty coconut shell!

(p. 73)

Let the discerning reader imagine Dinakrushna's plight from the above lines. The poet was chastised several times as a 'dishonest stupid scholar', sometimes he turned a deaf ear to the vilification and harsh public criticism. Poverty robs a man of all his strength. Had he not been constantly plagued by poverty, a talented poet like him would have achieved even greater fame as a poet. Apart from enduring deprivation, he was also subjected to attacks by the intelligent-sia. The following lines from *Rasakallola* substantiate the point made above:

1   To sing the praises of fools,
    Is a shame like no other.
    It would be better to plunge
    A knife into one's own heart.

(p. 74)

2   Camphor and sandal can not
    Dispel the stench of garlic.
    However hard you may try,
    A wicked mind can never be good.

(p. 73)

3   How I wish I enriched my voice
    Chanting His many names.
    What a pity, I asked a mean miser for favour.
    My desire for Chintamani
    Is still an unfulfilled dream.
    Now I wonder,
    Why I live this despicable life?
    How blissful it is to take refuge at Krishna's feet
    And learn noble things. Krushna Das says,
    To sing the praises of a wicked man
    Is as bad as
    Stabbing oneself.

(p. 103)

4   The king who accepts the biased views
    Of a pandit, who expresses them swearing by God
    Is a man without a conscience.

(p. 104)

5   Doesn't the street dog who barks
    At a lion appear ridiculous?
    Doesn't the attempt of the firefly to shine
    Before the sun seem ludicrous?

(p. 104)

These verses make it clear that the poet did not receive the attention of worthy readers and listeners. During Muslim rule in Odisha, the state of education was lamentable. Most people were unlettered. Unsurprisingly, therefore, not many were equipped to appreciate the beauty of his poetry.

"Songs do not soften small minds" (p. 72). What do ignoramuses know about poetry! Yet, whenever the wise and intelligent start following a creed, they usually follow the herd and bring ruin. That the pandits and the minor poets of those days did not appreciate Dinakrushna's poetry is clear from the above verses. Whenever a new literary or religious movement is initiated, conservative masses stubbornly resist it. However, pioneers overcome such resistance and assert themselves. Something similar happened in the case of Dinakrushna. His intense devotion to Vaishnavite faith and immense patience enabled him to overcome such obstacles. One may think of two possible reasons for the hostile response to Dinakrushna. First, no other poet before him had written a poem on such a scale on Radha and Krishna. The Vaishnavite element in literature was found only in a small number of short poems and songs. The depiction of the love between Radha and Krishna in Jagannath Das's *Bhagabata* differs significantly from Dinakrushna Das's portrayal of the same. During the reign of Ganga kings, most people in Odisha, especially the inhabitants of Puri, were devotees of Vishnu, and worshipped Krishna as His avatar. But at this point in time, they did not focus entirely upon the divine lovers, Radha and Krushna. Around the time of Chaitanya, Vaishnavism underwent reformation. As one initiated into the new order, Dinakrushna felt the need to transform prevalent religious orientations. In the process, the literary sensibility of the masses also underwent radical change. Earlier, almost everyone read devotional texts like the *Bhagabata*. The language of these puranic texts was unadorned and simple. It is likely that the new style and subject matter introduced by Dinakrushna failed to appeal to readers who had grown accustomed to the works of poets such as Sarala Das, Jagannath Das and Balaram Das. Secondly, acute poverty often rendered the poet desperate. For that matter, as is clear from his statements, he had to live on charity. As a result, the general public looked upon him as an object of pity and overlooked his brilliance. It is also believed that the king did not give him due respect. Impoverished poets like him are known to have suffered such fate during their lifetime. The Sanskrit poet Bhavabhuti, too, is believed to have undergone similar suffering for setting a new trend in Sanskrit literature and his poetry remained unappreciated for a long time. Similar was the plight of the Bengali poet, Michael Madhusudan Dutta. If the author of *Rasakallola* had not radically reworked the life of Krishna, he probably would not have suffered such ignominy. It appears from what the poet himself said that his depiction of the love between Radha and Krishna was not appreciated by the readers of his time:

(1) I pray to you all.
     Do not let anger and pride enter your hearts.
     Always be kind.
     Fix your mind only on Krishna.
     Talk sweetly, and
     Charm the devotees of Krushna.

                                                          (p. 142)

(2) Why feel bad if the atheists
    Taunt you? They are supposed to do so –
    To cast aspersions on others;
    No advice will change their mind.

(p. 72)

Piety and poetic skill

During Chaitanya's sojourn in Puri, Jagannath Das (popularly known as Atibadi) promoted a new Vaishnavite sect. This community is now called "Atibadi". Odia Math in Puri was established by the propagators of this creed. The poet Dinakrushna belonged to this sect. Among poets after Jagannath Das and Balaram Das, Dinakrushna and Banamali Das embraced this new cult. After these two *Karana* young men joined the above sect, they engrossed themselves in meditating on the divine pair and their poetry acquired new grace and loveliness.

> They wear such holy marks on their body
> But no one knows the sins that lie within.

(*Rasakallola*)

Our poet was definitely not a Vaishnava like this. He, truly, had experienced the love of God in his heart. Thus, his heart overflowed with feelings of divine bliss which found expression in ecstatic poetry. However, it needs to be ascertained whether this unique self-realization was the only source of his poetic inspiration. Educating popular sensibility is one of the chief objectives of poets in all ages and places, but they also sought to serve some secondary purposes. Since poets in olden times modelled their works on Sanskrit texts, it would be in order to discuss relevant aspects of Sanskrit poetics. The scholars of Sanskrit rhetoric stated that Sanskrit poets composed poems with the purpose of earning fame and money as well as to teach rules of conduct, and ways of overcoming illness and washing away sins. Of these, the desire to earn fame happens to be the most prevalent. Instances of poets writing in order to be cured of diseases and absolving themselves of sins are more numerous in Odia literature than in Sanskrit. In order to attain salvation and achieve absolution, many writers spent years composing a single, substantial text. Mallinath, the famous writer of Sanskrit commentaries, stated that several Sanskrit writers authored texts in order to alleviate physical suffering resulting from leprosy. It is likely that Dinakrushna also started writing poetry with the above-mentioned aim. Legend relates that, when the poet was afflicted with leprosy, he, in utter desperation, used to stand at the Garuda pillar to sing the "Artatrana Chautisha" to pray to the Lord for deliverance. This *chautisha* is the poet's first major literary work. With the grace of God and nourished by knowledge, gradually this blossomed into a beautiful lotus and won people's admiration.

Here, some might wonder if the poet composed poetry in order to mitigate the pain caused by leprosy. No, it is not just that. "The fear of punishment after Death will break the chains of worldly attachments" (p. 114). Even though the attainment of moksha or the washing away of sins was the prime objective of the poet, that the dreaded disease had taken his mind away from all kinds of physical pleasures and led him on a spiritual path is undeniable. Having fallen prey to this disease, the poet, in the prime of his life, suffered immense hardship and everyone in disgust started shunning him. To make matters worse, the heartless king banished the poet from the city. This incident is referred to in the following lines from *Rasakallola*:

(1) If you merely sleep there
    You get the fruit of the highest kind of devotion.
    Your wife, son and servants
    Will attain salvation.
    Oh how Dinakrushna wished he had stayed there!
    But he could not, as it was not God's desire.
    He followed the path fate laid for him.
    No one can change it unless
    Merciful God, the Maker of my destiny
    Shows mercy to me.

                                                                    (p. 103)

(2) O Lord of the Universe, who is
    As beautiful as the blue water-lily!
    Why are you so harsh on me?
    You fill my heart with longings and then dash my hopes
    O Pleasure-giver!
    Are these the ways of God?

                                                                    (p. 73)

(3) In times of misfortune,
    The wise, too, turn a deaf ear
    To the voice of truth.
    ....
    Who knows what will befall whom?
    Only Time will tell.

                                                                    (p. 111)

In this way, the poet, suffering in several ways, gained vast knowledge about the strange ways of people but at the same time he himself changed for the better. Even though he was tormented and attacked in many ways, he expressed no anger and even though he was a man of immense learning among illiterates, he showed no pride. "Doesn't the street dog who barks / At a lion appear ridiculous? / Doesn't the attempt of the firefly to shine

/ Before the sun seem ludicrous?" (p. 104). Let the wise judge and see for themselves how this statement, which bears testimony to the genius of the poet, is an expression of his humility and greatness. The religious faith and values of the poet appear faultless and are of an elevated nature. "The world is Krishna, know this". He definitely was not an idolater; idol worship did not satisfy him. "Brahman is all pervasive". He had realized this ancient truth and also that the omnipotent God is of unbounded greatness and His will prevails in the universe and makes it blissful.

> Chanting Krishna's name destroys
> Sins more than a sinner can ever commit.

After his banishment from Puri, nothing is known about where and how he spent his last days. There is no way of knowing this nor are there any legends relating to this part of the poet's life.

Question 2

Discuss the subject matter, structure and style of composition of *Rasakallola* with reference to the *bhavas* and *rasas* it seeks to convey, and highlight the *kavya*'s strengths and shortcomings.

Answer

Structure

The analysis of the subject matter of *Rasakallola* may be divided primarily into three parts: childhood, youth and adulthood. The principle underlying this tripartite division is that, just as in the first section of the *kavya*, there is abundant description of childhood innocence and the natural state of blissful happiness, in the second section, there is the effulgent beauty of youth, the craving for love and the growth in vigour and vitality, and, in the remaining part, the focus is on the description of adroitness, courage and intelligence. In the first ten cantos, there is a chronologically ordered account of the birth of Krishna, the killing of Putana, the slaying of the serpent Kaliya, the divine sport in Gopapura and other matters pertaining to Krishna's childhood. This section is steeped in *vatsalya* [filial love] *rasa*. In the ten cantos that follow, Krishna's pastimes in Vraj, wanderings in the forest, the stealing of the gopis' clothes, and other such youthful indulgences evoke the *sringara rasa*. In this context, the poet also describes the six seasons. The remaining few cantos delightfully depict the conversation between Krishna and Akrura, the journey to Mathura, the killing of demons such as Kubalaya, and Kamsa, the meeting with Kubja, the exchanges between Krishna and Uddhab, and such other incidents from Krishna's adult life. The style of description in this part is strikingly unusual, blending as it does the *veera*, *karuna* and *shanta rasas*. The account of Krishna's life and deeds comprise thirty-four sections. Although *sringara rasa* dominates the narrative of *Rasakallola*, it avoids excessive eroticism as it centers on divine characters, Radha and Krishna. To say anything critical of them would be deemed audacious. However, the poet, by mixing his description of the reprehensible behaviour of ordinary men and women with simple religious counsel, has diminished the poetic appeal of his work. It would not be appropriate here to elaborate on this any further.

Language and style

As has been mentioned earlier, Dinakrushna introduced a new mode of expression in Odia literature and gave a new direction to language use. These innovations infused his writings with a new vitality. The high lyrical quality of Dinakrushna's devotional poetry continues to have an enduring appeal for readers. If he happened to be a contemporary of Upendra Bhanja, this achievement would be deemed even more remarkable. The music of Dinakrushna's *kavyas*, especially of *Rasakallola*, has a distinctive quality. Whether or not the subject of the poem is important and the values therein are lofty or it has qualities befitting a kavya, it is the lyricism of its language that has endowed it with transcendent beauty. Before discussing the shortcomings and the qualities of the composition, one feels tempted to illustrate this lyrical quality of the verses. But wherever in *Rasakallola* this quality finds expression, the instances happen to be of an erotic nature, and cannot be presented to discerning readers. However, some examples are given below to describe the lyrical quality of the verses:

> (1) His feet are softer than the morning sun.
>   See, they are full of divine signs.
>   His toenails look as radiant
>   As a constellation of stars.
>   What to speak of his thighs!
>   They are softer than
>   The trunk of a young plantain tree **made of emerald.**
>   The middle portion of his body charms so,
>   His wide chest is irresistible.
>
>   (p. 20)

> (2) The Gopi is curly-haired, clever and lustful,
>   Lotus-faced, full-breasted
>   Red lips, teeth as beautiful as the bud of kunda flower
>   Throat like a conch
>   Her gait is as majestic as that of an elephant

Dressed in silken finery
She speaks so softly, it fills one with rapture.

(p. 38)

(3) Their smile is as sweet as the fragrance of lotus
They look like swans at play
Like anglers they tug at
The fish that is Krushna's mind.
O they, the noble and beautiful
How splendid the earth looks
As they walk on it gracefully.

(p. 64)

(4) Everyone's dress, at the waist,
Is in disarray. Drunk on desire
They totter. They look like
Golden creepers trembling in the breeze.
Like swans, they waddle.

(p. 102)

(5) Amid all this playfulness, dawn breaks,
The cock crows and the sun rises,
The cuckoo's song fills the air,
The sheldrakes cross the river to make love
After a night of painful separation.
Temple priests blow conches
The Brahmans go for bath,
The skies look a vermilion red
As the consort of Chhaya appears.
The wind carries the scent of flowers
The doves begin to sing
The owls, in fear of crows, enter
The hollows of the trees.

(p. 59)

How fantastic the word arrangement is in all of the above! In several cases, poets who focus too much on painting word pictures deviate from the naturalness of description. But even when one comes across instances in Dinakrushna's poetry of such self-indulgence, the poems mostly do not lose their liveliness and appeal because of these. (Excerpt 4) The use of alliteration in these verses does not inhibit the expression of emotions; rather, it renders the description more fascinating. Also see how the beauty of language is enhanced because of it. (Excerpt 2) In these verses, to lend the language lyrical grace, the poet goes against the rules of grammar and use words such as *kambukanthini* [throat like a conch]. Such words are imports from Vaishnavite literature of Bengal. In their writings, there is widespread use of words such as *gopini, bhujangini, bihangini, utsukini.* (Note the -ni morpheme.) Over time, poets have got used to violating the rules and have come to the point where they do not shy away from using words such as *kavi-kavini.* To maintain the lyricism of the poems, Dinakrushna, in places, ignored the rules of grammar, and, in the process of his adhering to the ka-initial rule, poetic felicity is lost. Anyway, wherever the poet did not get carried away by the lure of alliteration, the descriptions turn out to be pleasing and captivating. Consider the following description of Krishna's childhood pastimes:

> The son of Yashoda grows
> Like the waxing moon.
> Soon he begins to crawl
> And the jewelled waistband tinkles.
> Wisps of hair on his forehead
> Look like bees swarming over a lotus.
> Necklets adorn his conch-like neck,
> Bracelets cover his wrists
> Lines of collyrium blacker than the cuckoo
> Adorn his beautiful eyes.
>
> ....
>
> Sometimes he smears his body with dirt
> Then dusts it off and goes back.
>
> ....
>
> His mother feeds him with milk
> Others, fondly, carry him away
> And feel happy caressing him.
> Some say: You are mine.
> Some comfort him: Do not weep,
> What is troubling you my child?
> Someone says: O you of the colour of dark new cloud
> Of black curly hair
> You are a string of emeralds around my neck.
> You are the destroyer
> Of my sorrows and the source
> Of my joy. You are the killer
> of the evil breast-giver Putana, the shrewd woman of sharp claws.
> Someone says: You are the flowers on my bun
> and the collyrium on my eyes.

(pp. 7–8)

Here, see how these lines convey *vatsalya rasa* and make the image of child Krishna come vividly alive. Elsewhere, these descriptions have been presented similarly, which deserve praise.

> He holds butter in his palm.
> See how he slurps it. Curls on his forehead
> Look like lotus on a reef.
> His dark body is covered with dust.
> He wears a waist-band, but no clothes.
> The round face covered with beads of sweat
> Looks resplendent.
> His irises resemble black bees on a lotus.
> The string of emeralds glows on his neck.
> The Gopis plead: Come, dance
> We will give you plenty of butter.
> They clap, and he begins to sway.

(p. 18)

Instead of 'Wisps of hair on his forehead / Look like bees swarming over a lotus', it is 'Curls on his forehead / Look like lotus on a reef' which captures with greater clarity the image of a child's face encircled with curls of hair. It has been seen in several instances that the vehicles used by Sanskrit poets have not always adequately represented the tenor. In those cases, it is as if the poets searched for comparisons and imposed them. But when such forced comparisons are made, feelings would not be evoked naturally. Most similes employed by Dinakrushna appear natural, effective and not forced. Poets who can display their virtuosity through the use of effective and unforced metaphors are poets in the true sense of the term. That is why in Sanskrit, Kalidasa is unrivalled as a poet. In Odia, similarly, no classical poet has surpassed Dinakrushna in the deft employment of figures of speech. On seeing a beautiful smiling woman, many poets have compared her white teeth to the seeds of a pomegranate, to the buds of the *kunda* flower etc. But how does Dinakrushna present them?

> Brighter than the kunda flower, shapelier than pearls
> and lovelier than the seeds of pomegranate
> The teeth are neatly lined
> like gems strung together in a necklace.

(p. 40)

The imagery used by all other poets pales into insignificance in comparison. The poet of *Naishadha* described the thirty-two teeth of King Nala as thirty-two *rekhas* [lines]. Dinakrushna, perhaps, scoffing at Putana's teeth wrote this:

[Her] teeth as long as that of a comb
Make her look as beautiful as
the dark night of the new moon.

The poet has given enough evidence of jocularity as well. In the last line, we can almost see the sly smile on his face.

Another speciality of the poet's use of analogies is that he, having studied Nature and the character of the people very well, has drawn comparisons between the two. This is seen in no other classical poet. Through this, in many places, the real nature of things emerges clearly. The poet has this to say about the common seasonal cycle,

The *batachaakras* [wheels propelled by wind] begin to whirl
Like the black bee, a skilled dancer.
The sun fumes
like the irate servant of a miserly master.
The birds in the forest remain silent and still
Like yogis in deep meditation.

(p. 63)

The ripe crops in the field look as resplendent as
The yellow silken wrap on Krishna's body.
Like the mud wasp, the son of Nanda
Kills the Gopis by arousing their desire and then
Brings them back to life.

(p. 122)

Did the poet not lend an aura of novelty to objects described through well-chosen metaphors? The last simile seems to be the poet's favourite. This is because it occurs at several places in his poetry. Maybe, the perceptive poet witnessed this phenomenon several times; but we know little or nothing about it. All we have heard, however, is that the mud wasp, after killing its prey, which may be a bug or some flying insect, drags it to its nest and later enters its body and comes out of it looking like its prey; it is as if the prey itself has come alive. The truth of this matter is a subject of investigation.

The poet effectively conveys *sringara*, *karuna* and *vatsalya rasas* in his poems but fails when it came to expressing *veera rasa*. In the description of the battle between Sri Krishna and Hastipaka in *Rasakallola*, his language fails to communicate the vigour and vitality associated with the *veera rasa*:

On hearing such a thing,
The mahout braces for the battle
With an angry face and a stern look.

He lands a sharp blow on the elephant's tusk
To raise anger in the animal.
Strange are the ways of God.

Will such description enable the reader to experience *veera rasa*? Actually, no Odia poet other than Sarala Das has achieved success in this respect. Instead, in this case, Dinakrushna has focused more on maintaining a uniform metrical pattern than on the *rasa* to be depicted. One more point may be made here. The poet has used the word Keshihata to mean "Keshav" [one of the several names of Krishna]. If we take the word out of the line, the meaning will be entirely the opposite, that is, "one who was killed by Keshi". How can the suffix "-*ta*" or the active voice be possible from the transitive root "*hana*"? According to the rules of grammar, the word should be "hatakeshi" [one who killed Keshi]. But in such cases, not only Dinakrushna but several other poets have also blithely violated the rule. Therefore, the use of words such as "kundajitaradanā" (instead of *kundaradana* which means "having teeth as beautiful as kunda buds") is widely prevalent in Odia. Whatever the faults therein, through such choice of words, poets exercised their freedom in language use. The manner in which the poet of *Rasakallola*, through the use of words such as "dhāiparāṇakhiā" (literally, "the baby who kills the nurse"), "kekipuchhakhoṣā" ("the chignon held together by peacock quill"), "mandaratekā" ("one who held aloft the Mandara mountain"), "kulachharā bamśi" ("the flute which entices one away from his/her family"), brought forth the richness and variety of expression and used Odia and Sanskrit words to create a *maṇikānchan* style has not been bettered by any other Odia poet. Of course, because of this, while the language turns out to be felicitous at several places, it becomes unsavoury at others; however, through such innovations, it is as if the poet gives a fresh lease of life to the language. In our time, the poet Radhanath Ray has followed this style and enriched Odia. Be that as it may, we will take a break from the present discussion and conclude our response to the second question with a couple of statements. The *kavya* is seriously flawed in one respect; the depiction of love, having been essentially of a carnal nature, has made the poem obscene. The poem could have escaped the charge of obscenity had love been presented in abstract terms:

[Kubja] said: Come visit my home, be my guest
Sate my desire, set me free.
The lotus-eyed Krishna accepted the invitation
With a smile and said:
I will, after I settle matters with the king.

If he had adopted the manner in which Kubja [the hunchbacked woman] expressed her desire for Krushna in the rest of the *kavya*, the charge of obscenity would not have been levelled against the poet. However, the poet strove to subdue the erotic element in *Rasakallola*. He had no option but to reflect the tendencies prevalent in his time.

Translation: Urmishree Bedamatta

Note

1 Dinakrushna Das, "Talcher Padak Pariksha: *Rasakallola*" [The Talcher Medal-winning Essay on *Rasakallola*] (part 1), *Utkal Sahitya*, vol. 14, no. 1, Cuttack, 1910, pp. 1–16.

9 Sachchidananda Mishra

Baladeb Ratha and his experiments with poetic technique

Introduction

Sachchidananda Mishra (1930–2015) was an eminent scholar, literary critic, creative writer and translator. His father's love for medieval Odia poetry instilled in him an abiding passion for the study of the premodern literature of Odisha. A student of science and law, he combined logical precision and polemical rigour in his approach to literature. He relentlessly challenged received assumptions about authors and texts, and advanced views arrived at through meticulous examination and comparison of palm-leaf manuscripts. His work concentrated on Odia literature from Sarala Das to Baladeb Ratha, which was a largely uncharted terrain. Owing to the dearth of reliable evidence, scholarship on these periods in literary history was dominated by myths, legends and unverified formulations. His authoritative editions of Sarala Das's *Bichitra Ramayana* and Narasingh Sena's *Gopakeli* are substantive contributions to scholarship. He has a collection of poems titled *Ananya o Anyanya* [The Unique One and Other Poems] and two collections of stories, *Ruchira Rachanabali* [Writing Meant to Afford Pleasure] and *Nasta Debata o Anaynya Katha* [The Fallen God and Other Stories] to his credit. Sachchidananda also translated Fa Hsien's *Travels to India* and seventy tales of Sage Shuka. His books of literary criticism include *Baladeb Ratha Adhyayana* [A Study of Baladeb Ratha's Poetic Achievements] (1981), *Atitara Baranabaodha* [Understanding the Past] (2002) and *Sarala Das: Eka Adhyayana* [Sarala Das: A Study] (2006). In a world where criticism has become almost inescapably academized, Sachchidananda, though not an academic, established himself as a critic of the highest order.

The essay "Prayogbadi Kabi Baladeb Ratha" [Baladeb Ratha and His Experiments with Poetic Techniques] has been taken from Sachchidananda Mishra's book *Baladeb Ratha: Sahitya Sadhana o Siddhi* [Baladeb Ratha's Achievement as a Writer] (2005). It was serialized in *Jhankar* (vol. 26, nos. 1 & 2) in 1974. The book is a revised version of Sachchidananda's earlier work on the poet, published in 1981. It is an outcome of his intense and lifelong fascination for the poetry of Baladeb. His in-depth study of Baladeb's oeuvre leads him to interrogate some dominant assumptions regarding the

DOI: 10.4324/9781003224778-9

emergence of literary modernity in Odisha. This modernity is supposed to have originated in the negotiations with western influences in which Radhanath Ray and his contemporaries actively engaged in the late nineteenth century. Sachchidananda makes a convincing attempt to give this modernity an alternative genealogy by showing how Baladeb Ratha's poetic experiments conducted in the late eighteenth and early nineteenth centuries anticipate some its crucial aspects. He begins by emphasizing the distinctiveness of the historical and cultural milieu in which Baladeb's poetry is embedded. This milieu absorbed influences from diverse sources such as the Qutab Sahi rule in South Odisha, the colonial dispensation of the East India Company, and the strong impact of Telugu literary traditions. Sachchidananda shows how the milieu exposed the poet to diverse cultural, political and linguistic worlds, and led him to carry out innovative experiments. Baladeb is one of the earliest Odia poets to employ Perso-Arabic expressions in his poems, and he also created a space for colloquial expressions in otherwise highly stylized *kavyas*. Sachchidananda painstakingly draws up a fairly long list of such expressions which lent Baladeb's diction a supple liveliness. The use of humour, wit and satire in his poetry constitute yet another crucial element in Baladeb's contribution to literary modernity. This essay provides not only an insight into the poet's significance, but adds substantially to one's understanding of the history of Odia literature and language.

*

Baladeb Ratha and his experiments with poetic technique[1]

Sachchidananda Mishra

The writing style of Baladeb Ratha, the author of the iconic *kavya Kishorchandrananda Champu*, is essentially experimental in nature. Today, if one speaks of experimentalism – this consists in the introduction of something distinctively new into the language, feelings, techniques already established in a literature – some young litterateurs might think that it is a modern process imported from western literature into India sometime in the middle of the twentieth century. However, such a view is completely mistaken. The forms of a literature, its language, techniques and feelings keep changing from one age to another. Since this change does not occur on its own, it results from the efforts of an individual writer. This process unfolded in the ancient past and is taking place even today. Such transformations provide evidence of literature remaining alive. In fact, one finds the influence of experimentalism at the beginning of the history of literature. However, some writers focus less on demolishing the old and creating something new; others do the opposite. It is from this perspective that one may view the oeuvre of Baladeb Ratha.

Although Baladeb Ratha sought to conduct many experiments in Odia literature, not all of them succeeded. However, some of them bore fruit and quickly gained wide popular appeal. Today he is chiefly recognized in terms of those popular experiments which bear the stamp of his individuality. These include the attempts to place Odia *chaupadis* within the mould of Sanskrit *champus*, ingenious use of *tatsama*, *tadbhava*, indigenous and foreign (mostly Islamic) vocabulary, employment of diction befitting his characters, and spicing his poems with brilliant wit and humour. However, this is only one aspect of Ratha's achievement which is visible to the contemporary reader. The facets that are illuminated through a comprehensive approach to his works are no less important from a literary-historical point-of-view. This essay discusses the extent to which his innovative poetic practices succeeded or failed and how they constitute his uniqueness.

The need to examine Baladeb Ratha's poetic experiments assumes significance from the point of view of Odia literary historiography. Ratha appeared on the literary scene when the ancient literary tradition was coming to an end in Odisha. He led a richly creative life in different parts of Odisha and was honoured as a writer. If one places him in the context of his own time, it can be said without doubt that he was an accomplished 'modern' man. Apart from Odia, he acquired command of Sanskrit, Telugu, Urdu and Hindi (Kharotha). He also had a deep understanding of music. It can be surmised that he belonged to the top layer of the educated class in Odisha in his time; otherwise, the rare honour of becoming a court poet, serving Jalantara and Athagarh kingdoms as dewan and the kingdom of Mahuri as manager would not have been bestowed upon him. To this one may also add his appointment as the mentor of the prince of Paralakhemundi. It would be wrong to assume that all these distinctions came his way because the kings were connoisseurs of literature; for it was the East India Company, not the kings of Mahuri and Paralakhemundi who elevated him to these offices. If one harbours this erroneous notion, one would not be able to arrive at a correct estimate of his political acumen and administrative abilities. A close study of Ratha's towering personality, the innovations he introduced into the language, expressive resources and techniques of Odia literature in the era of transition from the old to the new assumes urgent relevance. He was born in the closing decades of the eighteenth century and it is in the first decades of the nineteenth (approximately 1800–1820 C.E.) that one witnesses the blossoming of his creative talent. (Kulamani Das in the biographical section of *Kabisurya Granthabali* [Collected Works of Baladeb Ratha] notes that Ratha was born in 1789 and died in 1845 but his calculations are incorrect. I have established with ample evidence in my essay titled 'Baladeb Rathanka Janmakala' that he was born after 1778 but before 1780.) By the time he was born, the Nizamshahi Muslim rule had come to an end in southern Odisha, the short-lived French political influence had disappeared, and the British East India Company had established its unchallenged control over it. (Politically, southern Odisha came to be cut off from northern Odisha and became a part of Hyderabad Nizam's kingdom in the seventeenth century. Maratha rule which was imposed on northern Odisha in the fifties of the eighteenth century was never extended to southern Odisha.) Seen from a political perspective, the modern age dawned in southern Odisha before it did in northern Odisha. No one had anticipated in the years preceding the modern age the emergence of literary modernity in Odisha or the advent of the Age of Fakir Mohan. It has also been argued that modern (for want of a better word, I am employing this rather vague term) Odia literature discarded its older literary traditions and chose to draw upon recently imported foreign (mainly English) literature. In fact, the borrowing was carried out through a heavy dependence on Bangla literature. To be accused of parasitism is a serious allegation against any literature. And yet, it cannot be said that this allegation is entirely base-less. Accustomed to reading *chhandas, chautishas, chaupadis, bolis, pois, bhajans, baramasis, koilis,* and *puranas,* Odias were naturally drawn to the freshly introduced English literary forms such as elegies, odes, ballads, lyr-ics, sonnets which were included in the school and college syllabi. But this allegation does not carry as much weight as is believed, and it is necessary to thoroughly examine the poetic experiments carried out by Baladeb Ratha to arrive at the above conclusion.

In addition to writing in Odia, Baladeb Ratha also wrote poems in some other languages. Palm-leaf manuscripts containing a few *chaupadis* in Telugu and Kharotha (Hindi) have recently been discovered. (I published an essay titled 'Sahityasadhak Baladeb Ratha' in the literary periodical *Sarathi,* to which I appended one of his Telugu songs with annotations.) His father Ujjwal Ratha was a Sanskrit scholar and poet, and his maternal grandfather Tripurari Ota was also a scholar of repute and his mentor. His birthplace Vijayanagar (situated seven miles from the fort of Digapahandi or Badakhemundi, which is now in complete ruins) was famous for its Sanskrit poets. Such a cultural milieu gave Baladeb Ratha a thorough grounding in Sanskrit literature. Notable among his Sanskrit writings are *Kishorchandrananda Champu, Rajiba Netrashtaka* and other songs. Relying on his deep knowledge of Sanskrit and in order to win the approba-tion of Sanskrit-knowing readers, he created an artificial language making extensive use of *samas* [conjugation] and *sandhi* [compound] which were never in common parlance. This may be termed Sanskritized Odia.

Baladeb Ratha found a novel way to introduce the *guru* [hard] and *laghu* [soft] rules of Sanskrit metrical schemes into Odia and employed them in many *chaupadis.* However, Odia language never recognized the distinction between *guru* and *laghu* metrical schemes. Literary historians of Odisha have claimed that Sanskrit metrical schemes were introduced into Odia by writers born long after Baladeb Ratha. However, as has been shown earlier, these were introduced by none other than Baladeb. Nonetheless the poet employed such Sanskritized Odia compounds in very few *chau-padis* and it does not appear as if he wanted to employ these extensively in

Odia. It appears that he wished to draw the attention of Odias well-versed in Sanskrit to a new aspect of language-use. Many Odia poets who had achieved command of Sanskrit in the last half of the nineteenth century and early decades of the twentieth (particularly in southern Odisha) accepted Baladeb as an ideal, and composed a plethora of poems, *chhandas* and plays in Sanskritized Odia. Such writings have been exiled from contemporary histories of Odia literature on account of their alleged ponderousness. The poets who emulated Baladeb in this respect include the renowned scholar Gopinatha Nanda Sarma, celebrated playwright and lyricist Raghunath Parichha, and Chikiti's court poet Radhamohan Rajendra. However, one must accept that Baladeb's experiments did not last long and were limited to a miniscule minority. And yet, it cannot be said to be a completely failed experiment. The advent of the printing press brought literature closer to the common reader. As a result, literature was no longer restricted to a highly educated section and Sanskritized Odia gradually lost its appeal.

Sanskrit is recognized as the mother of all Aryan languages. Thus, Odia always bore some resemblance to Sanskrit. Baladeb Ratha made this more pronounced by adopting artificial means. If it is true that Odia originated from Sanskrit, then the difference between the two would increase over time. The effort to Sanskritize Odia reverses this process. Though Sanskritized Odia has gone out of fashion in modern times, the Odia grammar taught in schools and colleges is modelled on Sanskrit grammar. For the creation of scientific terminology, Sanskrit was relied upon. The process of bringing Odia closer to Sanskrit takes place place even today. Any attempt to trace the origin of Sanskritized Odia must recognize the contribution of Baladeb's experiments.

The intermingling of two languages is nothing new. Instances of mixed languages can be found in literary texts even when one may not come across them in colloquial speech. Bidyapati, Chandi Das and many other famous Vaishnava poets nurtured a mixed language called Brajboli. Writers from different linguistic regions in eastern India such as Odisha, Bengal, Assam and Mithila employed Brajboli as a medium of literary expression although it was not their mother tongue. Elements of several languages went into the making of Brajboli. In many stone and copperplate inscriptions datable to the thirteenth century found in Srikurmam, Simhachala and other places in northern Andhra Pradesh, one comes across a language in which Telugu and Odia are mixed. This too was not the ordinary language used by common people.

It is possible that the literary tradition of the neighbouring Telugu-speaking areas inspired Baladeb Ratha to develop a Sanskritized Odia. Almost all the renowned Telugu *kavyas* and *puranas* were written in Sanskritized Telugu. Poetic texts written in this style were labelled as *marga* poetry. These *marga* poems are so Sanskritized that an average Telugu reader would not be able to understand them if they are not annotated by a Sanskrit scholar. It may be noted here that there was a movement in the final decades of the nineteenth century and the early part of the twentieth, to replace *marga* poems written in Sanskritized Telugu with those written in colloquial language.

Colloquial language

Odia poets, since the time of Sarala Das, favoured the use of unadorned colloquial language since sorrows and joys of the heart are more easily expressed through beautifully supple ordinary language than through an impenetrable language burdened with scholarly pedantry. Therefore, Baladeb Ratha accorded a lot of importance to everyday diction in his poetry although this was ridiculed by the pandits with whom he associated in the royal courts. And even before him, poets such as Abhimanyu Samantsinghar had demonstrated that easily understood and pronounced rural words could be infused with enchanting grace when employed in poetic expressions and this is the reason why the artificiality of Upendra Bhanja's diction fell out of favour. Likewise, the poet Brajanatha Badajena demonstrated how there was no need to discard the Perso-Arabic vocabulary which had passed into common parlance. Indeed, most evolving languages of the world have enriched themselves by assimilating words from other languages. Baladeb, for his part, chose to include words from other languages in order to enhance the expressive possibilities of Odia. His early works such as *Chandrakala* and later works such as *Kishorchandrananda Champu* contain a fascinating intermingling of rustic and Perso-Arabic expressions. A few such expressions from *Kishorchandrananda Champu* are given below:

Rustic: *anāuṇi* [glance]; *amala* [wine/liquor]; *ekā* [an expression to denote affirmation in southern Odisha]; *kashibā* [to inspect]; *kehi* [how]; *khalikar* [nomad]; *khārā* [sharp]; *gheniba* [to accept or to understand]; *chitta* [wish; the word is also in use in Telugu]; *chihnikāibā* [to frighten]; *jhimita* [a moment]; *tākara* [a recess in the wall]; *tikāe* [a little]; *tipibā* [sharing a secret]; *dāki* [small drum]; *dui* [guilty]; *dubibā* [to drown]; *thāpi* [to make steady]; *dharaṣibā* [to muster courage]; *dhūpibā* [to be ready to attack]; *nipata* [utterly]; *pahilu* [first]; *pālie* [once]; *hatibā* [to be stubborn].

Perso-Arabic: *ākhara* [final]; *ābur* [honor]; *kharāp* [bad]; *khiāl* [making fun]; *chākara* [servant]; *jahara* [poison]; *jura* [loot]; *jhagaṛa* [cares]; *tikāyita* [prince]; *thauraibā* [to guess]; *dhabā* [a pucca house]; *tanābi* [window]; *taras* [desire]; *tāj* [crown]; *darada* [pain]; *dāu* [harassment]; *dāni* [spittoon]; *dibālā* [insolvent]; *dhamkāibā* [to threaten]; *najara* [glance]; *fatuā* [one who is made fun of]; *fandā* [livelihood].

Modern Odia language has grown richer by absorbing rustic and Perso-Arabic terms. It also benefited from shunning the incongruous mixture of the elevated and the trivial that emerged in the middle ages and the sanitized idiom shaped under Bengali influence. Fakir Mohan Senapati carried this process forward by shaping and refining a distinctively new idiom. Short story writers and novelists who succeeded him followed his inspiring example. However, this idiom did not take shape in a vacuum nor was it a product of English influence. Its origin can be traced to Baladeb's experiments with Odia prose. True, like many of his contemporaries in other parts of India he was occasionally inclined to introduce into Odia obsolete and unnecessary Sanskrit words. However, on the whole, Baladeb accorded priority to the use of colloquial speech and this created conditions in modern Odia literature congenial to the extensive use of everyday diction.

Champu

Kishorchandrananda Champu is one of Baldeba Ratha's innovative poetic experiments. *Champu,* a literary form that used prose alongside verse, was in vogue in Sanskrit literature for a long time. In about tenth century C.E. *Nalachampu* written by Trivikram Bhatta was the first to attain popular acclaim. It was followed by the composition of hundreds of *champus.* Sanskrit *champus* comprise shlokas and between shlokas occur lines of Sanskrit prose. The *champu* form had achieved widespread popularity by Baladeb's time. However, all *champus* were composed in Sanskrit. The novelty of Baladeb's *champus* lies in weaving thirty-four *chaupadis* into a plot. Baladeb got rid of the deficiencies of his earlier efforts by giving it a plot and crafting it in the form of a *kavya* and a Sanskrit *champu.* Like a dexterous jeweller who makes a necklace matching different jewels, Ratha ingeniously combined Odia *chaupadis* with Sanskrit *champus.* *Kishorchandrananda Champu* remains an unparalleled achievement in the history of Odia poetry. Such a work of poetry using a language that blends both Sanskrit and Odia has not been composed since. In Sanskrit texts, especially in plays, there is a long tradition of incorporating *prakrit* dialogues and songs. For instance, Kapileshwardev's Sanskrit play *Parashuram Vijay* also contained an Odia song. But only Baladeb was able to blend Odia with Sanskrit harmoniously. However, just because the example of *Kishorchandrananda Champu* was not imitated later, one could not describe it as an unsuccessful literary experiment. It is a class apart and represents an inimitable and unattainable ideal. It affords pleasure to readers of both Odia and Sanskrit literature.

Wit

One comes across instances of wit in the fifteenth-century poet Sarala Das's *Mahabharata.* However, in medieval Odia literature that followed, the sources of wit and playfulness slowly began to dry up. In the modern age, wit is extensively deployed in plays, novels, and critical essays. In this respect, Baladeb Ratha's poetry anticipated literary modernity, gave it much validation and acted as a messenger to the upcoming generations. For instance, Lalita, the carrier of amorous messages in *Kishorchandrananda Champu,* is the living embodiment of wit. Lalita smartly conveys the idea to the hero and the heroine that they are not attracted to each other in order to intensify their longing. Not only this *champu*, but all his *chaupadis* have been enlivened with his scintillating wit.

Humour

Baladeb Ratha was also brilliantly adept at creating humour, which was conspicuous by its absence in ancient Odia literature. However, Upendra Bhanja provides an example of humour in his *Rasapanchaka* where he introduces various *rasas*:

> When Lakṣmaṇ cut off Suparnakha's nose and ears
> Her blood-splattered face made Sita
> Break into uproarious laughter.

This may seem strange to us today but in the feudal society to which Bhanja belonged, amusement was customarily derived from tormenting others. In aesthetic terms this laughter is perverse and tainted although obscene stories and such crude humour found favour with many. Biswanath Kaviraj in *Sahitya Darpan* states how portrayal of abnormality generates humour: "Bikritākārbāgbeś cheṣṭādeh kutukād bhabet" which means physical deformities, abnormal attire, ridiculous deeds, and risible speech provoke laughter. Baladeb Ratha's humour was unique in this regard as he did not attempt to generate humour by distorting dress or appearance. Unlike his predecessors such as Narasimha Sen, Banshi Das, Krushna Das and Brajanath Barajena, Baladeb never relied on the depiction of these to make readers laugh. Perhaps Baladeb took the view that the description of physical deformity and abnormal attire concerns clowns and buffoons, and lies outside the realm of literature in the true sense of the term. Instead, his emphasis on ridiculous deeds and risible speech indicates his refined literary taste. The source of the stream of wholesome humour which is getting deeper as it flows from Fakir Mohan to Faturananda and beyond is to be found in Baladeb's poetic experiments.

Satire

Satire consists in evoking laughter through exposing an individual, a group or a custom to ridicule. One rarely comes across satire in ancient Odia literature. As a matter of fact, ancient texts prescribing rules for literature did not recognize satire as a literary form. However, in the modern age, satire find unprecedented favour in all branches of literature including drama, poetry and prose. From *Babaji*, considered to be the first Odia play, to almost all the plays performed today, hypocritical abbots, village touts, money-grubbing merchants, dishonest political leaders and other such people have been used as targets of satire. In the same way, satire has made its presence strongly felt in poetic works such as Radhanath Ray's *Darbar* and Fakir Mohan Senapati's *Utkal Bhramanam,* and also in prose texts such as the latter's stories, novels and autobiography. However, this modern literary weapon was rendered much sharper by Baladeb Ratha. In this context, one may cite Mayadhara Mansinha's observation in relation to a satirical poem written by Baladeb: "When he was a young man, the poet was humiliated by some officials in the king's court. To avenge this insult the poet composed a biting satire." However, this fails to recognize the fact that satire was integral to Baladeb's poetic talent and was not a sudden response to accidental circumstances. It may be mentioned here that the poet wrote satires when he was much older and serving in the royal court of Athagarh. One can discover certain traits of modern satire in Baladev's *Hasyakallola* [Waves of Laughter]; its main character, a king, is portrayed as utterly stupid and insensitive, and his courtiers are even more so. If members of the ruling elite are stupid and callous, then how will they mitigate the sorrows of the subjects? Such people have not disappeared from modern society; they continue to oppress people disguised as bureaucrats. His bitter discontent with the feudal order which was latent in his poetry gave energy and direction to modern satire for a long time.

Blank verse

Blank verse is a notable feature of modern poetry ungoverned by metre, and of the poetry bound by metrical schemes which preceded it. It is commonly accepted that in India Michael Madhusudan Dutta employed blank verse for the first time in his Bangla epic *Meghanadvadh Kavya* which provided a model to later poets and inspired them to compose poems in blank verse. Before composing *Meghanadvadh Kavya*, Dutta, who was extremely well versed in western literature, had already used blank verse in his play *Padmavati* and in his long poem *Tilottama Sambhaba*, which were published in 1860. However, *Meghanadvadh Kavya* attained colossal fame on account of its poetic excellence. It is contended that blank verse made its first appearance in the Odia literary scene in Ram Sankar Ray's *Kanchikaveri* (1880). The author claims, "Blank verse was used in Odia earlier; I introduced it in *Kanchikaveri*." However, Madhusudan Rao refuted Ram Sankar Ray's assertion by crediting Radhanath Ray with having introduced blank verse in *Mahayatra*. *Kanchikaveri* being a play and not a poetic work might explain Madhusudhan Rao's claim regarding the introduction of blank verse even though Ram Sankar's work preceded Radhanath's. Furthermore, these two works were preceded by *Angada Vijay* (1879) where Chandranarayan Pattanayak used blank verse. However, one must recognize that Michael Madhusudan Dutta was a source of inspiration to these three writers. But it is Baladeb Ratha who truly pioneered the use of blank verse in Odia literature. Among his two hundred unpublished *chaupadis* collected in a palm-leaf *pothi* titled *Chaupadi Shiromani,* one comes across a *chaupadi* which is written in blank verse. (The *pothi* was discovered in Chikiti in Ganjam. It contains all the *chaupadis* Baladeb composed when he lived in Jalantara, i.e., between 1800 and 1810.) It is quite possible that Baladeb might have found models for composing poetry in Sanskrit literature or the Telugu literary traditions of the neighbouring province. Rhyme is not an essential element in Sanskrit poetry. Similarly, the use of blank verse is not uncommon in Telugu literature which one comes across in its earliest poetic texts. In order for them to be sung, songs depend on tunes, rhythm and beats; poetry, for its part, has to focus upon expression of feelings in order to acquire literary value. Baladeb certainly understood the distinction between songs and poems but while composing a song he carried out a bold experiment with writing in blank verse. Although we do not come across any other instance of Baladeb using blank verse and modern writers accept Michael Madhusudan Dutta as a pioneer in this regard, the credit for introducing blank verse in Odia literature should go to Baladeb. In this context, it should be remembered that Baladeb appeared on the literary scene at least half a century before Dutta did.

Thus, it should be recognized that Baladeb Ratha introduced many novelties in Odia literature such as the use of colloquial language, wit, humour, satire and blank verse. In this respect, he brilliantly anticipated the advent of literary modernity in Odisha, just before a new literary age was about to dawn.

Translation: Ujaan Ghosh and Amrita Chowdhury

Note

1 Sachchidananda Mishra, *Baladeb Ratha: Sahitya Sadhana o Siddhi* [Baladeb Ratha's Achievement as a Writer], Cuttack: Navoday Prakashan, 2005, pp. 124–142.

10 Krushna Charan Behera

Perso-Arabic influence on Odia literature

Introduction

Krushna Charan Behera (1932–2017) was a distinguished scholar, critic, institution-builder and creative writer. Educated at Visva-Bharati and Utkal University, he carried out in-depth research on prose fiction in Odia. He authored about twenty scholarly books exploring various aspects of Odia literature and culture which include the impact of the progressive movement on Odia sensibility, Jagannath in literary imagination, and the question of obscenity. One of his most notable contributions to scholarship consists in his intensive study of forms of popular performing art which resulted from Indo-Persian cultural exchanges during the seventeenth and eighteenth centuries in Odisha. Painstakingly collecting and collating various manuscripts of *Mughal Tamsa*, a multilingual farce which continues to be enacted even today, Krushna Charan brought out an authoritative edition of the play in 1966. The *Odia Gabesana Parisad* [Institute for Odia Studies] founded by Krushna Charan in 1982 is dedicated to advanced research on Odia literature and culture. The institute regularly organises seminars, symposia, conferences to undertake fresh evaluation of authors, texts and issues, and explore neglected areas of Odia literature. It brings out books, monographs, and scholarly editions of rare and out-of-print texts. *Esana*, a journal published by the institute, features research papers by young as well as senior scholars. Krushna Charan is also a noted poet and short story writer and has five volumes of poetry and eleven short story collections to his credit. His major publications include *Pragati Sahitya* [Progressive Literature] (1958), *Ashlilata Sapakshare* [A Defence of Obscenity] (1966), and *Natya Sahitya Parichay* [An Introduction to Drama] (1978). His autobiography titled *Akhira Dekha, Pranara Katha* [Life as I Have Seen it] was published in 2009.

The following discussion on aspects of Indo-Persian cultural exchange in the context of Odisha has been excerpted from Krushna Charan Behera's pioneering work *Odia Sahityare Islami Prabhab* [Perso-Arabic Influence on Odia Literature] (2007). This was originally serialized in *Jhankar* (vol. 25, nos. 11 & 12; vol. 26, nos. 1, 2, 3 & 4) in 1974. Although Odisha was under Afghan and Mughal rule for nearly two centuries, and was a site of

DOI: 10.4324/9781003224778-10

vibrant and multi-faceted Indo-Persian cultural negotiations, few scholars have explored aspects of this enriching transaction. In this context, Krushna Charan's book assumes special significance and deepens our understanding of this important but insufficiently mapped area of study. After sketching the socio-historical milieu, Krushna Charan traces the emergence of new literary forms such as *pala*, *tamsa* and *jatra*. A striking feature of all these genres is the use of a mixed language containing expressions from Odia, Bangla, Persian and Hindi. Krushna Charan shows with critical acuity how *Mughal Tamsa*, in particular, reflects social conditions prevailing in Odisha in the seventeenth and eighteenth centuries, and subjects figures of authority to hilariously scathing ridicule. He convincingly points out how the attempt to establish harmony between two religions led to the rise of a ritual called *Satyapir pala* which has significant literary consequences. As a form of performing art, *jatra* drew its intensity from this multicultural ethos; well into the early twentieth century, *jatra* performances opened with a Muslim dignitary summoning a zamindar to bring him gifts. Krushna Charan gives his account of Indo-Persian culture a whole new dimension through his bold and original suggestion that the obsessive preoccupation with formal devices in Odia poetry in the seventeenth and eighteenth centuries could be explained in terms of the influence of Perso-Arabic literary conventions on Odia writers. He also invites scholars' attention to the strong possibility of Sufi mysticism influencing the works of Vaishnava poets in Odisha.

*

Perso-Arabic Influence on Odia Literature[1]

Krushna Charan Behera

Unlike literatures in many other languages in India, Odia literature was not significantly influenced by Perso-Arabic literary culture. Compared to Hindi and Bangla literatures, the influence of this culture on Odia literature appears rather negligible. Some of the important reasons for this may be mentioned here. Firstly, Odisha was under Afghan and Mughal rule for a relatively shorter period, for about two centuries. Secondly, even during this period, the literary tradition of Odisha had acquired such strength and vitality that the influence of Perso-Arabic culture could not permeate it with ease. Sarala Das, the five saint poets of the sixteenth century, Upendra Bhanja, Dinakrushna Das, Abhimanyu Samantsinghar, and many others had already created a vibrant and popular body of literature in Odia. During this period, Sanskrit also continued to be used as a medium of creative writing and scholarly discourse in Odisha. Before 1568, many *kavyas*, plays, and treatises on aesthetics were written in Sanskrit. Thirdly, many scholars are of the view that a majority of Muslims in Odisha had not embraced Islam through conversion, unlike Muslims in Bengal. Even now, they use a distorted form of Persian and have rarely felt the need for developing a Perso-Odishan literary tradition. Fourthly, during this period the national character of Odias suffered a decline; once a proud and prosperous community, Odias lost their vigour and valour, and withdrew into their domestic world like cowards. At the beginning of the seventeenth century, Purushottam Dev of Khurda, the Gajapati king of Odisha and reverently addressed as the God-king, surrendered before Keshodas, the Rajput *jagirdar* of Odisha appointed by Emperor Jahangir, and offered lakhs of rupees and his daughter and sister as gifts. In the early part of the eighteenth century, the collective psyche of Odias received another terrible blow when Gajapati King Ramachandra Dev II embraced Islam, was rechristened Hafiz Qadir, and married the daughter of Murshid Quli Khan, the *naib-nazim* of Odisha. History tells us that oppressing and looting Odias, and attacking their religion for maximizing revenue collection was the order of the day. Therefore, under such painful circumstances, Odias grew increasingly insular and shunned all forms of external influence. So, it was but natural that they would resist the influence of Perso-Arabic culture.

Yet, enquiries reveal that Odia literature did get influenced in some ways by Perso-Arabic culture. Even today, one comes across more than two thousand Persian, Arabic, Turkish and Urdu words in Odia. Literary texts, absorbing this influence, although their number is not very large, appeared on the cultural landscape. All living literatures depend on reciprocal influences for their growth and survival. Odia literature is no exception to this rule. Such literary exchanges require conducive social conditions; such conditions were not wholly absent in Odisha at the time. Odisha did not remain entirely untouched by the feeling of Hindu-Muslim amity which then defined the prevalent milieu in India. It is also true that religious animosity soured the relationship between the two communities now and then; a temple was built where a mosque stood and a mosque was erected where a temple was. Under the charismatic influence of Sri Sri Rasikanand Dev Goswami, hundreds of Muslims in Banapur embraced Vaishnavism and Ramachandra Dev II was forcibly converted to Islam. But such instances disappeared like passing clouds and did not leave any lasting impact. However, the messages of tolerance, generosity and love preached by prophetic visionaries like Kabir (fifteenth century), Nanak (fifteenth century) and Chaitanya (sixteenth century), who visited Puri, proved profoundly enduring. Qadam-e-Rasool – a mosque built by Sujauddin, the son-in-law of Murshid Quli Khan at Cuttack in 1712 – was a place of worship sacred to both Hindus and Muslims. Gobind Ratha gives the following description of the mosque in his poem "Cuttack Darshan" [A Tour of Cuttack] (1884):

Here at Qadam-e-Rasool
Muslims bow to the Almighty.
Moved to devotion, a few Hindus
Rub their foreheads with its soil.

The temple is visible through the grand entrance.
A charming garden full of trees enhances its beauty.
To this garden Muslims bring their dead
And bury them respectfully.

O Friend, if you stay long enough in Cuttack
You'll witness the colourful *tajia* procession.
This ancient monument, built by the emperor in Delhi
Could have been made by no one else.

Similarly, the sacred burial place of Dhusa, the wrestler of Dhanapala village located on the outskirts of the town of Bhadrak, is a place of worship for both Hindus and Muslims, and at the holy shrine of Bukhari Baba in village Kaipadar in Puri district, devotees from both communities offer prayer together. In Manikgoda village, the Muslim *dalabehera* [headman], dressed as a Brahman, offered worship to the goddess during the Dussehra festival. Although some Hindus like the zamindar family of Rupsa were compelled by circumstances to convert to Islam during the reign of Mughal emperor Aurangzeb, they continued to observe Hindu rites at home. Evidence relating to Hindu-Muslim amity which prevailed in eastern India even during British rule in the nineteenth century is to be found in the writings of Syed Amir Ali. His father, Saadat Ali had relatives in Sambalpur and a house in Cuttack. Saadat Ali settled in Kolkata to give his son a good education. A brilliant and far-sighted intellectual, Syed Amir Ali observes,

> There was then no conflict between Hindus and Muslims. No untoward incident took place when drums were beaten in front of a mosque nor was anyone killed when cows were slaughtered on the occasion of Bakra Eid. At that time Hindus and Muslims had not learnt how to quarrel over elections.[2]

Pala

The worship of Satyapir or Satya Narayan which began in the early part of the eighteenth century in Odisha is an important event. Satyapir worship was introduced in Bengal in the sixteenth century. This was meant to promote amity between Hindus and Muslims. The *Skanda Purana* written in Sanskrit recounts episodes relating to Satya Narayan. This deity is blended with *pir* [a Muslim saint] to create Satyapir.[3] An idea of the pervasive influence and immense popularity of Satyapir worship in Odisha can be gained from the following verses of Baishnab Pani (1887–1956):

> Recite again and again the name of Satya Narayan.
> Realize that he is the supreme being.
> In the Kaliyug, he has assumed the form of Pir to release you
> From from sins and suffering, and to fulfil your wishes.

Fond of eating sirini [sweet dish offered to Satyapir], he imposes his authority,
Lays the wicked low on the earth.
Dressed as a fakir, miracles he performs
And saves you from danger the moment you remember him.

Hindus and Muslims are equal in his eyes.
Your devotion can make him your slave.
Says poet Baishnab, he belongs to one who chants his name.
No one can pay back his favours even in seven births.

Palas are literary narratives recounting stories of observance of vows, and are recited to celebrate and propitiate Satyapir. Kabi Karna of Midnapore is the earliest writer of *palas*. He introduces himself as "a Brahman devotee of Satyapir". He wrote sixteen *palas* in a mixed language in which Bangla, Odia and Urdu expressions co-existed. Many wondrous stories celebrating the miraculous deeds and greatness of Satyapir are woven into these *palas*. Some of these can be found in local legends and folktales, and some others occur in pre-modern Odia *kavyas*. The plot of Kavi Karna's eighth *pala* bears a striking resemblance to Pratap Ray's *kavya Shashisena* (c. late sixteenth and early seventeenth centuries). Outlines of the stories narrated in *Dardhyata Bhakti* [an eighteenth-century collection of lives of famous devotees] resemble those told in the *palas*.[4]

Tamsa

Mughal Tamsa can be regarded as a direct outcome of Perso-Arabic influence on Odia literature. *Tamsa* is a highly popular form of performing art. Every year at the end of the month of Chaitra (March–April), *Mughal Tamsa* is staged in Bhadrak. It is therefore also known as *Chaiti Tamsa*. *Mughal Tamsa* shares striking similarities with Marathi *tamsa* performed in western India. In the last part of the eighteenth century, the poet Banshi Ballabh Goswami wrote a number of *tamsas*. Although Odisha was then under Maratha rule, the Persian language had lost none of its importance and the impact of Perso-Arabic culture was not insignificant. In his *tamsas*, Banshi Ballabh employed Persian, Hindi, Bangla, Odia and some other languages, and portrayed a number of Muslim characters.

Although it is difficult to ascertain the number of *tamsas* Banshi Ballabh authored, manuscripts of seven of his *tamsas* are available. These are: *Bhil Tamsa, Radhakrishna Tamsa, Chauda (Chohada) Tamsa, Jogi Tamsa, Fakir Tamsa, Lolin-Majabai Tamsa* and *Mughal Tamsa*. Of these, *Mughal Tamsa* is extremely popular and continues to be enacted. Given below is a brief summary of the plot of *Mughal Tamsa*.

A *chopdar* [royal attendant] enters the stage announcing the arrival of Mirza sahib. Riding a palanquin and surrounded by his retinue, Mirza sahib arrives. Swaggering imperiously, he goes and seats himself on the throne.

Then he summons his attendants – water-carrier, sweeper, the one who pre-pares hookah, the one who pulls fans, and others – one after another. They come and pray for favours, and go about rendering services. From time to time, Mirza sahib would voice his curiosity about the villages and districts ruled by them, and the people living there. He would then boast before the audience about his elevated position, his servants, his gardens and orchards, and his own vast knowledge and superior wisdom. After this, his highness bestows gifts on minstrels and Sikh saints. A palace servant now rushes in bearing news of the demise of his chief queen; he also informs his majesty that his palace has been auctioned off. Mildly upset, Mirza sahib summons local zamindars and orders them to bring him "provisions" such as girls, goats and mosquito nets. But he is dissatisfied with whatever the zamindars arrange for him and scolds them pouring derision on Odias. A milkmaid is summoned, who brings jugs of milk and curd. Using florid language, an amorous Mirza seeks her favour. The milkmaid vigorously repels his advances by singing a hilarious song.

Mirza sahib is the central character of *Mughal Tamsa*. Banshi Ballabh aims at portraying the way he conducts himself and presents his activities. From this point of view, it may be regarded as a character-centric play. The *tamsa* hilariously delineates Mirza sahib's unrestrained hedonism, his stupid eccentricities, and his complete dependence on his courtiers and attendants.

During Maratha rule, a Muslim called Mirza sahib was the *subedar* [governor] of Odisha between 1752 and 1759. It is very likely that Banshi Ballabh modelled the central character of *Mughal Tamsa* on him.

Chintamani Mohanty (1867–1943), a famous poet who lived in Bhadrak, in his *kavya Salandi* (1911) writes about *Mughal Tamsa*,

> During the time when the Mughals ruled
> In the country, Persian was used widely.
> Writing songs in Persian, he won the hearts
> Of his own people and those of outsiders.
> In the beginning of the month of Mesha [April]
> *Mughal Tamsa* authored by Ballabh gets performed.
> The *tamsa* portrayed the Mughal king's reckless hedonism
> And his tyranny and stupidity.
> The poet presents a vivid picture
> Of the terrible misrule of the king.

In *Mughal Tamsa*, except Mirza Sahib, everyone else is a minor character. All his attendants and employees are addicted to some intoxicant or other. Some of them have fallen prey to women of easy virtue. These attendants tell the audience that they have been living in distress for they have not received their wages or salary. Mirza sahib's dealings with the Odia zamind-ars remind one of the negotiations between Dildar Mian and Ramachandra Mangaraj in Fakir Mohan Senapati's novel *Chha Mana Atha Guntha* [Six

Acres and a Third]. The character of the milkmaid is brilliantly crafted by the playwright. The character conveys powerfully the idea of how women belonging to trading communities of Odisha conducted themselves with dignity and a sense of honour. On the whole, *Mughal Tamsa* provides us with details concerning how our rulers, their cronies and employees, and people belonging to the lower orders of society lived and behaved about two hundred years ago.

Jatra

In eastern India, especially in states like Odisha, Bengal and Assam, there exists a long and rich tradition of *jatra*. Some scholars trace the development of *jatra* as a form of popular performing art in Odisha to the period of Afghan and Mughal rule, and contend that it was enriched by Perso-Arabic influence. Girija Sankar Ray in *Odia Natyakala* [Odia Dramaturgy] (1943) observes that *jatra*, like *pala*, arose as a literary form during Afghan and Mughal rule (p. 27). Harekrushna Mahatab in *Odisha Itihas* (1948) shares Girija Sankar's view saying that *jatras*, which flourished during this period, also carry the imprint of that milieu (p. 423). Regrettably, the text of the earliest Odia *jatras* are not available and there is no way of finding out who wrote *jatras* in Odisha and what kind of *jatras* they wrote. All the well-known writers of *jatras* are younger than Banshi Ballabh Goswami. Krupasindhu Mishra, the author of many Odia *jatras*, was born in Midnapore in 1832. Other acclaimed writers of Odia *jatras* include Jagannath Pani (1836–1897) from Bhadrak, Baishnab Pani (1882–1956) from Kothapada, and Gopal Das (1889–1935) from Kendrapada. A major author of Bangla *jatra* Gopal Chandra Das (also known as Gopal Ude[5]) was born in 1859.

So, Banshi Ballabh's *tamsas* can be regarded as early forms of *jatra*. For two hundred years after him, the persistent presence of Perso-Arabic influence can be noticed in Odia *jatras*. Until the close of the nineteenth century, even in some cases during the first three decades of the twentieth, a fascinating introductory scene was enacted before the performance of a *jatra*. An actor dressed as a Muslim dignitary appears on stage and asks the musicians, "Why are you making a noise here? Who'll be responsible if thieves slip away?" The musicians reply, "We have taken the permission of the chowkidar for this performance." Then the dignitary sends for the chowkidar and demands gifts from him which include a woman and the director of the *jatra*. On the orders of the dignitary, they open the performance by singing a song. However, this convention of introducing a *jatra* has been discontinued.

Poetry dominated by devices of embellishment

During the medieval period, especially during Upendra Bhanja's time, Odia poetry set a high value on embellishments. Many poets of the period paid more attention to the outer beauty of poetry than to its inmost essence. In works like Dinakrushna Das's *Rasakallola*, Upendra Bhanja's *Baidehisa Bilasa*, Abhimanyu Samantsinghar's *Bidagadha Chintamani*, Bhakta Charan Das's *Mathura Mangala*, Jadumani's *Prabandha Purnachandra* which were based on religious and puranic themes, and imaginative compositions such as Arjun Das's *Kalpalata*, Narasingh Sena's *Parimala*, Pratap Ray's *Sashisena*, one finds excessive wordplay, ostentatious display of erudition, and the use of musical rhythms and metrical schemes. Until now, critics have argued that the influence of Sanskrit literature on medieval Odia literature accounts for its obsessive preoccupation with formal devices. While accepting their view, we should also acknowledge the influence of Perso-Arabic poetic conventions in this context. Historians express the view that the lives of Muslim rulers in India were dominated by a hedonistic pursuit of pleasure. They also looked upon art and literature as sources of this pleasure. Towards the end of the sixteenth century, under the influence of Muslim courts, in Odisha too, literature came to be regarded as a means of savouring and enjoying life. In the courts of kingdoms such as Khurda, Ghumusar, Nayagarh, Sonepur, Paralakhemundi, Kendujhar, Mayurbhanj and Bamanda, literature was created and appreciated from this point of view. Thus, the unbridled use of formal devices became indispensable in Odia poetry. A literature that is defined in terms of poetic embellishments expresses an intense love of luxury and pleasure. It is worth noting here that Sarala Das did not prioritize the employment of formal devices although he was deeply versed in Sanskrit. The same is true of the *Panchasakhas* [five saint-poets of the sixteenth century] who were also erudite Sanskrit scholars. A possible explanation for this may be found in the fact that during the period in which they wrote, the influence of Perso-Arabic conventions on Odia literature had not been felt strongly. It may be that under this influence Odia literature became more form-centric towards the end of the sixteenth century. So, it is difficult to accept the view that the partiality for formal devices in Odia poetry can be explained entirely in terms of the influence of Sanskrit literature.

The poetry of the Perso-Arabic world foregrounds formal devices such as the artful composition of words, musicality, and sophisticated employment of similes and metaphors. It cannot be denied that Perso-Arabic influence entered the world of Odia poetry indirectly through Hindi. One may also try to discern the influence of Sufi mysticism on medieval Vaishnava Odia literature. The way poets such as Dinakrushna, Abhimanyu, Bhakta Charan, Gopal Krushna Patnaik established a harmony between physical love and the love that transcends the body, and surrendered themselves to the ecstasy of adoring God distinctly echoes the tenets of Sufi mysticism. This influence too must have permeated the poetry of Vaishnava authors through contact with Bangla and Hindi literatures.

Translation: Sangram Jena

Notes

1 Krushna Charan Behera, *Odia Sahityare Islami Prabhab* [Perso-Arabic Influence on Odia Literature], Cuttack: Srikantakumar Routray, 2007.
2 Makhanlal Raychaudhuri, *Banglar Manishi*, Kolkata, 1947, p. 68.
3 Detailed accounts of the influence of Satyapir worship and the rituals associated with it are given in *Purnachandra Odia Bhashakosha*, vol. IV (1934), pp. 4802–4803, and Kunja Bihari Das's *Odia Loka Gita o Kahani* [Odia Folk Songs and Tales] (1958), pp. 89–102.
4 Kunja Bihari Das, *Odia Loka Gita o Kahani* [Odia Folk Songs and Tales], Visva-Bharati: Santiniketan, 1958, p. 107.
5 Ude was a pejorative term used by Bengalis to refer to Odias.

11 Fakir Mohan Senapati

Michael Madhusudan Dutta and his *Meghanadvadh Kavya*

Introduction

Fakir Mohan Senapati (1843–1918) is widely acclaimed as one of the chief architects of modern Odia literature. He played a key role in shaping a new cultural sensibility in Odisha through his historic contributions to education, journalism, translation, poetry and prose. The initiatives he took in the field of journalism, which included setting up a printing press and bringing out a newspaper, and the textbooks he wrote on history, mathematics and grammar for schoolchildren, were part of a larger language movement which aimed at protecting Odia when it faced a crisis of survival. His translations of epics such as *Ramayana* (1884–1895) and *Mahabharata* (four *parvas* were published between 1887 and 1905) and other Sanskrit texts helped him acquire an in-depth understanding of ancient Indian traditions and hone his linguistic skills. In his famous poetic works such as *Utkal Bhramanam* [A Tour through Utkal] (1892) and "Hata Bahuda" [Upon Returning from the Marketplace] (1908) he subtly engages with the emerging new realities using a wryly satiric tone. In the latter, for instance, he vividly dramatizes the displacement of the traditional knowledge system by a western one sponsored by the colonial world, which he astutely likens to a bustling marketplace. However, Fakir Mohan's supreme achievement as a writer is to be located in his prose fiction where he inaugurated the tradition of social realism, crafted convincing and memorable characters, and employed the idiom of everyday life as the medium of literary expression. An irrepressibly subversive sense of humour leavens his prose and renders it delightfully unforgettable. His autobiography *Atma-jivan Charit* (1927) has attained the status of a classic.

In this essay, which appeared in the March 1905 issue of *Utkal Sahitya*, Fakir Mohan undertakes a pungent reassessment of the iconic Bangla epic *Meghanadvadh Kavya* (1861) written by Michael Madhusudan Dutta (1824–73). Fakir Mohan's response to *Meghanadvadh Kavya* reflects his abiding interest in epic as a literary form. It may be recalled here that he devoted a substantial part of his career to translating into Odia *Ramayana* and *Mahabharata*. This enabled him to carry out a sustained comparison

DOI: 10.4324/9781003224778-11

between Valmiki's epic and Michael Madhusudan's *kavya*, especially in the domain of characterization; this essay, therefore, constitutes an early attempt at adopting a comparative critical approach. Another point worth mentioning here is that the impressive achievement of modern Bangla literature was an inescapable reference point for Odia writers and critics in the late nineteenth and early twentieth centuries. Moreover, as a pioneer in the field of realistic prose fiction, Fakir Mohan felt inclined to analyse *Meghanadvadh Kavya* in the light of emerging conventions governing realistic prose narratives, especially that of plausibility. At the same time, he evaluated the *kavya* employing *rasa* theory. His irreverent humour enlivens the essay. Fakir Mohan focused upon the following deficiencies of *Meghanadvadh Kavya*. Michael Madhusudan's portrayal of major characters of the epic such as Pramila, Sita, Hanuman received Fakir Mohan's harsh censure; he found them unconvincing and sometimes utterly ridiculous. The language of *Meghanadvadh Kavya* Fakir Mohan found unpleasantly masculine. He criticized Michael Madhusudan's depiction of heaven and hell for it conveyed, in his view, Christian ideas of the world beyond death. He took Michael Madhusudan to task most severely for his failure to create ideal characters worthy of emulation. He looked upon Valmiki's *Ramayana* as primarily a Hindu religious text and therefore mounted a trenchant attack on Michael Madhusudan's attempt to rewrite it as a purely literary epic. Fakir Mohan expressed the view that most readers were not yet ready to distinguish between sacred and literary texts. It may be mentioned here that Fakir Mohan's provocative reassessment of the celebrated Bangla *kavya* drew an impassioned and detailed rebuttal from Dhirendra Nath Chaudhury which was published in the April 1905 issue of *Utkal Sahitya*. It may be noted here that before professional/academic critics appeared on the scene, major creative writers contributed to shaping critical discourse in Odisha.

*

Michael Madhusudan Dutta and his *Meghanadvadh Kavya*[1]

Fakir Mohan Senapati

Michael Madhusudan Dutta (1824–73) wrote many *kavyas* in Bangla and *Meghanadvadh Kavya* is the chief among them. His reputation as a poet rests primarily on this *kavya*. Many educated Bengalis celebrate it as a *mahakavya* or great epic. To them it contains many defining features of an epic. The subject matter of the epic is not i.e., not a product of the poet's imagination, but can be seen as a grafted branch from the huge spreading tree of Valmiki's *Ramayana*. Valmiki's world-famous epic shines like the radiant sun in the sky of literature. Planets circling it include *Uttararamacharita*, *Anargharaghava*, *Mahanataka*, *Bhojachampu*, etc. Although they are illuminated by the sun, these planets emit their own radiance in the firmament. We now have to decide what place can be assigned to *Meghanadvadh Kavya* among these celestial bodies.

Renowned Bengali scholars have elevated him to the highest position in the pantheon of poets. No one dares deny that Dutta was a polyglot possessing extraordinary talent. So, it would be audacious on the part of a man of little learning like me to comment on his *kavya*. Yet, distorted representations of an epic which we worship as holy scripture, which depicts incidents we regard as absolutely true, and which portrays images that have been indelibly etched in the heart of every Hindu, would deeply hurt our sentiments. So, we will be entirely within our rights to voice an opinion on *Meghanadvadh Kavya*. Errors and omissions are but expected of someone as insignificant as the writer of this essay; I would be grateful if someone points them out.

It may be in order here to discuss some aspects of the *kavya* before commenting on it.

Meghanad: He is the protagonist of the *kavya*. Meghanad is endowed with all the qualities that aestheticians consider desirable in the central character of a *kavya*. But in our view, while Meghanad may have conquered Lord Indra and be a mighty warrior, he lacks cardinal moral virtues. He never tried to reason with his father, a mature person of vast experience and who is celebrated in the three worlds, when he abducted the chaste wife of a wanderer in the forest and kept her in confinement. On the contrary, he heartily supported his sinning father. The poet spares no effort to present Meghanad as a noble figure but fails in projecting him as an ideal person.

Pramila: She is Meghanad's wife and thus qualifies as the heroine of the epic. Valmiki describes her as the daughter-in-law of a royal family and specifies the inner wing of the palace as her proper place of residence. The splendid portrayal of Pramila in *Meghanadvadh Kavya* provides an example of the richness and power of Michael Madhusudan's imagination. It seems as if the poet paints her using all the colours in his palette. The *kavya* owes much of its grandeur to the presence of Pramila in it; in fact, she proves more essential to the architecture of the narrative than Queen Mandodari, Ravana's consort. One comes across Pramila in the very first canto of the *kavya*. When Meghanad prepares to set out for the battlefield, Pramila clasps him to her bosom and wails, "How would this slave of yours survive in your absence?" It seems as if she has doubts about his manly valour and is apprehensive that he may not return alive. To have fears about a dear one's safety on the battlefield is natural on anyone's part; however, coming as it does from the wife of a warrior, who defeated Lord Indra, such fears appear strangely out of place.

Let us now see how her actions are depicted in the third canto. The return of Meghanad from the battlefield is delayed, and she is incoherent with fear and cries inconsolably. Her friend Vasanti takes her into the garden to solace her. After picking flowers and weaving garlands, Pramila breaks down again and indulges in another bout of weeping. But suddenly she is filled with boundless energy and is ready to give battle to Sriramachandra. Led by her, a multitude of demonesses armed to the teeth swarm out of the palace. She, King Ravana's daughter-in-law, lets out an ear-splitting battle-cry. Her cry is so terrifying that all creatures – the king, the palace women, birds, lions and elephants in the forest, aquatic animals – tremble in fear. Accompanied by her army, Pramila enters Srirama's camp. There she sends Nrimundamalini as an emissary to Rama with the message that he could choose between combat and truce. Her dreadful appearance scares the monkey-warriors. At the sight of the bow Nrimundamalini carries, Rama muses, "I have broken the bow of Lord Shiva but I cannot even string this bow." So, overwhelmed with fear, he lets her through. Then Pramila is reunited with her husband. Dear readers, you may note here that the army of demonesses gets ready for combat in a trice as if they were all trained experts in the art of war. This brings to one's mind *nidarshana bhava* [an impossible connection of things in this context]. If someone deserves praise for the employment of this figure of speech the poet should receive it in ample measure.

In the ninth canto, Pramila, like a Hindu wife, chooses to give up her life when Meghanad is slain and ascends his funeral pyre. This custom is unheard of among the rakshasas. Thus, one notices some incongruities in the portrayal of Pramila. There are times when Pramila is faint-hearted like a housewife and at others, she displays violent belligerence and shamelessly strides into the camp of the enemy at night. One might consider another incongruity here. Given the topography of Lanka presented by Valmiki as well as Michael Madhusudan, it is difficult to imagine Pramila getting anywhere near Rama's camp. It seems as if the poet, in order to highlight Pramila's martial prowess, ignores all considerations of plausibility relating to time and place bent upon as he is to bring her anyhow near the enemy camp. Moreover, Pramila is ready to engage in a battle against the enemy in the dead of night; the battle-cries make the earth quiver but it appears strange that neither Ravana nor Meghnad get any wind of it and even the palace guards are utterly oblivious of what is going on. What is even funnier is that Meghanad fails to recognize his wife when she approaches him carrying arms. What a shining example of conjugal love!

Srirama and Lakshman: Hindus believe that Lord Vishnu assumed the avatar of Rama in order to lighten the burden oppressing the earth. Valmiki portrays Rama as Vishnu's incarnation. But in *Meghanadvadh Kavya* he is delineated as no more than an ordinary human being. Here, he quails at the sight of a bow held by a mere female menial of Pramila. This is a glowing instance of Rama's dauntless courage! Unable to vanquish Meghanad in face-to-face combat, the truthful Rama, the fair-minded Bibhisana, and the dutiful Lakshman have no scruples about slaying an unarmed Meghanad. We have come across hundreds of instances of Lakshman's incredible martial prowess and moral steadfastness. But the same Lakshman steals into someone else's house like a thief in the night. Look at the heroic combat that ensues; an unarmed Meghanad hurls metal pots used for worship at Lakshman which renders him unconscious and he crashes to the ground below. Meghanad is not killed by Lakshman for there is barely any fight; it is Mayadevi who kills him and Lakshman is merely her instrument.

The sight of his nephew getting killed reduces Bibhisan to tears and Lakshman also follows suit. Rama keeps anxiously waiting for news of the battle. Should not one expect someone to return to the camp post haste and convey the news of his momentous victory? How awkward it is to see Lakshman cry at a moment like this?

Deep darkness throws effulgence into sharp relief. Valmiki lets Rama's divinity shine through by contrasting it with the diabolical qualities of Ravana, an implacable enemy of gods and humans. But Michael Madhusudan diminishes the divine and diabolical dimensions of both Rama and Ravana respectively and tries to place them on a footing of equality.

Hanuman: The term *Mahavir* [mighty warrior] is applied to Hanuman as a proverbial epithet. To him are attributed astounding feats such as leaping across the ocean and burning down Lanka single-handed. Now consider his "heroic" deeds in Michael Madhusudan's *kavya*. The bow in the hands of Nrimundamalini makes him shiver with dread. Ravana chases Lakshman to slay him; he shoots an arrow at Hanuman who blocks his way. The arrow may or may not have struck him but Hanuman turns tail and runs away with his father's name on his lips. While Rama's army cannot boast of a single intrepid warrior, among the rakshasas one finds many who are well-versed in the *Vedas*.

Sita: Valmiki's Sita, the daughter of King Janak, the embodiment of Goddess Lakshmi and the incarnation of chastity, is unequalled as an epic character. All the ideal women characters created by authors of *puranas* and *kavyas* have more or less been modelled on Valmiki's Sita. Every Hindu desires to have a daughter and daughter-in-law like Sita.

I would like to say a few things about Valmki's account of the time Sita spent as Ravana's prisoner in the garden of *ashok* trees because *Meghanadvadh Kavya* includes a description of only this phase of Sita's life. Sita in Valmiki's epic has no one to share her grief with and is surrounded by dreadful she-demons. Rama pervades her heart and his name is constantly on her lips. Ravana, who strikes terror in gods and humans, humbly stands before her and offers her the wealth of all the three worlds; Sita remains stonily unresponsive to his entreaties. The she-demons make hideous faces and threaten to devour her but nothing shakes or frightens Sita. Valmiki beautifully demonstrates the infinite power of pious virtue. In Sarama alone, among the she-demons, Sita finds a well-wisher who can offer her comforting words only occasionally. Now compare this with the portrait of Sita painted by Michael Madhusudan. Sita leads the life of a prisoner in a garden of *ashok* trees. In Sarama she finds a compassionate confidante. Her misery flows chiefly from her being confined in an alien place. She is unhappy because she has been deprived of the congenial company of the wives of hermits in the forest of Panchabati on the banks of the Godavari. She sorely misses playing with forest does and humming bumblebees, and joyfully wandering around, singing. Moreover, the poet endows Sita with immense patience and ample leisure, which enable her to recount five cantos of the *Ramayana* to Sarama. The poet displays remarkable ingenuity in enlarging the body of the *kavya* through this device. It is obvious here that he has misrepresented the basic essence of Sita's character. The three forest settings – *ashok* garden, the forest of Panchavati and Valmiki's hermitage – are ideal sites for manifesting Sita's glory in Valmiki's epic. Valmiki's hermitage finds no mention at all in *Meghanadvadh Kavya* and we have already described how Sita conducts herself in the other two settings. Valmiki's Sita provides an inspiring model which every Hindu woman seeks to emulate. A luminous image of Sita resides in the heart of even those who have never read Valmiki's epic. It is unfortunate that Michael Madhusudan has created such a misleading portrait of Sita.

Up to this point, we have focused on the portrayal of a few leading characters in the *kavya*. But character portrayal is just one component in the architecture of an epic; language forms its body, emotions breathe life into it and rhetorical figures embellish it. Let us now discuss in brief the above.

Language: Bangla is naturally simple and mellifluous like the women of Bengal. However, it seems the author of *Meghanadvadh Kavya* has rendered it somewhat convoluted and given it a harsh and masculine texture. It is patently obvious that the poet endows it with the luminescence of a fearless Rajput woman.

Rhetorical devices: Michael Madhusudan richly decks out the *kavya* with splendid, enchanting and exquisitely crafted rhetorical devices gleaned from foreign as well as native sources. At the same time, we cannot help observing that the *kavya* walks unsteadily under the crushing weight of the rhetorical devices.

It is time we touched upon yet another aspect of the *kavya*. The war between Rama and Ravana takes place in the Treta Yuga; the Kauravas and Pandavas fought the *Mahabharata* war in the succeeding era. Yet we find characters like Srikrishna, Arjuna, Kichaka, Brihannala and Hidimba in *Meghanadvadh Kavya*.

In the seventh canto of the *kavya*, the episode of the disruption of Shiva's meditation in *Kumarasambhava* is distortedly re-enacted. He gets Mahadev to do things that even a human being will shrink from. Goddesses such as Parvati, Indira and Indrani are presented as petty intriguers. Kartikeya, the commander of the celestial army, is but a tender-limbed infant. Devotees attribute noble qualities to the gods and goddesses they worship or they seek to emulate their heavenly virtues. Has the poet not given enough scope to foreigners to get the impression that the deities Hindus worship are outrageously revolting?

The description of heaven and hell in *Meghanadvadh Kavya* lacks originality. It is also largely unnecessary, for readers are already familiar with portrayals of heaven and hell in Hindu epics and *puranas*. There is nothing new about Michael Madhusudan's description of heaven and hell. However, one discovers in it hints of the infinity and eternity associated with Christian ideas of heaven and hell. Hindus believe that heaven and hell belong to two utterly different spheres. In *Meghanadvadh Kavya*, Yamapuri [the dominion of death] neatly divides into two departments of judicial administration: *dewani* [civil] and *fauzdari* [criminal]. This division is reflected in Michael Madhusudan's representation of heaven and hell.

Struck by Ravana's powerful weapon, Lakshman lies unconscious and thus Rama has to journey to the dominion of death to meet Dasharath and learn from him the way of reviving his younger brother. Oddly enough, he does not go straight to Dasharath; on his way to heaven he visits every nook and corner of hell and collects details about what punishment has been meted out to the sinners. Heaven is populated by all the noble figures of the earth; he makes a point of exchanging pleasantries with them. As for Lakshman, arrangements have to be made to bring him back to his senses before the night comes to an end. But Rama keeps himself busy touring heaven and hell.

Let us consider the episode in which Lakshman is hit by a lethal weapon. Ravana rushes at Lakshman to avenge his son's death and Rama intercepts him. Ravana tells him, "O, the consort of Sita! I would like to let you live for one more day. Your life, I will take tomorrow. Today I am bent on killing your barbaric younger brother." On hearing this, Rama quietly makes his way to his camp to rest for the day. This should count as a magnificent display of brotherly love!

It would be surprising indeed if, in spite of the points made above, someone wishes to accord *Meghanadvadh* the status of a national *kavya* or an epic.

Another question suggests itself here: why should the reader take the trouble of going through *Meghanadvadh Kavya*? Reading this *kavya* affords great pleasure and allows one to spend time without doing anything wrong. However, pleasure can also be derived from playing a game of dice or strolling in a garden. In this *kavya*, the poet depicts with uncommon effectiveness aesthetic emotions such as terror, anger, sorrow and courage. In this respect, he is unsurpassed by any other Bengali poet. There is no doubt that readers would experience fear, wonder and thrill while reading the text. In the light of this, one would not hesitate to accept *Meghanadvadh Kavya* as an epic and Michael Madhusudan Dutta as a great poet. But the reader expects more than mere delight while reading a *kavya*; to them, what matters more is receiving moral instruction. *Kavyas* serve as teachers and advisors to people. Portraits of ideal characters in *kavyas* provide readers with inspiring role models. Can one single out a character featuring in *Meghanadvadh Kavya* who is worthy of emulation? What scene from the *kavya* will rise before us when we experience sorrow or joy, prosperity or adversity? Is there anything in the text that provides us with companionship in a moment of crisis? Does any scene depicted in it have the power to instil in us feelings of noble generosity or stir and awaken our conscience? In other words, does it convey any instructive message which would strengthen the moral bonds that sustain social life? Or does it have the power to make us feel the existence of the all-pervading and infinite *brahma*? If the answer to all these questions is a "no", why should we read a distorted version of our sacred epic? Let the ideas that the Hindus have formed of Valmiki's epic remain unchanged forever; even if the ideas are wrong, they still remain desirable. When we read Valmiki's epic, the events featured in it come vividly alive before us and the images remain etched indelibly in our hearts. The mind continues to dwell on the events long after the reading comes to an end. The characters embodying the highest ideals of a community are portrayed in a *kavya;* they, in turn, contribute to the process of building the character of a nation.

It will take some time before an ordinary Hindu learns to distinguish between a religious text and a literary one. We are not speaking here of western-educated Hindus; in any case, they constitute a minority. To a Hindu, *Ramayana* is both a literary work and a religious book. Even the life of a Hindu who has not gone through the epic is shaped by the moral principles embodied in it such as reverence for one's father, parental affection, brotherly love and a wife's devotion to her husband. A Hindu desires to have a son like Ramachandra. He blesses his daughter and daughter-in-law saying, "Be chaste like Sita". Man's true strength lies in his pious virtues and performing his duties. Everywhere in *Ramayana* is this principle magnificently exemplified. Take the *Ramayana* out of the Hindu world, it will be emptied of all qualities that make it Hindu.

The *Vedas,* the *Ramayana* and the *Mahabharata* are the only possessions that Hindus can be truly proud of. Political turmoil and tyranny have robbed Hindus of everything. But the tower of Hindu glory soars high above all these disasters and remains undamaged. The firm foundation of this tower lies in the heart of every Hindu; the summit of this tower reaches celestial worlds; the glitter of gems studded in its walls gets reflected in every drop of a Hindu's blood. It is therefore to be expected that Hindu sentiments will be hurt if its holy temple and the hallowed images installed in it are presented in a distorted way. This made me reflect upon the *Meghanadvadh Kavya* and express certain opinions about it.

Translation: Jatindra Kumar Nayak and Animesh Mohapatra

Note

1 Fakir Mohan Senapati, "Kavi Michael Madhusudan Dutta evam *Meghanadvadh Kavya*" [Michael Madhusudan Dutta and his *Meghanadvadh Kavya*], *Utkal Sahitya*, vol. 8, no. 12, Cuttack, 1905, pp. 365–371.

12 Debendra Dash

System of patronage and attribution of authorship in colonial Odisha: the case of Gangadhar Meher

Introduction

Debendra Dash (b. 1954) established his reputation as a scholar and critic by undertaking an intensive study of Odia literature written in the nineteenth and early twentieth centuries. His critical method is distinguished by extensive archival research and analytical rigour. The collected works of iconic authors he meticulously edited such as *Radhanath Granthabali* (with Prasanna Kumar Mishra) and *Fakir Mohan Granthabali* (in four volumes, of which the first was prepared in collaboration with Krushna Charan Behera) bear evidence of his close attention to detail, and painstaking sifting of facts from legends and hearsay. He has been actively engaged in the retrieval of out-of-print but significant texts from neglect and oblivion. Notable among such initiatives is the publication of the unexpurgated version of Fakir Mohan Senapati's *Atmacharita* (2016). Two other important initiatives in this regard include the collected works of Ramakrushna Sahu (1861–1918) and Madanamohana Pattanayak (1890–1967). The extended scholarly introductions he included in his edited texts offer objective, unsentimental and insightful perspectives on authors, and the milieu from which they drew their vitality. He has written several essays which examine literature in the light of eastern and western aesthetic theories. He stands apart from the confines of his discipline, and takes a lively interest in issues relating to history, politics, society and culture, which helps him build a richly interdisciplinary perspective on literature. This informs the books he wrote and edited on thinker-statesmen like Madhusudan Das, M.K. Gandhi and Gopabandhu Das. His *Utkal Sammilani, 1903–1936* (2005), which comprises the proceedings of Utkal Union Conference and includes an exhaustive introduction, is a valuable contribution to historical research. He has also co-edited an encyclopaedia of Odia literature, *Sahityakosha* (Sambad–Aama Odisha, 2018). His major works include *Gotie Phula Phutibara Kahani* [Story of the Blossoming of a Flower] (1992) and *Gangadhar: Kabita o Kabi Atma* [Gangadhar Meher: The Soul of a Poet] (1995).

The present essay, selected from his above-mentioned book on Gangadhar Meher (1862–1924), examines the conditions of production of literary texts

DOI: 10.4324/9781003224778-12

in nineteenth-century Odisha. In pre-colonial Odisha, writers and artists for their survival had no option but to depend on financial support of wealthy and powerful patrons such as kings and zamindars. In return for such favour, many of them took recourse to the practice of *bhanati*, the attribution of the authorship of their own compositions to the patron. This practice was prevalent in the southern part of Odisha which had come under the heavy influence of literary conventions of Telugu-speaking areas. Debendra Dash gives here the illustrative instance of Baladeb Ratha (1779–1840) who attributed the authorship of some of his poems to his royal patrons. He goes on to show how the system of patronage underwent significant transformation under the impact of economic and administrative policies introduced during colonial rule, emergence of an upstart middle class, and the advent of print culture. He places Gangadhar's attribution of some of his works to his patron Nruparaj Singh, the zamindar of Barapali, against this background and demonstrates how the poet's relationship with the evolving system of patronage under colonial rule was a shifting and conflicted one. Debendra Dash convincingly argues that a misunderstanding of this relationship and an overemphasis on the poet's poverty has resulted in a grossly distorted assessment of Gangadhar's extraordinary literary achievement. The essay derives its significance from the way it illuminates the integral link between a literary text and the matrix in which the text and its author are embedded.

*

System of patronage and attribution of authorship in colonial Odisha: the case of Gangadhar Meher[1]

Debendra Dash

I

Nandakishore Bal (1875–1928), known as *pallikabi* [poet celebrating villages], wrote a poem titled "*Indumati* Kavya Praneta Shri Gangadhar Mehernka Prati" [To Gangadhar Meher (1862–1924), the Author of *Indumati*]. The poem was published in the magazine *Prajabandhu* in 1903–4. Here, one Odia poet pays a glowing tribute to another poet who is his contemporary. This famous poem of Nandakishore was later appended to the second edition of *Indumati*. It has contributed significantly to the formation of a certain idea of Gangadhar, the poet and the person, in the minds of readers. However, not many readers and critics seem to have understood the poem fully. No one has really explained the significance of the closing couplet – "However hard one may try, one can never conceal the flames of a burning fire / Could the identity of Baladeb Ratha, the composer of *champus*, remain concealed?"– in Gangadhar's life or poetry. Thanks to a partial understanding of the poem, several myths concerning not only Gangadhar but also Baladeb have gained currency.

Nandakishore's poem comprises four parts. He makes it clear at the outset that he was introduced to Gangadhar's poetry through *Indumati*. It is likely that he had not read the other poems, long and short, by Gangadhar published before *Indumati*. On the basis of this single poetic work, Nandakishore elevates Gangadhar to the pantheon of great writers and places him alongside Kalidasa. Nandakishore's views relating to Gangadhar's personal life are based mainly on hearsay. The accounts he heard concerning Gangadhar's life full of deprivation and extreme misery from his contemporaries aroused Nandakishore's sympathy for the poet. To Nandakishore, poverty can never destroy the truly gifted. The obstacles facing a poet actually serve as a test of his talent. The kings and zamindars who exploited Gangadhar would ultimately share the fate of even beggars and disappear from the face of the earth; however, a poet never sinks into oblivion. The genius of a poet can never be smothered by the ash heaps of adversity. A poet does not perish even when his poetry is published under someone else's name. In the fullness of time, the very same poems bring the poet to public attention as their real author. Baladeb Ratha's (1779–1840) *Champu*, in accordance with the prevailing custom of *bhanati*, was attributed to the king of Athagada. As time passed, however, the king's name was overlaid in public memory by the name of its real author. Likewise, Gangadhar's poems published under the names of his patrons must one day be recognized as his own creations. Nandakishore urged Gangadhar to compose excellent *kavyas* like *Indumati* taking no notice of the dire deprivation that accompanied his poetic genius.

At one point in time, *Indumati* was the most widely circulated work of Gangadhar. After Nandakishore's poem was appended to the second and successive editions of *Indumati*, Gangadhar's "poverty" receive considerable publicity. Some of Radhanath Ray's (1848–1908) remarks and Gangadhar's self-effacing expressions reinforced his image as a poor man. In his foreword to Gangadhar's *kavya Kichaka Badha*, Radhanath wrote,

> It is Gangadhar's misfortune that he is born in Odisha. In the world of imagination he has Vyasa and Valmiki, the high priests of sublime natural beauty, for his close companions. Alas, to earn his livelihood, he has to engage in the menial task of record-keeping.

Radhanath's comment finds a strong echo in Gangadhar's own statement: "The pond of my life is choked with the mire of poverty" (*Tapaswini*).

Like accounts of Gangadhar's life, those relating to Baladeb's (popularly known as Kabisurya or the Sun among poets) were also replete with legends and hearsay; they have been dispelled by the meticulous research and objective analysis carried out by the eminent critic Sachchidananda Mishra. Earlier accounts suggested that Baladeb's poetic achievement could be explained in terms of persistent poverty, divine grace and royal patronage. It is true that Baladeb was employed by many feudatory chiefs and kings, but not as a court poet but as an administrator. But poets like Radhanath blithely assume that benevolent royal patronage enabled Baladeb to lead a comfortable and carefree life as a court poet. Hence, he has been the target of Radhanath's envy in *Chilika:*

Fortunate are the children of goddess Saraswati
The great poets, Baladeb, and Upendra Bhanja.

As the inflated legends have it, Baladeb, driven by financial compulsions, attributed the authorship of many of his poems to his patrons in the hope of receiving royal favours. *Kishorchandrananda Champu*, his most celebrated work, is an illustrative example of this. Though he attained some affluence later in life, he had to pay a heavy price for it. Two key points emerge from these popular accounts: (a) his appeal for royal patronage to find relief from poverty; and (b) the attribution of authorship to feudatory chiefs. Countering the above claims, Sachchidananda writes,

Baladeb Ratha did not make a living by writing poetry; he supported himself by relying on other sources of income. Of course, he could have led a trouble-free life holding the position of a court poet but he chose to serve the states Athagada and Jalantara as manager/dewan instead and led a reasonably affluent life. He even served a stint as the tutor of the eccentric prince of Paralakhemundi. Baladeb also possessed qualities of an able administrator. These were recognized by the British East Indian Company, which had little or nothing to do with literature, and it appointed him as the manager of the feudatory state of Mahuri. Many other dewans of Baladeb's time, who had no interest in literature, were entitled to considerable prestige and financial benefits. And so was Baladeb.[2]

But Radhanath and Nandakishore firmly believed that Baladeb attributed the authorship of his poems to his patrons in order to fulfil his personal needs. Nandakishore superimposed this conventional account of Baladeb's life on Gangadhar in the poem cited above. He was convinced that, owing to his poverty, Gangadhar too, like Baladeb, attributed some of his works to his benefactors. In subsequent discussions of Gangadhar's life and work (other than the one written by Gobind Chandra Udgata), his poverty, and not the question of attribution of authorship to his patrons, is highlighted. In consequence, Nandakishore's paean to Gangadhar led to critics in our time approaching the poetry of Gangadhar, who was a modern poet endowed with a modern sensibility, through obsolete attitudes and critical tools.

II

Gangadhar immortalized the zamindar of Barapali, Lal Nruparaj Singhdeo. Nruparaj achieved memorability through his association with the poet. Gangadhar, for his part, authored a biography of the zamindar,[3] which was published in 1905. In this the poet threw light on various facets of the zamindar's personality, his literary achievements and his love for literature. Gangadhar writes,

> Even though Nruparaj Singh failed to obtain any higher academic degree, his penchant for Odia literature has earned him an elevated place in the world of letters. His two texts *Balaram Dev* and 'Amod' [Delight] have enabled him to adorn a special throne there. Besides, the prestigious literary periodical *Utkal Sahitya* has published quite a few of his poems. The prizes and awards he has given to writers have always encouraged and inspired them. The royal favours he bestowed upon Nilamani Bidyaratna, the editor of the newspaper *Sambalpur Hitesini* and the author of several books, and this writer, bear testimony to his generosity and appreciation of literary talent.[4]

As Gangadhar composed this biography while on official leave, we suspect that this biography was written at the behest of the zamindar.

Gangadhar simply mentions the two long poems authored by Nruparaj and does not provide any details regarding his short poems. Moreover, no information on the prizes Gangadhar received from Nruparaj is furnished. As his benefactor, Nruparaj Singh is painted in this biography in glowing terms. It may be viewed as a document proclaiming Gangadhar's loyalty to his master. However, Gangadhar has not distorted facts to impress his benefactor, and thus, there is a vague generality about the quality of his literary outputs.

Gangadhar himself never claimed the authorship of the works published under Nruparaj's name and whenever someone presented him as their author his response was ambiguous. But his contemporaries were absolutely sure that Gangadhar was their real author. Gangadhar had sent *Balaram Dev* to Radhanath for revision and his comments. In a letter dated 18 March 1895, Radhanath writes, "I am glad to read the poem composed by the King of Barapali. The description of Goddess Samalai demonstrates his impressive creative power. I noticed many similarities between your poetry and this work."[5] Gangadhar's answer to this is not available. But Radhanath, for his part, is convinced that the author of *Balaram Dev* is none other than Gangadhar himself. His letter dated 27 March 1895 makes this abundantly clear: "Things became clear as soon as I went through the text. I shall be happy if such a great sacrifice is duly acknowledged."[6] Similarly, after reading the poem "Amod" in *Utkal Sahitya*, Radhanath wrote to Gangadhar, "A few days back I fondly recalled you while reading a poem in *Utkal Sahitya* on Rama and Sita's trip to the forest. And I thought of writing to you to convey my joyous excitement about the same."[7] Apart from Radhanath, Nilamani Bidyaratna and Biswanath Kar, editor of *Utkal Sahitya*, also knew who the real author of *Balaram Dev* and "Amod" was. Nilamani was well acquainted with both Gangadhar and Nruparaj. He is silent about the literary achievements of Nruparaj while writing about him or reporting news concerning Barapali estate in *Sambalpur Hiteisini*. The newspaper published a long eulogy on Nruparaj not long after the publication of *Balaram Dev*.[8] However, the eulogy does not contain any mention of the poem. In that piece, Nruparaj is described as a lover of literature, and an astute judge and promoter of talent. Moreover, Biswanath exchanged letters with Gangadhar regarding the works published or to be published under the name of Nruparaj in *Utkal Sahitya*.[9] He even wrote to Gangadhar complaining about the money the zamindar owed to *Utkal Sahitya*.[10] There are a couple of additional instances regarding the above. Fakir Mohan Senapati, even before he came in contact with either Gangadhar or Nruparaj, in the second edition of *Utkala Bhramanam* praised the king:

O Nruparaj Singh, the king of Barapali
I sing your praise for nothing.
Scholar, poet and a king
In you come together precious stone and gold.
Ever mindful of the welfare of your subjects
You perform your duty sacrosanct.

But on becoming aware of the truth, Fakir Mohan left out the above lines from the 1916 edition of *Utkala Bhramanam*.[11] Nandakishore, too, while discussing the poems included in *Kabita Kallola* in a letter, mentioned Gangadhar as the author of the three poems earlier attributed to Nruparaj. However, Gangadhar, while sending a copy of Nandakishore's letter to Braja Mohan Panda and while writing a preface to *Kabita Kallola*, left these three works out.

That Gangadhar published some of his own poems under the name of Nruparaj Singh does not need further elaboration. Kulamani Das's biography written shortly after Gangadhar's death, attributed "Amod" to Gangadhar.[12] A comparative analysis of the diction and style of *Balaram Dev* and "Amod" with the works of Gangadhar would in itself substantiate Kulamani's claim. Gangadhar's description of nature, his distinctive outlook, awareness of recent scientific inventions can be found in works attributed to Nruparaj. Now the question arises whether the attribution of authorship to another person was driven only by material needs or can be explained in terms of complex socio-economic factors. I shall attempt to answer the question in the section that follows.

III

The dissemination of literature and the social recognition of the writer are deeply interconnected. In order to disseminate their texts and achieve recognition, the writer has to seek favours from the establishment. Sometimes the establishment obliges the writer on its own; at others, the writer has to plead for patronage and has to become complicit in its acts of injustice. When writers find themselves at odds with the social power centres, the establishment contemplates exiling them. Writers, for their part, sometimes choose to militate against centres of power and ally themselves with alternative power centres. In the process, writers either turn into rebels or abandon the pursuit of literature altogether.[13]

Before the nineteenth century, the social system prevailing in Odisha was feudal in character. In such a society, feudal chiefs controlled the centres of power and authority. In this world, therefore, literary culture revolved around feudal chiefs. For his daily subsistence the poet needed a benefactor; and for the promotion and circulation of his works he needed a patron. Therefore, poets composing in Sanskrit and those writing in the vernacular sought favours from the king and looked for a profitable position in the court. If they did not perform any administrative duty, poets as courtiers were confined to the outer margins. Sometimes they turned themselves into pitiable eulogists[14] and at others, they attributed the authorship of their works to their royal patron. The nature of literature and taste of the reading public were shaped by feudal lords; they also decided who would be recognized as the author of a literary text. The attribution of authorship of a text to one's patron is an accepted medieval practice. It was quite prevalent in Sanskrit and old Telugu literature. Sachchidananda Mishra contends that this practice gained currency in Odisha through its contact with the Telugu literary world:

> The practice of attributing the authorship of a work to a patron was more widespread in the Telugu-speaking regions and is datable to the works of the first great poet Nannaya. Since southern parts of Odisha lie close to Andhra Pradesh, Odia kings ruling over these areas emulated their Telugu counterparts in their love for literature. In Telugu literary tradition, a *kavya* is the daughter of a poet. As it is the duty of a father to find a suitable groom for his daughter, the poet should find a deserving candidate, a king or a minister, for a *kavya*. ... After proffering the *kavya* to him, the poet is bestowed with money, land and other gifts in the form of bride price.[15]

In the world of Odia literature, Baladeb Ratha was the most energetic practitioner of this convention. Many of his predecessors such as Bishnu Das and Upendra Bhanja had attributed authorship of their works to patrons; and some of Baladeb's contemporaries like Brajanath Badajena and Jadumani Mohapatra also followed this practice. Upendra Bhanja referred to such works as *dattakavya* [a kavya that is given as an offering] in *Chitrakavya Bandhodyaya*. Following this tradition of *kruti samarpana*, Gangadhar attributed the authorship of his works like *Balaram Dev*, "Amod", "Puskarini", "Tarubara" and "Nidagha Rajatva" to Nruparaj Singh.

Poverty was not the only factor responsible for poets attributing the authorship of their works to patrons. In medieval times, literature, for its effective dissemination, depended on its reception at a royal court or its circulation at a place of worship. Shucking, in his study of the social background of European literature, comments, "The history of literature is in large part the history of beneficence of individual princes and aristocrats."[16] In this context, one cannot do better than quote Sachchidananda Mishra's perceptive observations at some length:

> Before the advent of the printing press, publishing and disseminating literary texts was an expensive affair. If a poet sat at home and composed *kavyas* he could not expect these to find a readership on their own. To ensure wider dissemination of his texts he had to take recourse to certain strategies. Let us suppose a poet writes a *kavya* that runs into one hundred leaves. If a scribe copies out four leaves a day, it will take him twenty-four days to reproduce the full manuscript. A few more days will also be needed to put together materials such as blank palm leaves, flat wooden binders and thread. Thus, it would take a scribe an entire month to prepare a single copy of the manuscript. If the poet undertakes this task himself, someone else will have to support his family. ... A poet, therefore, cannot accomplish this task without generous help from a patron. However, mere financial assistance is not enough for a poet's work to gain wide recognition. Cultivating his art in splendid isolation will not enable a poet to achieve fame. For this, he has to establish his poetic credentials among other poets and scholars. ... In those days, kings were to poets what publishers are to modern authors today. So, the possibility of a literary text achieving a wide circulation was enhanced if its authorship was attributed to a king.[17]

Thus, it becomes clear that there were other factors than the purely economic for attributing authorship to a patron. In traditional Odia *kavyas*, greater primacy was accorded to form rather than content. So, the content of a *kavya* did not have an intimate and organic relationship with the experiences of the poet. Thematic innovation did not define the greatness of a work. Poetry was not the expression of the poet's personality. Therefore, its authorship being attributed to someone else did not really hurt the poet's sentiments. Not the author but the patron who exercised ownership over the text was more important. Therefore, poets deliberately attributed the authorship of their works to famous poets and gods. Thus, on occasions, identifying the real authors of ancient and medieval literary texts proves impossibly difficult.

This practice has all but disappeared in the modern era. Commercial publishers have replaced royal patrons. Novelty of subject matter rather than convention-bound narratives and description emerged as the new criterion of good literature. To link the poet's personality inextricably with his poetry has become an established critical practice. As a result, the recognition of the poet as an individual takes precedence over the fame of his work. Therefore, the practice of attributing authorship to one's patron has come to an end. In modern times, attribution of authorship is seen as evidence of the poet being exploited by his patron. Nandakishore views Gangadhar's attributing authorship to Nruparaj Singh in this light. Is poverty the only reason why Gangadhar took such a decision? Gangadhar's poetic development and his background may provide an answer to this question.

IV

Gangadhar was born into a rural middle-class family of *bhulia* caste [weavers] in the western region of Odisha in 1862. His family occupations included farming on a small scale, business, weaving and money-lending. Sometimes the *bhulias* served the local community as *baidyas*. Combining all these activities, the *bhulias* became a reasonably affluent community in western Odisha. Even though they do not occupy a high rung in the caste hierarchy, their economic prosperity has helped them belong to the middle class. Gangadhar's father Chaitanya Meher was adept at weaving but he did not feel drawn to this activity. He placed a high value on learning, and not on wealth. So, he took to teaching children at a *chatshali* [village primary school]. His family suffered financial hardships for some years on account of his indifference to his ancestral occupation. Gangadhar inherited his father's passion for learning. Therefore, through his own exertions, Gangadhar acquired as much modern learning as possible in spite of his limiting circumstances. His teacher Ghanashyam Mishra transformed his passion for learning into an unceasing perseverance. That is why, although he received formal education in a modern school up to class five (opportunities for receiving education beyond this level were not available in Barapali), at his own initiative he became conversant with ancient Sanskrit and Odia literature, and mastered the intricacies of Sanskrit grammar. Moreover, he remained warmly responsive to modern ideas.

Krushna Kar, a celebrated poet of the time, lived in Barangapali which lay close to Gangadhar's village. It is perfectly possible that in his youth Gangadhar came in contact with this poet. Although Gangadhar has not mentioned Krushna Kar in his autobiographical fragment, the probability of the senior poet having influenced Gangadhar's early poetry cannot be ruled out. Krushna Kar's *kavyas* such as *Kunjabihar*, *Pandarapoi* and *Raghunath Bilasa* lack originality, and yet the fame of these works must have inspired Gangadhar to pursue a career as a poet. Gangadhar's early *kavya Rasa Ratnakar* [Sea of Delight] is an outcome of a synthesis of the following factors: his father's passion for learning, his teacher Ghanashyam introducing him to Sanskrit *kavyas* and grammar, knowledge of ancient and medieval Odia literature acquired on his own, and the influence on him of Krushna Kar.

During his school years, Gangadhar came close to his teacher Lakshman Mishra.[18] Lakshman's *kavya* may have been derided by Radhanath Ray as "the work of a poetaster" but his passion for literature cannot be underplayed. Lakshman, who occasionally wrote poems employing the techniques and rhythmic patterns of Sanskrit *kavyas*, must have sharpened Gangadhar's poetic abilities. Moreover, friends like Akshay babu,[19] who was then the tutor of the prince of Barapali, and Madan Mohan Pradhan's enthusiastic support strengthened Gangadhar's resolve to become a poet. This resulted in the publication of the poem "Ahalyastaba". His poetic ambition sought to overcome his financial difficulties and constraining circumstances.

In all likelihood, it is Lakshman Mishra who introduced Radhanath Ray's works to Gangadhar. Lakshman did not entertain a high opinion of Radhanath's poetry, as evidenced by his "*Parvati* Samalochana" [A Review of *Parvati*].[20] In the review published in *Sambalpur Hitesini*, he dwells on grammatical errors in Radhanath's *kavya*. Lakshman's criticism, however, did not deter Gangadhar from admiring Radhanath's poetry. Enthused by a letter he received from Radhanath along with his works, Gangadhar sent him a copy of "Ahalyastaba". Radhanath's characteristic cordial response to the poem opened a new chapter in the history of literary friendships in Odisha. It may be mentioned here that writing letters, praising someone's work and creating the illusion of intimacy were part of Radhanath's familiar strategy. Radhanath's letter encouraged Gangadhar to find his own voice as a poet. Gangadhar already possessed the ability to employ novel perspectives and styles of expression. He could connect with the larger literary world of Odisha and consciously chose literary models that suited him. Gangadhar's literary endeavour reminds one of Ekalavya learning archery.

Around 1894, the encouragement received from *Hiteisini*, warm approbation from Radhanath, moral support from friends and his tenacity of purpose combined to make Gangadhar's poetic career flourish. *Kumar Janmotsav* and *Indumati* were published and attracted the attention of the contemporary intellectual elite. He received a prize of twenty rupees from the king of Mayurbhanj for the opening sections of *Indumati*. His poetic talent was recognized and profusely praised by Nilamani Bidyaratna in an editorial in *Hiteisini*.[21]

Appreciation and evaluation of literature does not entirely depend on an individual's choices; it is also influenced by the prevailing socio-cultural milieu. This principle equally applies to Gangadhar. The successful pursuit of literature calls for intensive study, deep contemplation and perseverance which cannot be sustained without a measure of financial stability, access to books and leisure. Then there is the additional challenge of publication and distribution of literary texts. A small but supportive literary circle In Barapali created a milieu favourable for Gangadhar's poetic growth. By 1893–94, he had achieved a degree of financial stability through his skill as a weaver and his clerical job in the zamindar's estate. However, three important amenities were not easily available to Gangadhar in Barapali: access to books, leisure and opportunities for publishing his works. To enjoy these, writers mostly had to seek the patronage of a powerful elite who guarded the gates of the hall of fame. No writer could afford to incur their disfavour. Those who defied them and yet wanted to earn fame as writers had to join a religious sect which opposed this elite or form a new sect. Instances of writers becoming famous without the support of the royal court or the religious centres are therefore extremely rare. The unavailability of such institutional patronage in western Odisha may explain why before the nineteenth century few major writers appeared on the literary scene here. Thus, it was an arduous task for Gangadhar to nurture his literary interests in Barapali.

The way in which colonial economic and administrative policies transformed Odisha in the nineteenth century is well known. The feeble attempt made by a few members of the emerging middle class during this period to cope with the cultural turmoil resulting from these policies is known as the Odia Renaissance. During this period, the feudal socio-economic order which was prevalent in Odisha had to enter into a conflict and collaboration with the colonial and capitalist dispensation. This process led to the rise of an upstart elite loyal to the British, who lacked a coherent worldview and a genuine spirit of enquiry. Moreover, British economic exploitation led to uneven development of regions in Odisha. This resulted in the emergence of a cultural power centre which was keen to dominate other parts of Odisha. Some members of the new middle class which benefited from this cultural centralization and uneven regional development started adopting the modern style of literary expression. In order to deal with the resulting identity crisis, they started imagining a new community on the basis of their language or religion. Hence, people who were associated with the colonial administration and education system such as Gouri Sankar Ray, Gobind Chandra Patnaik, Bicchanda Charan Patnaik, Fakir Mohan Senapati, Radhanath Ray, Madhusudan Das, Gopal Ballabh Das, Biswanath Kar and Nandakishore Bal established themselves as journalists and writers. Their generosity or sympathy enabled cultural figures like Gobind Ratha and Nilamani Bidyaratna, who had received a traditional education, to do reasonably well under the new system. But they were exceptions. This system, however, left places like Sambalpur, especially a village like Barapali largely unaffected. In spite of the constraints, Gangadhar strove to produce literary works in the hazy light of modernity. In his early career, he had to negotiate the disquieting tension between his broadening worldview and the narrow confines of his existence. This tension informs all his writings. In order to find relief from this tension, he looked for appreciation and encouragement from people close to him. Radhanath's letters provided this to him. The kind of praise Radhanath lavished on the poet Gangadhar he showered on many other authors. But not a single recipient of his praise attained the heights of imagination which Gangadhar scaled. For example, Damodar Mishra, who had enjoyed the patronage of kings, newspaper editors and eminent persons like Radhanath, sank into oblivion.

As a poet, Gangadhar faced four major challenges around 1893–94: (1) availability of leisure; (2) opportunity to interact with other writers; (3) financial stability which would enable him to buy books and periodicals; and (4) finding publishers for his works. Working the looms at home and doing the clerical job in the zamindar's estate left him with very little leisure. His financial stability depended on fulfilling both the tasks. Social and financial mobility was unimaginable for Gangadhar without the patronage of the zamindar of Barapali. The zamindar was also related to the king of Bamanda and the king of Mayubhanj, who brought out *Sambalpur Hiteisini* and *Utkal Parbha* respectively. He composed *Kumar Janmotsav* on the occasion of the birth of Nruparaj Singh's grandson, perhaps to win his favour. In it, Gangadhar writes, "Many dependents would benefit from his munificence, but what he will bestow on me only the Almighty knows."[22] However, no benefit seems to have come Gangadhar's way. Neither did he get a promotion nor did the zamindar help him publish his work. He published *Indumati* with the prize amount of twenty rupees he had received from the king of Mayurbhanj, and money borrowed from his friends. At that time, his financial situation did not allow him to publish *Utkal Lakshmi*. Hence, Gangadhar wished to devote himself whole-heartedly to his cloth-making business. In an advertisement published in 1894, the tension between his unfavourable socio-economic circumstances and his modern outlook surfaces visibly:

Advertisement

The silk cloth woven at Barapali is famous throughout India. This has been highly praised in London and the weaver has received a certificate of appreciation and a silver medal. Many who wish to buy silk cloth produced at Barapali face difficulties in doing so. We offer here a solution to overcome this difficulty. Dhotis, sarees, shawls, etc. can be ordered by post. We shall send the items by V.P.P. ordered within 15 days of receiving the letter. The postage cost has to be borne by the buyer. Those interested in finding out about prices of various items can contact us at the address given below:

Sri Gangadhar Meher, Barapali, Sambalpur, Madhyapradesh [Central Provinces][23]

One wonders if this advertisement brought Gangadhar any financial benefits. However, the subsequent course of events indicates that despite his abilities as a weaver, Gangadhar was unable to improve his financial condition. Although Gangadhar possessed a modern outlook which cherished progress, he had to depend upon a stagnant feudal order for realizing his talent. The crisis he faced as a writer and his failure to achieve financial stability compelled him to cultivate the zamindar.

In the nineteenth century, the British government created a group of loyal local zamindars in order to weaken the anti-colonial resistance led by Surendra Sai, Chakra Bisoi, Ratnakar Nayak and others. These local kings and zamindars were granted limited administrative autonomy and were encouraged to promote arts and literature. This was part of a larger mission of "civilizing" the restive tribal communities. Some feudatory chiefs in western Odisha – especially those of Kharial, Bamanda, Balangir-Patna and Sonepur – began patronizing art and literature. Even if they themselves did not pursue literary ambitions, they became patrons. This helped them receive titles from the colonial government. (However, the British government's attitude to ancient art and literature varied from province to province. What might be true of the Central Provinces in the Bombay presidency may not hold good for other parts of the country).

The zamindar of Barapali was loyal to the British. Gangadhar's account of the family bears testimony to this:

> After Narayan Singh's demise, Surendra Sai, Ujjawal Sai and a few others staked their claim to the throne, and rebelled against the British. Some Gond zamindars joined the rebels and committed depredations in the area but they did not dare enter the zamindari of Barapali out of fear of and respect for the zamindar. … Bhawani Singh (grandfather of Nruparaj Singh) longed for peace and helped the British suppress the rebellion. He got a few Gond rebels captured and handed them over to the British. For his services, he received a letter of appreciation from the then Commissioner, William Robert Forster.[24]

It appears very likely that the interest Nruparaj Singh displayed in arts and letters reflects his loyalty to the British and may not have sprung from a genuine love for these. Therefore, Gangadhar's eulogy *Kumar Janmotsav* made no impact on him. However, at the instance of his well-wishers, Gangadhar attributed the authorship of two long poems and three short ones to Nruparaj Singh. In return, Gangadhar landed the additional job of a judicial clerk (which had fallen vacant at the death of Swapneswar Panda). This enabled him to buy eight acres of arable land in Barapali, relieved him from the arduous task of weaving and helped him publish some of his books at his own expense. In short, the attribution led to three congenial outcomes: (a) landing a dependable and more remunerative government job; (b) leisure required for literary pursuits; and (c) financial stability that allowed him to publish his own books.

V

Although many poets engage in the attribution of authorship to patrons, they often appear less than willing to completely erase their authorial identity. However, Gangadhar never claimed the authorship of the works he attributed to Nruparaj Singh. Whenever the question of their authorship was raised, he preferred to maintain silence. This must have caused him intense mental agony. Therefore, after 1898, he considered attribution not only demeaning but also a hypocritical act. This probably accounts for his rejection of Nilamani Bidyaratna's proposal to attribute one of his works to a patron. He described the proposal as "ridiculous" in a letter written to Braja Mohan Panda. Nilamani, however, interpreted Gangadhar's rejection of his proposal as the poet's indifference to getting his works published. To quote Nilamani,

> He does not write poetry to achieve fame but to spend his leisure time pleasantly. He is not interested in the least in seeing his works in print. He was roused from such apathy only when his friends pressed him to publish his writings.[25]

Those days, writers who did not have the means to get their works published had to compromise their dignity, and Gangadhar was not one who would do so. Therefore, many of his books remained unpublished.

Gangadhar never turned down a warm and sincere gesture of friendship from a king or zamindar. He, in fact, looked forward to such gestures especially after he retired from his government job. In a letter dated 24 December 1920, Narayan Bahidar writes,

> After being disappointed in all quarters, I have presented your case to his majesty, the king of Kalahandi. His response was not entirely discouraging. His Majesty is now away on a pilgrimage. He has assured that upon his return to Kalahandi he would give a definite response to my request. What the king's response would be depends on our luck. ... However, His Majesty wondered if an honorarium of rupees thirty a month would induce you to take up residence in Bhawanipatna.[26]

Gangadhar accepted the job of an auditor in the zamindari of Bodasambar. *Sambalpur Hiteisini* described it as an honour bestowed upon the poet:

> Poet Gangadhar is from Barapali but he is known and admired all over Odisha. A divinely gifted poet, he has filled readers' hearts with pure bliss. Recently, he has retired from government service on a pension. ... The zamindar of Bodasambar, Ray Lal Rajendra Singh Bariha Bahadur has promised to offer the poet accommodation in the headquarters of the zamindari and provide financial support for the rest of his life.[27]

Although it was presented as an honour, Gangadhar actually worked for a living in Bodasambar, for he was averse to survive on someone's charity.

Compared with his contemporaries, Gangadhar was less given to deferring to people in positions of power and authority. At the same time, he remained loyal to his employers. Moreover, he was deeply attached to his birthplace, Barapali. The letters he wrote to Braja Mohan (dated 21 November 1910 and 27 November 1912) make it amply clear that he was not blind to the virtues of kings and zamindars: "The zamindar of Barapali is more generous than others of his kind. Unfortunately, God has not granted him as much wealth as He has bestowed on others."[28] These conflicting tendencies constitute the essence of his personality. He was neither enthusiastic about nor hostile to the circumstances in which he lived, and this attitude informs and shapes his works.

Later in life, Gangadhar's rationalist outlook made him critical of the zamindar family of Barapali. Nruparaj Singh might have acted unfairly towards the poet but he had a liberal outlook. But his grandson Suryoday Singh did not inherit this quality. This led to friction between Suryoday and Gangadhar. The poem "Ishwar Drohi" [Enemy of God], which Gangadhar composed towards the end of his life, perhaps offers a covert criticism of Suryoday's misrule. Gangadhar refused to compromise his ethical principles in order to curry favour with the zamindar.

Gangadhar's poetry did not depend on any patronage to manifest its brilliance. He faced many obstacles and overcame them in his own way. He could have resolved the dilemma that confronted him around 1894–95 in a different manner, but considering his meagre resources and following the advice of his well-wishers, he attributed the authorship of some of his poems to the zamindar between 1895 and 1898. Therefore, it would be patently unfair to evaluate his life and works in the light of the decisions he took during this critical period in his life. Pandit Raghav Mishra gave the following misleading opinion regarding Gangadhar: "Gangadhar never found the opportunity to pursue a hassle-free literary career. Financial misery often smothered his creative faculties."[29] However, only financial hardship did not overwhelm Gangadhar's poetic career; he had to contend with many other constraints. Gangadhar always resumed his writing after dealing effectively with temporary disruptions. But the exaggerated and distorted accounts of the poet's personal life presented by writers and critics from Nandakishore Bal to Raghav Mishra have led to gross misinterpretation of Gangadhar's literary achievement.

Translation: Umasankar Patra

Notes

1 Debendra Dash, "Luchile ki Champukabi Baladeb Ratha", *Gangadhar: Kabita o Kabi-Atma*, Rourkela: Pragati Utkal Sangha, 1995, pp. 96–120.
2 Sachchidananda Mishra, *Baladeb Ratha Adhyayana* [A Study of Baladeb Ratha's Poetic Achievements], Cuttack: Granthamandir, 1981, pp. 8–9.

3 Gangadhar's "Sri Nruparaj Singh" (1905) represents one of the earliest efforts at writing biography in prose in Odia. Before this, small biographical pieces were included Odia textbooks; some had also attempted to present short narratives of the lives of a few kings in verse. Gangadhar for the first time employed a historical method for writing a biography.

4 Hemant Kumar Das, ed., *Gangadhar Granthabali* [Collected Works of Gangadhar Meher], Berhampur: Pustak Bhandar, 1977, p. 462.

5 Debi Prasanna Pattanayak, ed., *Kabilipi* [Letters of Poets], Santiniketan: Visvabharati Gabesana Bibhag, 1957, p. 71.

6 Ibid. p. 72.

7 Ibid. p. 73.

8 *Sambalpur Hiteisini*, 27.10.1897, vol. 9, no. 22, pp. 85–87.

9 Bhagaban Meher, *Pitruprasanga* [About My Father], Cuttack: Odisha Book Store, 1977, p. 218.

10 Ibid. p. 220.

11 Natabara Samantaray, *Vyasakavi Fakir Mohan*, Bhubaneswar: Gangabai Samantaray, 1972, pp. 93–101.

12 *Utkal Sahitya,* vol. 24, no. 3, p. 103.

13 Debendra Dash, "Sahitya o Samaj" [Literature and Society], *Nabapatra*, vol. 16 (January 1988) no. 3 & vol. 17 no. 2 (October 1989), Rourkela.
    Dasarathi Das, *Bibidha Prastab* [Miscellaneous Literary Issues], Cuttack: Friends' Publishers, 1993, pp. 143–149.

14 N. K. Sidhanta, *The Heroic Age of India*, New Delhi: Oriental Books Reprint Corporation, 1975 [1929], p. 63.

15 Sachchidananda Mishra, *Baladeb Ratha Adhyayana* [A Study of Baladeb Ratha's Poetic Achievements], Cuttack: Granthamandir, 1981, p. 149.

16 Levin Ludwig Shucking, *The Sociology of Literary Taste*, trans. E. W. Dikes, London: Kegan Paul, Trench, Trubner and Co., 1944, p. 9.

17 Sachchidananda Mishra, *Baladeb Ratha Adhyayana* [A Study of Baladeb Ratha's Poetic Achievement], Cuttack: Granthamandir, 1981, pp. 8–9.

18 Poetic influence of Lakshman Mishra on Gangadhar has not been adequately discussed by scholars. Many sources including his autobiographical fragment suggest the profound impact he had on Gangadhar's literary growth. Lakshman was somewhat ambitious and had a hunger for adulation. He did not seem to share a cordial relationship with Radhanath, who made adverse comments on his *kavya Sahitya Sundari*. Mishra's bitter feelings towards Radhanath must have spilled over to Gangadhar. However, the influence of a connoisseur of literature like Lakshman Mishra on Gangadhar cannot be ruled out.

19 It is popularly believed that Surya Kumar Mitra, the tutor of the son of the Zamindar of Barapali, introduced Radhanath's works to Gangadhar and encouraged him to write poetry in the modern style. However, Surya Kumar played no role in shaping Gangadhar's poetic career. This myth was probably propagated by historian Shiv Prasad Dash and was accepted by Natabara Samantray, Asit Kabi and others. Surya Kumar came to Barapali around June 1894 and Gangadhar had already grown close to Radhanath by then. Gangadhar's *Indumati* was published in 1893 and the *kavya Utkal Lakshmi* had already been composed by the time Gangadhar got to know Surya Kumar Mitra.

20 *Sambalpur Hiteisini*, vol.2, no. 17 & 22.

21 *Sambalpur Hiteisini*, 2.5.1894, vol. 5, no. 48, p.189.

22 Hemant Kumar Das, Ed., *Gangadhar Granthabali* [Collected Works of Gangadhar Meher], Berhampur: Pustak Bhandar, 1977, p. 425.

23 *Sambalpur Hiteisini*, vol. 6, issue 27, Appendix. This advertisement was reprinted in the numbers 28 and 30 of the same periodical. Who is this famous weaver lauded in London? Could he possibly be Gangadhar himself?

24 Hemant Kumar Das, Ed., *Gangadhar Granthabali* [Collected Works of Gangadhar Meher], Berhampur: Pustak Bhandar, 1977, p. 454.
25 *Utkal Sahitya,* vol. 28, no.1, p. 14.
26 Bhagaban Meher, *Pitruprasanga* [About My Father], Cuttack: Odisha Book Store, 1977, p. 264.
27 *Sambalpur Hiteisini,* vol. 29, issue 10, p. 36.
28 Shiv Prasad Dash, Ed. *Gangadhar Patrabali* [Letters of Gangadhar Meher], Berhampur: Odisha Publishing House, 1955, p. 126.
29 Raghab Mishra, *Meher Kabi* [Gangadhar Meher, the Poet], Cuttack: Utkal Sahitya Press, 1925, p. 44.

13 Sudarsana Acharya

War of words: aspects of a literary controversy

Introduction

Sudarsana Acharya (b. 1939) is an eminent critic, translator and scholar. Initiated into the world of literary criticism by his legendary mentor Natabara Samantaray, he carried forward the latter's objective and systematic study of literature with unprecedented rigour. While Natabara focused primarily on Odia literature written in the nineteenth and early twentieth centuries, Sudarsana engaged in an intensive study of medieval Odia poetry. In this endeavour, he was ably aided by his thorough command of Sanskrit. In *Odia Kavya Kausala, 1500–1850* [Rhetorical Devices Employed in Odia *Kavyas*] (1983) he vividly sketches the historical background which shaped literary culture in Odisha and perceptively examines the diverse influences which the poets absorbed during this period. He insightfully analyses aspects of craftsmanship that lend a distinctive character to medieval Odia poetry. Sudarsana has also made his mark as an accomplished translator. His translations include Somadeva's *Kathasaritsagara* in five volumes, the *prakrit* writer Haribhadra Suri's *Dhurtakhyana,* and the Kannada writer Mirji Anna Rao's novel *NIsarga.* Sudarsana's scholarly investigations constitute substantive contributions to knowledge. His authoritative editions of Upendra Bhanja's first *kavya Chitralekha,* Ballabh Narayan Mohapatra's *Bishnupurana,* Krushna Singh's *Sriram Rasayan* etc., painstakingly retrieved from palm-leaf manuscripts, have helped literary historians build a fuller account of the history of Odia literature. The collected works of neglected but important authors he edited include Gopinath Nanda Sarma (1869–1924), Padmanabh Narayan Deb (1872–1904), Ramachandra Acharya (1895–1934), and Benimadhab Padhi (1919–2006). Moreover, by salvaging lost, forgotten and rare nineteenth-century Odia periodicals, *Utkal Madhupa, Pradipa* and *Indradhanu,* he has placed the study of modern Odia literature on a stronger footing.

The following piece has been excerpted from Sudarsana Acharya's long introduction to *Indradhnau: Unabimsha Satabdira Eka Bismruta Patrika* [Rainbow: A Forgotten Magazine of the Nineteenth Century]. This magazine was published irregularly between 1893 and 1897 to celebrate and

DOI: 10.4324/9781003224778-13

defend Upendra Bhanja, an early eighteenth-century poet and emerging symbol of Odia pride, who came under severe attack on account of the advent of a new literary sensibility. Many of the critics hostile to Upendra Bhanja found in the modern Odia poet Radhanath Ray (1848–1908) a powerful and convenient rallying point, and brought out a magazine titled *Bijuli* [Lightning]. The two rival camps in the controversy received enthusiastic support from the two leading newspapers of the time, *Utkal Dipika* and *Sambalpur Hiteisini*. In this controversy, obscenity, allegedly found in profusion Upendra Bhanja's *kavyas*, formed the core issue. It may be mentioned here that the puritanical Brahmo intellectuals in Odisha lent vigorous support to the *Bijuli* group. In retrieving with great difficulty, the extant issues of *Indradhanu* (not a single copy of *Bijuli* has survived), Sudarsana Achrya not only performs an extraordinary scholarly task, but in his richly insightful introduction he illuminates the historic role the magazines played in shaping Odia critical discourse in its formative phase. In other words, he presents this controversy as an exciting drama of a crucial shift in taste and sensibility in Odisha in the closing decades of the nineteenth century. He goes beyond meticulous documentation to demonstrate how the opponents of Radhanath who began by subjecting the poet's work to stinging critique ended up recognizing and emulating his achievement as the harbinger of modernity. Sudarsana also highlights the way in which literary magazines in Odisha helped create a community of young writers and the role controversy played in giving critical discourse new impetus and direction.

*

War of words: aspects of a literary controversy[1]

Sudarsana Acharya

The magazine *Indradhanu* [Rainbow] was launched in August 1893 with the express aim of defending the greatness and glory of Odisha by celebrating the achievement of the poet Upendra Bhanja. However, prevailing circumstances compelled it to counter the sustained initiatives of two other magazines, *Utkal Prabha* [The Light of Utkal] and *Bijuli* [Lightning], which projected Radhanath Ray (1848–1908) as a model of literary excellence. Odisha in the latter half of the nineteenth century witnessed several significant developments such as the spread of modern education, the emergence of an educated middle class which got exposed to western literature and culture largely through its contact with Bengal, the rise of Brahmoism, the catastrophic famine of 1866, and the movement against the attempt to abolish Odia language from schools and courts. All these combined to heighten the sense of Odia identity. As Natabara Samantaray observes, the appearance of *Indradhanu* should not therefore be viewed as an accident. But Lala

Ramnarayan Ray's essay "Kabi Upendra Bhanja" provided the immediate provocation for the publication of *Indradhanu*. Had this essay not been published, perhaps this fierce literary controversy would have assumed a different form, and the feelings and views of the partisans involved in it would have found other modes of expression. In other words, this historic essay created a unique opportunity for triggering a clash of conflicting literary tastes. In some contemporary periodicals, Ramnarayan's essay was identified as the source of this controversy. Golakdhanda (Gopal Ballabh Das' Pseudonym) wrote, "the origin of this controversy can be traced to my serious disagreements with Ramnarayan babu's views on Upendra Bhanja expressed in his article on *Baidehisha Bilasa*."[2] The observation of someone writing under the pseudonym Madhyastha Brahma [Brahma as Mediator], published in *Balasore Sambad Bahika* on 12 December 1893, deserves to be quoted here:

> What is funny about this battle is that the onlookers who should be enjoying the spectacle are actively engaged in the combat and the real warriors have stayed away from the battlefield.
>
> In this battle, the role of sage Narad is played by Ramnarayan babu. In *puranas*, Narad used to serve as an instigator of conflicts and watch them with relish. However, Ramnarayan babu has himself stepped into the battlefield as a warrior.

"Kabi Upendra Bhanja" was serialized in *Utkal Prabha*. Its first part came out in the ninth issue of the first volume of *Utkal Prabha* (December 1891). In this, he spoke of the use of *jatipata* [pauses made at intervals while singing and reciting a poem; something like a caesura] and *upadha* [the penultimate vowel sound in a poetic line]. In subsequent parts of the essay (vol. 2, no. 1; vol. 2, nos. 6 & 9), he discussed the rhetorical devices, aesthetic sentiments expressed and the issue of decorum in Upendra Bhanja's poetry. The essay published in five parts was devoted to an analysis of *Baidehisha Bilasa*.

It may be in order here to take a look at the history of the reception of Upendra Bhanja after the advent of print culture to understand why Ramnarayan focused on *Baidehisha Bilasa*. A systematic discussion of Upendra's poetry began in the magazine *Utkal Madhupa* [The Honeybee of Utkal] in 1878. Before this, only Reverend J. Long[3] (1859) and Rangalal Bandyopadyay[4] (1864) had prepared a list of works written by Upendra and given a brief sketch of his biography. Based on hearsay, these lacked the rigour of John Beames's article on Dinakrushna Das's *Rasakallola*.[5] Thus, *Utkal Madhupa* made the first attempt to present Upendra's poetry accompanied by commentary and critical notes. But the writers of these commentaries who happened to be Brahmos found Upendra's poetry outrageously obscene and discontinued publishing these. It may be added that such reservations about ancient Odia poetry had already been voiced in the magazine *Utkal Putra*. In the 3 June 1874 issue of the magazine, its editor Pyari Mohan Acharya (1851–1881) expressed the following view:

> Whatever exists in this category [literature] comprises merely the *kavyas* composed with the iron stylus of poets from a bygone era such as [Upendra] Bhanja, Brahma Das, Abhimanyu Samantsinghar; such poetry is famous for its ornate wordplay, religious thought and is replete with obscene language, though interspersed with occasional passages narrating natural human feelings expressed in heart-warmingly lucid and simple language. But these books are not such as could be handed safely to innocent children or adolescents.

Such a puritanical attitude must have led to *Utkal Madhupa*'s decision to stop serializing *Labanyabati* accompanied by commentary after publishing only five cantos. In the second year, the magazine began publishing a piece on *Kotibrahmandasundari* [A Beauty Celebrated in a Million Worlds]. Proposing the definition of an ideal *kavya* and what constitutes obscenity, the writer observed,

> Authors of *alamkakara-shastras* [treatises on figures of speech] recognize that *kavya* as ideal which consists of faultless words, appropriate meanings and uncorrupted qualities. ... Obscenity refers to crude and vulgar sentences that arouse feelings of embarrassment and revulsion. Employing rhetorical dexterity, a poet can work obscenity into the texture of a *kavya* and render it deplorable. The many explicitly erotic scenes depicted in *Labanyabati* provide examples of such ingrained obscenity. ... Physical love should be portrayed within certain limits. The transgression of these leads to immorality and erosion of religious values. Such *kavyas*, therefore, should not be considered works of art in the true sense of the term.
>
> ("Kotibrahmandasundari", *Utkal Madhupa*, vol. 2,
> nos. 3 & 4, July 1879)

The moral outlook of the Brahmos which was articulated earlier in *Utkal Madhupa* finds a more resounding echo in Ramnarayan's essay. Since *Labanyabati* and *Kotibrahmandasundari* had been dismissed as examples of true *kavya*, he chose to evaluate *Baidehisa Bilasa*, and sought to prove that three-fourths of it were undeserving of the appellation, *kavya*. Thus, it is to be expected that *Utkal Dipika* [The Lamp of Utkal] which had earlier countered the opinions on Upendra's poetry voiced in *Utkal Putra* and *Utkal Madhupa* would now rise to the poet's defence. By the time *Indradhanu* appeared on the literary scene, the critique of Upendra's poetry had grown more sharply hostile under the increasing influence of powerful Brahmo intellectuals such as Biswanath Kar and Bijoy Chandra Mazumdar. In response to this, a group of young writers, under the leadership of

Gourisankar Ray (1838–1917), the editor of *Utkal Dipika*, came forward to resist the assault on Upendra Bhanja, who had by then become a symbol of Odia pride. Many contemporary writers vehemently refuted the arguments advanced by Ramnarayan against Upendra Bhanja. The attack on the essayist was so fierce that another group of writers rose to support him by pointing out even more and more instances of obscenity in Upendra Bhanja's works. These attacks and counter-attacks made a dark cloud of obscenity descend on the critical world of Odisha. This obscenity reached a new low in the responses of Ramakrushna Sahu and Dasarathi Rout.

At this juncture, *Indradhanu* was brought out to provide a useful platform to the champions of Upendra Bhanja. Though many essays critical of Ramnarayan found a place in *Indradhanu*, it was Golakdhanda, who relentlessly exposed the weaknesses of Ramnarayan's arguments, through his insightful and coherent pieces. It must be admitted that Golakdhanda's contributions to the debate gave a new dimension to the interpretation and evaluation of Upendra Bhanja's poetry. Before he entered the fray, he had already obtained a master's degree and was familiar with more advanced methods of critical analysis. His contributions bore evidence of his ability to present ideas in an organized, logical and persuasive manner. Time and again, he urged his opponents to present their arguments in a more focused and coherent way, and reminded them of the expertise and specific skills that a critic and a participant in a literary debate must possess. He posed the following fundamental questions to his adversaries:

(a) Are there differences of opinion regarding the number of books Upendra Bhanja authored?
(b) Which *kavyas* do you think Upendra Bhanja composed?
(c) Which *kavyas*, in your opinion, were not written by Upendra Bhanja and what are the grounds for your claims?
(d) Have you read all the *kavyas* composed by the poet?
(e) Should we interpret and evaluate a literary work with reference to its poet's time and place or in terms of modern taste and disposition?

Unable to respond to these questions effectively, Ramnarayan felt compelled to withdraw from the arena. During the period between John Beames (1872) and Monmohan Chakravarti (1897), no one seems to have made a systematic and scientific study of medieval Odia poetry. Had he not come under the spell of an aggressive nationalism, Gopal Ballabha perhaps would have written a valuable and sophisticated critical study of Upendra Bhanja's oeuvre.

Ramnarayan severely criticized Upendra Bhanja for violating the rules governing *upadha milan* [the rhyming of penultimate vowel sounds in two lines in a poem]. Gopal Ballabh, in response, furnished several examples from Indian literature in different languages to assert that *upadha milan* was just another figure of speech which added to the aesthetic appeal of a poem but was not a defining characteristic of great poetry. It may be noted here that the effective use of *upadha milan* was considered the most significant yardstick for assessing a *kavya*. Ramnarayan discussed at length this aspect of a poem in his "Mitrakshar"[6] and the first part of "Upendra Bhanja", and set out to evaluate the works of the medieval Odia poet on the basis of his employment of this figure of speech. The loyal admirers of Radhanath Ray lavished praise on him on the basis of his masterful deployment of *upadha milan*. The importance assigned to *upadha milan* can be easily gauged from their instructions to contributors: "We are not interested in publishing poems that do not observe rules of full *mitrakshar* [the rhyme of the last two syllables in a verse]". *Sambalpur Hiteisini* also followed a similar principle.[7] Therefore, Golakdhanda cited instances of *upadha milan* in Upendra Bhanja's poetry and also persuasively demonstrated how the absence of this figure of speech did not diminish the aesthetic value of a *kavya* in any way. This can be seen as a first step towards initiating a systematic and scientific study of literature.

Many other writers also contributed articles to *Indradhanu* in defence of Upendra Bhanja's poetry. *Labanyabati*, which was considered unsuitable for publication by the editor of *Utkal Madhupa* now came to be serialized in *Indradhanu* accompanied by critical commentary. After *Bijuli*, the magazine brought out by the detractors of Upendra Bhanja, was discontinued, a few writers attempted a soberer assessment of Upendra Bhanja's poetic achievement. Although these cannot be considered major contributions by modern critical standards, their significance in the early phase of modern Odia criticism cannot be gainsaid. They concentrated on the subject matter, metrical scheme and the sources of aesthetic appeal in Upendra Bhanja's oeuvre. Those who subsequently sought to promote Upendra Bhanja celebrated these three aspects in his poetry with greater finesse. It may be said that, they built on and continued the legacy of *Indradhanu*.

Golakdhanda's interventions in the above-mentioned controversy led to two key consequences in the field of scholarly study of ancient Odia literature: the awareness of the need to prepare full biographical accounts of Upendra Bhanja and other pre-colonial poets; and the attempt to publish their works. The absence of the biographies of the poets and the unavailability of their works in print may be the reasons why the controversy did not achieve much depth and failed to advance critical discourse substantially. Since a well-documented book on the life of Upendra Bhanja had not been published by then, Gobind Chandra Mohapatra and Lala Ramnarayan were criticized for expressing two mutually contradictory opinions on the poet.[8] Similarly, the unavailability of all Upendra's *kavyas* in the form of printed books compelled them to base their judgements on only a handful of his works. Moreover, had the works of other pre-colonial poets been available in print, the writers associated with the magazine *Bijuli* would not have singled out Upendra Bhanja for mounting a trenchant attack on him on the grounds of obscenity, grammatical errors and obscurity.

After *Bijuli* ceased to be published, the contributors to *Indradhanu* gradually stopped writing on Upendra Bhanja. It appears incredible that, with the demise of these two magazines, critical interest in Upendra Bhanja should disappear almost completely for about half a century. It seems as if critics sought to keep a safe distance from Upendra Bhanja's *kavyas* until 1944, when Arta Ballabh Mohanty published an annotated edition of *Labanyabati* with a long introduction. One comes across no critical essays on Upendra Bhanja other than Mrutyunjay Ratha's "Odia Pothi"[9] and Nilakantha Das's "Labnyabati"[10] during this period. Bijoy Chandra Mazumdar, an ardent member of the group that supported *Bijuli*, included his views on Upendra Bhanja in the introduction to the second volume of *Typical Selections from Odia Literature* (1923). Around the same time, portions from *Labanyabati* were removed from the syllabus of Patna University at the instance of Bijoy Chandra. For this, he was taken severely to task by Braja Sundar Das in his editorial in *Mukur* titled "Bhanja Nirbasana"[11] [Bhanja Exiled]. This drew a spirited rejoinder from Biswanath Kar who vigorously defended Bijoy Chandra in his editorial titled "Bhanjakavya Prasanga"[12] [Matters Pertaining to Bhanja's *Kavyas*], published in *Utkal Sahitya*. Another interesting fact deserves mention here. The essays – the topics were chosen by the functionaries of the Utkal Sahitya Samaj – that won the annual Talcher Medal were published in *Utkal Sahitya*. Surprisingly, *Utkal Sahitya* did not publish Kulamani Dash's essay on the topic "Kabi Upendra Bhanja and *Baidehisa Bilasa*" which had won the medal in 1921. ...

From the above, it becomes apparent that even in the third decade of the twentieth century the controversy that raged between *Indradhanu* and *Bijuli* in the 1890s had not completely died down in the field of the criticism of Upendra Bhanja's poetry. Arta Ballabh Mohanty too was not able to escape the influence of this fierce debate. In the second half of the twentieth century, many new facts about Upendra's life came to light, several of his hitherto unpublished manuscripts found their way into print and efforts were made to study his works from varied perspectives. However, even now, critics of Upendra Bhanja seem to be following closely the footsteps of Golakdhanda and Ramnarayan in their approaches to Bhanja's poetry.

The importance of biographical accounts of precolonial poets and the study of their complete works for a meaningful study of precolonial literature was stressed by the *Indradhanu* group; these motivated contemporary critics to take a lot of initiatives in this regard. For instance, Ramnarayan actively engaged in research on the ancient history of Odisha and Damodar Pattanayak set to work on collecting songs written by precolonial Odia poets. The contributions made by Monmohan Chakravarti in this field are commendable. He succeeded in collecting accounts of the lives of many poets who wrote in Odia and Sanskrit, and offered astute evaluations of their works. The efforts of Shyamsundar Rajguru, Apanna Panda, Tarini Charan Ratha and Mrutynjaya Ratha in this direction are pioneering in nature. The need for publishing pre-colonial texts stressed by the *Indrdhanu* group inspired Gobind Ratha, Paralakhemundi Gajapati Press and Prachi Samiti to take necessary and fruitful steps. Thus, the significance of the part played by *Indradhanu* in the sphere of the critical evaluation of Upendra's works cannot be underestimated.

Although *Indradhanu* was published with the specific and limited objective of celebrating and defending the achievements of Upendra Bhanja, its role as a major literary periodical of the time needs to be emphasized. After *Utkal Madhupa* and *Pradipa* ceased publication, writers found a ray of hope in *Utkal Prabha*. However, the apathy of patrons and partiality of editors disappointed the writers; its activities remained largely confined to publishing a translation of *Mahabharata*. Thus, in 1893, *Sambalpur Hiteisini* and *Indradhanu* offered the only sources of hope for Odia writers. But even these were reduced to mouthpieces of two groups of fiercely combative partisans. But after *Bijuli*'s disappearance from the scene, the objective of these two magazines underwent salient change. It is interesting to note here that the partisans now had no qualms about publishing articles of their earlier antagonists. For example, the poems of Madhusudan Rao and Sadhu Charan Ray appeared in *Indradhanu*. And moving beyond the controversy over Upendra Bhanja, Gopal Ballabh Das published a brief biography of Nanda Kishor Das, parts of which appeared in *Sambalpur Hiteisini*.

The partisans associated with *Indradhanu* were English-educated young men. However, they were passionate about establishing the excellence of ancient Odia literature. Influenced by the ideas cherished by Gourisankar Ray (1838–1917), members of the *Indradhanu* group tirelessly strove to bring about the all-round development of Odia language and literature, and Odisha. Therefore, anything that impaired the interests of Odisha was anathema to them. It is their intense love and concern for Odisha that led them to vociferously celebrate ancient Odia literature and drew them into the venomous controversy. Although they adopted pseudonyms such as *Adirasia* [votary of the erotic], *Piratia* [someone obsessed with love] and *Prachinapanthi* [worshipper of the old and obsolete], their outlook on life and literature was unmistakably modern. Thus, it would be wrong to present them as writers averse to modern literature. They turned against the modern poet Radhanath Ray for a variety of reasons but they never held the view that Radhanath's poetic style was inimical to the growth of Odia literature. In fact, they themselves tried to modernize it. Thus, one comes across all aspects of modern literature covered in *Indradhanu*. These include descriptive poems, elegies, *kavyas* written in *amitrakshar chhanda*, social novels, sonnets, jokes, one-act plays and essays on scientific subjects. The same Golakdhanda, who was an ardent admirer of Upendra Bhanja, published a *kavya* employing *amitrakshar chhanda*; the same *Piratia* who was an energetic advocate of ancient Odia poetry, wrote a novel titled *Rajabibi*; and the same Ram Sankar who published an annotated edition of *Labanyabati*, wrote the novel *Unnmadini* [The Mad Woman]. The writers belonging to the *Indrdhanu* group carried out several lively experiments with modern forms of literature. However, underlying all these lay a reluctance to acknowledge Radhanath Ray's achievements.

The devoted followers of Radhanath placed a high value on *upadha milan* as a poetic device. The *Indradhnau* group, therefore, rejected it vehemently. One frequently comes across *upadha baisamya* [violation of rules relating to *upadha milan*] in their poems. In his invocation of goddess Saraswati in *Tarak Samhar* [Slaying of Tarak], Golakdhanda paid homage to his poetic ancestors such as Upendra Bhanja, Abhimanyu Samantsinghar, Dinakrushna Das, Balaram Das and Jagannath Das, who depicted the deeds of avatars like Rama and Krishna. However, Golakdhanda's choice of subject matter had little to do with the themes explored by the above-mentioned poets, who focused not on the heroic deeds of mythic characters but predominantly on the erotic. Therefore, *Tarak Samhar* can be more appositely described as a *kavya* like Radhanath Ray's *Mahayatra*, which was modelled on Michael Madhusudan Dutta's *Meghanadvadh Kavya*. Moreover, Gopal Ballabh employed *amitrakshar chhanda* to depict heroic sentiment in his *kavya*. Though he expressed his indebtedness to Michael Madhusudan for this, he was reluctant to acknowledge Radhanath's all-too-ostensible influence. [It may be mentioned here that Radhanath Ray is credited with pioneering the use of *amitrakshar chhanda* in Odia poetry.] However, it was Radhanath's boldly innovative experiments with subject matter and technique that opened possibilities for the *Indradhanu* group to write a new kind of poetry. Thus, the determined opponents of Radhanath ironically established that it was he who introduced modern sensibility in Odia poetry. A dramatic change of attitude is evident in an essay titled "Deshiya Sahityonnati [Improving the quality of Literature of the Land]" which paid glowing tribute to Radhanath and was published in the penultimate issue of *Indradhanu*.

In conclusion, it may be observed that *Indradhanu* played a crucial role in shaping modern Odia literature, although it was published irregularly over four short years. It not only aroused in the young in Odisha a profound interest in literature, it also inspired some of them to become writers themselves. It motivated writers to retrieve ancient literary texts and, engage in a close and systematic study of them. It served to confer a degree of stability on critical practices in Odisha. Through its initiatives the realization dawned that no matter how rich an ancient literature might be, it can never fulfil the aesthetic needs of a new, changing world. Even when the contributors to *Indradhanu* venerated Upendra Bhanja, their writings reflected a departure from the conventions of ancient Odia poetry. Although they harshly criticized Radhanath Ray, they acknowledged, in spite of themselves, that his poetry embodied the modern sensibility more effectively. They also helped Radhanath shift his focus away from his preoccupation with conveying aesthetic pleasure to more sensitively exploring his own world and its social values. In short, in spite of originating in a viciously narrow-minded literary controversy, *Indradhanu* did succeed in widening the horizon of modern Odia literature.

Translation: Animesh Mohapatra

Notes

1 Sudarsana Acharya, "Introduction", *Indradhnau: Unabimsha Satabdira Eka Bismruta Patrika* [Indradhnau: A Forgotten Magazine of the Nineteenth Century], Berhampur University: Berhampur, 1991, pp. xxxv–xlix.
2 *Indradhanu*, vol. 1, no. 7, 9 November 1893.
3 *Journal of Royal Asiatic Society*, vol. XXVIII, no. 3, 1859. pp. 189–190.
4 Rajendralal Mitra, ed., *Rahasya Sandarbha,* vol. 2, no. 16, 1864.
5 John Beames, "Notes on the Rasakallola, An Ancient Oriya Poem", *Indian Antiquary*, vol. 1, 5 July 1872, pp. 215–217; 4 October 1872, pp. 292–295.
6 *Sambalpur Hiteisini*, vol. 4, no. 11, Bamanda, 17 August 1892.
7 *Sambalpur Hiteisini*, vol. 4, no. 33, Bamanda, 18 January 1893.
8 *Utkal Dipika*, Cuttack, 14 October 1893.
9 *Utkal Sahitya*, vol. 8, no. 10, Cuttack, 1905.
10 *Satyabadi*, vol. 1, no. 8, Satyabadi, 1916.
11 *Mukur*, vol. 18, no. 3, Cuttack, 1923, pp. 123–124.
12 *Utkal Sahitya*, vol. 27, no. 5, Cuttack, 192–193.

14 Biswanath Kar and Chandra Mohan Maharana

The need for a literary periodical

Introduction

The publication of *Utkal Sahitya*, a monthly literary magazine, in January 1897 is an event of immense cultural significance for Odisha. It enjoyed uninterrupted publication for almost thirty-eight years, a fact remarkable in the context of the extremely short life-span of Odia literary magazines which had appeared in the previous two and a half decades or so. Significantly, it carried the term *samalochan* (criticism) on its cover page, thereby emphatically indicating the role it intended to play in shaping Odia critical discourse. It not only featured established creative writers but also nurtured, and created a space for, young and aspiring authors. In the process, a community of writers appeared on the scene, which found in *Utkal Sahitya* a vibrant platform for self-expression. More importantly, it provided a forum for critics to interpret and evaluate literary works, ancient and modern, and engage in educating the sensibility of an expanding reading public. It reflected and produced a restless milieu in which an educated middle class was actively seeking to carve an identity for itself and negotiate with colonial modernity. The essay given below comprises two parts; the first is written by Biswanath Kar and the second, by Chandra Mohan Maharana. The authors seek to provide justification for bringing out a literary monthly in Odia.

Biswanath Kar (1864–1934) began his career as a school teacher. He embraced Brahmoism under the influence of Madhusudan Rao (1853–1912), which led him to interrogate existing social conventions and practices. His essays, focusing mainly on issues of social reform, were brought out as a volume entitled *Bibidha Prabandha* [Miscellaneous Essays] in 1896. In 1897, he founded *Utkal Sahitya* and continued to edit it until his death. The first issue of *Utkal Sahitya* opened with a brief note by its editor in which he emphasized the crucial role literature plays in infusing a community with new energy and vitality. Undeterred by the premature demise of several literary magazines in Odisha, Biswanath launched *Utkal Sahitya* with the following objectives: to broaden and diversify the scope of literature by making it encompass different forms of knowledge such as science, agriculture, philosophy and industry; to strike a balance between ancient

DOI: 10.4324/9781003224778-14

and modern literatures by accepting what is valuable in the former and celebrating what embodies the spirit of the new age in the latter; and to engage in a project of reforming society by combating superstition and corruption.

Chandra Mohan Maharana (1870–1928) was an eminent educator, grammarian and author. He wrote highly acclaimed textbooks which include *Kathabali*, *Odia Byakarana* and *Rachana Shiksha* [How to Write an Essay] and contributed essays and poems to well-known periodicals of the time. Biswanath Kar invited Chandra Mohan, a highly respected cultural figure of the time, to explain the utility of literary magazines in the inaugural issue of *Utkal Sahitya*. Chandra Mohan's brief essay appeared as a companion piece to Biswanath's statement of editorial policy. Chandra Mohan began by distinguishing between books and magazines and dwelt on the special benefits offered by the latter. Magazines, unlike a book, explore a diversity of subjects and therefore relax the mind of readers and engage their interest. Readers can easily afford to buy magazines for these are less expensive than books. The most important advantage that magazines have over books lies in their ability to motivate young readers to become writers in their own right.

These two essays give us an idea of the growing awareness of the role literary magazines played in building a critical discourse in Odisha. They also highlight Biswanath's conscious attempt to give critical discourse new direction and substance through the sustained publication of a literary periodical.

*

The need for a literary periodical

Biswanath Kar and Chandra Mohan Maharana

I. A note on the need for publishing *Utkal Sahitya*[1]

Biswanath Kar

The first issue of *Utkal Sahitya* has appeared after much careful deliberation. We have taken this initiative bowing reverentially to the infinitely benevolent Almighty. We do not feel the need to explain at length the usefulness and relevance of a monthly literary magazine. These have been spelt out in our public declaration of purpose; and moreover, this issue of *Utkal Sahitya* features an article on this subject by an esteemed writer.[2] We do not mean to suggest that, in spite of the pervasive indifference to Odia literature, the absence of and necessity for a literary periodical have not been felt by others in Odisha earlier. If we do so, it would amount to underestimating the intelligence of educated Odias. However, to feel the necessity for something and to act in order to meet this are two different things. Although the former has been experienced in Odisha to some extent the latter has hardly been noticeable. In our humble opinion, the apathy and inertia of Odias is responsible for this state of affairs, has retarded the progress of this land, and accounts for their appalling misery. Success smiles on those who are enterprising and industrious. Unless we overcome apathy and lethargy, we will be deprived of many things that are desirable and cherished by human beings. We are aware that, given our insignificance, we are not equal to the task of rousing Odias from their deep slumber. Many who are far more accomplished and capable than us have made attempts in this regard and met with disappointment and failure. A number of literary magazines in Odisha have appeared in the past and died untimely deaths for want of support and encouragement. Their failure disheartens and terrifies us. One might ask, why then have we ventured into this perilous terrain? Who knows if we would not meet the same terrible fate that overtook our predecessors? Many well-wishers have warned us about the frightful consequences of our decision to launch a literary magazine. But why have we not paid any heed to their sensible advice? Our earnest response to these disturbing questions is that, overwhelmed by a powerful inner urge, we have undertaken this task. Our heart is also stirred by the cry of agony of our land which has nourished and nurtured us. Our life would be fulfilled we could serve our land. Life loses its meaning if we fail in doing this. We devote our energy to furthering our self-interest but what have we done to nourish our souls? What is then the point of remaining alive like *rakshasas*, drawing nourishment from one's mother and not giving her anything in return for her sacrifice? We thought that we should do something to the best of our ability to render service to our land. The prospect of failure does not perturb us. We are not worried about the prospect of the untimely demise of our magazine for within such death lies the possibility of a new life, a renewal. Should we retreat into a dark corner just because failure stares us in the face and spend our days shedding silent tears? Is such a response worthy of a human being? Without worrying about the outcome, perform whatever little task is within your power to accomplish. This is what great sages have advised us to do. This is also what the Almighty directs humanity to carry out. Thus, it would be futile to spend time speculating about the future.

Western education has transformed many areas of life in our country; it has also reshaped the world of literature. The changes that have taken place are desirable and welcome for human society and no culture can remain static forever. Stasis is absolutely unacceptable for any society that wants to remain vibrantly alive. It will be utterly foolish to resist the forces of progress out of blind loyalty to the past. At the same time, however, it would be equally terrible to dismiss ancient traditions out of immoderate admiration for the modern. Only those who can successfully negotiate between these two worlds are wise. The great and the good in all enlightened ages and developed lands have upheld this ideal. So long as we remain alive, we would sincerely follow this golden precept. Though the repository of ancient Odia literature does not have an abundance of invaluable works of art it is not entirely devoid of these. A few attempts are also being made at present to create a literature embodying the spirit of the new age. *Utkal Sahitya* aims at representing both these literary worlds. We deem it our duty to offer our readers what is valuable in ancient literature, and the thoughts and feelings that define a more advanced age. We hope to accomplish this sacred task with generous help from our enlightened authors.

Literature encompasses everything relating to human life and society. The vast and expansive domain of literature can include *kavyas*, plays, science, philosophy, education, industry, agriculture, commerce, religion and ethics. We cannot afford to ignore any one of these. Since progress is the goal towards which humanity strives, it is the duty of every individual to focus on whatever ensures all-round development. The other objective of *Utkal Sahitya* concerns a relentless effort to combat corruption, evil practices, superstition and promote honesty, good practices and genuine religiosity. Regardless of the outcome, we will perform these sacred and serious duties with unwavering dedication. We seek, in all humility, the support and blessings of the people of Odisha. May God who endows devotees with success bless our endeavour.

II. The utility of literary magazines[3]

Chandra Mohan Maharana

Pursuit of knowledge is unique to mankind and should be engaged in most actively. There are many ways in which knowledge can be acquired, of which two are most prominent: experience and reading. Knowledge gained through the above two methods is refined and enriched through close analysis and, the exercise of discrimination and judgment. One method complements the other. One gains access to knowledge generated by someone else through reading; at the same time, one also learns lessons from experience through techniques of close observation.

Knowledgeable or ignorant, human beings, of necessity, have to take the help of others in performing tasks, for they cannot do everything on their own. This is true of the process of acquisition of knowledge as well. A person learns new things by listening to another person or by reading books written by his predecessors. Recorded knowledge can be accessed through the reading of books and magazines. However, the former differs from the latter slightly. A book usually focuses on a single subject but a magazine contains pieces on a variety of subjects. Therefore, in a sense, reading a magazine amounts to going through several books. Moreover, buying five books may be an expensive proposition for a person who is not financially well off. But they may find magazines more affordable. The diversity of subjects dealt with in a magazine may prove mentally less taxing for readers, and engage their interest more effectively. Everybody knows how one derives happiness from seeing something pleasantly new, eating something differently flavoured, and listening to something beautifully unfamiliar. This is also true of the experience of reading an essay. One comes across instances of a few readers collectively subscribing to a magazine but one rarely, if ever, finds an example of a few readers buying one book. One has to invest more mental effort in reading a book than in going through a magazine. In saying this, we do not mean to devalue the importance of reading books and assign primacy only to reading magazines. No one can overlook the undeniable utility of reading books but this does not fall within the scope of the present discussion. Let us touch upon a few more benefits that accrue from going through magazines. The essays published in a magazine motivate the reader in a way that books cannot do. Readers, especially the young among them, reading an article with the author's name inscribed at its end, might feel inspired to write an article and get it published. This desire among young readers to write and publish articles contributes significantly to the growth of a literary culture. In more civilized countries, young and inexperienced speakers and writers acquire the rudiments of the art of speaking and writing in this manner, and in due course mature into accomplished orators and authors.

Magazines may be classified into two types: one includes dailies and weeklies, and the other, monthlies, etc. Both are important but in different ways. Dailies and weeklies are primarily concerned with topical issues whereas magazines belonging to the second type focus upon issues of deeper significance. Among the latter, monthlies are greater in number and enjoy wide circulation. From these monthly magazines, people acquire some knowledge about subjects such as science, history and literature. Magazines also satiate their need for pleasure to be derived from literature. Monthly literary magazines play a heroic role in the development of literature, and the promotion and appreciation of these serve as an index of the richness of our literary culture.

Translation: Aditya Nayak

Notes

1 Biswanath Kar, "Suchana" [A Note on the Need for Publishing *Utkal Sahitya*], *Utkal Sahitya*, vol. 1, no. 1, Cuttack: Sahityika, 1972 [1897], pp. 1–3.
2 See Chandra Mohan Maharana's essay which immediately follows this piece.
3 Chandra Mohan Maharana, "Sahitya Patrikara Upajogita" [The Utility of Literary Magazines], *Utkal Sahitya*, vol. 1, no. 1, Cuttack: Sahityika, 1972 [1897], pp. 3–4.

15 Gopal Chandra Praharaj

Two Odia books: a review

Introduction

Gopal Chandra Praharaj (1874–1945) contributed significantly to the development of modern Odia prose. A versatile man of letters and a lawyer by profession, Gopal Chandra wrote essays, poems, books for children satirical pieces, literary criticism, biographies, an unfinished autobiography, edited literary magazines, collected folktales and legends, and compiled a monumental dictionary of Odia. In the world of letters, he is celebrated as a belletrist, who acknowledged his indebtedness to the American author Oliver Wendell Holmes (1809–1894). Notable among his numerous collections of essays are *Bhagabata Tungire Sandhya* (Evenings at the Community Prayer Room in a Village, 1903) and *Bai Mohanty Panji* (Bai Mohanty's Journal, 1913). In the public imagination, however, he is remembered primarily as the compiler of *Purnachandra Odia Bhashakosha*, a seven-volume dictionary comprising about ten thousand pages. This quadri-lingual (Odia, English, Hindi and Bangla) lexicon which lists about 185,000 entries was part of the initiative to consolidate Odia identity through conferring stability upon Odia language. This concern with stabilizing Odia language is reflected in the review given in translation below which explores the question of developing a desirable diction for modern Odia literature.

Gopal Chandra reviews here two books by his senior contemporaries: *Chha Mana Atha Guntha*, a novel by Fakir Mohan Senapati (1843–1918) and *Yugadharma*, a play by Ram Sankar Ray (1857–1931). Fakir Mohan laid the foundation of realistic prose fiction in Odia and pioneered the use of colloquial idiom in the literary domain. Rama Sankar Ray emerged as the most distinguished playwright in the closing decades of the nineteenth century in Odisha. Both these authors were deeply concerned with social reform. The issues Gopal Chandra's review, titled "Duikhandi Odia Pustak", focuses upon are the moral world the characters of the two books inhabit and the diction appropriate for literary use. The moral worlds depicted in the two books problematize the nature of poetic justice to the discomfort of the reviewer. The advent of realism as a technique in Odia literature perhaps lies at the root of such discomfort. It may be mentioned

DOI: 10.4324/9781003224778-15

here that Gopal Chandra is more critical of the way poetic justice operates in *Chha Mana Atha Guntha* than it does in *Yugadharma*. In Fakir Mohan's novel, several innocent characters meet a terrible fate although evil is also punished. The choice of diction constitutes another key aspect of realism as a technique and the reviewer dwells upon it at great length. He turns to the wider question of the kind of language used in modern Odia literature and singles out for censure the habit of using bookish, high-sounding and foreign words. He lauds the two authors for having employed a home-spoken idiom in their books and hopes for this trend to grow more pronounced. He uses the review as a pretext for developing a general theory of diction suitable for modern Odia literature. While advocating the use of an "unalloyed home-spoken idiom" as the medium of literary expression, he recommends the eschewal of narrowly dialectal elements and the speech of people from lower social strata. In the process, he hopes a standard home-spoken idiom will emerge. Thus, even as he seeks to democratize literary diction, Gopal Chandra baulks at giving the democratic spirit free rein. This review is significant for its insightful discussion of the implications of the advent of realism in Odia literature. It also illustrates how book reviews shaped modern critical discourse in Odisha.

*

Two Odia books: a review[1]

Gopal Chandra Praharaj

Recently, two books, Fakir Mohan Senapati's social novel, *Chha Mana Atha Guntha* [Six Acres and a Third][2] and Ram Sankar Ray's social play, *Yugadharma* [Spirit of the Age], have been published.[3] We are convinced that these works have ushered in a new era in modern Odia literature and strengthened its foundation. *Chha Mana Atha Guntha* was earlier serialized in the periodical *Utkal Sahitya*. Though the books belong to two different branches of literature, there is no doubt about the distinctive merit of each. The works depict the demoniac machinations of two powerful men who are, in fact, rapacious and lecherous demons, Ramachandra Mangaraj and Mahanta Uddhav Das. Their fiendish deeds and the fatal consequences thereof, the victory of *dharma* and the defeat of *papa* [sin], the contemptible malevolence perpetrated on simple and virtuous characters by wicked men and women – all these are vividly depicted in the books. One cannot fully fathom the extent to which the two authors have rendered exemplary service to modern Odia society and literature, unless one goes through the books. Once we start reading the two books, we just cannot put them down until we reach the concluding passages of the last chapter or scene. The authors have impressed us with their skilful portrayal of characters, lively images of Odia households, and vibrant pictures of social life. Upon reading

Utkalara Kahani,[4] an accomplished young man remarked that writing such books was a waste of effort and intelligence. One would not be surprised if some Odia readers express similar disapproval after reading these books. We are seated on no such high pedestal, nor can we advise the general reading public to occupy such lofty heights.

There is a saying in English, "art lies in concealing art". We tend to use, to a greater or lesser extent, the refined diction current among the educated class of people, because of our frequent intercourse with them. The more frequent such interaction, the greater will be the threat to the "pure home-spoken idiom". Here, we do not argue against the use of such "refined" diction. We simply urge everyone to use "pure home-spoken idiom" wherever it is capable of conveying our feelings and thoughts. In situations where "pure home-spoken idiom" is not adequate or acceptable (there may arise occasions where it might violate norms of decorum and decency), the employment of refined, borrowed or conventional (decorous) diction is understandable. But one comes across instances in most books and writings in periodicals where the author, eager to display his learning, introduces a decorous word or sentence in places where he could have done with an ordinary spoken word or sentence. It is as though, had he not done so, the reader would have doubted his knowledge and intelligence. Interestingly, however, advanced languages of the world tell a different story. Take the case of English: books written in this language where words of Anglo-Saxon origin are used more extensively than those derived from Greek and Latin (or borrowed foreign words) achieve greater popularity. But, the precepts and practice of leading modern Odia writers have so far been just the opposite. In more recent times, however, attempts are being made to remedy the situation; how long these will take to bear fruit one cannot say.

Having used the bookish and high-sounding words for so long, we have forgotten, to some extent, our colloquial idiom. In fact, many educated but candid Odia young men would admit that they habitually let slip a few English, Hindi and Bangla expressions even while conversing with uneducated and uncultured housewives. The pure home-spoken idiom, for some, is lowly and worthless. A few in the higher echelons of our society are infected by this contagion. But let some of us try using the household idiom to write four lines; we shall then see that this is not as easy as is assumed. Much artistic skill is required to do this. Such skill is significant precisely because it easily escapes notice. A few highly educated Odias place Nandakishore Bal's poems, "Pallichitra" and "Nirjharini" in the same category as the folksy "Chandravati Harana" and "Ramlila" etc.[5] They might find it surprising that Englishmen appreciate the literary merit of writers such as Wordsworth, Tennyson, Dickens, Thackeray and George Eliot, and do not consider them as mere providers of popular entertainment.

Does this mean that there is no difference between the "pure home-spoken idiom" and that which is used by people belonging to untouchable castes? If, under the pretext of preferring home-spoken idiom, distorted word formations used by these people from lower social strata are employed, we are helpless. We consider the language spoken in cultured families which incorporates a few elements from refined diction and some imported words as a desirable model. It is an indisputable fact that Odia language has lost its simplicity and purity through contact with the languages of foreign rulers over centuries. The linguistic situation now needs to be remedied and at least efforts should be made in this direction.

It will be wrong to say that the two books under discussion are wholly free from such blemishes. The authors of these earnestly strived to turn home-spoken idiom into a medium of literary expression. It is futile to expect complete success in these early endeavours. The day when the golden rule "write as you speak" practised by English authors is followed here will be a momentous one. The current stage of development of Odia literature can be dubbed "where percheth the ghee?" era. Let me recount an amusing anecdote. A highly-educated man of refined taste asked his father, "Where percheth the ghee?" The amused father replied sarcastically, "Its Highness the Ghee percheth in the container that is reposing in the yarn-hanger."[6] Be that as it may. In these two books, we can sense the beginning of a new era in Odia literature. We do not dare to name the writers who are engaged in such a venture for fear of offending self-important authors rendering service to Odia literature. There is no doubt that the names of those worthy writers will be writ in gold in times to come in the annals of Odia literature. So, they should not feel discouraged just because we have not named them here.

Both the writers demonstrate exemplary skill in portraying characters. "Hold a mirror up to nature", instances of this time-tested dictum are amply furnished in these two works. As characters, Champa in *Chha Mana Atha Guntha* and Radhimata in *Yugadharma* closely resemble each other. However, Champa is a cunning she-devil. We dare not compare her with anyone other than Tamora[7] in Shakespeare's *Titus Andronicus*. Radhimata is also a demoness, but she is somewhat timid; Radhimata is a slave to the mahant Uddhav Das but Ramachandra Mangaraj is Chamapa's slave. Radhimata is the villainous fallen woman, Bawd[8] of Shakespeare's *Pericles*. It is hard to believe that if the Queen had fallen into the hands of Champa, Haridas and Premababu would have succeeded in rescuing her. We might find many Radhimatas in our society, but it is difficult to come across one Champa in a million. Though Ramachandra Mangaraj can be said to possess a few human qualities, he is both avaricious and wicked. As for the mahant, he is the devil incarnate; for only he can gift an *hamaru* sari[9] to a gypsy woman. It is only in the presence of the mahant that the scene of the boy-dancer and Keluni seems apt. The speech made by the mahant in the presence of the veiled "Rani" [actually the illusionist Haridas in female disguise], is indeed quite impressive. There is no hope for a society where characters like Champa and the mahant Uddhav Das flourish.

The authors have deftly depicted the terrible consequences that Champa and Uddhav Das eventually suffer. But what is the point? Champa moves about freely after destroying Bhagia and Saria, and ruining the life of Saantani, a noble soul and an innocent woman, adopting devious means. The mahant, who looted public funds and sent vast sums of money to his native place, indulged in pleasure and ruined the queen by dethroning her, roams freely with impunity. The writers have tried to convey the twin truism about the rich getting richer and there being many ways of evading the punitive powers of law. But which of the two writers has succeeded in doing so, it is for the readers to judge.

The author of *Chha Mana Atha Guntha*, after showing us how the forces of evil are defeated, leaves the readers to wait for the victory of virtue in life in the hereafter. But the author of *Yugadharma* has dramatized the defeat of evil and the victory of virtue in this life. After going through *Chha Mana Atha Guntha*, tears of disappointment well up in our eyes; whereas, after going through *Yugadharma*, we feel like dancing for joy. Selfless love and service to humanity are ardently celebrated throughout the play. In the closing chapter of *Chha Mana Atha Guntha*, we no longer feel amused by the chief *baidya*'s risible distortions of Sanskrit *shlokas* by the deathbed of Mangaraj. However, in the concluding section of *Yugadharma*, in the Brahmo wedding ceremony, we are filled with ecstasy thinking about the happy course of events in the recent past and share Prembabu's blissful joy.

We notice another flaw in *Chha Mana Atha Guntha* (someone has pointed out a similar blemish in Fakir Mohan's short story "Rebati"); almost everyone in the novel – Champa, Jaga, Mangaraj, Bhagia, Saria, Saantani – dies. The only character who survives is Makunda, the farmhand. But in *Yugadharma* all the good characters – Nityanand, Rani, Yashoda, Prembabu, Haridas – survive to affirm the triumph of virtue, and the villains and wrongdoers such as Radhamata and the mahant perish to signal the defeat of evil. However, Fakir Mohan's depiction in *Chha Mana Atha Guntha* of life in the inner wings of Odia households has an air of authenticity which is beyond the author of *Yugadharma*. No one can surpass Fakir Mohan in this regard. There is no nook and cranny in Odia households which has escaped his piercing eye. From the household of the high and mighty to that of the poor and the humble, be it Mangaraj's inner chambers or Saria's spinning and weaving verandah, he has seen it all, and has shown us everything.

A well-known American intellectual observes that it is only in fiction, and not in life, that sinners are punished and tyrants, defeated. Why else would men covet another man's wife? Pembabu comes forward to alleviate the grief of Nityanand and Rani in *Yugadharma*? But in the real world, who comes to the rescue of the many Ranis and Nityanands undergoing acute suffering behind closed doors.

It is our aim to bring the two books to the attention of the reading public. Our assessment of these books might appear biased; but we hope that the reading public will form their own opinions after going through the books themselves. Our humble views might be erroneous; but the educated Odias, instead of getting biased by them, would do well to arrive at their own judgments.

The books have their fair share of shortcomings. We have some reservations about the idiom used and the portrayal of characters in both the texts. Since not many good books get published in Odisha, we do not wish to demotivate the authors of these two books by giving a long list of their flaws. We earnestly request the two writers to continue their endeavour and not disappoint their readers' natural expectations of them. We have already seen how a young Odia writer, unable to take the sharp criticism of his literary efforts, gave up writing altogether. We had pinned high hopes on this young friend.

A writer who is able to use fewest possible words to express his thoughts and feelings, and portray characters successfully, deserves a high place in the literary pantheon. We are disappointed to find the above principle not followed in either of the two books. Brevity of expression is a necessary virtue. In this respect, *Chha Mana Atha Guntha* is more flawed than *Yugadharma*. Had the authors done away with a few passages from their texts, the quality of characterization, and expression of thoughts and feelings would not have been affected at all. To be able to set limits to creative expression is desirable in a writer. A true artist is someone who can make the audience cry and laugh without laughing or shedding tears himself.

Moreover, home-spoken idiom varies from place to place, even within the same language. In order to deploy this idiom, one may have to use local dialects. However, from among these, a standard form should be fashioned. But one need not be in an anxious hurry. For, once the habit of using home-spoken idiom is firmly established in Odia literary practice, the principle of the "survival of the fittest" will itself ensure the evolvement of a model home-spoken idiom before long. Words and expressions borrowed from foreign languages and narrowly dialectal elements will gradually disappear from that model linguistic register, and a fully developed model home-spoken idiom will emerge. All major languages of the world have been shaped through this process. Nowadays, no Bengali writer uses the spoken idiom of East Bengal or Dhaka while deploying "home-spoken" Bangla. Similarly, no English writer would employ the Welsh or Cornish dialect in the name of using pure, home-spoken English. Yet, at times, depending on the demands of the situation, the need to make characters mouth narrowly dialectal expressions may necessarily arise. We do not wish to pronounce a verdict on this matter. In *Yugadharma,* the playwright has made Barhmans from Berhampur in the southern part of Odisha speak a specific dialect. This eminently suits the given context. Similarly, if someone from Puri speaks the dialect prevalent in Balasore, people will laugh at him. A "model home-spoken" idiom in some form has already struck roots in Odisha. However, in order to grow stronger and gain stability, it must achieve wider currency and acceptance.

The two writers discussed here are far superior to us. We have expressed our views above fully convinced that they will not be upset with us for having spoken our mind freely and with good intentions. There is no doubt that the common reader is an abler judge of the merit of the books than we are.

Translation: Sumanyu Satpathy

Notes

1 Gopal Chandra Praharaj, "Duikhandi Odia Pustak" [Two Odia Books: A Review], *Utkal Sahitya*, vol. 6, no. 6, Cuttack, 1903, pp. 130–135.
2 Fakir Mohan Senapati, *Chha Mana Atha Guntha* [Six Acres and a Third], Tr. Rabi Shankar Mishra et al., Berkeley: University of California Press, 2005.
3 [Translator's note] Both the novel and the play were published in book form in 1902.
4 [Translator's note] *Utkalara Kahani*, a collection of Odia folktales compiled by Gopal Chandra Praharaj, was published in 1901.
5 [Translator's note] These two works belonging to the domain of popular or folk culture were thought to be infra dig.
6 [Translator's note] Odia sentences which mix *tadbhava* and colloquial words are hard to translate. I have pointed out the ridiculous incongruity by using bombastic English equivalents.
7 [Translator's note] Tamora is the Queen of the Goths turned Roman Empress in William Shakespeare's *Titus Andronicus*. After Titus ritually sacrifices her eldest son, Tamora makes it her mission in life to viciously torment Titus and his family. She accomplishes this through her good looks, sensuality, and ability to manipulate those around her.
8 [Translator's note] Bawd is the wife of Pander, the keeper of the brothel in the play *Pericles*.
9 [Translator's note] An expensive and exotic sari from Homboru.

16 Ashraf Ali Khan
Fakir Mohan Senapati's *Mamu*: a review

Introduction

Ashraf Ali Khan (1875–1959) was a distinguished man of letters who was well versed in Odia, Sanskrit, Persian, Urdu and English literatures. A vibrantly multi-cultural ethos had evolved in northern parts of Odisha, especially in Balasore and Bhadrak, in the seventeenth and eighteenth centuries. This resulted most notably in *tamsa*, a form of polyglot theatrical performance, and *Satyapir pala*, a syncretic religious ritual. In view of the wide range of works Ashraf Ali authored such as *Islam, Muharram Itibruti, Pradosh Padmini, Bruhat Gadyapadyamaya Champu Kavya* and *Bebak Galat*, he could be considered as a living embodiment of this rich Indo-Islamic heritage. He also wrote a farce titled *Adbhut Sakshya* [A Strange Witness] (1927). A collection of his poems was published under the title *Abasara Ranjana Hrudaya Nirjhara* [Emanations of the Heart to Fill Leisure Hours with Amusement]. Asharaf Ali was a close friend and great admirer of Fakir Mohan Senapati. In recognition of his contributions to literature, the title Kavya Ratnakar was conferred upon Ashraf Ali.

The essay given below was published as a review of Fakir Mohan Senapati's novel *Mamu* [The Maternal Uncle] in *Utkal Sahitya* (vol. 18, nos. 2 & 3) in 1914. Although modestly presented as a review, it should be recognized as a major contribution to Fakir Mohan criticism. Ashraf Ali Khan's astute reading of this classic Odia novel displays his sharp critical acumen, and embodies a rich contemporary response to the text. The essay is imbued with the exuberant irony and robust humour one inevitably associates with Fakir Mohan's narrative voice. Ashraf Ali, with playful self-deprecation, presents himself as a Muslim trespasser in the sacred precincts of Odia literary criticism. He locates *Mamu* firmly in the category of realistic novels but is quick to point out that idealistic elements do find their way into the fabric of the narrative. He singles out for praise Fakir Mohan's dexterous use of simple, rustic language which contributes to the unimpeded flow of the narrative. However, he celebrates the novelist's ability to distance himself from the rustic narrator and employ an elevated diction when the occasion demands it. He draws the reader's attention

DOI: 10.4324/9781003224778-16

to the novelist's remarkable success in fashioning a unique idiom which ingeniously blends colloquialized Sanskrit, Perso-Arabic expressions, English words and the home-spoken idiom of rural Odisha. Here, Fakir Mohan's modernity consists in using this composite diction as a medium for major art. In his analysis of the novel, Ashraf Ali employs *rasa* theory, traditionally applied to *kavyas* and *natakas*, to a nascent literary form for which a critical method of appreciation was in its early stage of development. At the same time, his attempt to understand the novel as a means of presenting a history of contemporary society moves beyond questions relating to aesthetic appeal and character portrayal to illuminate aspects of the novel as a picture of a society in motion. There is no doubt that this essay helps us glimpse the contours of an initiative which gives novel criticism a new direction and rigour by deftly negotiating between traditional and modern approaches.

*

Fakir Mohan Senapati's *Mamu*: a review[1]

Ashraf Ali Khan

Many readers would be astonished to see a strange new name at the end of this review; some would also be shocked to find that a *pathan*[2] is its author. Detecting the smell of onion, garlic and meat, a few might give evidence of their refined literary sensibility. But the fact is, when someone finds something terribly exciting, he thinks nothing of propriety and makes a fool of himself in public. As the great Persian poet Hafiz sings, "Ke Ishq aaj purdaye asmat berun aarad zolekha ra" [the power of love made a woman of incomparable beauty like Zolekha step out of the confines of her palace and court dishonour]. My delight knew no bounds when I went through Fakir Mohan's newly published novel *Mamu* [The Maternal Uncle][3]. I, therefore, could not restrain myself after reading discussions relating to it in the last few issues of *Utkal Sahitya*. The great writer Fakir Mohan wrote in his famous novel *Chha Mana Atha Guntha*, "When a *sankirtan*[4] is in progress, even a dumb person opens his mouth to join the singing." Getting carried away, I am also behaving like that dumb person. I hope that when a sword-wielding *pathan* intrudes into the sacred literary temple of pen-wielding Odias, he will not be bitterly ridiculed.

I read *Mamu* as soon as after it was published and eagerly wanted to write a review. But I was distracted by official and personal obligations and could not do so. In the meantime, Madanmohan Pattanaik and Shibanarayana Nayak have published their comments on *Mamu*. I have no intention of behaving like a sergeant to the literary foot-soldiers; I would like to serve them as an orderly. Instead of engaging in useless repetitions, I wish to supplement their views. In a circus, after the skilful actors perform their fascinating acts, the clown entertains the crowd by executing a few somer-saults. Like the clown, I hope to provide the reader with comic relief.

Here, some might express the view that there is no need for yet another comment on *Mamu*. To this my answer is, cannot a melodious song be sung hundreds of times without wearying the listener? Have people stopped commenting on and annotating canonical texts? Nothing deterred a critic to publish yet another review of Bankimchandra's famous and much-discussed *Krishnakant's Will* in the magazine *Bharatabarsha*. *Mamu* is the greatest Odia novel and has been brought out only recently. In this democratic age, why would I let go of an opportunity to publish my opinions in *Utkal Sahitya* (no matter how ordinary a writer I am)? Eminent lawyer Madhusudan Das[5] would support me in this argument.

Prose fiction can be of two types: idealistic and realistic. *Mamu* belongs to the latter. In the past, people used to be much more naïve; much like the immature children who readily believe in the western fairy tales and our folktales, people in the past credited everything that they came across in a well-written book, especially poetry, no matter how fantastic. Not only did they read it with much interest but also accepted it without a shred of doubt. But the new generation of readers with a scientific and rationalist bent of mind is increasingly disinclined to swallow the bitter pill of improbable nar-ratives. Such books continue to find favour only with the old, immature children and people with little education.

The exceptionally astute "Sahitya-senapati"[6] [commander in the field of literature], during the first phase of his career, wrote *Ramayana*, *Mahabharata*, *Purana* etc. Now with the weathercock of literary taste changing its direction, he has also adapted himself to the change. Hence, his novels *Chha Mana Atha Guntha* and *Mamu*, and his short stories belong to the category of realistic literature and have endeared themselves to the educated section of modern society.

Let me now draw your attention to some notable aspects of *Mamu*. Though *Mamu* is presented as a realistic novel, it also features elements of idealism. Saraswati Dei's expertise in running the household, love for children, generosity; Pitambar Aridamana's views on government jobs; the virtuousness of Gelhei in spite of her humble origins, her fortitude in the face of danger and her diligence; Pratapudita Malla Uttararay's aristocratic propriety, composure in the face of hardship, his moderation and efficient management of the zamindari; Chandamani's simplicity; and the loyalty of the servant, Karuna represent idealism in its highest form. The Odia reading public has immensely benefited from the lofty ideals celebrated by Fakir Mohan, the moralist who dramatizes the triumph of virtue over vice.

I feel completely lost when I undertake a close study of this fascinating novel. As every paragraph, every page is worth mentioning, I am confused as to what is to be discussed and what is to be left out. Since I have volun-teered to carry out this task, I will try to do my best.

Style of writing

Mamu is written in a style that is simple and effortless, which may even be described as rustic. The narrative flows like an unimpeded stream. So, it bears no trace of obscurity that one finds in many other texts. It, therefore, offers a very pleasant reading experience; one never feels fatigued while going through it; on the other hand, as she reads on, the reader feels more and more deeply involved. In engaging the readers in this way, Fakir Mohan is a pioneer in Odisha. A few writers have now started following his example.

Exceptions to the rule

The novelist abandons his rustic idiom at places and adopts an elevated style (as if distancing himself for a while from the rustic narrator). Here, his language becomes Sanskritized, his emotions assume a lofty dimension and his thoughts acquire a philosophical depth. This affords the reader much pleasure; had the novelist not done so, philosophical theories expressed in Sanskritized idiom through a rustic narrator would have appeared incongruous and improbable. Filial love, a comparative depiction of the joys and sorrows of the rich, the poor and the middle classes, differences in the dispositions of brothers and sisters, marital love, absence of perennial happiness in the world, the generosity of the master, inherited nobility, reflections on the success and failure of the *nazar* and the *peskar*[7] – these are the priceless gems that enrich the novel.

Diction

The novelist deliberately makes use of colloquialized Sanskrit, Persian and English words in order to enliven descriptions. These include *manish, bebasa, beusa, gerasta, bida, uaasa, saha, mukhya, ashra, adhya, chanchi, chotra, bibha, taskar, gahaki* etc. The word "prayaschita" becomes "praschita" in the mouth of the half-educated astrologer and even becomes "prachita" in the utterances of the unlettered Saraswati Dei. "Commissioner" is uttered as "commistan" by the barber Haribola. These transformations sound natural; the literary substitutes for these would have been utterly inappropriate.

Words of Perso-Arabic origins

Words such as *musalam, magdur, eenam, mamuli, dikdar, tofan, surukhuru, tarafsani, hemat, malmata, rosam, dasturi, haal, samjiba, eesara, mulak, hukum tamil, khapa, khuni kharap, sabari, barad, sataranj, mulakat, nishap, tahakharacha, aktiyar, naukar, tanakhi, bemani, adana, sailabi* are employed profusely throughout the novel. Needless to say, these render the text livelier. Owing to centuries of intimate familiarity, these foreign words have become so imperceptibly assimilated into Odia that to discard them now would only reek of a narrow mindset, extreme literary parochialism and hatred for everything foreign. This would also rob the narration of its natural beauty and liveliness. Among the major languages of the world, English probably has the largest vocabulary. This happened because the English race possesses, among other good qualities, a liberal literary outlook. At least a quarter of the English lexicon comprises words of foreign origin. Indian words like *deva*, *shastra*, *Allah*, *bismillah* have found their way into the English dictionary. The fact that people in our country who know English prefer to write letters in English, and not in their mother tongues, provide evidence of the richness of its vocabulary. Similarly, certain English words like rail, slate, bench have gradually entered Odia vocabulary within a hundred years of British annexation of Odisha. Getting rid of these foreign words in order to create an uncontaminated Odia vocabulary would be a difficult task and the newly coined Sanskrit words would be awkward to use. Like in other spheres of life, reciprocal exchange is an indispensable part of literature. Hence, loan words or the use of foreign words in Odia vocabulary is not undesirable; in fact, it is convenient and enhances its aesthetic appeal.

The use of Cuttack lingo

Even though the novelist hails from Balasore, he extensively uses words such as *saupa*, *garada*, *jhua*, *boila*, *basanda* which are peculiar to Cuttack. Especially, whenever he uses "kyan" or "jaiin", a resident of Balasore like me finds it shockingly unacceptable. However, one should not object to the use of local dialects in literary texts in view of the need to expand the literary sphere in Odisha.

Idioms

The employment of idiomatic expressions like *na chaa bhabi chinti* [thinking about all possibilities], *un chun kariba* [to murmur], *naaka pochibaku tara nahin* [there is no time even to wipe one's nose], *charkhi pari ghuru thibe* [moves like a spinning wheel], *kau ka thu* [from the time when the crow caws; break of dawn], *halila pani re goda diye nahin* [one who is scared of stepping into running water; very careful] immensely enriches the novel.

Rasa

Karuna rasa [pathos] is the prevalent *rasa* of the novel. The humiliation of Narubabu in the presence of his maternal aunt, Narubabu weeping in front of his maternal uncle, the Vaishnavas' praise showered on the zamindar before partaking of the *prasad*, the moneylender Sadhu Sahu expressing his loyalty to the zamindar's family – all powerfully evoke the sentiment of pathos. The description of the shaving of Raghab's beard is an example of the grotesque and other matters related to it are instances of comedy. I cannot help citing another example of the use of *hasya rasa* [the comic sentiment]. Discussing weighty philosophical matters at the gathering of pandits, the royal pandit of Badagada, Rangabhatla Venkat Pantulu draws a hilarious comparison between philosophy and hot, green chillies. ... Barber Haribola's brilliant ingenuity towards the end of the twenty-fifth chapter also provokes laughter. *Adirasa* [the erotic sentiment] has not been left out altogether. It is depicted decorously; the intimacy of the royal couple is full of tender eroticism whereas in the chapters titled "Pratijogini-Pratijogita" and "Dharma Bhai" vulgar eroticism is implicitly present. In the dramatic presentations of the fight between two characters, one finds *raudra rasa* (anger). Other *rasas* are also depicted in the novel.

Proverbs

The use of proverbs by village women at the bathing ghat to describe the Nazar's[8] wife with irony and sarcasm is hugely entertaining. Besides, the novelist also incorporates local proverbs, poems, similes and Sanskrit *shlokas* at appropriate places in the text. I desist from multiplying instances for fear of unnecessarily lengthening the essay.

Depiction of physical appearance

In this matter, the novelist adopts a pleasantly innovative technique. Generally speaking, writers focus on depicting the physical beauty of their young heroes and heroines. But since Pratap Udit and his wife Chandamani are of the age of his son and daughter, the elderly novelist refrains from presenting them as sexual beings and emphasizes their endearing qualities. Moreover, the author treats their parents and elders like Dasharathi Das, Menaka Dei and Saraswati Dei like his own relatives, and highlights their caring and loving nature, shying away from dwelling on their looks. This gentlemanly attitude of the writer towards ladies is consistent with rules of decorum; however, literary conventions demand that a writer depict the physical appearance of women. Here, faced with a dilemma, the author adopts a golden mean. He elaborately describes the appearance of the heroine as a child and leaves the reader to imagine her beauty as she comes of age. It is possible to imagine how beautiful a flower would turn out to be by just looking at the bud. Although the author observes admirable frugality in the portrayal of the physical appearance of good characters, he has given his imagination free play while delineating the evil ones. The author seems to be experiencing unconcealed delight while describing the looks of characters such as the evil Chitrakala and the stupid Raghab.

Lively descriptions

Description of the beauty of the newly born Chandamani, preparing the *panchuati*,[9] the dispositions of the cowherd, portrayal of Gelhei, the picture of Madhuban orchard, portarait of *abadhana* Sadashiba Khadiratna, Chandamani's feigned indifference when her marriage proposal is discussed and her amusing behaviour, the fight between Chitra and Nakaphodiama, Nazarani's entry looking like a ghost, Chitra's attempt to prove her innocence at the end of the fight, and the ecstatic dance of rival *kirtan* singers are presented with vivid aptness and are immensely enjoyable. The conversation among Saraswati, Menaka and Dasharathi presents a lovely picture of domesticity. The account of Chitra's many-layered vileness is quite impressive.

Portrayal of sin and virtue

Mamu is essentially a story of sin. Like the all-devouring Rahu, the *nazar* Natabara takes away the little money his ailing mother spent on her opium. His foster mother, his widowed younger sister who had inherited vast property and her family members face starvation due to his machinations. He robs his sister of everything she owned; her son Naru is made to face extreme hardship and the tenants of Naripur estate are subjected to all forms of tyranny. He even tries to fraudulently take possession of the estate. However, inscrutable are the ways of *dharma*; the boat overburdened with sins begins to sink. Faced with misfortune, the darkness of ignorance is suddenly dispelled from the *nazar*'s heart. The seed of virtue could not sprout in him who was born into a good family as it lay under the crushing weight of youth, the arrogance of authority, and love of erotic pleasure. It suddenly puts out leaves as he becomes aware of the consequences of his sinful actions. Natabara's soliloquy in the jail is a lesson for all. He remembers each of his heinous acts, burns in penitence and experiences hell. Hence, it is said, "The mind is its own place, and in itself can make a heaven of hell, a hell of heaven".

After suffering like this for some time, Natabara surrenders to the merciful Almighty. He experiences a strange kind of divine bliss and is filled with a new strength. This leads him to sing an ecstatic song of repentance which captivates fellow inmates as well as the guards. In the end, Natabara accepts his guilt at the sessions court but suddenly loses his reason. Hence, instead of imposing on him a heavy sentence, the judge send him to the lunatic asylum. The other accused are also awarded sentences commensurate with their guilt. Thus is virtue triumphant and sin, defeated. The prayer of *chaprasi* Khodabaksh who had been deceived by the *nazar* addressed to God provides another good example of the victory of *dharma*. Other charming incidents dramatized in the novel include Narubabu's loving and benevolent uncle refusing to accept his nephew's scholarship money for three months and paying all his expenses, Narubabu sending this scholarship amount home to help his cash-strapped mother and foster mother to meet household expenses, his foster mother spending this money to feed the poor and the pious at the temple of Jugal-Kishor in spite of her indigence, devoted tenants carrying gifts of vegetables for the feast, the ecstatic dance of *kirtan* singers and village women blowing conches and ululating.

Plot of the novel

The events of the story have been imaginatively woven together. The narrator describes the physical appearance and conduct of Bishakha Dei, who belongs to a good family, through the gossip of village women at the bathing ghat instead of presenting the details himself. Similarly, the misery of tenants of Naripur village is conveyed through the conversation between Shyam Samal and the barber, Haribol. Most notably, information on Natabara Das' machinations and exploitation of the tenants of Naripur is transmitted through Gokul Pattanaik's letter. These instances reveal the incomparable craftsmanship of the author.

Miscellaneous matters

Mamu contains a history of how the Khandayat caste came into being and the establishment of *chaupadhis*.[10] The author's previous novel *Chha Mana Atha Guntha* [Six Acres and a Third] presented the most vivid portrait of Odisha as it was nearly sixty years ago and *Mamu* offers an excellent picture of contemporary Odisha. It would not be easy to come across such realistic accounts even in the highly-developed Bangla literary world. Through this novel *Mamu* and his short story "Birei Bishala", Senapati infuses the word "Mamu" with a new connotation – a deceptive and selfish blood-relation.

The concept of dharma

The fifteenth chapter titled "Panditsabha" [a conference of pandits] can be regarded as the heart of the novel. Through the scholarly discourses of the pandits, the pious author discusses the following points of philosophical import: the atheism of Charbak and other *nyaya* philosophers; the scepticism of Kanada, Jaimini, John Stuart Mill and Herbert Spencer, and other schools of philosophy such as *Mayavad* and *Sunyabad*; the nature of the Brahman in Upanishads; the teachings of the Advaitas and Buddhists; Patanjali's Yoga; the difference between *karma* and *gyana*; the position of the theists, sceptics, the superstitious and the atheists in the religious world; the lack of devotion to god among philosophers. At the end of the chapter, the deliberations focus on the need for monotheism to attain salvation. The author discusses these issues with remarkable brevity and depth within the space of only eleven pages. Irrespective of caste or religion, this chapter should be read by all those who wish to espouse a liberal religious outlook.

Shortcomings

Some good characters are not rewarded for their virtues and some wicked characters are not penalized for their vices adequately. Saraswati Dei's generosity and her unalloyed affection for her kin; Banabara's innocence, his respect for teachers and the absence of greed in him; Chandamani's joyous simplicity; Pitambar Aridamana's diligence and commitment to duty; Narubabu's many aristocratic virtues; Prabhudayal's chicanery; the peshkar's kindness and love for his near and dear ones – one would have liked to see the positive consequences resulting from these. Moreover, the villainy of Gokul Pattanaik, the loyalty of the moneylender Sadhu Sahu and the deep concern of barber Haribol for others' well-being needed to be etched out more fully. Perhaps, the author desisted from developing these peripheral characters for fear of the novel growing too voluminous. He therefore restricted himself to the main task of demonstrating how characters like Natabara and a few others receive the wages of their sins. I heard from a reliable source that the novelist, in future, would remedy these minor deficiencies and present a fuller narrative.

The last word

There is no doubt that, in spite of these inconsiderable limitations, this novel is undoubtedly one of the finest in Odia. In view of its admirable style of narration, impressive scope and moral depth, the novel deserves to be taught at the higher classes of the university. I am told that some of the learned professors have already included *Mamu* in the college syllabus.

Translation: Umasankar Patra

Notes

1 [Editors' note] Ashraf Ali Khan, "*Mamu*–Samalochana" [Fakir Mohan Senapati's *Mamu*: A Review], *Utkal Sahitya*, vol. 18, nos. 2 & 3, Cuttack, 1914, pp. 111–115, 149–152.
2 [Translator's note] A Muslim in colloquial Odia.
3 [Translator's note] Fakir Mohan Senapati, *Mamu* [The Maternal Uncle], Tr. Jatindra Kumar Nayak, Bhubaneswar: Rupantar, 2007.
4 [Translator's note] Communal singing of devotional songs usually celebrating the love between Radha and Krishna.
5 [Translator's note] Madhusudan Das (1848–1934) was a renowned lawyer and the chief architect of modern Odisha in the colonial period.
6 [Author's note] Dear reader, I do not feel inclined to use the age-old epithet "Sahitya-rathi" (literary-charioteers) as except gods and goddesses no one uses *rathas*. Instead, I wish to refer to the middle-aged writers as "Sahitya-sadi" (literary-horse riders) as the use of horses is still in vogue and the college-educated young writers as "Sahitya-cyclists" (these fortunate ones enjoy wide popularity now-a-days). However, a veteran writer like Fakir Mohan Senapati should not be given such trivial labels. In every respect, he is a "Sahitya-senapati" [literary commander].

Readers might think – as it is, the *pathan* has intruded into the sacred literary temple and on top of it, is objecting to the well-established sobriquet, "Sahitya-rathi." Moreover, he is trying to employ absurd terminology. How insolent! How foolish! How can a *pathan* give up his congenital irreverence! If a pandit were around, he would instantly add a shloka: "*swabhabam naiba muchyate*" [One's disposition never changes]. But whatever you may say, I would like to make it clear that I pay the least heed to what you think. (Esteemed Editor, before you publish this essay, weigh the possibility of your magazine *Utkal Sahitya* losing readers.)

7 [Translator's note] Court officials. The *nazar* and the *peskar* are important characters of the novel.

8 [Translator's note] Nazar was a court official and one of the primary characters of the novel, the maternal uncle, is the Nazar at the court.

9 [Translator's note] An offering of five kinds of fried grain distributed on the fifth day of a child's birth.

10 [Translator's note] *Khandayat* literally means a sword wielder. They were traditionally the warrior caste who also cultivated land when the kingdom was not at war. *Chaupadhi* was a place where the four Vedas were studied. Over centuries, it came to stand for a school, especially a school where Sanskrit was taught. It also came to suggest a pavilion or a square hall with four doors.

17 Surendra Mohanty
Literature and morality

Introduction

Surendra Mohanty's (1922–1990) extraordinarily versatile career combined several facets. A renowned novelist and short story writer, he wrote biographies and an autobiography, a multi-volume history of literature, literary criticism, a travelogue, a radio-play in twelve acts, and numerous columns and journalistic essays. In each of these genres he displayed rare virtuosity and exemplary excellence. His literary achievement was supplemented by his more than three-decade-long active political life. He was elected to Parliament on four occasions. The disenchantment that set in after Independence forms the central theme of many of his short stories and novels, most notably in *Andha Diganta* [Dark Horizon] (1964). He achieved unprecedented popular acclaim writing *Nilashaila* [Blue Hill] (1968), a historical novel depicting a crisis of survival which Odia society faced in the eighteenth century. Many of his short stories dramatize agonizing moral dilemmas confronting the modern man and, depict contemporary social and political realities with biting satire and insightful irony. His *Fakir Mohan Samiksha* [Fakir Mohan Senapati: A Study] (1955) opened up new perspectives on the novelist's many-layered achievements. Notable among his contributions to literary criticism include *Odia Sahityara Adi Parva* (1963) and *Odia Sahityara Madhya Parva* (1968). His biographical novels – *Satabdira Surya* [The Sun Illuminating a Century] (1970) and *Kula Briddha* [The Grand Old Man] (1978) – based on the life of Madhusudan Das (1848–1934), the architect of modern Odisha, received both popular and critical acclaim. Travel literature in Odisha was enriched by the account of his experiences in China, which was published under the title *Peking Diary* (1959).

In this essay originally titled "Aphimara Phula" [Poppy Flowers], Surendra focuses upon the searching question concerning the complex relationship between literature and morality. With novelistic flair, he begins this discussion by analyzing the photographs of two canonical Odia authors Fakir Mohan Senapati (1843–1918) and Radhanath Ray (1848–1908), included in the autobiography of the former and the collected works of the latter. Astutely interpreting biographical evidence, he goes on to show how the

DOI: 10.4324/9781003224778-17

decision to present these authors striking a prayerful pose is redolent of sanc-timonious hypocrisy. He argues that this decision is shaped by a desire to make literature obey the oppressive dictates of a puritanical moral outlook. This, he contends, led to devaluing truly great works written by Radhanath such as *Parvati* and privileging his mediocre texts like *Chilika*, which dispense comforting moral platitudes. The scope of the essay now expands to include instructive examples from world literature to examine the question of morality in literature in greater depth. Particular attention is paid to Radhanath's crea-tive reworking of Percy B. Shelley's *The Cenci* and Aeschylus' *Agamemnon* in portraying a world where poetic justice, so keenly valued by moralists, does not operate. Thus, in Surendra's opinion, great literature is created when the distinction between sin and virtue is transcended by artists. He brilliantly displays here the bold irreverence and playful innovations of a gifted creative writer. The essay, therefore, departs from the conventions of academic criti-cism and appeals to the sensibility of the general reader. It also introduces a refreshingly new element in Odia critical discourse by challenging narrowly moralistic interpretations of literary texts. See, for instance, Gopal Chandra Praharaj's "Two Odia Books: A Review" included in this volume which takes Fakir Mohan to task for the absence of poetic justice in his novel *Chha Mana Atha Guntha* [Six Acres and a Third] (1902). The essay derives its signifi-cance from the skilful deployment of biographical information as a critical tool and placing the discussion of Odia literature in a broader comparative framework.

*

Literature and morality[1]

Surendra Mohanty

One doubt I entertain concerning Radhanath Ray and Fakir Mohan Senapati remains unresolved; this doubt has to do with the former's photograph included in *Radhanath Granthabali* [Collected Works of Radhanath Ray] (3rd ed., 1916) and that of the latter featured in *Atma-jivan Charita* [An Autobiography] (1927). One wonders why the author of fine lyrics of the col-lection titled *Lekhabali* and such lively *kavyas* as *Nandikeshvari, Jajatikeshari* and *Parvati* sits contritely on bended knees on a length of leopard skin, his face afflicted with sorrow and his moustache drooping. Radhanath's works offer no evidence to suggest that he was ever drawn to yoga or pranayama, or if he was a person of deeply devout disposition. Why, then, such an unre-alistic image of Radhanath is presented to the reading public?

Radhanath was possessed of an immense zest for life. In his autobiogra-phy, Fakir Mohan recounts an interesting anecdote concerning a journey he and Radhanath undertook by steamer from Balasore to Cuttack. They travelled in a second-class cabin. As the steamer sailed into river Ghadiamal,

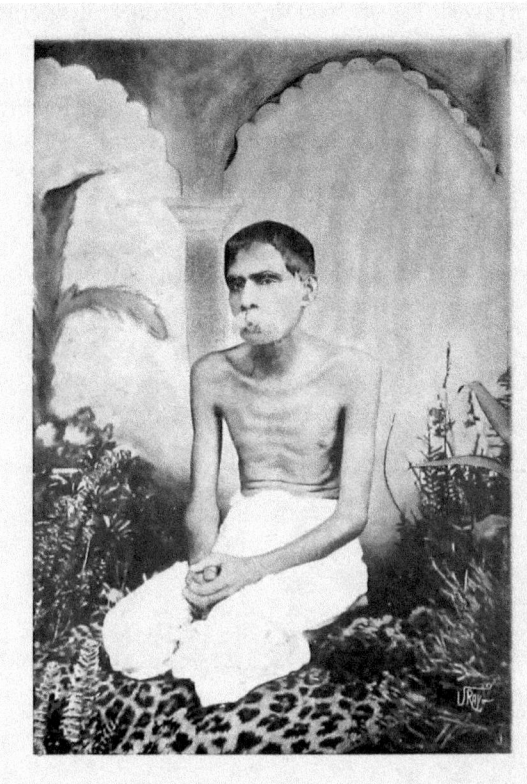

Figure 17.1 Photograph of Radhanath Ray as a humble devotee. Source: Radhanath Ray, *Radhanath Granthabali* [Collected Works], Cuttack: Shashi Bhusan Ray, 3rd ed., 1916 [1902].

a violent rainstorm blew and almost sank it. (Radhanath had not yet composed his *magnum opus*, *Mahayatra* [The Great Journey] (1896); and Fakir Mohan's novel *Six Acres and a Third* (1902) and short story "Rebati" (1898) existed only in the realm of possibility.) Fakir Mohan writes that as the storm raged, Radhanath covered himself with the end border of his *dhoti* and hurriedly tied into it a quantity of opium. It was clear that Radhanath was more scared of the opium getting drenched than by the prospect of the steamer going down into the river. Only an utterly humourless puritan could present a person who in the midst of a terrible storm would not pray to god but try to keep his opium dry as someone absorbed in meditative prayer.

In the same way, the picture of Fakir Mohan included in his autobiography completely misrepresents him for he was a hedonist whose life was more fascinating than a novel and for whom living itself was an "art". The picture shows him wearing sacred marks on his forehead, a holy scarf thrown over his neck, hands joined in a prayerful gesture. Does this accurately depict Fakir Mohan's emotional self?

Does this picture convey a convincing impression of a Fakir Mohan who, when a schoolteacher, asked his colleague to expand the line "the bashful girl is reluctant to go there" into a *shloka*? The *shloka* runs as follows:

> With bosom high and buttocks heavy
> hair as lovely as clouds
> always adorned in nectars
> of a smile, unwilling is she
> to come to thee
> because she is shy.[2]

Figure 17.2 Photograph of Fakir Mohan Senapati in a prayerful pose. Source: Fakir Mohan Senapati, *Fakir Mohan Senapatinka Atma-jivan Charit* [Autobiography of Fakir Mohan Senapati], Cuttack: Mohini Mohan Senapati, 1927.

It may be mentioned here that the *shloka* describes a young girl called Sharada who was Fakir Mohan's student at Balasore Mission School. It is also worth recalling that the same Fakir Mohan also skillfully crafted women characters such as Champa and Saria, and wrote a bold satire like *Utkal Bhramanam* [Travels through Odisha].

After much thought, I have found an answer to this question. It is likely that the publishers added such images in order not to offend the sensibilities of the reading public. They believed that without the pompous veneer of devotion the readers would have completely rejected the works of these authors. This belief grew firmer when an enlightened friend took me aside and said, "You write reasonably well but the characters you draw in your fiction are immoral and irresponsible, and contribute nothing to the task of nation-building. Nor do they provide any moral education which would ennoble the reader's character."

To this I replied,

> I am not too sure of my own character. Is it not natural, then, that the characters in my fiction are "characterless" and immoral? But if great men, like the Buddha, Christ, Ramakrishna, and Gandhi, even the chief guests at school prize distribution ceremonies could not improve human character, why a poor writer should be tasked with straightening the crooked timber of humanity?

The manner in which King Dushyanta entered into an intimate relationship with Shakuntala in the absence of sage Kanva in *Abhijnanashakuntalam* may not find the approval of the custodians of morality. Who can be more irresponsible and unethical than King Lear; and can anyone be more wavering and weak-minded than Hamlet? Ananta, the widow's son, a wayward and stubborn character created by Fakir Mohan, furnishes yet another example. A list of such characters would easily swell into an entire volume. World literature would be terribly impoverished and our aesthetic sensibility would be severely distorted if such characters were expelled from literature. If one looks at Gopabandhu Das's poem "Jane Sahakarminka Prati" [To a Close Associate] from the narrow point of view of decorum, one would find it nauseating. But this certainly counts among the small number of excellent poems he wrote. No other poem he composed reveals the same depth of feeling and warmth of emotion.

A puritanical perspective has enfeebled our creative literature; it has also equally devitalized our critical tradition. In the past, this led to the exclusion of Bishwanath Khuntia's *Bichitra Ramayana*, an early eighteenth-century work rich in aesthetic appeal, from the school syllabus. Moreover, the obsession with the obscenity-decorum divide continues to pervade critical discourse relating to medieval Odia literature. Similarly, *Chilika*, an anaemic literary text, is projected as Radhanath's crowning poetic achievement and is prescribed for students, instead of *Parvati*, a brilliant work of art.

Chilika is deemed worthy of attention for it is studded with moral sayings and adages. No wonder then that couplets from *Chilika* adorn the walls of lower and upper primary schools in villages in Odisha. However, one should not forget that *Chilika* may be morally uplifting, but in terms of artistry it is distinctly inferior.

In view of this, until literature is purged of moralistic and puritanical attitudes, neither the development of modern literature nor bold experiments within it will be possible. Just as hypocrisy, self-aggrandizement and priestly pomposity have corrupted contemporary politics, these have also rendered some enormous volumes written by established writers insufferably unreadable. In literature, as in life, the quest for truth is full of mystery and hazardous. One fails to discover the truth of life if one abandons this quest out of fear; similarly, the same fear prevents the writer from perceiving the beautiful and the eternal.

To the best of my knowledge, it was Percy B. Shelley who, in the preface to his play *The Cenci* (1819), first addressed the issue of morality in literature. In this context, it may be remembered that *The Cenci* was an audacious attempt in early nineteenth-century English literature. Critics have recognized this play as Shelley's most accomplished work. Additionally, the subject matter of this play was so outrageous that it could not be enacted on stage. The action of the play revolves around a horrifying sequence of events: Count Francesco of Cenci rapes his daughter Beatrice, who hires two servants to kill him, and is in turn executed when her crime, patricide, is discovered. I will not go into a detailed analysis of the play as it lies outside the scope of this essay. The story of Count Francesco's diabolical lust for his daughter Beatrice and her pitiable death has made it one of the most heart-rending tragedies in the world. In *Parvati*, Radhanath deftly combines elements from Shelley's *The Cenci* and Aeschylus' *Agamemnon*. (In *Agamemnon*, a father sacrifices his young daughter to propitiate gods and ensure success in battle.) *The Cenci* provides a rare instance in world literature of the solemn universality of suffering, the oppressive nature of religion, the wanton excesses of incompetent tyrants, and the corruption of the so-called guardians of justice. The play also movingly depicts the heroic defiance put up by the victim against these dark forces. However, in the play, the most terrible punishment is meted out to the guiltless and unblemished Beatrice. On the eve of her execution, Beatrice tells her mother,

> Here, Mother, tie
> My girdle for me, and bind up this hair
> In any simple knot; ay, that does well.
> And yours I see is coming down. How often
> Have we done this for one another; now
> We shall not do it anymore. My Lord,
> We are quite ready. Well, 'tis very well.

These lines bring the play to an end. There is no "poetic justice" here. Count Francesco thus becomes like a naked sword in the right hand of the Goddess of Justice and he, despite committing heinous sins, appears innocent in the eyes of the Pope.

Therefore, the following question suggests itself: what principle of morality or justice does Shelley, who influenced virtually all European literature, uphold through a play in which Beatrice, "as pure as speechless infancy", is punished so brutally? Moreover, given the availability of a vast array of themes, why did Shelley choose to dramatize such an utterly odious story in his play? This question is so overwhelmingly profound that it calls for a separate study. Shelley has the puritanical critics in mind when he states the following on the nature of literature in the preface to *The Cenci*:

> The highest moral purpose aimed at in the highest species of the drama is the teaching the human heart, through its sympathies and antipathies, the knowledge of itself; in proportion to the possession of which knowledge every human being is wise, just, sincere, tolerant and kind. If dogmas can do more, it is well: but a drama is no fit place for the enforcement of them.

In other words, great literature strives to discover the meaning of life between the extremes of sin and virtue. Through such self-knowledge alone humans become wise, considerate, powerful and generous. If, in the interest of morality, some adages can serve the greater good, then so be it; but these lie outside the province of literature.

If poets and artists fail to discern the all-pervading divine presence in the manifest mundane world, if in the midst of overwhelming ugliness they fail to perceive beauty, if they fail to glimpse a sliver of truth in a world engulfed in lies, if in the midst of evil they fail to hear the faint music of goodness, and if such goodness does not get reflected in their creations, then they will remain mere scribes and illustrators, and never achieve true greatness. Just as the light of the spotted moon lends majestic beauty to the unruly waves of a great ocean, art adorns even a mucky puddle with visual splendour. For that reason, a composition that does not reflect the soul's discontent, a quest for the unknown, a search for the meaning of life, may, with the aid of sophisticated writerly craft and sweet-sounding diction become "good writing" but such a work can never become literature of lasting value. Hamlet is a weak-minded, vacillating and faint-hearted character; however, in virtually every era of human existence, man has discovered in Hamlet's character ever new dimensions of significance for humanity. In real life, however, to be called a "typical Hamlet" is to be criticized harshly. (I must have used the same expression to describe Prime Minister Jawaharlal Nehru at least a hundred times). Similarly, King Lear, Othello and even Count Francesco each points to routes of access to the meaning of life. These routes differ radically from the metaled highways brightly lit up by hypocritical moral principles. However, unless one stumbles along the dark alleyways one will never understand the true significance of life that lies concealed behind masks. The defining feature of timeless literature consists in its ability to realize, analyze and depict the realm of experience that transcends the crippling distinctions between sin and virtue. Such a realm of experience provides a meeting point for religion and literature. The presence of "Vishad Yoga" [the canto depicting Arjun's dejection] in *The Gita* and of psalms in *The Bible* raise them to the level of great literature. Epics like *Ramayana* and *Mahabharata*, for their part, are as much religious texts as they are works of literature. In the same way, Tolstoy's *War and Peace* and Pasternak's *Dr. Zhivago* have attained the status of timeless classics.

What is sin? Where lies virtue? What is true and what is a lie? These profound questions have engaged the human mind since time immemorial; these have agitated human beings since at least the time of the *Upanishads*. In *Kena Upanishad*, the disciple raises such questions:

> *Kenesitam patati presitam manah?* [At whose behest does the mind move toward its object?]
> *Kena prana preti yuktah?* [At whose instance does the life force express itself]
> *Kenesitam bacham shama badanti chakshu?* [At whose command do men utter words]
> *Srotram kabah debojunakti?* [And which God makes the eyes and ears pulse with life?]

Replying to these questions the teacher says that whatever transcends life, and yet is its stay and support is the *brahma*, who is not the one you offer worship to.

The mind being drawn to the red lips of a woman and those of Lord Krishna cannot be accused of either practising virtue or committing sin. Similarly, the mind attracted by the jingling anklets of a woman on an amorous mission or the sacred sound of someone chanting "Om" has nothing to do with sin or virtue. For in all these, the *brahma* is immanent; it is present as much in a libertine as in a saint. Everything is relative; sin and virtue are but the two sides of the same coin.

Where, in contemporary Indian literature, can one find such a mode of apprehending life? Like politics, literature, too, appears to be shackled by a powerful propagandist tendency. In poetry, we fight like intrepid heroes and achieve martyrdom on the battlefield but in the battleground of real life we turn tail and scurry for safety. However, such hypocrisy can never form the basis for great literature. Perhaps illustrating such a truth, the critic Cyril Connolly writes in the introduction to Albert Camus's *The Outsider*,

It is not enough to love life. We must teach everyone else to love it. We must appreciate that happiness is consciousness, and consciousness is one, that all its manifestations are sacred and it is from this newer school of novelists and poets in all countries that one day we will learn it.

Perhaps India is not yet ready for the development of such an outlook on life. It is therefore likely that Radhanath Ray and Fakir Mohan Senapati struck those sanctimonious poses in the photographs mentioned earlier. (It is as if writing is impossible without practising piety). It is time we rescued these two authors from their pious outfits; it is time we made Radhanath hold a sprig of Ashok blossoms and Fakir Mohan wear a colourful scarf.

Translation: Aruni Mahapatra

Notes

1 Surendra Mohanty, "Aphimara Phula", *Surendra Bichitra,* Cuttack: Friends' Publishers, 2nd ed., 1983 [1967], pp. 291–297.
2 John Boulton, tr., *My Times and I: Atma-jivana Carita of Phakirmohana Senapati*. Bhubaneswar: Odisha Sahitya Akademi, 1985, p. 22.

18 Girija Sankar Ray

Odia drama: a study of its social background

Introduction

Girija Sankar Ray (1886–1967) came from a family which played a historic role in shaping modern Odisha. Nephew of Gourisankar Ray (1838–1917), the legendary editor of *Utkal Dipika*, and son of Ram Sankar Ray (1857–1931), pioneering playwright and novelist, Girija Sankar Ray was educated at Ravenshaw College and Calcutta University, and spent the best part of his career teaching English literature at the former. He was one of the earliest English teachers who devoted their energies to an intensive study of Odia literature. His essays were published in the leading literary magazines of the time such as *Utkal Sahitya*, *Bhanja Pradip* and *Nababharat*. The areas he accorded special attention to included dramatic tradition in Odisha and Odia language. *Odia Natyakala* (1943), an acclaimed study of Odia dramaturgy, traces the emergence of modern dramatic forms in Odisha and the influences they absorbed. Here, he classifies Odia plays into various categories, throws light on their prehistory, examines in detail the stagecraft employed, and the plot and setting of the plays, and explores the changing relationship between drama and performative spaces. His book *Sahitya Sandarbh* [Essays on Literature] (1933) discusses questions relating to aesthetic experience. *Sarala Bhasatattva* (1933) introduces the reader to the fundamentals of linguistics. In one of his early essays, published in *Utkal Sahitya* in 1919, Girija Sankar presciently reflects upon the state of Odia criticism and stresses the need for widening its perspective.

"Odia Natakara Samajika Prusthapata" [Odia Drama: A Study of its Social Background] constitutes a chapter in Girija Sankar's seminal book on Odia dramaturgy. Modern Odia drama as a literary form began taking shape in the 1870s. Before this, dramatic art in Odisha consisted in forms of popular entertainment. Modern Odia drama, like its counterparts elsewhere, withdrew from open spaces into indoor stages and catered to the changing tastes of the English-educated audiences. The new form in Odisha awaited a literary historian, who would trace its origin and chart its progress. This task was accomplished by Girija Sankar in his ground-breaking book *Odia Natyakala*. In this chapter, he enumerates and examines various sources of

DOI: 10.4324/9781003224778-18

influence – English, Sanskrit, Bangla and indigenous folk performative traditions – on modern Odia drama in the early phase of its evolution. In doing
so, Girija Sankar develops a comparative perspective from which Odia literature could be fruitfully approached. He also goes on to convincingly
show how imitative dimensions of Odia plays in their early phase gradually
gave way to a lively portrayal of the socio-economic life of contemporary
Odisha. Thus, Girija Sankar adroitly maps the movement towards realism
in the emerging genre. Plays now sought to dramatize the unfolding of social
and political change in Odisha. Many important contemporary events such
as the auctioning of feudal estates, an imminent famine in 1880, the vote
war caused by election to the Governor General's Council, Madhusudan
Das setting up a factory and the Non-Cooperation Movement found their
way into modern Odia drama. The playwrights also displayed an acute sensitivity to the cultural shifts taking place in the world around them. Their
plays presented characters who spoke Odia mixed with English and Bengalis
speaking a mangled Odia, and deftly captured new forms of corruption taking root in modern institutions like law courts and government offices. In
other words, modern Odia playwrights actively engaged in writing the history of the present.

*

Odia drama: a study of its social background[1]

Girija Sankar Ray

Drama presents a reflection of society and the dramatist offers a picture of
this to the audience. The more vividly the texture of daily life is rendered in
a play, the greater becomes its appeal. Unrealistic portrayals fail to leave a
powerful effect on our minds. The poet composes songs inspired by a vision
of the future. Captivating the mind of the listener through sweet rhythm and
rhyme, the poet makes the listener oblivious to reality for a time. Enthralled
by the music, the listener ceases to care for its truth or unreality. It is true
that the novelist depicts society as it is; however, employing deft narrative
techniques s/he manages to make something unreal appear real. But if anything unreal is introduced into a play while it is being staged, people in the
audience feel disconcerted and alienated. As the dramatist has to remain off-
stage, s/he cannot use their skills to give the unreal the appearance of reality.
It will therefore be necessary to discuss the portrayal of social life in plays.

Four major sources of influence on modern Odia drama in the early stage
of its evolution may be discerned. English Drama, especially the plays of
Shakespeare, influenced many Odia playwrights. The plot of *Banabala* (1882)
by Ram Sankar Ray is modelled on that of Shakespeare's *The Tempest* and
the character of Raja Chitrasen clearly reminds one of Prospero.[2] Even the

opening scene of the play *Samaleswari* (1924) by Ashwini Kumar Ghosh carries distinct echoes of *The Tempest*. In the play *Purusottama Dev* (1880) the
episode of Padmabati and Kanaka passing through a forest and Sumantra
carving his name on trees is based on a scene in *As You Like It*. Again, in
Dhrubacharitra, the song of *yoginis*, "Oh! Sister, let's eat", seems to have
been influenced by the songs of the witches in *Macbeth*. Many of the words
used in the play *Susila* (1917) are an imitation of expressions used in English
plays. The influence of Sanskrit dramatic conventions is visible in the following areas: the description of royal courts, the portrayal of *vidusakas* [court
jesters], the art of making the audience experience various *rasas* and the
introduction of the *sutradhara*.[3] The conversation *sakhis*[4] engage in while
picking flowers and the presentation of dance and music in *Sitabibaha* (1899)
by Kamapala Mishra and some other Odia plays are based on Sanskrit dramatic conventions. In the play *Kartrabirjya* (1931), the growing attachment
between Sumitra and Padmini in Jamadagni's hermitage and their love for
one another is reminiscent of the plot of *Abhijnanashakuntalam*. Before the
advent of modern drama in Odisha, *jatras*[5] were extremely popular, and
their influence on Odia plays is clearly visible. For instance, in *Bhaktamani*
(1929), the scene where the king seeks a report on the welfare of his kingdom from his ministers is based on the *rajyasamachar* [news of the king-
dom] convention prevalent in *jatras*. Similarly, in *Prabhas Milana* (1931)
by Bhagirathi Mahapatra, Radha saying in her songs, "O friend! I cannot
bear this pain any longer, I feel as if I am on fire" or "O sage! This grief-
stricken soul knows nothing but verses about Krishna" carries echoes of
jatra. The presentation of fights on the stage and the description of the death
of the opponent also rely on *jatra* conventions. Modern Bangla drama has
influenced Odia drama in several significant ways. The influence of Bangla
drama on Odia plays can be seen in the following areas: the prevalence of
amritakshar chhanda [blank verse], dance duets, design of the stage, and
the extensive use of music. The depiction of feelings of a terrified citizenry,
of guards' reluctance to perform their duty, soldiers' ineptitude in the battlefield constitutes another major influence of Bangla theatre. Permanently
settled Bengalis had established theatres in Odisha, wrote plays, and formed
and patronized troupes of actors. Since educated people of Odisha were also
familiar with the literature of Bengal, the influence of Bangla plays becomes
evident.

    While looking at the social background of Odia drama, it is necessary to
understand the external influences shaping it and the impact of *jatra* because
most of the plays were imitative in nature and the subjects they explored
had little to do with the social life of Odisha. Even when a few plays did
not imitate any non-indigenous dramatic traditions, they introduced unreal
incidents in order to provide excitement to the audience. It would be wrong
to conclude that court jesters, dance duets, singing of songs while picking
flowers, and sleepy guards were present in Odia society just because they
featured in plays. These merely reproduced alien dramatic conventions and

have no links with lived reality in Odisha. However, in many Odia plays, we do get glimpses of authentic glimpses of social life.

The emergence of modern Odia drama was preceded by the *Na'nka* famine which devastated Odisha in 1866. It is impossible to estimate how many people perished in this famine.[6] Since modern literary forms such as drama and the novel had not arisen at this time, depiction of the famine finds no place in the literature of the period. In the immediate aftermath of the famine, landowners became debt-ridden, and many even went bankrupt as they had tax arrears and lived idle lives. The beginning of the oppression by moneylenders and peoples' reluctance to treat them with respect can be traced to this period in history. A great sensation was caused when many estates were auctioned off in quick succession by creditors. The Kujanga[7] estate was the first to be auctioned. This happened on 18 May 1868, and finds mention in Ram Sankar Ray's novel *Bibasini* (1891). Gradually, other big estates met with a similar fate. In 1895, when Puri Kotha Desha[8] estate was auctioned, it created a feeling of outrage in the minds of dramatists. This found expression in the play *Bisamodaka* [The Poisoned Sweetmeat] (1900) by Ram Sankar Ray. Everybody in Odisha knew how the collusion between the clerks of creditors and those of landlords brought ruin upon the traditional aristocracy. *Bisamodaka* shows how in paying income tax the creditors resorted to fraudulent accounting practices. When the play was staged in 1903, the greatest son of Utkal, Madhubabu[9] acknowledged the reality and prevalence of this dishonest practice. Among modern Odia dramatists, two happened to be lawyers, and consequently, their plays feature many incidents relating to the court of law.[10] However, the portrait of lawyers that obtains in *Bisamodaka* and *Sansarchitra* (1915) by Bhikari Charan Pattanaik, is an unflattering one. In *Sansarchitra*, a character says,

> No lawyer in the bar could match them. In a moment they will turn black into white and white into black; in no time at all they will cut your head and place it in your own hands; and this will take place even before you realise what has happened to you. If need be, they will throw themselves at the feet of powerful men. They would not bother to look at law books. Day and night they visit the judges' residences and salute them.[11]

Although the above account appears exaggerated, the attitude of the dramatists towards the legal profession is absolutely clear. They focus upon the judges' lack of generosity, touts making money through deceit and all manner of corrupt practices pervasive at the court of law. *Kali Kala* (1883) by Ram Sankar Ray shows how at one point in time, lots of people in Odisha tried to speak Bangla.[12] As times changed, they made efforts to speak English and this has been ridiculed in the plays *Irani* (1937) and *Susila*. Modern students' habit of speaking Odia mixed with English has been mocked in *Pariksha Phala* (1915) by Laxmikant Mahapatra and *Premika Chhatra*

(1916) by Ashwini Kumar Ghosh. At the same time, Bengalis speaking mangled Odia has been presented humorously in several plays.

The relationship between landlords and their tenants form the subject matter of many Odia plays. In 1880, another devastating famine loomed over Odisha and demands for exempting people from paying taxes were voiced. Although the government acceded to people's demand, landlords for their part compelled them to pay taxes. This resulted in people agitating against landlords. Hence, in 1891, the government directed landlords not to collect the whole amount due from their tenants and the landlords signed an agreement to this effect. This conflict is dramatized in the play *Rama Banabasa* (1891)[13] by Ram Sankar Ray. In the play *Yugadharma* (1902) by the same author, we come across statements such as "the settlement took away all the profit – landlords found themselves in deep trouble, and cases were filed against tenants to realise tax arrears"[14]. These reveal the dramatists' remarkable powers of observation and present a realistic picture of Odia social life. Aspects of the contemporary rural life of Odisha are illuminated in the same play through references to the oppressive methods of collecting water tax and *chowkidari* tax. Although newspapers carried articles criticizing such tyrannical practices, the idea that no blame attached to the British government and that "the landlords' cronies were responsible for the tenants' misery" had gained currency.[15] Moreover, the plays show how landlords felt scared when they were summoned to serve as assessors and how their failure to obtain a medical certificate from a *sahib* doctor to be exempted from this duty made life difficult for them. *Utkal Dipika* published a report on this problem on 23 June 1894.

The picture of Odia village life presented in *Yugadharma* is vibrant and is remarkable for its authenticity. Therefore, the audience found it enthralling when the play was enacted on the stage. The corruption of officials was common knowledge in Odisha at the time. In the play *Vishwajajna* (1916), Ram Sankar Ray recounts his own experience of the *amin's* tyranny during the revision settlement of 1913: "If peace prevails in a village, call a few *amins* to measure land. In no time there will be an explosion of animosity among the people of this village and peope of this village and those of the neighbouring one will be at each other's throats".[16] In 1912, the magistrate of Cuttack went to inaugurate the girls' high school established by Gourisankar Ray in his village, Dikshitpada and during this time the controversy[17] surrounding the issue of sporting a moustache raised by Nilakantha Das also caused quite a sensation. The play *Lilabati* (1912) portrays these incidents.

The awakening of national consciousness in Odisha can be traced to the establishment of *Utkal Sammilani* in 1903, and the writing of the play *Kanchanmali* (1904) by Ram Sankar Ray was inspired by this historic event. The adoption in this play of a *nolia's*[18] daughter Kanchanmali by the king of Odisha is based on Madhusudan Das's adoption of Miss Shailabala Das. The promotion of the practice of wearing *pagas* [turbans] at the meetings of *Utkal Sammilani* and the proposal of uniting Odisha with the Central Provinces featured in this play.[19] Madhusudan's name finds a mention in the play *Susila* and also in *Deshara Daka,* which was written to launch a movement for uniting Odia-speaking tracts. This is a measure of the tremendous influence of Madhusudan on Odia social life. His establishment of a factory and the *latsahib*'s[20] encouragement of workers on his visit to the factory have been portrayed in the play *Badalok* (1913) by Ram Sankar Ray.

The attitudes of the people of Odisha towards the British find expression in many Odia plays. For instance, plays like *Bisamodaka*[21] and *Yugadharma*[22] celebrate the British respect for learning and their commitment to cleanliness. In *Yugadharma,* the white doctor's issuing a wrong medical certificate is hinted at and made light of.[23] Again, in the play *Susila,* an account is given of the white sahib's response to Odias aspiring to be like the British. The plays *Hindu Ramani* (1937) and *Irani* hold up to ridicule the attempt of Odias to ape the ways of sahibs.

The uneducated imparting knowledge in village schools are shown in plays like *Kanchanmali*[24] and *Sansar Chitra* and the dramatist mocks the newly educated in plays such as *Premika Chhatra* and *Pariksha Phala.* These portraits are also based on contemporary social reality; however, it is thought that the situation would change as a result of modern education. In the play *Lilavati,* the theme of girls' education is explored since resistance to it had grown weaker. If one looks at the history of the establishment of the girls' high school in Cuttack, one realizes how fiercely it was opposed in the past.

Odia *jatras* depict the tyrannical behaviour and deceit of Odia village chowkidars. Although the guards are appointed to serve the villagers, they actually worked as spies of the policemen and because of them, people faced a lot of trouble. We see vivid portraits of such characters in ancient *jatras* such as *Bohu Baidya Suanga.*[25] Since the villagers came directly in contact with them, the depiction of their misconduct had greater appeal. In the play *Badalok,*[26] there is a description of the cudgel of the chowkidar and his various mischiefs, and as this play was influenced by the *jatra* tradition prevalent in Odisha, the character of a guard figures prominently here. The name *Jhutapur* [a place of lies][27] given to a jail in the play *Satya Vijay* reveals the negative attitude of people towards the police.

The play *Vishwajajna* tells us of a funny incident which once took place in Odisha.[28] The desire of Ray Bahadur Nimai Charan Mitra to get elected to the Governor General's Council led to a vote war and a Muslim voter was secretly moved from one place to another. This caused much hilarity and a lot of controversy. In writing the play, the dramatist relied on this real incident. After the Non-Cooperation Movement was launched in Odisha, non-violence was preached and attempts were made to allow untouchables entry into temples. One can feel the impact of this movement in plays such as *Bhanja Bhujanga*[29] (1936) by Ashwini Kumar Ghosh and *Matru Puja.*

Thus, the social circumstances of modern Odisha are mirrored in Odia plays. And this is to be expected. The theme of premarital love which is explored in Odia plays has no basis in the reality of Odia social life. Society affords many instances of a wife's devotion to her husband, her eagerness to support him in his distress, and virtuous deeds; these naturally find a place in the world of Odia drama. Had there been no relationship between Odia drama and Odia social life, the portrayal of conjugal love on stage would not have held such a powerful appeal. The impact of a surge in patriotic feelings in Odisha can be discerned clearly in plays like Ashwini Kumar Ghosh's *Paika Pua* (1933) and Ram Ranjan Mohanty's *Gouda Bijeta* (1931). As puranic[30] narratives are immensely popular in Odisha, dramatists have authored many plays based on these.

Translation: Haramohan Nayak

Notes

1 Girija Sankar Ray, *Odia Natyakala* [A Critical Study of Odia Drama up to 1939], Cuttack: Shashank Sankar Ray, 1943, pp. 124–132.
2 Ram Sankar Ray, *Ram Sankar Granthabali*, Cuttack: Bani Bhandar, 1930, p.114.
3 [Translator] In Sanskrit drama, a person whose job is to introduce the characters and the setting of the play at the beginning of the performance.
4 [Translator] A female friend or companion.
5 [Translator] A form of folk theatre.
6 [Editors] According to Bidyut Mohanty about one million people died in the 1866 famine ("Orissa Famine" 55–56).
7 [Translator] Name of a permanently settled estate on the sea-board of the district of Cuttack.
8 [Translator] Name of a *pragana* [fiscal subdivision of a district] in Puri.
9 [Translator] The popular name of Madhusudan Das (1848–1934), the first Odia to become a lawyer; he is also the founder of *Utkal Samilani* in 1903, an organization instrumental in unifying Odia-speaking tracts as a separate province.
10 *Utkal Dipika*, 10 March 1903.
11 *Sansarchitra*, p. 39.
12 *Ram Sankar Granthabali*, p. 164.
13 Ibid, p. 205.
14 Ibid, p. 616.
15 Ibid.
16 Ibid, p. 938.
17 [Editors] A reformist movement launched by Pandit Nilakantha Das (1884–1967), against the superstitions prevailing among the orthodox Brahmins who disapproved of keeping a moustache without a beard.
18 [Translator] A class of Telugu fishermen.
19 *Ram Sankar Granthabali*, pp. 656, 667.
20 [Translator] The provincial Governor or the Viceroy of India.
21   *Ram Sankar Granthabali*, p. 542.
22 Ibid, p. 612.
23 Ibid, p. 613.
24 Ibid, p. 668.

25 [Translator] It is a musical performance which is humorous in nature.
26 *Ram Sankar Granthabali,* p. 917.
27 *Satyabijaya,* p. 51.
28 *Ram Sankar Granthabali,* p. 966.
29 *Bhanjabhujanga,* p. 83.
30 [Translator] Mythological; based on Hindu legendary work by Vyasa and other sages dealing with creation, destruction, genealogy, the different ages and family history of ancient times.

19 Basant Kumar Satpathy

Accounting for literary change: a survey of modern Odia poetry

Introduction

Basant Kumar Satpathy (1913–1994) occupies an important place in the literary world of Odisha as a leading short story writer, an illustrious translator and a perceptive literary critic. His short stories offer a unique blend of humour and pathos, and explore moral dilemmas confronting a middle class emerging after Independence with nuanced irony. A deep, abiding compassion for the underdog finds memorable expression in many of his stories; this extends even to the animal world in his imaginative universe. The rich legacy he inherited from Fakir Mohan Senapati enabled him to employ a vibrant colloquial idiom in his short stories with uncommon effectiveness. In many of his stories, an apparently trivial anecdote recounted with effortless ease often leads to a moment of unsettling epiphany. He has to his credit eleven collections of short stories which include *Anti-romantic* (1966), and *Mansasimananka Udesyare* [For Non-Vegetarians by Meat-eaters] (1982) and *Pua Pain Jhia* [A Bride for my Son] (1996). Basant Kumar translated *Othello* and *Tales from Shakespeare*, and innovatively adapted a number of English one-act plays in Odia. His stage adaptation of Fakir Mohan's iconic Odia novel *Chha Mana Atha Guntha* [Six Acres and a Third] (1902) titled *Champa* (1970) offers a boldly unconventional interpretation. A life-long fascination for Fakir Mohan's achievements as an author led Basant Kumar to write insightful studies of his fiction. Sahitya Akademi commissioned him to edit a collection of Odia poetry which was published under the title *Sanchayan* [An Anthology of Odia Poetry] (1974). His autobiography *Maneapde* [Recollections], published posthumously in 2008, received warm appreciation from literary critics and lay readers alike.

The excerpt given below is taken from the introduction Basant Kumar included in the anthology of Odia poetry mentioned above. It may be noted here that after Bijoy Chandra Mazumadar's three-volume *Typical Selections from Oriya Literature* (published between 1921 and 1925), *Sanchayan* represents the first major attempt to undertake a magisterial survey of Odia poetry. While compiling *Typical Selections*, Bijoy Chandra had laboured under two circumstantial constraints: firstly many ancient

DOI: 10.4324/9781003224778-19

Odia literary texts were not available to him because they had not been retrieved and printed; secondly the chronology of ancient Odia poets had not been established by scholars with a reasonable degree of accuracy. Therefore, almost half a century later, Basant Kumar set out to present an updated and alternative history of Odia poetry. In his preface to the volume, he self-consciously explains and justifies his principles of selection, especially those relating to the poets and texts of the modern period. Everywhere in his comprehensive introduction, a refreshingly new attempt to convey the singularity of a literary text by locating it in its historical context is impressively evident. This is amply illustrated by the excerpt we have selected for our purpose here. For instance, Basant Kumar seeks to account for the advent of the Sabuja era in the 1920s and 30s in Odia literature which was dismissed earlier as ephemeral and escapist, but the sensation they had caused had never been explained quite convincingly. By referring to the vacuum created in the literary world when the Satyabadi poets joined the Gandhian freedom struggle, he shows how this was filled by energetic young writers heavily influenced by the escapist and mystical tendencies prominent in Bangla literature of the time. His observations on Brajanath Badajena (c. 1730–1800) choosing a historical incident as the subject matter of his *kavya* and Bhima Bhoi (c. 1850–1895) anticipating the Gandhian idea of non-violence are remarkably insightful.

*

Accounting for literary change: a survey of modern Odia poetry[1]

Basant Kumar Satpathy

Brajanath Badajena and Bhima Bhoi occupy a distinctive place in the three-hundred-year history of Odia poetry, which was dominated by religiosity and intricate ornateness. For the first time since the composition of Purushottam Das's *kavya Padmavati*, a historical event forms the central theme in a *kavya* written by Brajanath Badajena. His account of the Maratha invasion of the kingdom of Dhenkanal, coloured by nationalist sentiment and patriotism, found eloquent expression in *Samar Tarang*. The lively description of war preparations and the deft reproduction of the speech of Maratha soldiers contribute significantly to the impression of realism created in the poem. In his childhood Bhima Bhoi was an unlettered (blind?) cowherd. The simplicity that characterized early Odia poetry under the influence of Buddhism and Jainism resurfaced in his remarkably spontaneous verses. Bhima Bhoi was endowed with supernatural poetic talent. His poetry, which preaches "non-violence", predates the propagation of the Gandhian doctrine. Bhima Bhoi's poetic achievement brings the ancient and medieval traditions of

Odia poetry to a glorious end and marks the advent of the modern era in Odisha's literary history.

However, the modern era emerged out of an experience of excruciating agony. Odia language, which rested on firm foundations having enjoyed an uninterrupted existence of almost a thousand years, suddenly faced a terrible crisis of survival in the middle of the nineteenth century. A similar crisis also confronted the Odia community. The Kalinga empire which extended from the Godavari to the Ganga, lost its glory and [during British rule] was appended to Bengal or Bihar depending on administrative convenience. It was even claimed that Odia was not a language in its own right. The memory of Maratha misrule was still fresh; the benefits of British occupation were yet to be experienced. Matters were made worse by the devastating famine of 1866 which was followed by an epidemic. All this broke the back of an already enfeebled community, and darkness and despair engulfed its art and literature.

In the midst of this impenetrable darkness shone three luminaries: Fakir Mohan Senapati, Radhanath Ray and Madhusudan Rao. Through dedicated effort, the trinity rescued Odia language and literature from the threat of extinction. Fakir Mohan, Radhanath and Madhusudan in their works focused on man (truth), nature (beauty) and God (goodness) respectively. In doing so they opened up new possibilities of creative expression and gave Odia literature a radically new direction. Modern literature was created out of a unique synthesis of Sanskrit literature, medieval Odia literature and western literature. Puranic and medieval Odia literature abounded with innumerable ornate accounts of the deeds of Rama and Krishna. Such accounts went out of fashion in the modern era and literature now descended from the realm of deities to the human sphere. This development did not mark a break with tradition; on the other hand, it expanded its possibilities. Fakir Mohan established a printing press in Balasore and took several initiatives to save and nurture Odia language. If Sarala Das is regarded as the father of Odia literature, Fakir Mohan can be celebrated as its ablest defender. Although he achieved fame primarily as a short story writer and novelist, he is popularly known as *Vyasakavi* [a great poet like Vyasa]. He is brilliantly adept at seamlessly blending irony, humour and pathos in his works. His *Abasara Basare* features lyrics which eschew intricate ornamentation and religious subject matter to express secular themes with unfettered ease. Fakir Mohan also wrote books for children. A learned man and connoisseur of music, Radhanath Ray possessed a deep knowledge of western and eastern literary classics. He adapted some western classics with such amazing skill that they read like original works. He transposed texts such as "Atlanta's Race", "Apollo and Daphne", *Twelfth Night, Lady of the Lake* and *The Fairie Queene* into Odishan settings with such dexterity that they came to be accepted as local legends. Widely travelled, he entered into an intimate relationship with nature and wove a fascinating narrative around everything he saw and adored. He made use of traditional *ragas* (rhythmic patterns) in his poetic compositions. He pioneered the employment of blank verse in Odia poetry. His poetry portrays and celebrates every aspect of Odisha's natural landscape, its shrines, and places of historical interest. It was Radhanath who introduced the Romantic sensibility in Odia literature. Madhusudan Rao is chiefly known as a writer of devotional poetry. His poems have the solemn rhythmic quality of Vedic hymns chanted by sages. They have the sublimity associated with serene, unclouded skies and have the power to move even a heartless person. The works of the trinity exude an intense love for their motherland. In Gangadhar Meher, popularly known as Kalidasa of Utkal, and Nandakishore Bal, the poet who depicts village life, the trinity finds its worthy successors. Despite being born into a poor weaver family and bereft of formal education, Gangadhar composed a few but memorable *kavyas*. The heroines of Kalidasa's works such as Shakuntala, Sita and Indumati are portrayed as ideal Indian women in Gangadhar's writings. Nandakishore Bal, for his part, drew the reader's attention to a hitherto neglected area of experience in Odia poetry. A melancholy portrait of the rural world depicted vividly by the poet enthralled readers. One, of course, comes across such portraits of Odisha's rural world in Fakir Mohan's prose fiction. Nandakishore's lullabies and other songs for children lent fullness to the multi-faceted achievements of the writers of the Radhanath era. Although the tastes and personal experiences of these writers varied significantly, the imaginative worlds they created shared deep affinities. It may be noted here that Madhusudan Rao introduced the sonnet form into Odia literature and composed odes of high literary quality. Radhanath's successors developed a new perspective on nature and Odias grew increasingly responsive to issues and events of national importance.

The political world of Odisha experienced a new awakening even before the Radhanath era came to end. In 1903, exactly one hundred years after the British annexed Odisha, a movement to unify Odia-speaking tracts was launched. An organization called Utkal Sammilani was established under the leadership of Madhusudan Das to fulfil this collective aspiration. This was the first time the demand for the formation of a province on the basis of language was articulated in India. Inviting Fakir Mohan to preside over the Conference before he passed away in 1918, the leaders of the new age paid homage to the older generation. Although the followers of the Radhanath tradition continued to write well into the 1930s, the literature they produced had lost its vitality by the first decade of the twentieth century.

The nationalist fervour which filled the hearts of Indians between 1903 and the Non-Cooperation Movement led by Gandhi in 1921, found expression in Odisha under the inspiring leadership of Gopabandhu Das. One comes across a remarkable fusion of nationalist spirit and literary sensibility in his works. He founded a model school in a forest in Satyabadi near Puri and tried to infuse the ideas cherished by Vedic sages into the existing education system. He used literature as a means of inspiring young students to dedicate their lives to the task of building a new nation. His thought-provoking essays aiming at social transformation were disseminated through *The Samaj*, a weekly he himself had founded. His close associates included Nilakantha Das, Godabarish Mishra, Acharya Harihar Das and Krupasindhu Mishra. They were major writers, historians, social reformers and patriots. The literature of the Satyabadi era drew its vitality from these five close associates (popularly known as the Panchsakha). Social reform, patriotism and service to the poor – in one word, Gandhism – lent a distinctive character to the literature of this era.

Gopabandhu's deeply felt humanism informs and animates every line of his poetic compositions, especially in *Bandira Atmakatha* [Autobiography of a Prisoner] and *Karakabita* [Prison Poems]. The poet's powerful emotions and feelings expressed in simple diction stir the hearts of readers. Nilakantha Das's "Konarke" [A Visit to Konark] constitutes a brilliant achievement in the field of modern Odia poetry. In this long poem, intense patriotic feelings blend harmoniously with lofty flights of imagination. His *kavya Kharavel* awakens readers to Odisha's lost glory and inspires them to build a new world. Godabarish Mishra is famous for his ballads. Expressed in simple folk idiom, his poems recount various legends and historical incidents, and fill one's heart with deep pathos and a sense of patriotism. His ballad "Kalijai" is an unforgettable contribution not only to Odia literature but also to the ballad tradition of the world.

Around the same time, the freedom movement led by Gandhi swept through India. The whole country fervently responded to Gandhi's nonviolent battle against untruth, injustice and untouchability. It is not surprising that these five associates who had waged a war against religious hypocrisy and superstitions would respond enthusiastically to Gandhi's call to action. The movement aimed at unifying the Odia-speaking tracts was now made a part of the larger struggle for India's Independence. From now on, the school at Satyabadi resonated with the sound of *charkhas* [spinning wheels], and the poets transformed themselves into Gandhi's loyal foot-soldiers. The end of the Satyabadi era in the history of Odia literature created an aching vacuum in the literary sphere.

Around this time, not far from Odisha, appeared in the eastern sky a luminous new sun, Rabindranath Tagore. Just as the political realm in India was radically transformed by Gandhi's influence, the literary world was illuminated by Tagore's radiant poetic achievement. Tagore won the Nobel Prize in 1913; however, his impact was not felt in Odia literature until 1920. Although most of the members of the Satyabadi group had received higher education in Kolkata they fiercely resisted being influenced by Bengali literature and culture. Annada Shankar Ray, Kalindi Charan

Panigrahi, Baikunthanath Patnaik and a few others, all undergraduate students at Ravenshaw College, felt drawn towards Tagore's works, formed a group called "Sabuja Samiti" and engaged in literary experiments. They published numerous short stories, poems, travelogues and critical essays in the magazine, *Yugavina*, which was modelled on *Sabuja Patra* [Green Leaf] brought out from Santiniketan. Biswanath Kar, editor of the *Utkal Sahitya*, who had a liberal and progressive outlook, lent them support and encouragement. A collection of poems titled *Sabuja Kabita* [Green Poems] came to be published in 1931. A spirit of rebellion and exuberance animated these poems. The poem beginning with the words "Agnikana! agnikana!" [sparks of fire] vividly conveys the spirit of rebellion. In the poem "Puri Mandir" [The Temple at Puri], Kalindi Charan Panigrahi addresses the deity as a piece of lifeless wood and defiantly declares his lack of faith in Hindu religion and celebrates humanity. His poem "Patha Kahin?" [Searching for a Path] expresses a sense of scepticism and spirit of renunciation. In the works of Sabuja poets, especially in those written by Annada Shankar, one finds a fascination for change, emotional fervour and deep excitement. The Sabuja poets sang ecstatic paeans to love, beauty and youth; with the same fervour, they loudly fulminated against the old and the effete. In the end, however, the harsh realities of life compelled these lotus-eaters to beat a retreat. All the same, it must be accepted that in spite of their shortcomings they left an indelible imprint on Odia poetry. They expanded the possibilities of Odia literature by introducing new rhythms, innovative word-combinations and a cosmopolitan outlook.

Odia poetry moved in a new direction in the fourth decade of the twentieth century. Although the freedom struggle led by Gandhi had generated an intense political awareness in the 1930s, his impact on the literary realm was surprisingly limited to only a few patriotic songs, elegies and lamentations, and propagandist lyrics. The movement to unite all Odia-speaking regions which was launched in 1903 achieved partial success in 1936 when Odisha became a separate province. The desire to consolidate the nascent province and bring about its all-round development excited the imagination of people. Therefore, bringing into being a classless society, promoting the dignity of the individual, removing social inequality and uplifting the downtrodden emerged as the central concerns of a new literature inspired by socialist ideals. Gandhi had already upheld these ideals; however, surprisingly, the young writers turned to Karl Marx as a source of inspiration and began creating new literary organizations to disseminate his ideas. As a result, an international outlook now came to shape literary sensibility in Odisha. The socialist era in Odia literature was ushered in by Bhagabati Charan Panigrahi, younger brother of Kalindi Charan. The organization Navayug Sahitya Sansad, founded by Bhagabati, spread socialist ideas through the short-lived periodical *Adhunik*. Anant Patnaik, Manmohan Mishra and Sachidananda Rautray were notable among the left-leaning poets of the time. Manmohan Mishra rose to fame composing deeply moving and fiery revolutionary songs. Left ideology has little to do with Anant Patnaik's truly memorable poems of high quality.

Translation: **Niroj Kumar Sethi**

Note

1 Basant Kumar Satpathy, "Odia Kavya Sahityara Suchana" [A Survey of Odia Poetry], *Sanchayan* [An Anthology of Odia Poetry], New Delhi: Sahitya Akademi, 1974 [2013], pp. 27–32.

20 Natabara Samantaray
Netramani's diary

Introduction

Natabara Samantaray (1918–2000) is arguably the most outstanding critic of modern Odia literature. Although he wrote essays and books on pre-modern Odia literary tradition, it is his boldly original and insightful readings of late-nineteenth and early-twentieth-century literary texts that gave new direction to critical discourse in Odisha. Meeting the eminent archaeologist Paramanand Acharya, when Natabara was a young college teacher of Odia literature, proved to be a turning point in his career as a critic. Paramanand made him aware of the exciting possibilities that the study of modern Odia literature offered, and encouraged him to find answers to the intriguing question as to why the literary and cultural landscape of Odisha changed so dramatically in the nineteenth century. Following Paramanand's advice to diligently explore archival sources, he laid a firm foundation for historical interpretation of modern Odia literature. His critical practice powerfully combated sentimentalism and impressionist tendencies through logical rigour and archival explorations; and, unlike many of his contemporaries, he remarkably resisted the temptation to cite western/British critics even though his work reflects a rich awareness of western scholarship. He authored as many as twenty-four books of literary criticism and numerous essays. Notable among these is his ground-breaking *Odia Sahityara Itihas, 1803–1920* [A History of Odia Literature, 1803–1920] (1963) where he has convincingly demonstrated the reciprocal relationship between text and context. For instance, in this book, school textbooks, dictionaries, missionary tracts and government reports yield fresh and fascinating perspectives on literary change.

In the essay translated here, Natabara reads Kalindi Charan Panigrahi's iconic novel *Matira Manisha* [Born of the Soil] (1931) against the grain. The novel achieved unprecedented popularity for its depiction of the influence of Gandhian ideals on rural Odisha. It celebrates the noble sacrifice of its central character when faced with selfish rapacity and conflict over property, and, as the eminent Hindi critic Namwar Singh aptly observed, imaginatively reworks the story of self-sacrifice unfolding in *Ramayana*. Idealism in

DOI: 10.4324/9781003224778-20

the novel is embodied by its noble central character Baraju, and this sharply contrasts with the selfish pettiness of his younger brother's wife Netramani. Writing in 1958, when neither feminism nor deconstruction nor even subaltern studies had struck roots in the domain of literary criticism, Samantaray gave an eloquent voice to a much-maligned woman and resonantly presented her point of view. Certain stereotypical responses to the novel had already crystallized by the time Natabara choose to subject it to fresh interpretation. So, he sought to challenge and undermine these stereotypes by trying to inhabit the consciousness of a "negative" character, Netramani. No one in the world of Odia criticism has performed this unusual function of a critic with such aplomb. It may be mentioned here that Samantaray attempted something similar in the case of Bhagia, a victim-figure in Fakir Mohan Senapati's famous novel *Chha Mana Atha Guntha* [Six Acres and a Third] (1902). The English translation of *Pagala Bhagiara Jawanbandi* [Mad Bhagia's Testimony] has been included in *Natabara Samantaray: A Reader* (2017). Netramani's Diary assumes significance in the context of critical discourse for it represents the attempt of a critic to step into the shoes of a creative writer by reimagining a fictional character's motives and responses. Presented in the form of a diary, this essay illuminates aspects of criticism as a creative activity.

*

Netramani's diary[1]

Natabara Samantaray

I was born as a fictional character in 1931; I do not remember the exact date and month. What I remember is that my creator, the great novelist Kalindi Charan Panigrahi, introduced me to his countrymen in this inauspicious year. Since then I have been reborn fourteen times in the wombs of printing presses and have found and place in various textbooks taught at high school and degree classes. No other fictional character in the history of modern Odia literature has enjoyed the good fortune of being introduced to so many readers in such a short time.

However, to my utter misfortune, I have been much maligned and subjected to universal ridicule. School and college teachers have habitually represented me as a quarrelsome woman, the wrecker of a happy family, and as proud and scornful. By contrast, my husband's elder brother and his wife are routinely presented as compassionate human beings and god-like persons possessing all divine attributes. Every year, students appearing for examinations eloquently denigrate me.

Let me now ask my creator with utmost humility – what glory has he earned by humiliating me publicly? I was the daughter of a tax collector, and could do as I liked in my own little world. Did the author do the right thing by pulling me out of that world and painting my character black? I have no clue as to why he drew such an unflattering portrait of mine, but the fact that such a portrayal made me a much-maligned character is beyond doubt. In order to rectify that mistake and offer an unbiased account of my character, I hereby record my side of the story in this diary. I cannot adequately express myself in the language which my creator made me speak in the novel. Therefore, I will now adopt a different manner of speaking. This will help people get to know my real self and wash away the dark stains disfiguring my character.

Today is New Year's Day in Odisha, the first day of summer. The premises of Biharibag in Cuttack are reverberating with the voices of writers. This is the opportune moment to ask them if I was the only one who wrecked homes, and to insist that they look at their own lives and tell me if there are honest men among them. Would they be bold enough to assert that they have been able to keep their families together? Biharibag is frequented not just by poets, storywriters, novelists and dramatists, but also by literary critics. I suspect that most of these people are not sincere and that they merely pretend to be dedicated to the causes of literature and aesthetics. I request them to find out why no one has taken Kalindi Charan Panigrahi to task for crafting a character like me and passing all the blame to it. I would also like to know if the yardstick various critics have used to judge me is universal or region-specific? I sincerely hope that the next generation will find the time to evaluate in an unbiased manner what I am going to write in my diary after due deliberations over my creator's psychological universe.

Let us consider the curious case of my creator. He is one of the members of the so-called Sabuja [Green] group comprising only five poets: Sarat Chandra Mukherjee, Annada Shankar Ray, Harihara Mohapatra, Baikunthanath Patnaik and Kalindi Charan Panigrahi. In July 1921, six months after Gandhi launched the Non-Cooperation Movement, these five joined Ravenshaw College as first-year students. All of them passed Intermediate Arts examination and came to the third year in 1923. In two years' time, Kalindi Charan and Harihara graduated from Ravenshaw. Similarly, Annada Shankar and Sarat Chandra passed from Patna College with English honours (first class first) and Economics honours (first class first) respectively. Baikunthanath, for his part, failed the exam that year and graduated in 1926.

Prior to 1923, none of them, with the exception of Kalindi Charan, had written anything significant. They wrote poetry, fiction, short stories, criticism, travelogues, but to their misfortune, critics started evaluating their work only on the basis of their contribution to poetry. Some of their poetic creations were inspired by Bangla literature, its rhyme schemes and rhythmic patterns. These poems betrayed their desire to move away from the local life-world and its stark realities, and escape and soar high in the sky. No doubt, this appeared like a devastating cyclonic storm in the contemporary cultural sphere, and, predictably, Sabuja poets became targets of extremely harsh criticism. Before the publication of the literary magazine *Baruni*, its editor Raybahadur Rajkishore Das described these poets in the following manner in his booklet "Parichaya":

> There are many poets in Odisha who are half-educated, hotheaded or mentally unbalanced. They read a few works written by Tagore and uncritically by slavishly imitate his style while producing meaningless, inaccessible, directionless writings. The same is true of the novelists. They write stories and novels stealing themes from Bengali literature, blindly imitating its style or by relying on the uncontrolled outpourings of their delirious minds.

One may not immediately identify Rajkishore Das's targets but he continues his tirade against contemporary poetry produced by Sabuja poets. He further cites lines from Baikunthanath's poems which mindlessly echo words and expressions from Bangla poetry.

It is to escape being labelled as an escapist that Kalindi Charan took to writing short stories. But nowhere did he create a life-like character like me who could be said to have been born of the soil. However, the same cannot be said of my husband's elder brother and his wife. It seems as if the dreamer Kalindi Charan countered his critics by bringing a character like me into being. With the passage of time, the greenness of the Sabuja poets faded away. Though there is more than one reason for such a change, the most important could be the rise of communism, which was already popular in Russia, and its realistic orientation. Signs of this change among Odia writers can be noticed around 1931. Kalindi Charan's novel *Matira Manisha* [Born of the Soil][2] where I appear as a character is the most visible example of this transformation of Sabuja writers. In fact, a character born of the soil like me saved a Sabuja poet like Kalindi Charan from the hostility of his critics but in the process I became disfigured.

Gandhiji began his historic Dandi March on 12 March 1930, which may be hailed as the auspicious beginning of his second Non-Cooperation Movement. The first phase of Gandhi's movement in 1921 and the second in 1930 deeply impacted the budding poet Kalindi Charan. Around the same time the response of writers unsympathetic to Sabuja poetry came to be marked by profound contempt. The milieu shaped by the confluence of communist and Gandhian movements created conditions under which a novel like *Born of the Soil* could be written. Although the novel embodies Gandhian values, these are not shared by characters who truly belong to the soil. Characters whose actions have been inspired by Gandhian ideals were in fact made of gold. I was not like them nor did anyone make any effort to make me golden. My world was a very limited one and defined by trivial mundanities. More than anyone else, I was the one who truly belonged to this world and remained absorbed in it. I was a stranger to publicly cherished grand ideals and I made no effort to embrace them. What was available and adorable in my narrow little world may be dismissed by others as trivial or meaningless, but they were my own and so I felt deeply attached to them. It is this intimacy with the soil which lends beauty to my existence.

In terms of age, my creator Kalindi Charan is younger than me. When I was hell-bent on wrecking a home, my creator was perhaps a high school student. This was the time of World War I (1914–18). The Non-Cooperation Movement had generated new hope among Indians, and this led Kalindi Charan to create a character like my husband's elder brother, Baraju. The sensation created by the influence of Gandhian ideals at that particular moment in history found its finest embodiment in Baraju. However, the circumstances of my birth were entirely different. I am not a fleeting bubble in the eternal stream of time. My birth was not an accident, and my relationship with time is as indivisible and endless as time's eternal relation to this land. I am universal and eternal. My identity cannot be defined only in terms of my being a daughter-in-law in Shama Padhan's house located on the banks of river Birupa; I also embody several other identities such as maternal aunt, paternal aunt, mother, mother-in-law, elder sister-in-law and younger sister-in-law. My identities are as diverse as they are colourful; one who has not grasped the significance of my character and the strange beauty of my inner life will fail to understand the novel *Born of the Soil*.

Delang is a non-descript railway station in Puri district, and not far from Beraboi village. A road running on the southern side of this village leads to Pattanaikia. A decaying leprosarium stands on one side of this road and opposite to it runs a mud path going in the southern direction. Once upon a time, there was a cooperative department office not far from this place. Perhaps it was during 1929–30 when an officer named Kalindi Charan Panigrahi came to this office for inspection. He was sitting outside the office and verifying documents when quite a few people assembled there in connection with activities of the cooperative. A farmer from Beraboi village narrated the story of his life to Kalindi Charan. I do not remember the name or surname of that farmer. He said,

> My father, before he died, made us, his two sons, promise that we would never divide our ancestral land. My younger brother was not happy and frequently quarrelled with me. Though he wanted to take his share, I did not agree out of respect for the parting words of our father. In the end, I was left with no alternative but to leave home for good. I now work with my own hands to make a living.

Kalindi Charan was deeply touched by this story. A few days later, the whole country found itself in the grip of the Satyagraha. Kalindi Charan could see in the life of this illiterate humble farmer, a worthy example of Gandhi's message of sacrificing one's life for the welfare of the multitude. This led him to instill Gandhian ideals in the character of this farmer, Baraju Padhan. This forms the backdrop of *Born of the Soil*.

Now let me ask if Netramani was the actual name of the wife of this farmer's younger brother or if the character is modelled on a real person. Certainly not. It is the conflict between the two brothers which provides the motive for the "magnanimous" farmer's act of sacrifice, and not the daily quarrels between the two daughters-in-law as depicted in the novel. However, the author used me as a potent tool to ensure the success of his fictional creation. I am the unique and beautiful embodiment of the author's imagination. To present Gandhian ideals, the novelist shifted Baraju's character to the banks of the Birupa and made him the son of Shama Padhan. This is how he gave the magical powers of fictional art free play. However, the literary greatness of the novel, the richness of its form and style, and the depth of its themes derive from the distinctiveness with which the author invests my character.

Idealism or theory always relies heavily on abstract thought and does not easily translate into concrete and visible reality. The world of thought is utterly dull and prosaic, and therefore does not enjoy popular appeal. It is because of the need to present the ideal in terms of the real, authors create a credible fictional world exercising powers of imagination. Only characters born of the soil invest the ideal with aesthetic appeal. If Gandhian values were realized through my brother-in-law, it must be acknowledged that this was made possible through me. My creator made me appear unpleasant and unappealing, and as an object of ridicule in order to dramatize the success of Gandhian ideals. I am offered as a sacrificial lamb at the altar of this great ideal. Puranas narrate the story of how the eight queens of Lord Krishna refused to offer the dust of their feet to help him recover from a dreaded disease fearing eternal damnation. It was Radha who thought nothing of the threat of damnation and offered him the dust of her feet. Thus, like Radha, do I not deserve the pity and affection of readers for my sacrifice?

Regardless of the reader's response to me, I am a highly successful and flawless creation in the world of art. To create a beautifully ideal world, the author chose to portray me as an unfeeling and unpleasant character. My brother-in-law became a character worthy of worship just by letting go four or six acres of land whereas I was made to appear despicable to endow his character with glory. In order to enable readers to properly evaluate my character, I feel compelled to present incidents from my miserable life.

If I assumed the role of a revolutionary, it was for the sake of liberating myself. It is understood that Gandhi's message inspired people to fight for the nation's independence; his message was universal and ideal. But then how can one blame me for fighting for my freedom in my own way and why should it be seen as shameful? People called me a shrew and a family-wrecker. I can easily refute such accusations. Let me ask people if I was the only one who quarrelled all the time? Is it not true that my sister-in-law was an equal partner in such fights? Over two-thirds of the novel, the author represented her in a positive light in order to project an ideal. He made her adopt methods such as fasting, renunciation and remaining silent – all part of Gandhi's strategy of Non-Cooperation. Everybody knows that parrots can be taught to speak and even wild animals can be tamed through care and affection. If one tries hard, one can change one's heart. Unfortunately, my sister-in-law could change herself, but I remained the same forever. One per cent of the effort made to bring about my sister-in-law's transformation would have proved that I was not born a devil. Unfortunately for me, my husband, sister-in-law and brother-in-law did nothing to expel the devil within me. How can I accept the judgment of those who labelled me as quarrelsome and created conditions for my descent into hell; how can I believe that they really understood me?

It is not entirely true that I am a home-wrecker. It would be equally wrong to imagine that the only aim I cherished in life was to break homes when I came to Shama Padhan's family as a daughter-in-law. Differences of opinion often lead to fights among brothers, which result in the disintegration of a family. As I am not solely responsible for the former, I cannot be the only person to blame for the latter. My sister-in-law was deliberately not given any role in the latter half of the novel to secure the triumph of a particular ideal. Otherwise the kind of life she was shown to be living in the first part of the novel would have naturally led to the family falling apart. I leave it to readers to decide whether it was right to put all the blame on me and remove her slyly from the theatre of the conflict.

The infighting among brothers and their drifting away from each other is caused by prevailing social circumstances as well as the aspirations of people embedded in those. The instinct to assert one's individuality within the community has been rooted in the human psyche since time immemorial. At the same time, in order to live in the world, the individual has to become a social animal. It is extremely difficult for an individual to stay outside the fold of society. The harmony of society is impossible to imagine without the soothing idea of a well-knit family. Human beings are committed to both family and society; it is within the confines of the family that one can promote the welfare of society. Similarly, both society and family shape the course of an individual's life. When an individual's relationship with society and family is intimate and harmonious, one experiences heaven on earth. It is not for nothing that the poet Madhusudan Rao wrote, "That home is heaven where mutual love binds people together." If a family is devoid of love and affection, it turns into hell.

If one goes beyond village Beraboi and reflects on the nature of Hindu society and family, one would understand the place of a stigmatized woman like me in these. As the daughter-in-law of the family, I am expected to maintain its dignity and put up with everything unpleasant that happens there. It should not surprise anybody that such norms prevail in a society that is patriarchal. It is always the man who supports the family through his earnings. The woman is usually confined to the four walls of the house and has no way of experiencing the world outside. If she adjusts herself to all that is good or bad in the family, she qualifies as an ideal homemaker.

While discussing family as an institution, we should not lose sight of the joint-family system. Say there are four sons in a family and in due course of time four daughters-in-law join them. None of these women shares a blood relation; upbringing and inherited family traits divide them. With an aim to uphold the reputation of an ideal daughter-in-law, these four women, in spite of their differences, try to run the house. Since the eldest son is treated as the head of the household, the eldest daughter-in-law is treated as the his female counterpart. The household runs as per their dictates. When they accommodate the needs and demands of the brothers and their wives, the house comes to resemble heaven. In the absence of trust and affection, the family begins to seethe with suspicion and discontent. As we know, vices often outnumber the virtues of humans. The eldest sister-in-law often behaves as if the house belongs only to her and runs it in her own way. If noble thoughts guide her actions, happiness and harmony descend on the house. But when she tries to lord over the younger brothers and their wives, conflicts erupt. Such desire to impose one's will on others is just a synonym for vanity.

The vanity of the eldest daughter-in-law may begin by harassing the servants and farmhands of the house but it eventually targets other brothers and their wives. A time comes when she is no longer satisfied with the tag of the lady of the house. Other sisters-in-law just take orders from her and are not treated any differently from the servants. Though at times people willingly submit themselves to the wish of the eldest daughter-in-law in joint families and work together happily, it is mostly due to her undiluted affection and her accommodating disposition. The younger daughters-in-law often choose to do her bidding rather than bear the burden of running the household. But when the power exercised by the eldest daughter-in-law is not accompanied by affection, the younger ones feel that they live entirely at her mercy. This situation generates resentment. In the beginning, the younger ones endure everything for the sake of maintaining family reputation. But when the tipping point is reached, these women turn into rebels like me.

It is said that when Telugus come by a substantial sum of money, they prefer to carry them on their bodies, in the form of gold ornaments. Bengalis deposit it in a bank. Odias instead prefer to buy land. It is because of this social practice that home and land form the core of rural life in Odisha. Since land is the only means of livelihood, it is intimately connected with the web of life. It is because of a small plot of land measuring six acres and a third, Saria lost her life [in Fakir Mohan Senapati's novel *Chha Mana Atha Guntha* (Six Acres and a Third)] and Sukru Jani along with his son had to toil as bonded labourers in moneylender Ramachandra's household [in Gopinath Mohanty's novel *Paraja*]. If these victims had possessed physical strength and mental courage, they could have taken up arms and rebelled like Bakshi Jagabandhu (1773–1829). Even when one does not have the economic means to fight oppression and exploitation, simple folks like Sukru Jani's son wield weapons to eliminate oppressors like the moneylender Ramachandra. Similarly, when such tyranny desecrates one's home, it leads to the emergence of a woman like Netramani, one who can always resist oppression through her sharp tongue. Other people may escape this oppression by jumping into the well or hanging themselves, but women like Netramani make good use of harsh words. Though such liberty with language is often disparaged in polite society, its relevance cannot be gainsaid....

Women like me who oppose the oppressive structure of joint families often resort to such disagreeable language. Readers who admire my brother-in-law and sister-in-law may not actually appreciate the value of individual liberty. The efficacy of the trick I adopted in wrecking a joint family cannot be underestimated. I did so to establish my individual liberty and protect my freedom. I am not willing to accept labels like 'devoted wife' or 'ideal daughter-in-law' as these very terms are used to confine women to the four walls of the house. These also make them remain ever dependent on men and lose the ability to make a living by working outside home. If we live such a debilitating life that does not allow us to live like human beings or if our very existence is thus denied, reaction to such dehumanization is inevitable. When animals grunt, it is understood that they are hungry and their owners give them food. But in a joint family such as ours, a woman like me cannot share her feelings with anyone, nor does anyone have the time to pay heed to her grievances. When a woman's place is lower than that of cats and dogs, where one's basic rights are not recognized, a home turns into a veritable prison. When one feels a sense of belonging to a family, one's humanity and individuality flourish. However, if one feels that her freedom is curtailed in a family, one tends to become selfish. The unfettered development of one's being leads to the full realization of one's humanity – the acceptance of this principle eventually helps one counter tyranny within a joint family. It may sound unpleasant, but it is true. I admit that I quarrelled with others and instigated my husband to part ways with his elder brother. Superficially speaking, all these actions betray my selfishness, but did anyone ever try to understand the situation of an oppressed woman like me?

You must accept that I am a human being and like everybody else. I too feel entitled to some basic facilities within the family. I expect that my family members recognize my contribution and respect me as a member of this family, even though I understand that I am not its head. All my quarrels were intended to find answers to my questions. It is no surprise that when my brother-in-law and sister-in-law decided to leave, I started rebuilding my home. This is because, for the first time, I felt that this house was mine. Unfortunately, my brother-in-law and sister-in-law appeared to be even nobler after their departure. Nobody tried to appreciate that I had initiated the plan to secure basic minimum dignity for myself.

Those who cite idealism and Gandhian values, and believe that my husband's elder brother and his wife are divine beings, do not fully understand those values. Gandhi's ideals were not abstract or theoretical, but action-oriented. There is nothing that Gandhi preached that he did not practice. It is because of this resolve, Gandhi dedicated his life at the altar of sacrifice. This world of clay and stone was his sphere of action, where he put these ideals to test. Whenever he translated his ideals into practice, he made sure that he did so for the welfare of his fellow human beings. He knew that to solve human problems, one needs to live among humans. This is the reason why he did not run away from society to the forest, nor did he seek to solve problems by cutting himself off from people.

Gandhi never resorted to sophistry while trying to establish brotherhood among Hindus and Muslims. In places like Nuakhali where such relationships had degenerated, he strove to revive that sense of brotherhood. We all know how he had to sacrifice his life in his mission to put ideals into practice. By contrast, my brother-in-law did not do anything substantive. Let us not forget that the ideal which he preached to Dharamu Das and people like him, he did not apply to his own household. If he had done so, our home would not have been split. I believe that his ideals were only confined to rhetoric and that he was preoccupied with worldly ambitions. He never cared to accord importance to the fire ravaging the house, let alone try to douse it. His indifference fed that raging fire. For something to burn, two things are necessary; one is fire and the other is some object to be consumed by it. Without a combustible object in the house, fire cannot be kindled. My brother-in-law dedicated his whole life to the transformation of the heart but such discipline was meant for the benefit of my sister-in-law, and not me. He should have understood that change in one person does not automatically translate into the change of heart in another. He should have tried to understand the interests of both the women. Since he did not do so, I came to be convinced that all that he was doing was eyewash, intended to show me in an unfavourable light.

When the fire started spreading, my brother-in-law never made any effort to extinguish it, but withdrew into a cocoon. Such escapism is not the mark of a true Gandhian. If the problem arises at home, the solution lies in staying there, confronting it and solving it. When one suffers from a disease, one's family members often dread the disease but never shun the patient. We know that the sick person is our own and so cannot be forsaken. We stay close to her and give her medicine. Running away from a problem, as my brother-in-law did, is not Gandhi's way. The unity of the family depends on the ability of its members, who have diverse attitudes towards life, finding something common binding them.

When this spirit of mutual dependence within a family is extended to the larger society, the latter stays strong and united. And when this coexists with a respect for individuality, the individual lives in harmony with society. For the individual, a sense of belonging begins at home and when such emotion permeates the larger society, freedom does not appear to be an abstraction. Unfortunately, this noble thought propagated by my brother-in-law from the precincts of the temple of goddess Mangala was mere rhetoric. First, he failed to create an environment at home conducive to a woman's freedom and individuality. Second, when such failure resulted in the fire of conflict, his attempts to quell it were nothing but escapism, and as such betrayed his defeatist attitude.

Born of the Soil is a social novel exploring social problems, but these are not caused by oppressed women like Netramani. Its protagonists are the heads of joint families and those who are at the helm of affairs. The undesirable result of these problems is the rise of rebellious women like Netramani. As we know, if we plant paddy we can harvest paddy and not millet. Similarly, nobody goes to harvest paddy only a few days after sowing the seeds. Successful harvest requires proper tilling and allied activities such as watering, using manure and weeding, and if these conditions are not met the field will yield only weeds. Similarly, the elders of a family are expected to steer it in a responsible manner without denying anyone the expression of her individuality. In the absence of such maturity of mind, the emergence of women like Netramani is only to be expected. Thus, it would be wrong to admire everyone else and treat me as the origin of all problems, and look upon me as an undesirable weed in a paddy field.

Trains run past village Beraboi; they not only carry people and goods but also transport knowledge to different regions. But no woman of this village has benefited from or been empowered by this knowledge. Society continues to keep women uneducated and uncultured, and fill their minds with superstitions. These women remain confined within the four walls of a house and are deprived of the knowledge and experience of the world outside. Their universe consists of broomsticks, reed mats, hand threshers and heaps of trash, which subjects them to a life of mindless drudgery. Given this limiting life-world, can you blame a woman like me for finding her voice in a way which society finds perverse? Can you then exonerate heads of households and celebrate them as paragons of virtue?

Translation: Jyotirmaya Tripathy

Notes

1 Natabara Samantaray, "Netramanira Diary", *Dagar*, vol. 21, no. 11, 1958, pp. 20–26.
2 Kalindi Charan Panigrahi, *Matira Manisha* [Born of the Soil], Tr. Bikram Das, New Delhi: Niyogi Books, 2017.

21 Gopinath Mohanty

Rabindranath Tagore and modern Odia poetry

Introduction

Gopinath Mohanty (1914–91) is arguably the most outstanding exponent of prose fiction in Odisha after Fakir Mohan Senapati. He studied English literature at the master's level at Ravenshaw College and served the Government of Odisha as an administrator for more than three decades. His job took him to the highlands of southern Odisha where he came in close contact with the lifeways of several tribal communities. He learnt their languages and wrote grammars of a few of them. Seven of his twenty-five novels, which include *Dadibudha* [The Ancestor] (1944), *Paraja* (1945), *Amrutara Santan* [Dynasty of Immortals] (1949), are set in this world and provide vivid insights into the tribal people's collision with encroaching modernity and their unique worldview. Until Gopinath's arrival on the literary scene, Odia novels were mostly set in villages and towns of coastal Odisha. In his fiction, Gopinath expanded the imaginative world of Odia fiction to include the lived experience of tribal communities living in the hinterland. In some other novels, especially in *Danapani* [Our Daily Bread] (1955), Gopinath masterfully explored the dilemmas and aspirations of an emerging middle class in the post-Independence period. He was an accomplished short story writer and has eleven volumes of stories to his credit; several of his stories feature memorable tribal characters. His versatility as a man of letters is reflected in the acclaimed biographies he wrote of two major political figures of Odisha, Gopabandhu Das (1877–1928) and Gopabandhu Choudhary (1885–1958). *Utkalmani* (1965) is based on Gopinath's conversation with Gopabandhu Das's personal attendant Ramachandra Barik. This may be regarded as one of the earliest attempts at writing oral history in Odisha. Gopinath also distinguished himself as a translator. His major translations include *Jogajog* [Tagore's novel bearing the same title] (1966), *Mo Vishwavidyalaya* [Gorky's *My Universities*] (1969), and *Juddha o Shanti* [Tolstoy's *War and Peace*] (1980). His autobiography in three volumes titled *Srotasvati* [The River] was published posthumously.

This essay was read at a seminar held at Santiniketan on the occasion of Tagore centenary celebrations in 1961. Here Gopinath Mohanty traces

DOI: 10.4324/9781003224778-21

the reception of Rabindranath Tagore's poetry in Odisha and uses this as a lens to provide an insightful perspective on the development of modern Odia poetry. Gopinath minutely examines several factors which help one explain why the poetry of Tagore, in spite of the acclaim it achieved worldwide, could not exert a powerful and shaping influence on modern Odia poetry. For one thing, the devotee's intense longing for a union with the formless divinity, which constitutes a major theme in Tagore's poetry, was already familiar to Odia readers on account of their contact with the poetry written by premodern mystics. Moreover, the fact that western education had not spread widely in Odisha in the first half of the twentieth century, explains why Odias remained overwhelmingly partial to traditional forms of literature and gave a lukewarm response to Tagore. Another source of resistance to Tagore's influence lies in the reluctance to emulate literatures from other regions in the context of growing assertion of Odia identity in the early twentieth century. Around the same time, the anti-colonial nationalist movement and an increasing awareness of class conflict promoted by Marxists began making their presence felt in Odia literature. As a result, a growing emphasis on action shaped the outlook of many Odia poets and diminished the possibility of Tagore's contemplative inwardness influencing them. Even when a few poets, like the members of the Sabuja group, chose to imitate Tagore's poetic style, they were spurned as escapists and some of them themselves consciously outgrew his influence. Gopinath discovers and illuminates key aspects of the Odia literary tradition through selective absorption and rejection of external influence.

*

Rabindranath Tagore and modern Odia poetry[1]

Gopinath Mohanty

Memories come rushing in.

He was the only Indian who won the Nobel Prize for literature in the last sixty years. It made him an illustrious figure in the world. It was a memorable event in the history of India. Every Indian felt proud of him.

Compared to the unprecedented tribute the world pays him and the reverence with which Indians look upon him on the occasion of the celebration of his birth anniversary, the glory of winning the Nobel Prize appears unimportant.

Bengal and Odisha share borders and close bonds of love and fraternity. The bond grew stronger after Sri Chaitanya's celebrated visit to Odisha. Although Vaishnavism had already struck roots in Odisha before Chaitanya, he gave it a whole new dimension. The Vaishnvite cult of Radha found a powerful expression in the works of later poets such as Dinakrushna

Das, Abhimanyu Samntsinghar, Gopalkrushna Patnaik, Baladeb Ratha and scores of other poets, even when some of them did not belong to the Vaishnava sect. In most of his poems, Tagore casts the human soul in the role of the beloved. But the lover is unknown, unseen and infinite. This mystical element invests his poetry with an aura of strange newness. This loving union of the human and the divine is expressed from different perspectives in his poems. The fine blending of imagination and intellect renders this expression significant in several ways. It paved the path for the more cerebral poetry that came to be written later.

One hears a similar mystic note in the poetry of the seventh-century Vajrayana saints. They sought to comprehend a world beyond human reach, a world bereft of sound and light, and a cosmic void that made the body its abode. They believed that the vast outer expanse enveloped a subtle inner one. Subsequently, *Shunyavadis* [the believers in the doctrine of the void] imagined the divine spirit as infinite and as the eternal lover. Poets in Odisha were intimately familiar with the idea of the union of the finite human soul and the infinite divine soul, long before Tagore appeared on the literary scene. Therefore, what is distinctive in Tagore's poetry is not this theme, but its treatment. He released this union from the confines of the local and the physical. Tagore's poetry is informed with the belief that God is omnipresent and one can achieve union with Him within and outside the body. The intensity of the desire to be united with the lover that is articulated in the poetry of Vaishnavas also finds expression in Rabindranath's poems. At times, the beloved eagerly waits to be united with the lover, and at others, she laments the absence of her lover. There are also times when the beloved is overcome by the ecstasy of the union. This sublime passion of being one with the lover was also symbolically expressed in the works of the *tantrik* or *yogic* poets [occult poets] of Odisha. The *pinda-bramhanda* [body as the universe] theory was a major theme in the poetry of the sixteenth-century mystic poet Achyutananda Das. Bhima Bhoi, a late nineteenth-century tribal poet and religious leader, also played a crucial role in popularizing this new cult. On the other hand, poets who did not engage in such spiritual or philosophical pursuits preferred not to draw upon such esoteric religious themes. The saint-poets of Odisha, however, had rarely described the Supreme Lord as formless. About a hundred and twenty years ago, poet Arata Das, a Matipanthi siddha [a saint who espoused the earth cult] of the famous monastery of Benupada near Delang in the district of Puri wrote,

> O wise one, opening your eyes of wisdom, see the image before thee
> Though to your mortal eyes it may not visible be.

Odia poets embraced either the Vaishnva view of life or that of the *Shunyavadis*. However, one comes across a unique synthesis of these two only in Tagore's poetry. The mysterious unknown being that exists at one end of the spectrum of human perception and the familiar form at the other blissfully merge with each other.

Although in Tagore the East harmoniously blends with the West, his poetry remains deeply rooted in cultural and philosophical traditions of ancient India. He drew heavily upon the *Vedas* and the *Upanishads*. In spite of the linguistic diversity prevailing in India, its cultural practices shared intimate affinities. In some way, Tagore's poetic sensibility was shaped by these affinities he inherited. The following example may be considered here.

The way the rising Sun is addressed in Tagore's poem that begins with the line *"Bhengechhe duara esechho jyotirmaya"* [the orb of radiant light has burst in breaking the door open] bears a striking resemblance to the tenth-century Odia poet Sarala Das[2] invoking the Sun in the *Sabha Parva* of the *Mahabharata*. Sarala Das uses the expression *timira bidarana* [one who tears darkness apart] to describe the rising Sun; Tagore who wrote about a thousand years after him employs the same phrase *timira bidara*. Surprisingly, the two poets, separated by a millennium, both visualize the Sun tearing darkness with his sharp nails. Furthermore, both the poets imagine the sun as Rudra or Shiva worshipped in the form of a phallus. While Sarala Das venerates the Sun as *gagana linga* [the flaming phallus of heaven], Rabindranath addresses the Sun as *"Prabhata surya esechho Rudra saje"* [The morning sun has arrived in the form of Rudra]. Thus, both the poets look upon the Sun and the Shiva as one and the same and dwell on their benevolent aspects.

Odisha has a long tradition of poets desperately seeking the mercy of the Lord and the bliss of divine love in their songs. These intensely moving songs are popularly known as *jananas*. These *jananas* were written not only by established poets but also by mendicants, and ordinary men and women. *Jananas*, however, do not present the Supreme Lord as formless; they recount the miraculous deeds He performed by assuming different avatars.

Odia poets could rarely imagine a formless God or One without attributes who did not perform miraculous deeds before the advent of Brahmoism in the nineteenth century.

In his autobiography, Fakir Mohan Senapati (1843–1918) mentions that Prasanna Kumar Bhattacharya, a Brahmo preacher, visited Balasore in 1867-68 and praised Fakir Mohan's poems saying that these were written by a *sadhaka* [one who has reached a higher level of spiritual attainment]. Though Radhanath Ray (1848–1908) and his associates disapproved of the portrayal of physical love in medieval poetry, in his own poetry, Radhanath himself does not eschew the depiction of such love. In his poetry, desire is delineated with a subtlety of expression while crude and gross details relating to it are discreetly excluded. However, his close associate, Madhusudan Rao (1853–1912), chose to concentrate on spiritual themes out of deep conviction. There is a saint-like serenity and simplicity about his poetry and an intense longing to merge with the divine. His poetry has a pervasive presence in Odisha and people sing them as prayers.

Take for instance his poem *Dhvani* (Sound) where he tries to listen to the divine voice amid many other voices which express joy and sorrow, kindness and cruelty, and so on:

Million kinds of sounds on this earth
Every moment resonate.
Have you ever heard that mysterious sound
That echoes the Eternal, the Ultimate?
Listen O world! In a mood exalted
The sound Ultimate that fills every molecule of this earth
And with a mysterious joy makes it vibrate.

In his poem "Nadi Prati" [Ode to the River], enticed by this mysterious sound the river flows out of the secret cavern. Some critics suggest that the influence of Tagore's *Nadi* [The River] and *Nirjharar Swapna Bhanga* [The Stream Awakens from a Dream] can be discerned in Rao's poem but this may not be the case. Inspired by Brahmo philosophy, Rao undertook a deep study of the *Upanishads* which gave him a rare insight into the nature of things. This accounts for the fundamental difference between Tagore's poetic vision and Rao's. Rao never construed the relationship of the human soul with the divine in terms of the one that binds a lover to his beloved. The ecstasy and agony that define a passionate romantic relationship are absent in Rao's poetry. Although he was not influenced by Tagore, his profound spiritual vision makes him share a poetic kinship with the latter. The same cannot be said of his successors.

The purpose of discussing the works of some Odia poets who wrote before Tagore is to examine the extent to which Odia literature was influenced by Tagore. Although Tagore brilliantly excelled in all genres of literature, his influence is not discernible in Odia prose. His novels, short stories, plays and essays were not read by many in Odisha. Only in Odia poetry can one find traces of his influence; even here, his influence on writers of lyric poetry was neither deep nor pervasive, and was limited to the employment of innovative rhyme schemes and rhythmic patterns. The reasons for Tagore not exercising a significant impact on Odia literature may be found if we examine the context in which Tagore's works were received in Odisha, the trends that were prevalent in Odia literature at the time, and dispositions and preferences of the Odia reading public.

Tagore received the Nobel Prize in 1913 and the attention of the whole world focused on him for he belonged to a country that was a colony. Although he was sympathetic to the Indian nationalist movement, he articulated the ideal of universal brotherhood in a new idiom. But by then, the Odia canon, nourished by the works of powerful writers such as Fakir Mohan Senapati, Radhanath Ray, Madhusudan Rao and Nandakishore Bal, had consolidated itself. In the latter half of the nineteenth century, Odia language faced a threat to its very survival. Odia writers, therefore, had to measure up to the challenge of establishing the rich distinctiveness of their language and celebrate its glorious past. At the same time, in poems like Radhanath Ray's *Darbar* and *Mahayatra* [The Final Journey] and Gangadhar Meher's *Bharati Bhavana* [Thoughts on the Motherland] anticolonial sentiments are fervently voiced. These sentiments grew even stronger when Madhusudan Das launched in 1903 a movement to unify Odia-speaking tracts under the aegis of Utkal Union Conference. A pan-Indian nationalist movement swept through Odisha in 1921 and it was spearheaded by great leaders like Gopabandhu Das, Nilakantha Das and Godabarish Mishra, who were also renowned Odia poets. They set up a national school at Satyabadi and ushered in a new era in Odia literature. Their writing exerted a powerful influence on the people of Odisha. They laid emphasis on freeing India from alien rule, the revival of ancient Indian values and the formation of the character of the young. Alongside this, they drew attention to the problems afflicting Odisha and instilled in Odias a love for their motherland. Odisha resonated with the stirring lines of Godabarish Mishra's song "Tunga shikharichula" [Soaring peak of the mountain] and "Ranjita asi dhare" [Blade of the bloodstained sword]. One comes across these moving lines in Gopabandhu Das's *Bandira Atma Katha* [The Autobiography of a Prisoner]:

The shadow of decay
That looms over Utkal
Haunts my nights and drives sleep away
Farmers once rich, and men of means
Now cannot get two square meals a day.

Sturdy, sinewy men
Who were once soldiers of Utkal,
Who belonged to the clan of Paiks
Now wander from door to door, begging.
Their bodies are reduced to tottering skeletons
Too weak to stand up on their own legs.

Wicked moneylenders
And cruel village guards
Strip them of whatever they earn
By the sweat of their brow,
Blood sucking landlords
Reduced people to paupers
Crushing them with
Whip-lashes and heavy blows.

Two aspects of modern Odia poetry now manifest themselves. The first relates to the growing preoccupation with the social dimension of human existence. One finds this preoccupation reflected even in Odishan art and sculpture. They project neither disembodied ideals nor mere physicality; they seek to bring these two into a harmonious relationship. In these the ideal and the universal emerge from the local and the individual. This vision informs and animates Odia poetry from Sarala Das to Sachidananda Rautray. The second aspect consists of an intense pride in Odishan heritage and a deep aversion towards the tendency to imitate others. The concept of universal brotherhood which the Jagannathdharma had preached centuries ago was not put into practice. The rise of Marxism, Gandhism and the idea of *Sarvodaya* [uplift of everyone] advanced by Binoba Bhave increasingly lent substance to this concept over recent decades. By the time Tagore's works reached the Odia reading public, they had grown so loyal to traditional Odia literature that they resisted Tagore as a model. Despite this resistance there were poets who preferred to abandon the traditional metrical pattern in favour of the syllabic-rhyming pattern adopted in Tagore's poems. This testifies to Tagore's poetic genius.

Another reason for the lukewarm reception of Tagore in Odisha concerns the literary preferences of the rural population which was not exposed to English education. It was given access to the riches of medieval literature by *pala* singers. They enacted episodes from medieval literature before an audience comprising farmers and labourers in villages, embellishing these with examples from famous texts and elaborated on their meanings. Villagers remunerated these professional singers by raising subscriptions. In *badipala*, two teams of *pala* singers enter into a contest, which was immensely popular in Odisha. The *pala* singers of each team recited verses written by well-known ancient and medieval poets. They explained and analyzed them to make them intelligible to the rural public, mostly unlettered. Large crowds thronged the sites of *pala* performance. The reading public of this state preferred to get introduced to the great poets of Odisha through such popular forms of entertainment. Any new style which did not bear the stamp of indigeneity was not accepted by them as it did not cater to their cultural needs. The situation described above prevailed in the 1920s when Tagore's works found their way into Odisha.

The influence of Tagore is clearly visible in the lyrics of the famous nationalist poet and musician Lakshmikanta Mahapatra. In his collection titled *Jivan-sangit* [The Song of Life], published in 1932 but written much earlier, he conveys intense longings of the beloved waiting eagerly for her lover. The poetic persona assuming a feminine form awaits her lover holding the doors of her heart open. A shiver of ecstasy runs through her as she hears the sound of His soft footsteps. One comes across a similar depiction in Tagore's *Gitali* (57):

The sound of You opening the door
Reaches the depths of my heart.

In Lakshmikanta's poems the tune of the unknown lover's song issues from
the veena the beloved plays. Rabindranath writes,

Play the tune pulling at my heartstrings
And usher in the morning.

This amorous connection between the deity and the devotee is explored in
the poems of Lakshmikanta, too. The beloved hears the inviting music from
the other side of the river which makes her grow restless. Lakshmikanta
also uses expressions like *ananad ghana* [merry clouds], or lines like *nikhila
vishwa nindita kari jagichhi nikhila chhanda, gagana bhubana spandita kari
bahuchhi malaya spanda* [as the celestial cadence begins to pulsate sending
a stir of joy through the cosmos whole, a throbbing swirl of joy runs along
it as the south-breeze begins to blow] in his poems.

Lakshmikanta Mohapatra was a great writer in his own right. So, even
when he borrowed ideas and themes from Tagore, he imaginatively transformed them. Therefore, the many inspiring lyrics he wrote to celebrate
India's freedom struggle, and the songs which were enriched by his inimitable humour and irony will have an enduring appeal. His poetry displays
a meditative inwardness and perfect mastery of craft. This enabled him to
capture the essence of Tagore's poetry, which has a spiritual dimension. But
those of his contemporaries, who were dazzled by Tagore's fame and slavishly imitated him, failed to do so.

Inspired by Tagore's example, a few college students in Odisha began
writing poetry in the second and third decades of the twentieth century.
They included Annada Shankar Ray, who later achieved fame as a novelist
in Bengal, Baikunthanath Patnaik and Kalindi Charan Panigrahi who subsequently distinguished themselves as poets in Odisha, Harihara Mahapatra
and Sarat Chandra Mukherjee. They set up the "Nonsense Club" and
brought out a collection of poems titled *Sabuja Kabita* [Green Poems] in
1931. Earlier, their poems were published in the literary monthly *Utkal
Sahitya*. *Sabuja* [green] is a Bangla word; its Sanskrit and Odia equivalents
are *harit* and *sagua* respectively. Tagore published many of his poems in a
Bangla literary periodical, *Sabujapatra* [Green Leaf]. Moreover, the word
sabuja also occurs in his famous poem "Valaka" [Cranes] in which the
young are presented as defiantly alive.

One may place Annada Shankar's poem "Pralaya Prerana" [The Inspiring
Apocalypse] alongside the eighteenth poem in Tagore's collection *Gitali*.
Annada Shankar writes,

O spark of fire! Ignite the lamp of my body
With my burning flame will I Pierce

The dense fog of stagnation ...
I am a hurricane and will sweep over Time and Space
To burn everything, animate or inanimate, with a fire merciless.

And Tagore writes,

In this temple of yours let my body be a lamp
And with your touch ignited be
May the magic-stone of its flame
Purge and redeem me.

However, as an Odia poet Annada Shankar did not realize his potential and later began writing in Bangla. Sarat Mukherjee and Harihara Mahapatra did not write many poems after contributing a few to *Sabuja Kabita*. As for Kalindi Charan, he turned to writing novels, short stories and essays after composing a few poems. His poetry is a quest for truth and beauty. It displays a fine blend of a subtle aesthetic appeal and sharp intellect. He won acclaim as the author of the famous novel *Matira Manisha* [Born of the Soil] and almost gave up writing poetry. In his poem "Puri Mandira" [The Temple at Puri], he writes: "I would not engage in a quest for salvation renouncing all my worldly affections". This echoes the sentiment voiced in the oft-quoted line in a Tagore poem: "Renunciation of worldly ties is not my way". In his poem "Lohita Vyatha" [Crimson Agony], Kalindi Charan writes,

What pain has cleft the soft-pink heart
Its cruel blow has torn the world apart
The crimson agony drifts through the vast space
And across the heavens the crimson pain throbs;
It fills the heart with such terrible woe
Has planted crimson kisses all over me
Which feel like a crimson blow.

The influence of the eighth stanza of Tagore's famous work *Urvashi* can be easily detected in this poem. The poems written by the members of the Sabuja group lack the depth of Tagore's spiritual vision. Spirituality, for Tagore, was part of a genuinely felt experience; with the members of the Sabuja group, however, it was a shallow gesture.

Baikunthanath Patnaik was the only member of the group who remained consistently engaged in writing poetry. He reminds one of Tagore when he writes,

Every day I string a garland of my tears
That the pain of separation from you brings
This, I offer to you as my gift.

or,

> Wiping my tears a tune on the veena I play
> With the hope that you might listen to it
> And make it your own some day.

Imagining the Supreme Soul as his beloved the poet writes,

> An enigma you are, perhaps a shadow
> You are the poet's bride
> But You are the Truth Ultimate
> You are the poet's pride.

In his famous "Sesha Geeti" [Last Song] he writes,

> How can I blame you for not being kind
> You have filled the pot of my life in so many ways
> You have dispelled my delusions
> May the raft of my life sail into your ocean.

On occasions, the influence of Tagore can be traced in the music of words one finds in Baikunthanath's poetry.

> *Shunya mora ghara aji re kharatara*
> *Timira hane chira sajani*
> *Ki katha nirabata kahii jalaye byatha*
> *Na dishe dura priya sajani.*
> [My empty house pulsates with hope, but the
> Piercing darkness seems to last forever.
> Silence speaks and torments me, I cannot see my love
> Who is so far away from me!]

Adolescents tend to follow uncritically someone they venerate. Baikunthanath managed to overcome this tendency to hero-worship Tagore. In the later part of his poetic career, his poetry achieved maturity by engaging with the real world more vigorously. The adolescent exuberance was replaced by a mature social consciousness and a revolutionary strain found its way into his writings. He protested against the existing social inequality, the sufferings of the downtrodden, and other social evils.

A poet who was not part of the Sabuja group and was their contemporary also came under Tagore's influence. She is the celebrated poet and novelist, Kuntala Kumari Sabat. She began publishing her works in the 1920s and her novel *Raghu Arakshit* [Raghu, the Orphan] and poetry collections such as *Anjali* [A Handful of Offerings], *Archana* [Worship], and *Sphulinga*

[Spark] enjoyed immense popularity. In her novels, she expresses deep concern over the miserable plight of women in rural Odisha. If a sublime spirituality informs her devotional poems in *Anjali* and *Archana*, the poems in *Sphulinga* convey the message of rebellion and nationalism. The structure and rhythm of her devotional poems sometimes reveal traces of Tagore's influence. In "Nirimakhi" [The Innocent] she addresses the lover who symbolizes the infinite:

> My tears have washed away my pride
> To dispel my despair at your feet I pray

One can hear Tagore's voice in these words. In her poem "Mo Karani" [My Deeds] she writes, "I do not pray at your feet to relieve the agony which torments me". One could compare it with Tagore's "Bipade moore rakhya karo ei nuhen prarthana" [I do not entreat you to save me from this danger!]. However, she differs from Tagore in that she does not implore God only to grant her fortitude to bear desolation but beseeches Him to make duty her religion. The impact of Gandhian thought is unmistakably obvious in her prayer. In her "Nara Narayana" [God in the Form of Man] she tells her Lover, who symbolizes the Infinite,

> Because I knew You would pass this way I spent a sleepless night keeping the door open. The whole universe woke up to welcome you, a fragrant breeze blew, and the birds sang paeans to you. But no one could know when you went past this place. You came in the guise of a poor man to fill your bowls and left unseen.

This reminiscent of Tagore.

Kuntala Kumari's poems, for the most part, reminded Odias of how their world had fallen into decay and she inspired them to revive their lost glory. Her poems were inherently musical and possessed an endearing aesthetic appeal. Unfortunately, this great poet died young.

The Sabuja era quickly came to an end and the direct influence of Tagore on Odia literature waned. Mayadhar Mansinha was primarily a poet of love. Occasionally, one can hear in his poems, distant echoes of Tagore. Mayadhar wrote a few poetic plays like *Sadhabajhia* [Merchant's Daughter] which were modelled on some of Tagore's plays. However, Tagore's influence on his poetry was confined to a few resonant images. Two other noteworthy poets whose poetry does not show any influence of Tagore are Radhamohan Gadnayak and Godabarish Mahapatra.

Modern poetry gradually moved away from the lyrical impulse that dominated traditional Odia poetry. This tendency grew more pronounced in Sachi Rautray's poems. As a teenager, he translated Tagore's *Varsha Mangal* into Odia. He was intimately familiar with Tagore's poetry and he received the blessings of Tagore who encouraged him to establish a close relationship between Bangla and Odia literatures.

Sachidananda Rautray's poetic development is complex and multifaceted. Consistent experimentation with innovative styles, exploring multiple and diverse poetic perspectives are remarkable features of his poetry. Combined with a sharp intellect and powerful creativity, these give his poetry a strikingly fresh flavour. At a certain phase of his poetic career, he borrowed elements from Tagore's poetic diction. For example, he employed phrases like *"jhara bakulara krandana"* [when fallen *bakula* petals weep], *"ghara chhada ei pathara kabita"* [the song of the road that leads away from home], *"matira malina buke"* [upon the pale bosom of the earth] and *"mauna dirghswas"* [silent sigh]. Lines like *"he mora niraparadha desha"* [o my innocent nation] are shaped in the mould of Rabindranath's "he mora durbhaga desha" [o my ill-fated nation]. In poems written before this phase and which brought him recognition, we find enchanting delineation of simple, guileless village life, sentimental love, and suffering humanity. The influence of the final stanza of Tagore's "Sesher Kabita", a poem that figures in the collection titled *Balaka*, is clearly visible in the following lines of Sachidananda:

This love of mine, this creation that bears my soul's signature
Recedes into oblivion like a torn page from the past
Future beckons me, invites me to take a long and exciting journey
For what I have left behind fills me with no regrets.

However, subsequently, under the influence of Marxism he wrote several poems charged with revolutionary ardour. At a later stage, he returned to his true poetic self and began writing poems that vividly conveyed intense and sublime emotions. He wrote about the aftermath of World War II. His poems were brilliant renditions of the postwar turbulence and disillusionment which had taken human existence in its crushing grip. His poetry came to be characterized by sparseness and an economy of expression. He achieved remarkable directness in his poems by using a simple and appropriate idiom. In this manner, Sachi Rautary inaugurated a new era in Odia poetry. His poem "Pratima Nayak" marks a distinct break with the tradition in Odia poetry that focused on lyrical fervor.

A dull moon in the sky like soap's lather, a pale-white
Has made a compromise between darkness and light,
In a distant mill somewhere, the chimney keeps wheezing
Crossing past the green-ladder of the paddy fields and the river
Rattled on the mail train at eight in the evening,
The sheldrake weeps at this hour I read in a poem years back
All of a sudden, I came across Pratima Nayak,
A leather bag in hand, a pimple-ridden face
Her pale gaunt cheeks held unmistakable mark of lostness,
An emaciated figure, the pallor of pimple-marks
Had settled on her face

Her once upright figure was flaccid now
And was concealed in a khaki dress,
On her body, like a Japan-made paper flower
Had settled the patina of advancing age
'Are you alright', I asked, with the husky gloom of dusk in my voice,
Pratima smiled ...
Far, far away where the blue bounds of the sky and
The ochre limits of the earth met
We both stood beyond the estuary where reality and dream merged,
Behind us a long span of two years lay slumbering
Grey, smoky, dark, war-worn and frightening

Another major Marxist Odia poet, Anant Patnaik, who makes effective use of the spoken idiom, is not indebted in any way to Tagore's style. And eminent modernist poets who include Guru Prasad Mohanaty and Bhanuji Rao find in T.S. Eliot, Charles Baudelaire, and seventeenth-century metaphysical poets, not in Tagore, their models and sources of inspiration. The razor-sharp irony underlying the texture of pleasant familiarity lends their poetry its distinctive character. They seek to tear apart the mask of sentimentality concealing harsher truths of the human subconscious.

It is not easy to foresee the future course of Odia poetry. Even in this modernist era in Odia literature, writers such as Gadadhar Singhsamant, Madhav Chandra Mishra Sharma and Golak Pradhan continue to compose poems in imitation of Upendra Bhanja, a pre-modern poet. These poets enjoy considerable popularity.

To conclude, Tagore's influence on Odia poetry did not last long. This influence may have been felt with some force for about a decade. And a decade appears negligible when placed in the context of the long thousand-year-old history of Odia literature. However, Tagore, the writer, has achieved immortality and his oeuvre is a timeless treasure cherished by the nation. Tagore's poetry, like that of Kalidasa, has become a part of every Indian's inalienable cultural inheritance. It has entered our collective unconscious. From this perspective, it can be argued that any Indian writer who has read Tagore's poetry must have assimilated his vision in some form or other. To put this in Tagore's own words,

My songs like clusters of water-hyacinths
Keep drifting wherever they grow
Put out leaves and flowers but no roots
Basking in the sun
Merrily dance floating across rippling water.

Translation: Snehaprava Das

Notes

1 Gopinath Mohanty, "Rabindranath" [Rabindranath Tagore and Modern Odia Poetry], *Rabindra Smaranika*, ed. Debi Prasanna Pattanayak, Santiniketan: Visva-Bharati, 1963, pp. 16–37.
2 Gopinath Mohanty was of the view that Sarala Das lived and wrote in the tenth century CE whereas many other Odia scholars place him in the fifteenth century CE.

22 Krishna Chandra Panigrahi

Commercial prospects of modern Odia literature

Introduction

Krishna Chandra Panigrahi (1909–1987) was a celebrated historian, an accomplished literary critic and astute chronicler of culture. Educated at Ravenshaw College and Calcutta University, Krishna Chandra began his career engaging in extensive archaeological excavations. The publication of *Archaeological Remains at Bhubaneswar* in 1961 (regarded as a classic) established his reputation as a leading archaeologist of India. His perspective on the past as a historian was remarkably free from sentimentality and chauvinism as it sought to separate history from legend. In fact, one of his acclaimed books written in Odia bears the title *Itihas o Kimbadanti* [History and Legend] (1963). Krishna Chandra enriched Odia critical discourse by bringing his skills as a professional historian to bear upon the interpretation of texts and contexts. This is vividly evident in his masterful study of the socio-political world of Sarala Das's *Mahabharata*. His erudite reflections on Odia literature also deepen our understanding of the sources and directions of literary change. His essays are distinguished by a consistent emphasis on analytic rigour and dispassionate objectivity. His autobiography *Mo Samayara Odisha* [Odisha of my Times] (1978) presents a searing critique of contemporary Odishan society and culture, and seeks to trace the roots of this pervasive cultural decline. His major publications include *Odishara Sanskruti o Itihasare Jajpur* [The Place of Jajpur in the History and Culture of Odisha] (1973), *Prabandha Manasa* [Essays] (1973), *Sarala Sahityara Aitihasika Chitra* [History in Sarala Das's *Mahabharata*] (1976) and *History of Odisha: Hindu Period* (1981).

The present essay titled "Adhunika Odia Sahityara Vanijya Mulya" [Commercial Prospects of Modern Odia Literature] was delivered as a lecture at Navagunjar Sahitya Samiti in Sambalpur in 1944. In this lecture, Krishna Chandra attempts to answer the question as to why modern Odia literature is not commercially viable. He focuses attention on the poetry written in the Sabuja era (1920s and 30s) to identify factors which led to this crisis. The experiments the Sabuja poets carried out with themes, diction and technique constituted a sharp break with tradition. Pre-Sabuja Odia literature,

DOI: 10.4324/9781003224778-22

Krishna Chandra argues, drew its vitality from being deeply rooted in local myths, legends and *puranas*, and adhering to popular melodic modes. These accounted for its powerfully pervasive appeal. Even when Radhanath Ray (1848–1908), who ushered in literary modernity in Odia poetry, introduced audacious experiments at the level of both form and content, he took particular care to draw upon established premodern poetic conventions. The Odia readership, therefore, never felt alienated from his poetry; on the other hand, they responded to it with avid enthusiasm. The undiminished loyalty of this readership to traditional Odia literature and the persistence of orality contributed to the bleak commercial prospects of modern Odia literature. However, Krishna Chandra's position in this lecture is not to be mistaken for the grim pessimism of a parochial conservative. He is keenly aware that to grow richer a literature needs to absorb influences from the world outside and introduce transformative innovations. But, he contends, such a task cannot be accomplished through slavish imitation of and fascination for transient fashions. This requires the exertions of outstanding writers endowed with genius and discipline, such as George Bernard Shaw and Rabindranath Tagore. Krishna Chandra urges modern Odia poets to consciously and painstakingly acquire Odisha's richly multi-layered literary tradition and not passively inherit or deliberately disown it.

*

Commercial prospects of modern Odia literature[1]

Krishna Chandra Panigrahi

Why does modern Odia literature lack a large readership? In my lecture, I will address this question. I discuss this not as a writer but as a reader. If these two things are kept in mind, the following discussion can be properly understood. Writers and journal editors are of the opinion that while there is no dearth of litterateurs in Odisha, a large readership is conspicuous by its absence. Everything in this world, from fine arts to science, is governed by the logic of the market. Anything that does not have a market value cannot simply sustain itself. These days, Odia literature is not commercially viable. How long can it be sustained just because of its fame and prestige? This sums up the present dilemma.

It is impossible to ignore this dilemma in an age dominated by technology and commerce. The way the periodicals of Odisha are dying one after another and writers are either giving up writing or becoming indifferent to the pursuit of literature bear out the above contention. Is the reader or the writer to blame for the failure of Odia literature to achieve commercial viability? This question merits serious attention. The number of writers in Odisha is small and its population and reading public are not very large either. It is necessary to maintain a proper ratio between readers and writers in order to help Odia literature survive and prosper. A look at the literary scene of our neighbouring state, Bengal makes us realise how the pursuit of literary activities is in close conformity with rules of the market. No poet or author of any consequence there faces a crisis of survival. Though the population and the literate readership of Bengal are far greater than that of Odisha, the number of authors there is also correspondingly big. However, establishing one's reputation as an author is no easy task in Bengal. Many a writer fail to find a market for their books; the fact that lots of books are sold as waste paper on the pavements of Kolkata makes this clearly evident. Then how can one blame only the readers for the failure of Odia literature to achieve commercial success?

The reason for this failure lies in the fact that Odia literature has not been able to establish itself as a national asset. This literature is developing without connecting to its readers and social context. It is not surprising therefore that it does not enjoy commercial success. No literature of any era has progressed by isolating itself from its social milieu and reading public. If we leave the early phase of Odia literature out of account, the remaining period can be divided into three broad phases: the Bhanja era, the Radhanath era and the modern or Sabuja era. If one makes enquiries at bookstores in Odisha, one learns that books by authors belonging to Bhanja and Radhanath eras sell in greater numbers than those written by modern authors. It may be mentioned here that books such as *Baidehisha Bilasa, Labanyabati, Bidagdha Chintamani, Rasakallola, Mathuramangala, Kishorchandrananda Champu, Radhanath Granthabali*, the novels of Fakir Mohan Senapati, Gangadhar Meher's *Indumati, Kichaka Badha* and Nandakishore Bal's *Nirjharini* find more buyers than the celebrated books of the modern era. If this claim appears unconvincing, I urge you to collect the data from the booksellers themselves. How does one account for the lesser popularity of modern authors? The literature of an age is widely received and appreciated in the age in which it is produced. After this, generally speaking, their reception becomes less and less enthusiastic, and they are gradually reduced to historical artefacts. However, there are exceptions like Shelley and Keats who did not receive recognition from their contemporaries but achieved fame later. If one looks at it from a holistic perspective, this appears to be the general norm regarding the reception of literary works. Since few among modern Odia poets rank with Shelley or Keats, one wonders why they fail to find a readership in their own lifetime.

Why is that the literature of the Bhanja era still enjoys wide circulation? One of the main reasons for this is that the literature of the Bhanja Era is looked upon as a national treasure of Odisha. Upendra Bhanja in his own time was like the sun and surrounding him shone many planets and satellites. Bhanja did not write in imitation of literature produced in neighbouring provinces. He was a poet and an innovator. His poetry was not a mere echo or pastiche of contemporary Bangla, Telugu or Hindi literatures.

It bore the unmistakable stamp of originality. Anyone who seeks to contest this claim may be invited to furnish examples from the literatures of neighbouring provinces which show that Bhanja followed literary models or conventions provided by any of them. Of course, he might have absorbed a few lessons from the ornate and intricate wordplay of Sanskrit poets such as Bharavi and Sriharsha. Nonetheless, the Sanskrit language is a national treasure of India and is the mother of many Indian languages. Furthermore, Bhanja borrowed only a few elements from Bharavi and Sriharsha; one easily realises this if one goes through his works. There was a long tradition of intricate wordplay in Odisha. If required, I will produce examples from copperplate inscriptions. Thus, the literature of the Bhanja era, even where it is obscene, is as representative of Odia culture as are the sculptures found on the temples of Konark and Bhubaneswar. This is the main reason it continues to be vibrantly alive.

The second reason why the literature of the Bhanja era remains widely popular is because it was composed in conformity with well-known *ragas* (melodic modes). His works were more than mere written texts; they were also enjoyed as songs. In Odisha, music and literature were traditionally inseparably linked to each other. Thus, when a poem was composed, the poet's primary task was to set it to music so that it could be sung. True, the poets of this age displayed a great fondness for rhetoric and their poetry was filled with eroticism but it must be admitted that literature and music together fulfilled deeply felt needs of Odia readers and listeners.

The third reason for the popularity of the literature of this era was its subject matter which was culled from epics such as *Mahabharata*, *Ramayana*, and *Harivamsha*. Thus, it could easily find its way into the heart of every Odia. The language and modes of expression of the works might have been difficult but their essence could be easily grasped. Moreover, Sita and Rama, Radha and Krishna have been worshipped as deities since time immemorial. The literature of this era is therefore also recited as religious texts.

The fourth reason why the literature of this period is regarded as a national treasure could be that it is loved and appreciated by the highly educated, the half-educated and the uneducated alike. Upendra Bhanja, Dinakrushna Das, Abhimanyu Samantsinghar and the like undoubtedly wrote for people who were learned and erudite. However, in reality, their poetry was also relished by people with very little education. Since the *kavyas* employed well-known musical modes and familiar characters they appealed to even unlettered readers who were able to learn something from them. In addition, the learned discussed these works in great detail in *chatuspathis* [public places] of villages and *palas* [popular performances] as well. Scholars discussed and debated these works; these debates and discussions were listened to, understood, and enjoyed by the unlettered.

Although verbal pyrotechnics characterizing this body of literature may be considered a limitation, they perhaps account for much of its popular appeal. A substantial number of readers have always been fond of such ornate wordplay and made it a focal point in their appreciation of literature. The study of rhetorical strategies in poetry in Odisha is datable to the seventh or eighth century and this is evidenced in copperplate inscriptions.

Thus, it is clear that the literature of the Bhanja era remains alive. People of rural Odisha know nothing about when the age of Radhanath in Odia literature began or when it came to an end, but for them, the age of Bhanja is not yet over. Therefore, those who denigrate the literature of the Bhanja era and want to wipe it out of existence, should be aware of the limits of their power. Long after many of the modern poets are dead and gone, the literature of the Bhanja era would continue to charm and fascinate Odia readers.

The age of Radhanath followed the Bhanja era. Radhanath did not introduce anything that was new; he popularized literary innovations such as the use of blank verse, simpler poetic diction and plausible metaphors employed by famous Bangla poets like Michael Madhusudhan Dutta, Hemchandra Bandyopadhyay and Nabinchandra Sen. Importantly, the link between the age of Bhanja and that of Radhanath was not severed. In this period, familiar Odia melodic modes were retained and epics such as *Ramayana* and *Mahabharata* continued to supply the subject matter of literary works. Though outlandish verbal acrobatics were discarded, writers of this period engaged in simpler wordplay and double entendre. It may be mentioned here that some lines in the fifth canto of Gangadhar Meher's *Kichaka Badha* remind one of the rhetorical devices employed in Upendra Bhanja's *Baidehisha Bilasa*. Radhanath, for his part, borrowed many themes and elements of plot from western literature. However, he blended them with local legends, historical and political events and integrated them so deftly into the natural and cultural landscape of Odisha that they appeared completely original and new. Intense love for his motherland formed an important part of his poetic vision. His poetry bears testimony to his deep love for the mountains, rivers and forests of Odisha. With him as their mentor, writers like Gangadhar and Nandakishore Bal joyously celebrated their motherland. Radhanath's adoration of Odisha deepened, as he grew older into a love for India. His love for India found eloquent expression in his unfinished epic *Mahayatra*. Thus, the poetry of the Radhanath era was a unique synthesis of older and newer components. It shared a close relationship with ancient literature and it took or borrowed newer elements which were infused with regional specificities of Odisha. This made it a national treasure and was received and cherished by both the highly educated as well as the half-educated reader. Only the uneducated failed to appreciate it.

Before the Radhanath era reached an end, the Sabuja Yuga had arrived. Annada Shankar Ray and a few other enthusiastic young men founded the Sabuja Samiti and became the torch-bearers of this age. The literature produced in this era was not marked by originality and bore distant echoes of contemporary Bangla literature, severing all ties with ancient Odia literary traditions. There was in Sabuja poetry a conspicuous absence of conventional melodic modes. The characters from *Ramayana*, *Mahabharata* and *puranas* with whom readers were intimately familiar no longer featured in the literature of the Sabuja era. Universally comprehensible religious elements, the legends and natural beauty of Odisha seldom found a place in it. This age specialized in depicting a world of fragmented thoughts and feelings. The tradition of writing *kavyas* thus came to an end. Radically new metrical patterns and styles of versification were introduced. The preference for *tatsama* words in the Radhanath era gave way to a partiality for a much simpler diction. New words were coined and a few were imported as well. Odia readers were not ready to accept and respond to so many changes taking place in such a short span of time.

I am not trying to suggest that Odia literature should forever follow older traditions. Clinging slavishly to existing traditions is a sign of weakness on the part of a community. However, in order to bring about a massive transformation in national life, politics or literature, the birth of a divinely gifted individual is necessary. Initially, the people of no country readily accept any radical change, but they do so when such change is brought about by a person who is immensely talented and profoundly disciplined. George Bernard Shaw had to suffer because he tried to create an entirely new form of literature. Rabindranath introduced a new style and was therefore ridiculed and mocked. But through their talent, discipline and erudition, they succeeded in convincing their readers, who came to value their writings as national treasures. The Sabuja era is not an outcome of the exertions of any supremely gifted Odia writer. It owed its existence to the achievement and influence of Rabindranath. But one should not overlook here the fundamental educational and cultural differences between Bengal and Odisha. Since Bengal was way ahead of Odisha in the fields of education and culture, it is but natural that the progress in the field of literature in the latter would be slower. Just as the emergence of highly gifted and courageous figures in the Maharashtra of sixteenth and seventeenth centuries gave the region a pride of place in the political history of India, the appearance of many gifted individuals in the Bengal of the nineteenth and twentieth centuries made it a renowned seat of literature and learning. After the fall of the Utkal empire, conditions were not created in Odisha under which a vibrant national life could flourish; rather, certain events contributed to its decline. I am not going to discuss these. Suffice it to say that the progress of literature depends on that of national life. The level of literature of a nation is determined by the level its education and culture have reached. For instance, long after the tradition of writing lyrical poetry had enjoyed an extended vogue in England, it struck roots in Bengal. Had someone so outstandingly talented as Rabindranath not taken birth in Bengal, lyrical poetry might not have appeared on its literary scene until today. Odia literature was also evolving at its natural pace but a few young men abruptly inaugurated the Sabuja era and thus like a premature baby it was cursed with unnaturalness and weakness, which remained its hallmarks. That it was the offspring of an association indicates its unnaturalness. Associations are formed for research, for deliberating upon literature and expanding existing literary traditions. However, literary eras can only be ushered in by a gifted individual.

In this brief essay, I am only trying to articulate my personal opinions. It is not my intention to present abstract formulations. I have not cited examples from any poem, which would have unnecessarily increased the length of the essay. And moreover attacking particular authors would have become unavoidable. However, I wish to demonstrate the weaknesses and elements of artificiality in the content and form of the literature of the Sabuja era without quoting from the poems. Sabuja authors claimed that they would simplify the poetic practices associated with the Radhanath era and, therefore, reach a wider readership. However, its artificiality was so deftly concealed beneath its diction, tone, styles of versification and modes feeling that it could not be easily detected.

Let us talk about its use of language. The authors of the Sabuja era sought to make the language of their poetry simple and tender. To achieve this, one needed extraordinary command of Odia and an ability to use it with great dexterity. Rabindranath could use Bangla with such virtuosity that it accounted for his spectacular success. In Sabuja poetry, the evidence of linguistic dexterity is absent. Rather, the preponderance of sounds such as "ḍa", "ṇa", "la" in Odia created difficulties for them and they composed poems which with minor alterations would sound like Bangla poems. *Tadbhava* and *deshaja* words were used extensively in ancient Odia poetry, rendering them very different from Bangla poetry. Even those which used a lot of *tatsama* words cannot be easily transformed into Bangla poems. How then can Sabuja poems, in spite of the profusion of *tadbhava* and *deshaja* words in them, read like poems written in Bangla? This can be explained by the fact that Sabuja poets read the poems of Rabindranath so avidly and absorbed their tone, idiom and style that they tried to model their poetry on his. However, they did not quite succeed in this endeavour and, by overlooking the subtle differences between Odia and Bangla, they merely made one resemble the other. At first sight, Bangla and Odia share a lot of similarities. In terms of style and speech patterns, both languages have much in common. Had it not been the case, Odia would not have been obliterated in the space of a century in Medinipur. Why did Odia not disappear in Ganjam in the same period? Therefore, those who are reducing the gap between Bangla and Odia are not only erasing its individuality and distinctive character, they are also destroying the market for Odia poetry as most educated Odias can read and comprehend Bangla.[2]

Sabuja poets were so enamoured with these borrowed expressions that they used them indiscriminately. There is nothing wrong with borrowing words from other languages but showing uncritical devotion to these and distorting modes of feeling to be able to accommodate them is highly undesirable.

Melodic modes constituted one of the key features of pre-modern Odia literature. Popular melodic modes such as *chokhi, todi, kamodi, asadh-shukla* fell into oblivion during the Sabuja era, and the modes that replaced those were unfamiliar to modern Odia readers. Renowned modern poets of Bengal like Rabindranath and Nazrul were not content with creating new melodies; they were good singers and therefore introduced new rhythmic patterns. Theatre, cinema, radio, gramophone and music schools popularized the new melodic modes introduced by Rabindranath and Nazrul. The poets themselves presented these new modes through songs. I cannot say whether any of the Sabuja poets was a good singer; none of them presented any poem in the form of a song. There is no harm if someone invents a melodic mode. Kabisurya Baladeb Ratha and Gopalkrushna Patnaik did so; you can categorize their poems as lyrics or as songs. For their part, these poets set their poems to music and sang them before an audience. In the cities and villages of Odisha, these poems live on as songs that are sung daily. One does not care to find out whether these melodic modes were created by the poets themselves or borrowed from neighbouring regions; these are now cherished as a national treasure. The poetry of the Sabuja era is silent about melodic modes and leaves the readers confused. Some words were unnecessarily lengthened to make them fit their *matrabrutta chhanda* [metrical schemes]. Such elongation of words was not resorted to by pre-modern Odia poets. Metrical schemes came to Odisha close on the heels of their use in Bangla literature but the phonetic differences between the two languages were not taken into consideration. Bengalis lengthen the compound letters while pronouncing them, but Odias do not do so. It is possible that in some texts of ancient Odia literature a metrical scheme is present; but the poets followed the sound systems of Sanskrit rather than those of Odia. Thus, one of the major reasons why the poetry of the Sabuja era is not appreciated is because it is bereft of proper formal and rhythmic patterns.

The modes of expressing emotions in Sabuja poetry were so complicated that it is difficult to understand which emotion the poet seeks to convey. To express a simple and fine thought in the most complicated manner was considered praiseworthy. As a result, this became one of the distinguishing features of Sabuja poetry. Those who have read the poems of Rabindranath and Sabuja poetry may notice that making sense of the former is comparatively easier. Sometimes, it appears that the poets themselves are not sure which emotions they want to express. The religious outlook and the feelings expressed in most Sabuja poems are cosmopolitan in nature. Therefore, the presence of quintessetial Odia elements is minimal here. However, in pre-Sabuja Odia poetry these elements were prominently visible. Take Radhanath Ray's *Chandrabhaga* for example; it features Odisha's religious culture, its gods and goddesses, its temples, trees, land, sea, and the attire and demureness of its high-born women. These are conspicuous by their absence in Sabuja poetry.

For the above-mentioned reasons, the most avid readers of Odia literature got alienated from modern poetry. They felt that since much of modern Odia poetry was a replica of Bangla poetry, they would rather do well to read the latter. If our own literature reads like a foreign literature, why not go through the latter? This is how readers responded to Sabuja authors. Not only the half-educated reader but even their teachers could not understand this poetry. If primary, middle and high school teachers are asked to explain these poems, most of them would be unsuccessful. For the less-educated, these were as unintelligible as the *Vedas*. Education in the nineteenth and twentieth centuries gave rise to a class division among readers in India. For the highly educated readers, Sabuja poetry occupied the highest rung in the ladder. The presence of gods and goddesses, kings and queens in ancient literature put Sabuja authors off. In their writings, the masses figured as heroes and heroines, and the plight of the poor, social injustice and critique of superstition formed their subjects. Overall, Sabuja poetry reflected the problems besetting society; however, ordinary people understand the problems they face without having to read literature. Therefore, there is no need to teach them about these problems. This literature was offered to the masses just as *prasad* is offered to deities. Being denied access to the literature meant for the highly-educated, the little-educated rural folks of Odisha have turned to Baishnab Pani, Balakrushna Mohanty, Hamid and other popular poets; and some continue to derive enjoyment from the writings of pre-modern poets. Enquiries would reveal that the works of Baishnab, Balakrushna and others like them sell in large numbers in the market. They have helped in raising the level of literacy of people living in rural areas. There are some among the highly educated who dismiss their poetry as garbage, but nobody has explained how the habit of reading poetry would spread in villages without such "garbage".

Therefore, the self-conscious novelty of modern Odia literature, its absolute loss of contact with ancient and modern Odisha, and its elitism and rejection of existing religious faith have alienated it from readers of all classes. It thus becomes obvious why it would not find many buyers in the market. If Odisha were Bengal, and if contemporary Odia poets could create a readership like Rabindranath did in Bengal and abroad, this literature would have found a market. Those who think their poetry will receive acclaim with the passage of time, let this hope sustain them. However, history tells us that a literature created in a particular era receives appreciation in that era itself. How the poems of Upendra Bhanja were received during the Bhanja era is not easy to ascertain now. However, it is beyond doubt that Radhanath's poetry enjoyed enthusiastic acclaim during his lifetime. In Bengal, Michael Madhusudhan and others are not as highly appreciated now as they were during their lifetime.

Finally, to conclude this essay, I would like to say something about what can be done to increase the market value of contemporary literature. I do not feel qualified to act as an advisor. My age and knowledge of literature do not equip me to give people advice in matters concerning Odia literature; my expertise lies in other disciplines. Therefore, I offer the following suggestions only as a reader. In the meetings of poets and literary societies, there should be discussions on how to change the direction of contemporary literature.

At least in some areas there should be contact between ancient and modern Odia literature. What these areas should be would depend on the ability and judgment of the poets. It would be good if older melodic modes are reintroduced; these should be mentioned after the poem's title. It is the responsibility of those who are inventing or following newer rhythms to popularize them. Beneath the layers of antiquity, novelty never loses its vitality; rather, everywhere in the world novelty is nourished by antiquity. Rabindranath's outstanding talent first lay concealed under layers of antiquity and later found powerful expression. A glowing example of this is furnished by *Bhanu Singher Padabali*.

Those who aspire to be authors and poets in Odisha should study the evolution of Odia literature. When did Odia poetry begin to appear, like a torrential waterfall, is not easy to ascertain; however, the Buddhist songs and the *dohas* (couplets) of Krushnacharya from the eighth century were among first streams. After that, the stream began to swell. Contemporary literature will contribute to it and carry it further. However, if it tries to sever itself completely from the past it will suffer the fate of the hidden river Saraswati. Poets should receive patronage from the rich and powerful in Odisha. Such patronage was extended to poets till the age of Radhanath. The link between contemporary literature and patrons has snapped. In terms of language and culture, Odisha is a harmonious whole. It would not be wise to allow politics to affect its sense of unity.

Those who are unable to create poetry out of a sense of Odisha's cultural heritage, tradition and taste should write in English or Bangla. There is no reason for Odias to feel outraged about this, because it has become imperative that Odias should distinguish themselves abroad rather than inside.

Translation: Amrita Chowdhury and Ujaan Ghosh

Notes

1 Krishna Chandra Panigrahi, "Adhunika Odia Sahityara Banijya Mulya" [The Commercial Prospects of Modern Odia Poetry], *Prabandha Manas*, Cuttack: Kitab Mahal, 1972, pp. 71–87.
2 This was the case when the lecture was delivered in 1944; few Odias can now read and understand Bangla.

23 Chintamani Behera

The poetry of Sachidananda Rautray

Chintamani Behera (1927–2005) was an illustrious poet, critic, anthologist and translator. Educated at Ravenshaw College and Calcutta University, he taught Odia literature at several government colleges in Odisha. Eight collections of poems published between 1950 and 2003 established his reputation as a major modern Odia poet. These include *Shwetapadma* [White Lotus] (1950), *Trutiya Chakshu* [The Third Eye] (1975) and *Nije Nijara Sakshi* [Bearing Witness] (1996). His poetry presents an engrossing blend of melancholy and an abiding faith in humanity. He also edited four poetry anthologies, notable among which are *Adhunik Kabita* [Modern Poetry] (1964) and *Swara o Swakashar* [Modern Odia Poetry: Voices and Identities] (1974). He was Secretary, Odisha Sahitya Akademi from 1983 to 1985 and edited (from 1992 to 2000) *Shishulekha*, a highly popular children's magazine published by the Government of Odisha. He translated into Odia Rabindranath Tagore's *Bishwamanvara Pathe* [In the Footsteps of the Universal Man] and *Nibandhamala*, vol. 2 [Essays], and Santosh Kumar Ghosh's *Kinu Goalar Gali* [The Lane of Kinu, the Milkman]. Chintamani made a significant contribution to literary criticism in Odia by undertaking an intensive study of contemporary Odia literature, especially poetry. His major works of criticism include *Kavya o Kalakar* [The Artist and his Art] (1965), *Adhunika Kabitara "ka" "kha" o Anyanya Alochana* [ABC of Modern Poetry and Other Essays] (1973) and *Sahitya Chinta* [Reflections on Literature] (1996).

Chintamani Behera's "Kabi Sachidananda Rautray" [The Poetry of Sachidananda Rautray] was published in *Dagar* in 1956 as part of a series of articles titled "Mo Priya Lekhaka" [My Favourite Writer]. In this essay, he attempts an evaluation of the oeuvre of Sachidananda Rautray, arguably the greatest modern Odia poet after Radhanath Ray. The essay is at once an impassioned celebration and a spirited defence of Sachidananda. It assumes significance for the serious critical attention it devotes to the totality of a contemporary writer's works. One can discern in Chintamani's essay the influence of the New Critical practice of consciously dissociating a writer's work from the historical and social contexts in which it is embedded. It marks a significant point of departure from the dominant tendency in modern Odia

DOI: 10.4324/9781003224778-23

literary criticism towards a historical study of literature. Chintamani shows how Sachidananda rejected the mystical outlook and escapism of Sabuja poets and affirmed movement and struggle as the guiding principles of human existence. The humanism embodied in his works enables Sachidananda to powerfully combat feelings of defeatism and despair, and helps the reader glimpse the contours of a regenerated and egalitarian world order. However, Chintamani's evaluation of Sachidananda's achievement is not entirely laudatory. He concedes that the poet's passionate commitment to a particular political ideology sometimes makes his poems descend to the level of propaganda. But Sachidananda's supreme craftsmanship and depth of vision help him rise above ideology and create poems and stories of enduring appeal. Chintamani defends his favourite poet against his critics by pointing out how Sachidananda presents a richer worldview in his poetry by absorbing influences from world literature and reflecting a cosmopolitan outlook. He invites the reader's attention to a large number of brilliantly original images and metaphors which Sachidananda employs in his poems. These, Chintamani argues, introduce the Odia reader to a radically new sensibility and modes of expression. Importantly, in this essay, Chintamani highlights the provisional nature of his critical judgement and accepts the possibility of his approach to the poet evolving in course of time.

*

The poetry of Sachidananda Rautray[1]

Chintamani Behera

It is neither possible nor desirable to offer an assessment of the entire oeuvre of Sachidananda Rautray within the limited scope of a short essay. Here I do not intend to undertake a chronological survey of his works nor do I wish to locate them in their socio-historical context; instead, I choose to focus on his poetic credo and craftsmanship which enthral me. This essay embodies my intimate response to his poetry.

As a human being and reader, I belong to the contemporary world. So human beings who belong to this world are dear to me. Their hopes and aspirations, joys and sorrows, smiles and tears, struggle and perseverance, success and failure matter immensely to me. Therefore, I deeply adore a poet who so vividly portrays their triumphs and tragedies. I am convinced that in Sachidananda's poetry, the modern world and its realities find the fullest expression and the triumph of the human spirit seeking freedom is proclaimed. Sachidananda eloquently voices the thoughts, ideals, feelings, conflicts and uncertainties of his age.

> Heaven's gates are shaken today
> Kicked by humans, beastliness cringes.

Colours of glory adorn their foreheads
O humans! Conquerors of heaven! I bow to thee.

("Manav")

At a time when a number of Sabuja poets spurned the vitality of social experience and sought to create and escape into an enchanted ivory tower, the young Sachidananda celebrated inexhaustible human possibilities and sang a paean to a glorious future. It is true that one can find elements of a mystical outlook on life in his first collection of poems, *Patheya* [Resources for a Traveller] (1935). However, as the poet's expressive powers grew, the mist of dreaminess enveloping his poetry lifted, and was replaced by a realistic and ironic sensibility. This shift is evident in his subsequent works of poetry such as *Pallishri* [Portrait of a Village], *Baji Raut, Pandulipi* [Manuscript], *Abhijan* [An Expedition], *Hasant* [Laughter], and *Bhanumatira Desha* [The Land of Bhanumati], collections of short stories *Mashanira Phula* [A Flower in the Cremation Ground] and *Matira Taj* [The Monument Made of Clay], and his novel *Chitragriba*.

Life appears before me
Like a baffling riddle I cannot solve.
Sometimes, like a king, and at others, like a beggar
Who can open the doors of this world of mysteries for me?

or

Why did the heavens recede from the earth?
The stench of hell pervades it.
Who can unravel this mystery?
Why does the sea of time flow against the current?

(*Patheya*)

Sachidananda was, of course, overwhelmed by the wonder and mystery of life but the miseries of the world did not overpower him for he is determined to look for their sources. Rather than retreat from the dusty squalor of the harsh realities of life, he chose to use these to build a magnificent literary edifice.

In a dusty world full of sin and grief
Bursting with the pride of being alive
I have created a heavenly garden
And my heart overflows with bliss.

(*Patheya*)

Although one comes across the poet's realistic point of view in *Pallishri*, we find its fuller expression in *Baji Raut* and *Chitragriba*. His evolving poetic personality left a more visible imprint in his works such as *Pandulipi*, *Mashanira Phula* and *Matira Taj*. By the time he wrote *Chitragriba*, he had come under the powerful influence of Marxist philosophy and social realism. Therefore, in *Baji Raut*, his poetic voice grew fiery and combative as he launched a stinging attack on escapist and pacifist writers:

> O you escapists
> Where can you go tearing your bonds with the earth?
> O cowards, where can you find shelter?
> Can the lover's bower
> Offer you protection from danger?

One can clearly discern here a firmer control of form, a new strength of expression, and a transition from self-indulgent emotionalism that one finds in *Patheya* and *Purnima* to a socially-oriented realism. His sympathy for the suffering humanity grew more intense. His words "O workers, overcome your fear / And sing the glory of the oppressed humanity" echo Vladimir Mayakovsky's "On every single tear that is shed / I myself am crucified". Similarly, the following lines remind one of Whitman's "Comrade, this is no book / If you touch it you will touch a man":

> I am Sachi Rautra
> (Not Tagore or Shelley)
> I am the poet of this earth
> And the sky.
> My task is not to draw pictures on sheets of paper.
> Nor am I a professional singer.
> When you touch the pages of my book
> You touch the portrait of a new man.
> Everything that happens to human beings in this world
> Finds a place in my poems.
>
> ("Rajajema" ["The Princess"] in *Pandulipi*)

Sachidananda not only portrays the contradictions, complexities, and conflicts that characterize modern life and expresses sympathy for human beings in distress, he also engaged in the struggle to liberate them from bondage. The social consciousness of a progressive writer is powerfully present in his works. This profound sympathy and progressive spirit potently inform many of the poems in *Pandulipi* and quite a few stories in *Mashanira Phula* and *Matira Taj*. As Matthew Arnold observes, "What are the eternal objects of Poetry, among all nations and at all times? They are actions, human actions". But actions which do not lead human beings along the path of progress and enable them to live with dignity, are but empty and futile. Poetry that draws its intensity from such barren actions is bound to be lifeless and effete, and its creator impedes the march of human progress. Romain

Rolland describes such artists as worshippers of sterile and uninspiring art who are devoted to the luxury of cerebration and thought for thought's sake. They teeter on the brink of a fathomless abyss and their bodies exude the odour of cadavers. Sachidananda's outlook is instinct with dynamism and a living warmth. Humans in his poems are portrayed as always on the move and forward-looking; they do not long for "languid ease" and "a world of lyrical ecstasy". They want to discover "new ways of life and new templates for survival". They ask for the boon "Fill my empty quiver with two fatal arrows – one of revolt and the other of scorn; may struggle be my vocation". Or they ask for "a piece of land which my raised foot would rest upon". Two characters, Souri and Gagan, in Sachidananda's novel *Chitragriba* give concrete form to his ideals. Through the character of Souri, the author states,

> A human being inhabits a world lit up by the sun. ... They emerge from the whirling flux of life. ... And after death, they dissolve into the cease-less flux of ecstasy. ... Created out of a compact between the divine and the diabolic, humans embody the supreme truth of the world.

I firmly believe that Sachidananda is one of the pioneering progressive poets who takes great pride in celebrating the endless journey of human beings towards glory.

A number of his poems are animated by this energetic life-affirming vision; these include "Jhada" [Tempest], "Samkranti" [Transmigration of the Sun from One Zodiac Sign to the Next], "Pashu" [Beast], "Rakshas" [Demon], "Nabajatak" [The New-born], "Mukti" [Liberation] and "Rajajema" [The Princess]. The following lines express this vision most forcefully:

> I have to travel to a far-off destination and the road is a long one...
> Like a storm, I move forward for my road tells me that ceaseless move-ment is the supreme truth of life.

Thus, the poet refrains from shedding tears by the grave of a million dreams and the dead past. He chooses instead to emblazon the myriad possibilities of life and offers homage to vitality and progress. He is eager to discover "the new plan of the earth and the new maps of cultivated fields" and keen to accept the invitation of "the fresh crops raised in green minds". The desire to recognize the infinite possibilities of the future while showing respect to the glories of the past is eloquently voiced by Vinata in *Bhanumatira Desha*, who says to Tarang,

> Why won't you sing
> The glory of that flower blossoming triumphantly?
> This is how one learns to conquer life.
> And, if you, like Amit Roy in Tagore's *Shesher Kabita* [Farewell Song]

Stop by a flowering tree during your journey
You lose the battle.
What a terrible defeat it would be, Tarang!

As Lawrence Durrell says, "If art has any message, it must be this: to remind us that we are dying without having properly lived". This view of the function of art is projected emphatically in Sachidananda's poetry. The poet holds a particular social and political system responsible for the corrosive suffering endured by humanity, and dreams of a humane and egalitarian society rising out of a destructive revolution. It has to be conceded that on occasions, his poetry takes on the character of propaganda; however, no one can deny that he displays consummate ingenuity in reconciling expressive resources and the demands of form. As a poet who deeply engages with his own time, he records its failures, miseries, and feeling of futility with unerring dexterity. Poems like "Pratima Nayak", "Alaka Sanyal", "Matia Burujara Janha" [The Moon over Matia Buruj] and "Adina Barsha" [Unseasonal Rain] render this feeling memorably.

Youth turns deaf and mute.
The withering summons of summer dries up the silver-tongued stream of youth.
Where can we find nectar? Where is the world beyond death?
All we face is a gigantic question – an insubstantial mirage.
("Pashu" [Beast])

The barren dreams of the slum's prostitute …
The lonely soul of the night quietly descends …
Where is the way? Where is the way?
Far away yawns the chimney of a steel factory.
("Padmabhuk" [Lotus-eaters])

While painting a portrait of the oppressed humanity, the poet however never loses faith in its ability to build a golden future and sings,

The ochre coloured path peters out, in the womb of the sun
Forms a new life out of blood, tears, sweat and breath.
Awake, O great poet
And bloom like a scarlet oleander in the month of Shravana on the head of humanity.
("Padmabhuk")

I know, I know
Maybe this augurs the rise of the sun.
For the night is the womb of the dawn
and clouds cradle the rain.
("Matia Burujara Janha")

Like all gifted creative writers, Sachidananda rebelled against the stale conventionality espoused by the Sabuja poets, and achieved the remarkable feat of synthesizing idealism and realism in his own art. *Baji Raut*, *Pandulipi*, *Bhanumatira Desha*, *Mashanira Phula*, *Matira Taj* and *Chitragriba* illuminate aspects of this unique synthesis. Although written within the poetic conventions of celebrating village life established by Nandakishore Bal (1875–1928), the poems included in Sachidananda's *Pallishri* display a vibrant and lively individuality. Poems such as "Chhota Mora Gaanti" [My Little Village], "Palli Sanja" [Evening in a Village], "Rangoon Jatri" [Traveller to Rangoon], "Pahili Raja" [First Day of the Raja Festival], "Maluni" [The Flower Seller], "Shiva Puja" [Offering Worship to Lord Shiva], and "Grama Shmashan" [Village Cremation Ground] expertly combine excellent craftsmanship with the vivid depiction of the lived experience of villagers. In *Baji Raut*, the dreams of liberty cherished by the masses and their struggle to realize it are presented as vividly as the vicious tyranny let loose by the feudal elite. Every word in the poem bears the luminous imprint of the poet's genius. Nityanand Mohapatra's claim that *Baji Raut* occupies a place among *puranas* in Odisha and is as revered as a sacred text, is no exaggeration. Nityanand's observation conveys the insight of a true connoisseur of poetry. "One who displays fortitude in victory, and in defeat never loses hope" – Baji Raut is no longer a mere boatman boy of a village by river Brahmani; the poet transforms him into a deathless hero of the freedom struggle. Baji who "was small yet so colossal" and "whom life couldn't contain, and death yielded the right-of-way" will illuminate the path leading to freedom for humankind and kindle the spirit of resistance in its heart.

In his novel *Chitragriba*, we find a portrait of moral decadence, social disorder and uncertainty in the contemporary world along with a delineation of its dreams and ideals. It may not be regarded as a novel in the conventional sense of the term, but considered from the point of view of depiction of emotions, portrayal of characters and craftsmanship, it reveals remarkable originality and deserves to be categorized as a novel. Like his poems, his short stories in *Mashanira Phula* and *Matira Taj* reveal acute social awareness and a sharp ironic perspective on life. Characters like Jagu Tiadi and Jatiama's daughter-in-Law in "Mashanira Phula", Lochan and Sundari from "Mala Kain" [Dead Water Lily], Pahali in "Andharua" [Darkness], and Nakula in "Rajapua" [The Prince] masterfully expose the injustices and deficiencies inherent in our social life. The profound sympathy Sachidananda expresses towards characters like Jatiama's daughter-in-law, Pahali or Nakula render these realistic stories deeply moving. "Please do not sit in judgement over others. Can one human being truly understand another?" These words uttered by Jagu in "Mashanira Phula" magnificently define Sachidananda's compassionate and humanistic view of life.

Hasant introduces Sachidananda as a gifted humourist and satirist to the reader. In *Chitragriba*, published as early as 1930, one discerns his skills in generating humour through subjecting characters to ridicule. In poems like "Debalokare Ghoda Dauda" [A Horse Race in Heaven], "Hanumanra Gotra" [Hanuman's Lineage], Gopabandhunka Shraddha [Gopabandhau's Death Anniversary], "Ama Ganra Muralidhar Panda" [Muralidhar Panda of our Village] launch a subtle attack on our social and individual shortcomings and in the process induce laughter. He deftly blends pathos with humour and seeks to revive lost human values through lines such as "My old bullock, I gave to the butcher / Everything barring human life has grown dearer".

Bhanumatira Desha, a prose poem, provides a shining example of how poetic rhythms can be used with uncommon effectiveness in prose. This prose poem recounts the story of two lovers and ends in their separation. One looks in vain in it for features of a conventional *kavya*, nor does its subject matter display any novelty. Yet, its mode of presentation is distinguished by a rare innovativeness. The differences between the country and the city, the mental conflict characterizing modern life, and simple problems facing lovers are brought vividly to life by the artist. A romantic response to life which is yet informed by a sense of reality and the use of strikingly unusual images enthral the reader. One may notice in the poem the absence of a profound apprehension of life, nor should one expect to find here a great depth of feeling; all the same, a realistic outlook on the experience of love and Sachidananda's accomplished artistry make reading the poem a delightful experience. At the end of the poem, compelled by a sense of duty, its heroine Vinata deliberately distances herself from her lover, Tarang. The poem conveys the central idea that life is far greater than love. Although not presented as something to be dismissed with disdain, love is presented as trivial in the larger scheme of things. One does not hear the plangent utterance of a disappointed hedonist but the voice of a lover who is not paralysed by the pangs of separation:

> Since I know that I am greater than my love
> A mournful song I do not sing when I part from my beloved.
> No regrets does the past stir in my heart
> The glory of the journey fills me with a sense of plenitude.
>
> ("Prema o Jibana") [Love and Life]

The poem impresses the reader with an image of the lover's strong and dynamic masculinity. Similarly, Vinata symbolizes a powerfully assertive femininity. Through these characters, the poet rejects the defeatism of fatigue and affirms movement as the guiding principle of life. In presenting the experience of love, Sachidananda introduces a wholly new and life-affirming point-of-view. His love poems constitute a remarkable point of departure from the depiction of love in the works of major Vaishnava poets such as Vidyapati, Chandi Das, Abhimanyu Samantsinghar and Gopalkrushna Patnaik.

Sachidananda's originality is potently manifest in the images and metaphors he employs in his poetry. These splendidly serve to establish a harmony between thoughts and feelings, lend depth and range to the meaning of poems, and endow descriptions with a vibrant liveliness. Images employed in his poems such as "the green invitation of the sky", "the cold germs of apprehension", "silken slippery terror", "slumber luscious like fat", "the moon, a flaming scimitar", "the silken square of *jahni* flowers", "a heart hard like red sandalwood tree", "narrow streets winding like innocent lines on a palm", "the languid wine of leisure", "the vast and expansive lake of grass" captivate the reader. Such unusual metaphors and similes occur in large numbers in *Bhanumatira Desha* and immensely enliven the poem.

> These drowsy hills
> Curved like the hump of a camel
> Rise as if they were stupendous candelabra.
> And on it the sun burns
> in the morning and the evening.

or

> Tarang's face suddenly grew pale
> Like paper flowers in a living room
> Slowly fade in the light of the sun.

These images contribute to broadening and deepening the world of the reader's experiences and feelings. Only a great poet like Sachidananda can accomplish such an extraordinary feat of creative imagination.

His fascination for a particular political ideology affects the quality of his poetry on occasions but it is redeemed by the depth of his imagination and his superb craftsmanship. Sincerity, originality, nuanced expressiveness, and the variousness of the poetic universe are the distinguishing excellences of his art.

> Do the magic of dreams fill
> Vinata's wide-eyed gaze?
> Her heart hard like the trunk
> Of a red sandalwood tree,
> Exudes a fragrance
> That sends a strange shiver down every spine.
>
> (*Bhanumatira Desha*)

Numerous lines like "In a far-off land lies my temple built of stone, a wandering pilgrim I have lost my way" ("Banshi") [Flute], "Can the bulbul who belongs to the pear orchards of Iran, feel at home in the arid sands of Sahara" ("Nimba Gachhare Phula Phutichhi") [The Neem Tree has Come into Flower], and "The blind lane of life longs for wide open fields and the green sea of paddies" ("Mukti") [Liberation] exemplify the powers of his artistic imagination.

Some critics are of the view that Sachidananda's imitation of western models has run counter to the poetic principles cherished in traditional Odia poetry. One should, however, not forget that we live in an age of internationalism. The poet is constantly exposed to all kinds of influences; it is but natural that the poet cannot help acutely responding to these. What ultimately matters is the manner in which an artist internalizes these influences and effects a creative synthesis. T.S. Eliot's observation on the originality of an artist is eminently applicable to Sachidananda Rautray as a poet: "One of the surest of tests is the way in which a poet borrows. Immature poets imitate; mature poets steal; bad poets deface what they take, and good poets make it into something better, or at least something different".

Reservations have also been expressed regarding the obscurity and unintelligibility of Sachidananda's poetry. It must be conceded that sometimes his poems are focused more on cerebration than on expression of emotions. This might be an outcome of the impact of experimentalism in modern poetry and the harsh realities of modern existence. But, in this context, readers will do well to keep in mind C.D. Lewis's observation, "Learning to read poetry takes as much patience and concentration as learning to write it". Readers, therefore, have to be profoundly sensitive to the forces transforming life and society. It is impossible to create great art rejecting lived experience and social realities. The secret of the greatness of all great literature is that it is rooted in reality. As Herbert Read asserts, "To escape from society is to escape from the only soil fertile enough to nourish art". Since Sachidananda is a modern poet and embraces modern life in its totality, he has uses in his poems many unpleasant, unpoetic and coarse expressions. In the process, he has introduced a new aesthetic sensibility in Odia poetry. In Bertrand Russell's words "now-a-days he [the poet] must either ignore contemporary life or fill his poems with words that are stark and harsh", one finds persuasive justification for Sachidananda's poetic experiments.

Like in other spheres of life, a crisis of values afflicts literature. Therefore, philosophers and thoughtful leaders are engaged in finding ways of overcoming this crisis through the discovery of new values. Progressive writers, for their part, are striving to fashion new perspectives. Sachidananda has endeavoured to assert and express new human values, sometimes within the confines of individualism and at others, under the banner of socialism. One, of course, comes across images of decadence, exhaustion, disaster and delusions of the modern world in his works; at the same time, one also hears the resonant voice of a liberated, powerful and progressive artist. With the passage of time, many of his poems which preach an ideology or glorify revolution may lose their appeal, but his experiments with rhythmic patterns, his employment of distinctly innovative images and symbols, the singularity of his artistic perspective, and his responsiveness to world literature, will establish him as the creator of a new era in Odia literature.

I admitted at the beginning of this essay that it would be impossible to undertake a comprehensive study and evaluation of Sachidananda's achievement as a writer within the scope of this essay. Moreover, since I adore him as a writer whose work has deeply affected me, I have tried to explain why his writings so powerfully fascinate me. Furthermore, given my excessive fondness for poetry, I may not have been able to pay major writers of Odia prose fiction the attention they eminently deserve. It is possible that my worldview and literary taste might undergo change in course of time and I might disagree with the views on Sachidananda's work I espoused in this essay. If someone asks me why this happened, I would answer in the words used by Walt Whitman: "Do I contradict myself? Yes, I contain multitudes". Or, I would solace myself with the words of Sachidananda, my favourite writer: "Life moves like a whirling top outpacing knowledge, intelligence, ideas and experiences. Endless motion defines life. The more alive one is, the faster one moves". Thus, there is nothing unusual about my literary sensibility evolving over time.

Translation: Jatindra Kumar Nayak

Note

1 Chintamani Behera, "Kabi Sachidananda Rautray" [The Poetry of Sachidananda Rautray], *Dagar*, vol. 19, no. 8, Cuttack: Nityanand Mahapatra, 1956, pp. 26–32.

24 Nilakantha Das

Odia literature: a historical enquiry

Introduction

Nilakantha Das (1884–1967) was an eminent scholar, freedom fighter, poet and educationist. He was a member of the Panchasakha group which sought to bring about the regeneration of Odisha through cultural, political and social initiatives. He famously combined an impassioned pursuit of literature with an active and exciting political career. The latter encompassed his involvement in the movement for the unification of Odia-speaking tracts and his vigorous participation in the freedom struggle led by Mahatma Gandhi. The years he spent as a teacher at the Stayabadi School founded by Gopabandhu Das (1887–1928) led him to write books for children. He achieved fame as a poet writing two *kavyas Konarke* [At Konark] (1919) and *Kharavel* (1920) and through his exquisite adaptations of Tennyson's *The Princess* as *Pranayini* (1919) and *Enoch Arden* as *Dasa Naik* (1923). His incisively provocative essays interrogating obsolete social practices and ossified conventions established his reputation as an iconoclastic free thinker. He launched the magazine *Nababharat* [New India] in 1934, which created a vibrant forum for voicing and debating new ideas about society, politics, culture and religion. His immense erudition and intellectual independence are reflected in his extensive commentary on *The Gita*. His autobiography *Atmajivani* (1963), which recounts his eventful life and multi-faceted career with unforgettable acuteness, has attained the status of a modern classic.

The following excerpt is taken from the first volume of Nilakantha's *Odia Sahityara Krama-parinama* [Odia Literature: A Historical Enquiry] (1948) where he proposes a radically new framework for writing literary history. The book began life as a lecture he delivered at Balasore College (now Fakir Mohan College) on 29 September 1947. Invited to speak on the evolution of Odia literature, he chose to interpret "evolution" not in terms of a developmental scheme, in which the present is always superior to the past, but as the complex and non-linear unfolding of a historical process. Here, Nilakantha displays a bold originality of approach. Under the impact of colonial modernity and the pressure of identity crisis faced by Odias, an urgent need was felt in late nineteenth-century Odisha to redefine literature

DOI: 10.4324/9781003224778-24

as a category. An early attempt in this direction was made by Biswanath Kar, who in one of his editorials in *Utkal Sahitya* (included in this volume) enlarged the category to bring in science, philosophy, education, industry, agriculture, commerce, religion and ethics within its scope. Nilakantha goes a step further in emphasizing the centrality of language to culture and recognizing literature as embodying its fullest expression. He departs from the dominant tradition of writing a literary history of Odisha which focused on authors, texts and chronology by placing literature in a broader civilizational framework. As part of this approach, he traces the roots of Odia literature to its tribal past and shows how it is integrally linked with orality. He attempts to develop a theory of literature by elaborating three analytical tools which can be employed to account for literary change. These include *chahani* [ways of seeing], *chalani* [modes of life] and *chamak* [elements of novelty]. In employing these tools to develop a historical approach to literature, Nilakantha pays particular attention to the role of conflicts and disruptions in shaping the course of literary change.

*

Odia literature: a historical enquiry[1]

Nilakantha Das

Broadly speaking, literature can be defined as the expression of the development of society. Culture captures the tendencies of this development and through literature one analyzes and evaluates culture. For this reason, everything including social behaviour, art, poetry, criticism, science, painting, sculpture, etc. belong to the province of literature. Understood in these terms, the category of literature can be seen to encompass the social institutions, tales and legends embodied in the elephant sculpture at Dhauli; the caves in Udayagiri; the temples in Bhubaneswar, Khiching, Puri and Konark; the stone embankment of the Kathajodi; even in bell metal utensils and filigree artware made in Kantilo and Cuttack respectively. Moreover, literature embraces epics like Sarala Das's *Mahabharata* and contemporary poetry and prose fiction.

Chahani [ways of seeing], *chalani* [modes of life] and *chamak* [elements of novelty]

Culture evaluated in terms of thought and philosophy, effort and creativity, feelings and experience helps us arrive at a historical understanding of literature. In other words, ways of seeing, modes of life and elements of novelty render the cultural dimensions of society visible. Ways of seeing include systems of ideas, analysis and the process of discovery. By modes of life is meant all kinds of social transactions, the birth of necessity and the genesis of art. Elements of novelty consist in the unexpectedness of signs and the limitless effusion of emotions. These always find expression in ways of seeing and modes of life. They draw human beings towards the experience of delight through art, poetry, symmetry and beauty. Ways of seeing and modes of life constitute the body of literature; the elements of novelty are its soul.

Evaluation, description and significance

One can discern the development of culture in fine arts; one can also do so in the processes of scientific discovery and the genesis of necessity. However, language is the supreme vehicle of culture. Although ways of seeing and modes of life can find expression in diverse media, literary change is primarily manifested through the evaluation, description and significance embodied in language. Ways of seeing provide literature with its spine and its skeletal framework which enable it to grow like a living being. When this spine receives a blow or is afflicted by disease, it loses a sense of direction. If the spine is shattered, literature loses its individuality and its growth gets disrupted. Perhaps it acquires a new individual identity. Unable to express itself in a distinctive manner, it ceases to exist or it gets dissolved in a larger collective, or else, it retreats from view and awaits discovery like a secret, subterranean stream.

Changes shaping the course of Odia literature have to be understood from this point of view. This course can be mapped by taking into account evaluation, description and significance, and development and disruption expressed through language and keeping in view modes of life and ways of seeing. In order to comprehend the fullness of the context one needs to understand the way language has changed.

Orality and literacy

Literature is understood and appreciated better if it is presented in written form. Therefore, by "literature" is meant literature that is written. However, it is possible that songs, stories and tales transmitted orally may even be livelier and more enjoyable than written texts. Earlier, these were the dominant modes of literary expression. *Vedas* were called *shruti* in ancient India. *Shruti* meant what people memorized by listening. Vedic chants and hymns were committed to memory and were passed from one generation to another. In those days alphabets did not exist; so, there was no writing. Even after literacy gained currency *bratakathas*, fairy tales, folktales, songs meant to soothe children, *puranas*, etc. were orally circulated. One comes across instances of such oral transmission even today. Before the advent of print, the above-mentioned forms constituted popular literature and the *puranas* written in Sanskrit and Prakrit absorbed much from these. These folk narratives were quite popular in our country a generation ago. Many of these have now been lost. But some have managed to survive and these form a vital part of Odia literature.

Assault and influence

The literatures created in the languages of the Kandhas, Santals, Gandas, Bhils, Sabaras and others have disappeared either partially or completely. This has happened as a result of the assault they faced from other languages and literatures. This phenomenon is quite common in the history of human society. Such aggression is very similar to and sometimes accompanied by acts of conquest aimed at acquiring wealth and territory. In the midst of such assaults and mutual interactions, some literatures have survived by finding expression in robust and established languages. Wherever a language has not been able to sustain this literature, it has lost its individuality and become extinct.

Discovering elements of the literary

An enquiry into the languages and literatures mentioned above is essential to reach an in-depth understanding of the changing course of Odia literature. Among the above-mentioned 'backward' communities persist many folktales, festivals and social practices which one finds in unaltered forms or slightly modified versions in Odisha and Odia language. Although they do not possess a body of written literature, the images of love, domesticity and institutions one finds in their songs and dances are sometimes of great value. In the remote past, a young woman in a certain village wandered singing songs after unrequited love for a handsome youth drove her mad. In some other village, a young man had married a woman from another village in secret; later, the father of this woman had come with fellow villagers to forcibly take her back and lost his life in the ensuing fight. Maybe, the killing of her father led the woman to murder her husband and end her own life. Elsewhere, when a tiger or a bear devoured someone, a sorcerer practised magic by a hill stream to protect the villagers from such attacks. As a result of his spell, the tiger or the bear came out and got killed. These also tell us of which crops were grown first in which village and which feast propitiated a god, who increased the harvest. Perhaps sacrifices were offered to some gods to placate them. The stories describe how the sorcerers and priests protected the village from danger. Some people became hermits and taught people ways of living a good life and became one with God. All these incidents are still being presented with great simplicity, vividness and musical grace by forest-dwelling communities. Even today, one would be impressed by dormitories meant for unmarried men (*dhangda*) and women (*dhangdi*), and the warm hospitality they show to strangers. In many Kandha and Sabara villages, one still comes across autonomous institutions of village administration. These villagers continue to make arrangements for the board and lodging of the visitors in the above-mentioned dormitories and help them reach their destination carrying the luggage of the guests on their shoulders. Documenting these practices will provide us with invaluable evidence relating to processes of literary change. The forest-dwelling tribals do not have a script. Missionaries made attempts to transcribe their oral texts using the Roman script. The missionary Verrier Elwin collected priceless material from the oral narratives of the Gonds and Bhils. Calcutta University, for its part, has recognized Santali and Khasia as minor vernaculars and initiated a study of these. Utkal University and literary institutions in Odisha should immediately take up similar well-conceived projects.

The presence of folk elements in contemporary Odia language and literature

In Odia folktales and social practices, one can easily trace many of the elements mentioned above. These have also found expression in written literature in Odisha. However, contemporary Odia has moved away from the language of Sabaras and its Tamil roots. Odia-speaking people have embraced the language of the Aryans. Yet, if one would like to engage in a historical enquiry into Odia literature, one has to take into account the influence on it of the texts produced in the pre-literacy era. We have not collected our folktales, legends and songs. We should, therefore, make use of evidences such as a social practice or even a word in our attempt to account for literary change. Customs and unpublished folktales will also enrich our understanding. It has already been said that literature is generally understood to be a body of written texts. However, an account of the literary history of Odisha should not focus only on these. One should try to locate the distinctiveness of Odia life in folk culture and literature. One has to find out what identity Odia literature has assumed in the context of an evolving civilization. How this identity has been shaped by crises and conflicts can help one arrive at a proper understanding of the course Odia literature has taken. Therefore, this discussion is based on material and evidence collected from words, social and religious practices, folktales and customs.

Uses of a literary history of Odisha

We must keep in mind the fact that our civilization has a vast history which has found expression in its literature. Drawing inspiration from the encompassing context and at the same time influencing it, the robust Odia identity has made its presence felt in India as well as the world. The more the distinctiveness of this identity becomes pronounced, the identity of India and the world will be nourished through mutual interaction. Enriching our own literature and strengthening our society will constitute service to India and the whole of mankind. In the ecosystem of the world, Odias ought to give as much as they receive. Our identity is derived from and expressed through this intimate exchange. However, unless our literature and society are placed on a strong foundation of self-confidence, this process of give and take would not be possible; without it, both Indian and world civilizations would not be able to achieve wholeness. Therefore, we have to find the right perspective on the changing course of Odia literature and equip it to serve the world by nurturing it through the vibrant exchange mentioned earlier.

Translation: Jatindra Kumar Nayak

Note

1 Nilakantha Das, *Odia Sahityara Krama-parinama* [Odia Literature: A Historical Enquiry], Cuttack: Nababharat Granthalaya, 1948, pp. 1–4, 20–24.

25 Bipin Bihari Ray
Literature and philosophy

Introduction

Bipin Bihari Ray (1887–1975) was a teacher of philosophy and an eminent man of letters. Educated at Ravenshaw College, Cuttack and Scottish
Church College, Kolkata, he taught at the former for the best part of his
career. He was one of the three noted philosophy teachers in Odisha in the
first half of the twentieth century who enriched Odia literature by writing
essays on philosophical themes. While Mohini Mohan Senapati (his essay
"Odia Folktales" has been included in this volume) focused on western philosophical thought and Ratnakar Pati explored eastern philosophical systems in their writings, Bipin Bihari sought to integrate the two philosophical
approaches in his essays. He contributed numerous articles to major literary
periodicals of the time such as *Utkal Sahitya*, *Sahakar* and *Nababharat*. In
many of these articles, he explored contemporary issues relating to society,
politics and education. These were collected in volumes titled *Prabnadha
Sopan* [Selected Essays] (1937) and *Samajika Prabandha* [Essays on Society]
(vol. 1, 1942; vol. 2, 1944).

The present essay, which was included in the second volume of *Samajika
Prabandha*, examines the differences and affinities between philosophy and
literature, thereby, developing an innovative approach to critical practice in
Odisha. It may be noted here that Biswanath Kar in his attempt to revitalize
Odia literature and criticism brought within the scope of literature areas of
knowledge such as science, philosophy, commerce and industry. This essay
constitutes an important contribution to this initiative. Departing from the
traditional method of analysing a single text, author or genre, he reflects on
more general issues such as the nature of the experience of beauty, the source
of the aesthetic value of a literary work and enables the reader to look at literature from a larger philosophical perspective. Bipin Bihari warns against
the harms insularity can do to a literary culture and strongly recommends a
cosmopolitan outlook, demonstrating how a literature grows and prospers
by absorbing influences from other literatures. Moreover, he suggests a distinction between highbrow and popular literatures and emphasizes that no
great literature can rest on the foundation of only popular writing; for, the

DOI: 10.4324/9781003224778-25

latter can undermine social harmony by intensifying class antagonism. Bipin Bihari's observation can be understood by placing it in the social and political context of the 1930s and 40s, and its impact on literature. In this essay, Bipin Bihari lends another significant dimension to the evaluation of literary texts arguing that linguistic virtuosity and description of natural beauty cannot in themselves bestow enduring significance on a literary text. The timeless beauty of a text would emanate from the author's ability to comprehend and express deeper structures of feeling. Not content with operating at this high level of theoretical abstraction, Bipin Bihari convincingly illustrates his points by offering vivid examples from contemporary Odia literature. This essay explores the common ground shared by philosophy and literature and shows how the apprehension of truth is central to the experience of beauty.

*

Literature and philosophy[1]

Bipin Bihari Ray

Literature encompasses a vast universe of experience. The subject matter of literature comprises inner and outer worlds; the visible and the invisible; sentient beings and insentient objects; human joys and sorrows, hopes and aspirations; ethical and cultural values; and, life's movement and progress. The writer's task consists in expressing in appropriate language his personal responses – which include his thoughts and experiences – to the world he encounters. Differences with respect to content and technique account for the diversity of literary forms such as prose, poetry, drama, novel and epic; and each form has split into more generic categories. This process has also unfolded in Odia literature. So far as various literary forms are concerned, one notices differences between these forms in Odia literature and their counterparts elsewhere. But these differences do not obscure the inevitable connections they share. Literature is the essence of human imagination and writers belonging to every place and community go on creating it. However, in order to generate a richly multi-layered literature, these communities need to engage in a vibrant exchange of ideas. Although different communities and nations vary in terms of language, they all belong to one republic of knowledge. Thus, they enrich themselves through mutual influence. No good literature is created if its authors rely entirely on the cultural resources of their own community. Such an insular approach would diminish the quality of their literature. For example, it is obvious that Odia literature belongs to Odisha but it is addressed to and meant for the whole of humanity. In other words, it does not merely exist for itself. The aim of literature is to make individuals aware of the universality underlying their being and establish unity amidst diversity. In this sense, writers like Jayadeva, Dinakrushna Das, Upendra Bhanja and Gopal Chandra Praharaj should not be kept confined to Odisha but be regarded as precious assets of humankind. From this perspective, writers and philosophers share fundamental similarities. Both live in the world but are detached from it. They both worship and adore the universal, and serve as guides to humanity.

When we undertake a classification of disciplines, we emphasize the ways in which literature differs from philosophy. We stress that literature aims to create beauty, give delight and provide access to aesthetic experience whereas philosophy focuses on the quest for, and discovery and analysis of, truth. One is concerned with concrete particulars while the other engages in abstract thought. Subjectivity dominates literature and philosophy tends to be objective. These apparent differences, however, conceal deeper affinities. For what is true is also beautiful. Both contemplate the universal and imaginative patterns. Just as the philosopher has to go beyond concrete particulars in order to arrive at generalizations and analyse the particular in the light of the universal, the poet has to transcend the world of senses while creating beauty out of an intense engagement with sense-experience. Both the poet and the philosopher possess insight and a broad vision of the outer world.

Literature may be divided into two broad categories, highbrow and popular. Similarly, language is of two types, chaste and colloquial. Popular literature is associated with popular movements and aims at the improvement of the condition of lower classes. The principal task of popular literature is to make ordinary people aware of their rights relating to sustenance, education and health through the use of colloquial language. As popular literature is written in descriptive and accessible language, it enables the masses to awaken to the circumstances encompassing them and better their lives by overcoming deprivations. Since people belonging to lower classes lead a precarious existence characterized by poverty, writers of popular literature should ensure that it does not generate violent class antagonism. They should be sensitive to the need for promoting amity among various classes in a populous society based on class hierarchy. Kalindi Charan Panigrahi's *Muktagadara Kshudha* [Hungry Muktagada] and Kanhu Charan Mohanty's *Ha Anna* [A Handful of Rice] handle such issues with desirable sensitivity.

However, a nation's literature should not be confined to its popular literature alone. It is not that literature mirrors only the lives of uneducated or half-educated people; it also draws vitality from the lives of educated persons and intellectuals. Unless literature of high quality informed by elevated thoughts and feelings is written, society will fail to reach a high intellectual level. Just as a painter cannot create a work of art by drawing random lines on a canvas or splashing it with deep colours, a writer will not be able to produce good literature by simply describing external particulars of life or mere appearances. In the absence of insight born of philosophical contemplation and profound thoughts, literature degenerates into a misshapen clay image. Therefore, the spread of popular literature should be accompanied by literature of high quality. Excellence of literature depends on the depiction of refined experience. Experience is the soul of literature and language, its body. This refined experience finds expression in elegant diction and new experiences seek outlets in new modes of expression. For this reason, Odia literature, which is indebted to Sanskrit literature, must draw upon philosophical, grammatical and puranic texts written in the latter.

Even among canonical Odia texts one comes across various levels of intellectual and aesthetic attainment. Gopabandhu Das's narrative poem *Dharmapada* fills the heart with unalloyed delight. For, here the graceful progress of thought makes the heart overflow with bliss. To produce literature of lasting value one needs much more than ornate language or beautifully portrayed natural landscape. Decking up an ugly woman with jewels will not make her look beautiful; similarly, linguistic dexterity cannot imbue a lifeless text with vitality. Through the deft use of a certain kind of diction, one may be able to evoke a vivid picture of an enchanting place in the reader's mind, but the pleasure derived from this is transient. It only portrays physical beauty and lacks real depth. A text which contents itself with depicting external appearances is doomed to be repetitive.

The beauty of literature does not inhere in a display of linguistic virtuosity nor portraying natural landscapes but in conveying noble and elevated feelings. The beguiling charm of external appearance may immediately grab a reader's attention. However, literature that provides only this kind of pleasure is fit for children. The glamour of the surface appeals to and excites children but experienced adults look for inner beauty, which emanates from a grasp of imperceptible causes and relationships. Only poets and philosophers can perceive this relationship and share their pleasure with the reader. As a poet Gangadhar Meher was able to accomplished this. The beauty of *Tapaswini* lies in its lofty inner thoughts and its bringing the animate and inanimate worlds into an intimate relationship. Even the natural world empathizes with Sita when she is overwhelmed with grief:

> Upon hearing Sita's lament the wind dropped
> The earth and water were stricken with grief
> The waves of river Janhavi grew numb
> Birds in the forest stopped chirping and became mute.

Going through Radhanath Ray's *Chilika* [Lake Chilika] gives the reader an intense experience of beauty. Consider its opening lines:

> Adorned with swans, O blue-watered Chilika
> You are the pleasure lake of Goddess Lakshmi.

However, this description goes beyond the static depiction of physical attributes. It expands to include other associate thoughts, historical incidents and a vision of the future. Radhanath continues,

To the past you are an ancient witness.
You have seen human fortunes rise and fall.
So many capitals of kingdoms were founded
On your shores and then crumbled into dust.

Padmacharan Pattnaik's poem titled "Dhauli Pahada" (The Hill of Dhauli)
shares the quality that distinguishes *Chilika*. The beauty of the hill does not
lie in its physical appearance; it lies in the world of memory which is linked
to the radical transformation Emperor Asoka underwent there.

Dhauli hill, Dhauli hill!
What did you whisper into the king's ears?
What saga did you sing to him
That sent him into a deep trance?

The beauty of literature consists in its close link with the world of feelings;
it is defined in terms of creativity. Here, the writer is not concerned with
offering only a faithful copy of the natural world, but goes beyond concrete
objects, the visible universe, and the differences between *prakriti* (nature,
changeable material reality) and *purusha* (spirit, eternal and unchanging
consciousness) in order to create new possibilities of beauty and delight by
revealing inherent interconnections. This kind of newness is largely constituted by elements drawn from the real world. Literary inventions do not
create a mirage of illusions nor do they imagine a fairy-tale world. The poet
writes,

There is no need to visit a distant temple.
Look intently into your own heart opening your eyes wide.
And again,
Fathomless and vast, the ocean
Is filled with an unending resonance.
Drink the sweet music which the deep blue ocean,
Daughter of the sacred earth pours out.

Literature connects the human with the divine through an intense engagement with the created world and thus generates a sense of fulfilment. A true
poet, if fortunate, succeeds in penetrating the veil of the quotidian world
and gets a glimpse of the inner soul. He can hear the music of the universe,
which is drowned in the din of mundane life.

The same can be said of human society as well. Both literature and philosophy engage in presenting a realistic picture of society, evaluating the real
world and improving it by offering achievable ideals. Intoxicated by sensual
delight, when a society gets immersed in the here and now, thereby failing
to visualize the consequences of its actions, a writer through the power of
imagination traces the contours of an ideal world and a better future. A

writer cannot cut himself off from society and at the same time remain content with leaving things in society as they are. He tries to point out what is good and what is bad in the existing social order. If literature seeks to recast society in a new mould and guide the existing towards an ideal, it justifies its existence.

> One has to go door to door to persuade people to buy milk
> Whereas buyers throng the wine-seller's stall.

This is an illuminating comment on the character of society and its prevailing culture.

Ramachandra Mohapatra's play *Raghu Arakhit* (1934) paints the portrait of a society obsessed with money. It shows how terrible consequences follow from compulsive acquisition of wealth, how one violates the sacred marital bond and wants to marry another person out of a love of lucre, and tries to murder his blood brother. However, it also offers the possibility of moral redemption. Elements such as social history and analysis, adept characterization, and insight on character building account for the success of this play.

A careful analysis of literary texts reveals that writers differ from one another in terms of their philosophical orientation. Some of them are materialists, some are theists and others are idealists. Among modern writers, Mayadhar Manasinha strikes one as at once a theist and a reformist; his poems "Devapuja" (Worshiping a Deity) and "Vishwarupa" (The All-pervading Form of God) reflect this attitude towards the world. Naba Kishor Das is an idealist. Narayan Mohan De in his poems "Santwana" (Consolation) and "Chinmayi" (A Woman who is Spiritually Minded) visualizes a higher life for humanity. Kalindi Charan Panigrahi is a materialist. In his view, "man born of the soil will in the end mingle in it", and "Jagnnath is but a lifeless image made of wood and stone". Perhaps, overcome with pity for people belonging to the lower strata, he expressed such extreme feelings.

Not content with writing *Matira Manisha* [Born of the Soil] (1931), Kalindi Charan went on to create *Luhara Manisha* [The Man of Iron] (1947). He idealizes peasant life in Odisha and celebrates a poor farmer's capacity for self-sacrifice, service and virtue. Here, an elder brother gives up his claim to his share of family land to avoid conflict in the family. In *Luhara Manisha*, attention of the author shifts from the peasant to the worker.

Harnarayan Singh, a noted scholar, made the following oservationn in his presidential address delivered at the meeting of Odia Sahitya Parisad held recently at Puri: "The relationship of literature with life is not an external one; it is very intimate and runs very deep". He adds, "Our literature can be enriched only if we intensify our life and widen the circle of our experience". In other words, the writer's experience transcends the experience gained through the senses or that of the external world. Observing closely human activity unfolding in the real world, the writer transforms all this into something invested with timeless beauty. The beautiful always fascinates a writer. Beauty does not lie around us so that we can easily pick it up. Real beauty lies far below the surface; only a penetrating imaginative vision can capture it. Literature and philosophy are bound to pierce through the veil of time and place, and they possess the ability to do so. This is where literature and philosophy converge and one complements the other.

Translation: Asim Ranjan Parhi

Note

1 Bipin Bihari Ray, "Sahityare Darsan" [Literature and Philosophy], *Samajika Prabandha*, vol. 2 [Essays on Society], Cuttack: Saraswata Press, 1949, 2nd ed., 79–87.

Glossary

alamkara: figure of speech, poetic embellishment

amitrakshar chhanda: unrhymed lines of poetry; blank verse

baidya: a practitioner of Ayurveda or traditional Hindu system of medicine

bani: the tune of a song

baramasi: a song describing nature through the twelve months of a year; a song depicting thoughts of a woman separated from her lover during every month of the year; or a song composed in honour of a deity mentioning all the twelve months

bargi: Maratha horsemen or freebooters who used to raid and loot Odisha and Bengal in seventeenth and eighteenth centuries

bhajan: a devotional song celebrating a deity's glory

bhanati/bhanita: the concluding lines of a poem where the name of the author or the patron is mentioned

bhava: emotion, mood, or sentiment

boli: saying, proverb; the set phraseology for a song or musical instrument; dialectal forms of a language

bratakatha: a story about how a certain vow originated and how it is to be performed

brutta: the tune of a poem

chatshali: a traditional village school for young children where rudiments of reading, writing and arithmetic were taught

champu: an elaborate poetic composition interspersed with passages of prose

chaupadi: a song consisting of four couplets

chautisha: a poem comprising thirty-four couplets in which each begins with one of the thirty-four consonants of the alphabet and follows the sequence from *ka* to *ksha*; an abecedarian poem

chhanda: metre of a poem; poem composed in a particular metre

dattakavya: a *kavya* whose authorship is attributed to a patron

jatipata: pauses made at intervals while singing and reciting a poem; something like a caesura

jatra: open-air musical or theatrical performance

kahani: tale, fable, folktale

koili: a mournful song comprising thirty-four stanzas addressed to a cuckoo

pala: performance of religious and literary texts accompanied by music and dance

parva: the sections into which a long poem is divided; a festival

poi: a poem comprising couplets in which each line consists of twenty-two letters, and the person reciting it pauses after the sixth, twelfth, eighteenth and final syllables of each line. It is sung following *bhupal* raga.

pothi: a palm-leaf manuscript

prachina: old, ancient; in nineteenth-century Odisha, *prachina* referred to the pre-colonial era and often meant traditional with reference to literature

pragana: a group of villages constitute a *pargana*, a fiscal subdivision of a district. This fiscal division was introduced during the Mughal rule and is still in use

samkranti: advance; the transition of the sun from one sign of the zodiac to another

suanga: popular farce; mime

upadha: the penultimate vowel sound in a poetic line

Note

For most of the entries in this glossary, we have relied upon Gopal Chandra Praharaj's seven-volume encyclopaedic dictionary *Purnachandra Odia Bhashakosha* (1931–1940), which has been digitized by Srujanika and can be accessed at https://odiabibhaba.in/en/bhasakosha-e/.

Bibliography

Animesh Mohapatra, "The Local and the National in Oriya Public Sphere: 1866–1948", unpublished dissertation, University of Delhi, 2016.

Arabinda Giri, Ed., *Odishara Prathama Sahitya Patra: Utkal Darpan* [The First Literary Periodical of Odisha: Utkal Darpan], Rourkela: Pragati Utkal Sangha, 2007.

Bansidhar Mohanty, Ed., *Atharasha Chhasathi (Utkal Dipika)* [Eighteen Sixty-six (Utkal Dipika)], Cuttack: Friends Publishers, 1978.

Bansidhar Mohanty, Ed., *Prabodh Chandrika (1856)*, Vani Vihar: Utkal University, 1984.

Bansidhar Mohanty, *Odia Bhasa Andolana* [The Language Agitation in Odisha], Cuttack: Sahitya Sangraha Prakashan, 2nd Ed., 2001.

Bidyut Mohanty, "Orissa Famine of 1866: Demographic and Economic Consequences", *Economic and Political Weekly*, vol. 28 (1993), no.s 1 & 2, pp. 55–66.

Bijoy Chandra Mazumdar, Ed., *Typical Selections from Oriya Literature*, vol. 1, Calcutta: University of Calcutta, 1921.

Chakradhar Mohapatra, *Utkal Gaunli Gita*, Cuttack: Surama Mohanty, 2nd Ed., 1971 [1959].

Dasarathi Das, *Sahityaviveka* [The Conscience of Literature], Cuttack: Agraduta, 1996.

Dasarathi Das, Ed., *Odia Sahityachinta* [Literary Criticism in Odia], New Delhi: National Book Trust, 2012.

Debendra Dash, *Gangadhar: Kabita o Kabi-Atma*, Rourkela: Pragati Utkal Sangha, 1995.

Debi Prasanna Pattanayak, *Kabilipi* [Letters of Poets], Santiniketan: Odia Gabesana Bibhag, 1957.

Fanindra Bhusan Nanda, *Sambalpur Hiteisini: Eka Adhyayan* [Sambalpur Hiteisini: A Study], Bhubaneswar: Subas Chandra Mishra, 2002.

Gaganendra Nath Dash, *Odia Bhasa-Charchara Parampara* [Linguistic Study of Odia: A Historical Enquiry], Odia Gabesana Parisad: Cuttack, 1983.

Gaganendra Nath Dash, *Punascha Janasruti Kanchi-Kaberi* [Revisiting the Legend of Kanchi-Kaberi], Bhubaneswar: Rama Devi, 2014.

Gaganendra Nath Dash, *Naba Digantara Sandhanare* [In Search of a New Horizon], Bhubaneswar: Rama Devi, 2016.

Gary Day, *Literary Criticism: A New History*, Edinburgh: Edinburgh University Press, 2008.

Graham W. Shaw, "The Cuttack Mission Press and Early Oriya Printing", *The British Library Journal*, vol. 3 (1977), pp. 29–43.

Harry Blamires, *A History of Literary Criticism*, London: Macmillan, 1991.

Jatindra Mohan Mohanty, *History of Oriya Literature*, Bhubaneswar: Vidya, 2006.

Jayanta Sengupta, *At the Margins: Discourses of Development, and Regionalism in Orissa*, New Delhi: Oxford University Press, 2015.

Joseph North, *Literary Criticism: A Concise Political History*, Cambridge, Massachusetts: Harvard University Press, 2017.

Lalatendu Das Mohapatra, Ed., *John Beames and Orissa*, Rourkela: Pragati Utkal Sangha, 2007.

Mayadhar Manasinha, *History of Oriya Literature*, New Delhi: Sahitya Akademi, 1962.

Mayadhar Manasinha, *Odia Sahityara Itihas*, Cuttack: Grantha Mandir, 1967.

Monmohan Chakravarti, "Notes on the Language and Literature of Orissa", parts III and IV, *Journal of the Asiatic Society of Bengal*, vol. LXVI (1898), no. IV, Calcutta: Asiatic Society, 332–386.

Mrutyunjay Ratha, *Karmayogi Gourisankar*, Cuttack: Granthamandir, 2005 [1925].

Natabara Samantaray, *Adhunika Odia Sahityara Bhittibhumi*, Cuttack: Friends' Publishers, 1964a.

Natabara Samantaray, *Odia Sahityara Itihas: 1803–1920*, Bhubaneswar: Prafulla Kumar Dhala and Hrudananda Bhola, 1964b.

Nivedita Mohanty, *Oriya Nationalism: Quest for a United Orissa, 1866–1956*, Jagatsinghpur: Prafulla, Revised ed., 2005 [1982].

Nivedita Mohanty, *Ravenshaw College: Orissa's Temple of Learning, 1868–2006*, Jagatsinghpur: Prafulla, 2017.

Odia Samalochana Sahitya [Odia Literary Criticism], Bhubaneswar: Odisha Sahitya Akademi, 2015 [1989].

Pathani Patnaik, *Odishara Patrapatrika o Adya Prakashita Odia Pustaka* [Periodicals and Early Printed Books in Odisha], Bhubaneswar: Odisha Sahitya Akademi, 1982.

Pradipta Kumar Panda, "Prachin o Madhya-kalin Sahitya Samalochana" [Literary Criticism in Ancient and Medieval Odisha], *Sahityapatra*, Cuttack: Department of Odia, Ravenshaw University, 2016–17, 178–191.

Prasanna Kumar Mishra and Debendra Dash, Eds., *Radhanath Granthabali*, Cuttack: Grantha Mandir, 2010 [1998].

Pritam Mukherjee, "William Wilson Hunter and Colonial Bengal: Historiography, Literature, Modernity", unpublished dissertation, Jadavpur University, 2015.

Pritipuspa Mishra, *Language and the Making of Modern India: Nationalism and the Vernacular in Colonial Odisha, 1803–1956*, Cambridge: Cambridge University Press, 2020.

Priyaranjan Sen, *Modern Odia Literature*, Calcutta: Self-published, 1947.

Sachchidananda Mishra, *Baladeb Ratha: Sahitya Sadhana o Siddhi* [Baladeb Ratha's Achievement as a Writer], Cuttack: Navoday Prakashan, 2005.

Sachidananda Mohanty, *The Lost World of Sarala Devi: Selected Writings*, New Delhi: Oxford University Press, 2016a.

Sachidananda Mohanty, *Periodical Press and Colonial Modernity: Odisha, 1866–1936*, New Delhi: Oxford University Press, 2016b.

Sarala Devi, *Sarala Mahabharatiya Narichitra* [Portrayal of Women in Sarala Das's *Mahabharata*], Cuttack: Utkal University, 1952.

Sudarsana Acharya, *Odia Kavya Kaushal (1500–1850)* [Odia Poetry: A Study of its Techniques], Cuttack: Friends' Publishers, 2002 [1983].

Sudarsana Acharya, Ed., *Indradhanu: Unabimsha Satabdira Eka Bismruta Patrika* [Indradhnau: A Forgotten Magazine of the Nineteenth Century], Berhampur: Centre for Regional Studies, Berhampur University, 1991.

Sudarsana Acharya, Ed., *Pandit Gopinath Nanda Sarma Granthabali* [Collected Works of Gopinath Nanda Sarma], vol. 1, Cuttack: Prachi Sahitya Pratisthan, 2011.

Sudarsana Acharya, Ed., *Odishara Asmita Sandhan o Upendra Bhanja Kabyalochana* [Upendra Bhanja and the Search for Odia Identity], Cuttack: Agraduta, 2013.

Sumanyu Satpathy, *Reading Literary Culture: Perspectives on Odisha*, New Delhi: Rawat, 2007.

Sumanyu Satpathy, *Will to Argue: Studies in Late Colonial and Postcolonial Controversies*, New Delhi: Primus, 2017.

Sumanyu Satpathy and Animesh Mohapatra, Eds., *Natabara Samantaray: A Reader*, New Delhi: Sahitya Akademi, 2017.

Ujaan Ghosh and Amrita Chowdhury, "Refiguring Baidehīśa Bilāsa: Reading the Queer and the Erotic in Upendra Bhanja's Rāmāyaṇa", *Journal of the American Academy of Religion*, vol. 88 (June 2020) no. 2, pp. 569–593.

Umacharan Pujari, *Odia Samalochana Sahityara Kramabikash* [The Development of Odia Criticism], Digapahandi: Gitarani Devi, 1963.

William Wilson Hunter, *Orissa: Or the Vicissitudes of an Indian Province under Native and British Rule*, vol. 2, London: Smith, Elder & Co., 1872.

Index

For Product Safety Concerns and Information please contact our EU
representative GPSR@taylorandfrancis.com
Taylor & Francis Verlag GmbH, Kaufingerstraße 24, 80331 München, Germany